D1480593

How much impact did the Protestant Reformation actually have on such fundamental institutions as marriage? Until this study, many historians have attempted to answer this question by focusing on particular legal, theological, and, most recently, social aspects of marriage, but none has succeeded in creating a synthetic overview of this important institution. Combining extensive archival research and a broad array of scholarly monographs, Harrington presents us with the clearest and most comprehensive evaluation of the Reformation's impact on marriage currently available.

To assess fairly the degree of Protestant innovation, he compares reformers' goals and achievements for marriage to those of contemporary Catholics. All sixteenth-century campaigns to restore "traditional family values," Harrington argues, must first be viewed in the context of much more gradual social transformations of private morality, public authority, and familial relations. Seen from this perspective, the apparent innovations of Protestants in marriage – including the abolition of clerical celibacy and introduction of divorce – fade in comparison to their much greater adherence to the theological, legal, and social traditions they share with their Catholic ancestors and contemporaries. All more ambitious attempts by Protestant authorities to alter marital and sexual relations during the sixteenth century similarly met with widespread popular resistance. In his detailed comparison of marriage formation and sexual discipline among Lutherans, Calvinists, and Catholics of the Rhineland Palatinate, Harrington concludes that local custom and authority continued to prevail over all religiously inspired innovation.

The findings of this book carry significant implications for some of the most debated issues of Reformation historiography, including parallel "confessionalization" among sixteenth-century Protestants and Catholics, connections between religious reforms and early modern statebuilding, and especially the hotly disputed question of the Reformation's "success" in social transformation.

Reordering marriage and society
in Reformation Germany

Reordering marriage and society in Reformation Germany

JOEL F. HARRINGTON

Vanderbilt University

CAMBRIDGE
UNIVERSITY PRESS

PUBLISHED BY THE PRESS SYNDICATE OF THE UNIVERSITY OF CAMBRIDGE
The Pitt Building, Trumpington Street, Cambridge CB2 1RP, United Kingdom

CAMBRIDGE UNIVERSITY PRESS
The Edinburgh Building, Cambridge CB2 2RU, United Kingdom
40 West 20th Street, New York, NY 10011-4211, USA
10 Stamford Road, Oakleigh, Melbourne 3166, Australia

First published 1995
Reprinted 1997

Printed in the United States of America

Typeset in Ehrhardt

A catalogue record for this book is available from the British Library

Library of Congess Cataloguing-in-Publication Data is available

ISBN 0-521-46483-8 hardback

TO MY FAMILY

Contents

Contents

Tables and figures

Tables

Figures

Acknowledgments

Many individuals and institutions have helped me in the development of what began as a graduate seminar paper and over the course of ten years grew into something more. My research both in the United States and Germany would never have been possible without the generous support of the Fulbright-Hayes Foundation, the Germanistic Society of America, the Rackham Graduate School and History Department of the University of Michigan, and a Bernadotte E. Smitt Grant from the American Historical Association. A grant from the University Research Council of Vanderbilt University paid my illustration costs. I am also grateful to the staffs of all the archives and libraries I visited for their general helpfulness and courtesy, particularly the Badisches Generallandesarchiv Karlsruhe, Stadtarchiv Speyer, Landesarchiv Speyer, Landeshauptarchiv Koblenz, and the Bayerische Staatsbibliothek in Munich. Dr. H.-J. Köhler obligingly made all the records of his Special Research Project on pamphlets available to me on visits to Tübingen. The Graduate Library of the University of Michigan and particularly the Interlibrary Loan Department were indispensible resources during the years following my initial archival work in Germany, and the Interlibrary Loan staff at Vanderbilt similarly handled all requests I threw their way in a good-humored and expeditious manner.

Parts of this book have appeared in different form in *Fides et Historia* 22/3 (1990): 53–63, and *Central European History* 25/1 (1992): 52–75. I am grateful to Professor Frank Roberts and Humanities Press International, respectively, for their kind permission to make use of this material.

My list of scholarly debts on both sides of the Atlantic is equally great. From the time of my first *Hauptseminar* at the Universität Tübingen in 1984, Hans-Christoph Rublack has been a continual source of encouragement and research advice, including his timely suggestion to explore

Acknowledgments

the underused Generallandesarchiv of Karlsruhe. Further archival orientation and other suggestions were generously supplied by Lyndal Roper, Tom Safley, Laurence Duggan, Charles Donahue, and Volker Press. The members of my dissertation committee were instrumental in giving coherence and form to a previously amorphous collection of research directions and conclusions; Diane Owen-Hughes and Elaine Clark in particular forced me to reconsider the larger social origins and ramifications of my findings – all to the great benefit of the thesis. Gerald Strauss, André Burgière, Tom Green, Joy Wiltenburg, and my two anonymous readers all offered valuable suggestions at later stages and both Marc Forster and Herman Selderhuis shared unpublished research.

During my years of teaching at Vanderbilt, I have been blessed by an exceptionally warm, supportive, and intellectually stimulating department. It would be difficult to specify all of the collegial ideas and suggestions that have strengthened the book, but I would especially like to single out Margo Todd, Paul Freedman, and Jim Epstein for sporadic comments, which they have probably forgotten; Michael Bess, who boldly plowed through the unrevised dissertation at an early stage of revision; and Helmut Smith, for some last-minute stylistic advice.

Finally, two groups of people provided continual support throughout the project's long maturation. At the University of Michigan, Tom Tentler and Phil Soergel were unfailing reservoirs of new ideas, constructive criticism, moral encouragement, and edifying friendship. Since our graduate days, Phil has continued to help in the book's revision, particularly hoping to cure me of my penchant for laborious Germanic sentences (he should not, however, be held accountable for the end result). As a *Doktorvater*, Tom Tentler guided me through many a crisis while still allowing me to choose my own direction and pursue it. I will always value his personal example of scholarly integrity and human compassion.

In a different vein, I wish to thank the members of my family, all of whom contributed in one way or another to the successful completion of the book. Because of their unquestioning support in every conceivable area, I dedicate it to them: Jack, Marilyn, Susan, Tom, Jeff, Alyson, Nick, Michael, Maggie, Noah, Timmy, and Bridget.

All translations, unless otherwise noted, are my own. I have provided the original text in footnotes only for poetry and especially significant passages.

Abbreviations

AEKK	Archiv der Evangelischen Kirche in Rheinland, Archivstelle Koblenz.
BSB	Bayerische Staatsbibliothek München.
Calvin, Commentaries	John Calvin, *New Testament Commentaries*, ed. David W. Torrance and Thomas F. Torrance, (Grand Rapids, Mich., 1959–74).
Calvin, Institutes	John Calvin, *Institutes of the Christian Religion*, ed. J. T. McNeil, trans. Ford Lewis Battles, 2 vols. (Philadelphia, 1960).
CIC	*Corpus Iuris Canonici*, ed. Emil Friedberg (Leipzig, 1879–).
Collectio	*Collectio processum synodalium et constitutionem ecclesiasticarum Diocesis Spirensis ab anno 1397 usque annum 1720*, ed. Speyer Bischof August von Lindburg-Stirum. (Bruchsal, 1786).
CSEL	*Corpus scriptorum ecclesiasticorum latinorum* (Vienna, 1866–).
DDC	*Dictionnaire de droit canonique*, ed. A. Villem, F. Magnin, and R. Naz, 7 vols. (Paris, 1935–65).
Dieterich	Hartweg Dieterich, *Das Protestantische Eherecht in Deutschland bis zur Mitte des 17. Jahrhunderts* (Munich, 1970).
DTC	*Dictionnaire de théologie catholique*, ed. Albert Vacant and E. Mangenot, 15 vols. (Paris, 1909–50).

EGO	Ehegerichtsordnung (marriage court ordinance).
EKO	ed. Emil Sehling, *Die Evangelischen Kirchenordnungen des XVI. Jahrhunderts*, vol. XIV (Kurpfalz), ed. J. F. G. Goeters (Tübingen, 1969).
EO	Eheordnung (marriage ordinance).
Esmein	Adhémar Esmein, *Le mariage en droit canonique*, 2 vols. (Paris, 1891).
GLA	Badisches Generallandesarchiv Karlsruhe.
Grimm	Jacob Grimm, *Weistümer*, 6 vols., Göttingen, 1840–78, 2nd ed. (Reprint: Berlin, 1957).
GStSp	*Geschichte der Stadt Speyer*, ed. Wolfgang Eger, 2 vols., 2nd ed. (Stuttgart, 1983).
HQL	*Handbuch der Quellen und Literatur der neueren europäischen Privatrechtsgeschichte*, 2 vols, ed. Helmut Coing (Munich, 1973–).
HRG	*Handwörterbuch zur deutschen Rechtsgeschichte*, ed. A. Erler and E. Kaufmann (Berlin, 1964–).
HStAMü	Bayerisches Hauptstaatsarchiv München.
Kö	Walther Köhler, *Zürcher Ehegericht und Genfer Konsistorium*, 2 vols. (Leipzig, 1932–42).
LAK	Landeshauptarchiv Koblenz.
LAS	Landesarchiv Speyer.
LW	*Luther's Works, American edition*, ed. Jaroslav Pelikan and Helmut Lehman, 55 vols. (Philadelphia, 1955–).
Riedner I	Otto Riedner, "Das Speierer Offizialsgericht im 13. Jahrhundert," *Mitteilungen des Historischen Vereins der Pfalz* 29–30 (1907), 1–107.
Riedner II	Otto Riedner, *Die geistlichen Gerichtshöfe zu Speyer im Mittelalter*, vol. II (Paderborn, 1915).
Sammlung	*Sammlung der Hochfürstlich-Speirischen Gesetze und Landesverordnungen*, part I (1470–1720) (Bruchsal, 1788).

xiv

Introduction

~~~~~~

During the past thirty years the very validity of the historiographical term "Reformation" has come under attack as never before. To a large degree, the controversy reflects the declining preeminence of the periodizations of intellectual history as well as the simultaneous rising popularity of "social history." During the preceding half-century, the French *Annales* school of historians in particular with its focus on larger impersonal social and economic changes has succeeded in gradually redefining our understanding of the entire period.[1] As historians increasingly scrutinize aspects of sixteenth-century society other than religious doctrine, the significance of the Protestant Reformation as a defining event continues to recede accordingly. More recently, scholars such as Gerald Strauss have questioned the very social impact or "success" of sixteenth-century religious reforms, concluding that the effects of Lutheran attempts at popular indoctrination were minimal at best.[2] One need only consult the latest job bulletin of the American Historical Association to confirm that "Reformation" teaching posts (invariably paired with the intellectual sister, "Renaissance") are increasingly replaced by the more inclusive "Early Modern Europe."[3]

---

[1] Cf. Lucien Febvre's own work on the subject, especially *Au coeur religieux du XVIème siècle* (Paris, 1957); and *The Problem of Unbelief in the Sixteenth Century*, trans. Beatrice Gottlieb (Cambridge, Mass., 1982). On the preceding influence of Marx, Engels, Weber, Tawney, and especially Troeltsch, see summaries in P. Wichelhaus, *Kirchengeschichtsschreibung und Soziologie im neunzehnten Jahrhundert und bei Ernst Troeltsch* (Heidelberg, 1965), and Thomas Brady, "Social History of the Reformation," in *Reformation Europe: A Guide to Research*, ed. Steven Ozment (St. Louis, 1982), 161–81.

[2] *Luther's House of Learning: Indoctrination of the Young in the German Reformation* (Baltimore, 1978).

[3] See also R. Po-Chia Hsia, *Social Discipline in the Reformation: Central Europe, 1550–1750* (London, 1989), 1–9; and cf. William Bouwsma for a similar reevaluation of "Renaissance" as a distinct historical period in "The Renaissance and the Drama of Western Civilization," *American*

Introduction

Another striking and apparently inevitable consequence of the *Annales* influence has been the almost universal compulsion among Reformation historians of all varieties – intellectual, legal, as well as economic – to address in some way the issue of social context in discussing almost any aspect of sixteenth-century religion.[4] Most researchers have welcomed the departure from narrow theological and confessional evaluations of the Reformation, particularly in German scholarship, but at least one early advocate of historiographical change in this area has more recently questioned whether the "socialization" of Reformation scholarship has gone too far, creating a "sociologistic" monster worse than its predecessor.[5] For some, the importance of the "Reformation" as a historical watershed risks being lost in a sea of other "more significant" social changes regarding family and demography, State and political power, gender relations, and so forth.

At a deeper level, the decline of the Reformation in modern historiography also represents an ancient and insoluble philosophical division on the role of human agency in history. The school of interpretation that has sometimes been unfairly characterized as the "great men" approach in fact represents a more universal confidence in all individuals and their ability to significantly affect the course of social developments. This could be called a dynamic or "revolutionary" interpretation of history that predictably views the leaders and ideas of the Reformation as distinctively creative and influential. At the other end of the historiographical spectrum, we encounter a more collective, gradual, and "evolutionary" version of social change. Here, the *longue durée* of Fernand Braudel provides the central paradigm with the lasting impact of individual action much less likely in comparison to larger collective changes. Here too the Protestant Reformation represents only one aspect of a much more gradual social transformation and certainly not an abrupt divergence resulting from the ideas and actions of a few outstanding individuals.

Despite the somewhat artificial polarization of these two approaches,

Historical Review 84 (1979), 1–16; also Lewis Spitz, "Periodization in History: Renaissance and Reformation," in *The Future of History*, ed. Gordon Connell-Smith (Hull, 1975), 189–217.

[4] See historiographical overviews of all Reformation fields in Ozment, *Reformation Europe*.

[5] Cf. original call of Bernd Moeller for study of the "Reformation movement as a whole" in "Probleme der Reformationsgeschichtsforschung," *Zeitschrift für Reformationsgeschichte* 14 (1965), 246–57, and later reconsideration of the resulting historiography in "Stadt und Buch. Bemerkungen zur Struktur der reformatorischen Bewegung in Deutschland," in *Stadtbürgertum und Adel in der Reformation*, ed. W. J. Mommsen (Stuttgart, 1979), 25–40.

this interpretative division continues to shape our understanding of the peoples and societies of the sixteenth century. My purpose here is not to sway the reader to my own preference (like most, somewhere between the two poles) but to address the question of the historical significance of "Reformation." I believe that the term remains valid for discussions of sixteenth-century historical change, but not in terms of the immediate or broad-ranging social implications often associated with it. The religious reformers of this period did have an impact on the ideas and practices of their societies but not always in the manner intended. Nor were their own perceptions formed in an intellectual void. The right balance between long-term "evolutionary" and short-term "revolutionary" change therefore must be our objective, and I can think of no more suitable candidate for establishing this equilibrium than the institution of marriage.

Marriage in the sixteenth century – as today – defied easy categorization: It was at the same time a social, economic, religious, and legal institution. As a public joining of two individuals, it represented the fundamental link between the private and the public, making it for many contemporaries the very basis of all social order. Most important for our question of "Reformation" and social change, it was the focus of very specific criticisms and programs of secular and religious reform among all denominations. Clearly an evaluation of evolutionary and revolutionary change in sixteenth-century marriage would contribute greatly toward putting the Reformation in its proper social context. First, however, we must establish our historiographical and geographical perspectives.

The historiographical perspective

Despite a long historiographical tradition, the question of the Reformation's impact on marriage has consistently suffered from a fundamental problem of perspective. On the one hand, we confront a documentational obstacle familiar to medievalists and modernists alike, namely, limited access to sixteenth-century perspectives. Despite its rich social complexity, the institution of marriage during this period remains accessible to us in the twentieth century mainly through two kinds of sources: legal or administrative records and published literary or intellectual sources. On the other hand, we who study the development of this still extant social institution are often hampered by too much information about what happens after the Reformation. No matter how diligently we attempt to suspend such knowledge, five centuries of subsequent changes in Western marriage cannot help but influence our most basic questions about the Reformation's impact.

Though in some ways typical of all historical study, these two problems of primary sources and of teleological inclinations have produced an especially polarized approach to the question of marriage and the Reformation, similar to the more general historiographical debate already mentioned. At one end of the interpretational spectrum, we find those who theorize broadly using the limited primary sources and thus, not surprisingly, tend to support a revolutionary version of the Reformation's effects on marriage. At the opposite end of the same spectrum, we confront supporters of evolutionary explanations of changes in marriage, wherein individual reformers and the Reformation play only minor or peripheral roles. In both instances, moreover, interpretations of the nature and direction of all changes in marriage remain perceptibly shaped by the teleological preferences of the historians themselves.

Revolutionary interpretations of the Reformation's impact, for example, may have expanded considerably in scope over the past century, but have changed little in their basic disposition. For such scholars, the Protestant Reformation produced a marriage doctrine and practice fundamentally different from that of pre- and post-Tridentine Catholics, thus initiating a long process of "confessional formation" (*Konfessionsbildung*) in German society.[6] Ironically, in attempting to move beyond the boundaries of traditional works on marriage law[7] and theolo-

---

[6] Cf. influential interpretation of Ernst W. Zeeden, *Die Enstehung der Konfessionen. Grundlagen und Formen der Konfessionsbildung* (Munich, 1965); and *Konfessionsbildung* (Stuttgart, 1985).

[7] Most modern German legal scholarship on the subject of *Eheschließung*, or marriage formation and completion finds its origin in the debate between Emil Friedberg, *Das Recht der Eheschliessung in seiner geschichtlichen Entwicklung* (Leipzig, 1865; reprint: Aalen, 1965), and Rudolph Sohm, *Das Recht der Eheschliessung aus dem deutschen und canonischen Recht geschichtlich entwickelt* (Weimar, 1875). See especially the heated exchange between the two in Friedberg, *Verlobung und Trauung* (Leipzig, 1876), and Sohm, *Trauung und Verlobung: Eine Entgegnung auf Friedberg: Verlobung und Trauung* (Weimar, 1876); also Adolf von Scheurl, *Die Entwicklung des kirchlichen Eheschließungsrechts* (Erlangen, 1877); Hans von Schubert, *Die evangelische Trauung, ihre geschichtliche Entwicklung und gegenwärtige Bedeutung* (Berlin, 1890); and the more recent Siegfried Reicke, "Geschichtliche Grundlagen des deutschen Eheschließungsrechts, weltliche Eheschließung und kirchliche Eheschließung," in *Beiträge zur Frage des Eheschließungsrechts*, ed. Hans Adolf Dombois and Friedreich Karl Schumann (Gladbeck, 1953). On the development of German marital property law, see Richard Schroeder, *Geschichte des ehelichen Güterrechts in Deutschland*, 3 vols. (Stettin, 1863–74).

The classic on the Church's marriage law is still indisputably Adhémar Esmein, *Le mariage en*

4

gy,[8] many recent historians have produced an even more source-biased "social" representation than all of their predecessors. Steven Ozment, for instance, acknowledges that his evidence is "heavily-weighted toward self-conscious assessments by contemporary observers and participants."[9] Yet he proceeds to argue for the widespread emergence of a new Protestant married religious ideal in place of the traditional Catholic celibate ideal, resulting in fewer clerical abuses and a more affectionate view of the family overall.[10] Thomas Safley rejects a confessional distinction based on theology for one founded in law enforcement, particularly in the Protestant introduction of divorce.[11] Again, though, the

droit canonique, 2 vols. (Paris, 1891). Also valuable are Joseph Freisen, *Geschichte des kanonischen Eherechtes bis zum Verfall der Glossenliteratur* (1893; reprint: Paderborn, 1963); Jean Dauvillier, *Le mariage dans le droit classique de l'Eglise depuis le Décret de Gratian (1140) jusqu'à mort de Clement V (1314)* (Paris, 1933); and on the Protestant adaptation of the same: Rudolf Schäfer, "Die Geltung des kanonischen Rechts in der evangelischen Kirche Deutschlands von Luther bis zur Gegenwart. Ein Beitrag zur Geschichte der Quellen, der Literatur und der Rechtsprechung des evangelischen Kirchenrechts," in *Zeitschrift der Savigny-Stiftung für Rechtsgeschichte, Kanonistische Abteilung* 36/5 (1915), 165–413.

   Two recent works provide excellent syntheses on marriage law during the period. But while exhaustively researched, both Hartweg Dieterich, *Das Protestantische Eherecht in Deutschland bis zur Mitte des 17. Jahrhunderts* (Munich, 1970), and James A. Brundage, *Law, Sex, and Christian Society in Medieval Europe* (Chicago, 1987), overwhelmingly focus on the writings of contemporary jurists and other scholars alone.

8 The writings of Luther on marriage have expectedly received the greatest attention. Among the most thorough modern analyses of Luther's teachings on marriage: Olavi Lähteenmäki, *Sexus und Ehe bei Luther* (Turku, 1955); Ernst Kinder, "Luthers Auffassung von der Ehe," in *Bekenntnis zur Kirche. Festgabe für Ernst Sommerlath zum 70. Geburtstag*, ed. Ernst Heinz Amberg (Berlin, 1960); and Dieterich chap. 1. See also the earlier uncompleted work by Sigmund Baranowski, *Luthers Lehre von der Ehe* (Poznan, 1906). On other reformers and humanists, see Emile Telle, *Erasme de Rotterdam et le septième sacrament* (Geneva, 1954); Andre Biéler, *L'homme et la femme dans la morale calvaniste: La doctrine reformée sur l'amour, le mariage, le célibat, le divorce, l'adultère et la prostitution, considerée dans son cadre historique* (Geneva, 1963); Charles Pfeiffer, "Heinrich Bullinger and Marriage" (Ph.D. diss., St. Louis University, 1981); Herman Selderhuis, *Huwelijk en entscheiding bij Martin Bucer* (Leidem, 1994), forthcoming in English in the *Sixteenth Century Studies* series.

   On the medieval doctrinal precedents, see Gabriel LeBras, "La doctrine du mariage chez les théologiens et les canonistes depuis l'An Mille," in *DTC* 9:2123–220; Jean Leclerq, *Monks on Marriage: A Twelfth-Century View* (New York, 1982); and James Brundage, "Carnal Delight: Canonistic Theories of Sexuality," in *Proceedings of the Fifth International Congress of Medieval Canon Law*, ed. S. Kuttner and K. Pennington (Vatican City, 1980), 361–85.

9 Steven Ozment, *When Fathers Ruled: Family Life in Reformation Europe* (Cambridge, Mass., 1983), 2. Cf. similar criticisms of Ozment's use of such sources in reviews by Thomas Safley, *Sixteenth Century Journal* 15/1 (1984), 126–28, and Lyndal Roper, *Journal of Modern History* 58/1 (1986), 263–64.

10 See also Thomas Fischer Miller, "Mirror for Marriage: Lutheran Views of Marriage and the Family, 1520–1600" (Ph.D diss., University of Virginia, 1981); as well as the widespread influence of the Protestant Whig model of marriage in surveys and textbooks, evident even in the scholarly Brundage, *Law, Sex, and Christian Society*, 574–75.

11 Thomas M. Safley, *Let No Man Put Asunder: The Control of Marriage in the German Southwest: A Comparative Study, 1550–1600* (Kirkville, Mo., 1984). Safley's argument of confessional forma-

narrow and limited basis for generalization results in some distortions. For even Safley's more empirically founded conclusion that "Protestants achieved a more comprehensive and effective regulation of marriage in early modern Europe [than Catholics]" is unfortunately based on an unequal comparison of marriage litigation in the sprawling Catholic diocese of Constance with that of the highly centralized Reformed city-state of Basel.[12]

While most of these modern historians resist the simplistic confessional generalizations of earlier polemic,[13] many also resist establishing the full social context in which such reform agendas were formulated. Long-term development in any area other than the traditional concerns of law and theology is often hostilely discounted as dehumanizing.[14] The result is more of a caricature of social history in which the only role of Protestant and Catholic peoples is largely one of reactive acceptance or rejection of "new" marriage teachings, with almost all initiative for the timing and direction of change belonging to their religious and political leaders. Such scholars may differ on the legal or theological basis for confessional formation, but the elite source of change remains unchallenged.

Long-term developments in marriage constitute the almost exclusive concern of evolutionary interpretations of the Reformation's significance. Since the pioneering work of Philippe Ariès on childhood and the family, scholarship on the demographic and economic dimensions of

---

tion based on legal jurisdiction in many ways echoes the conclusions of Esmein, Wendel, Köhler, and Staehlin (see n.35 and also my discussion in Chapter 3). See also Judith Walters Harvey, "The Influence of the Reformation on Nürnberg Marriage Laws, 1520–1535" (Ph.D. diss., Ohio State University, 1972).

[12] *Let No Man Put Asunder*, 195. See Chapter 5 for a fuller discussion of his arguments and methodology.

[13] The revolutionary view of sixteenth-century marriage reforms in fact builds on a long tradition of confessional revision already current by the seventeenth century. Köhler, certainly no Catholic apologist, notes such historical revision in the Zurich *Ehesatzung* of 1698, which ahistorically attributes the city's long-anticipated break with the bishop's marriage jurisdiction to pious, Evangelical motives. In view of the pervasiveness of such assumptions, he writes, "Der erkannte Zusammenhang mit der Reformationsbewegung muß umgrenzt werden" (Kö I:2).

[14] Ozment approaches the animus expressed by other antiquantitative Reformation historians such as Hugh Trevor-Roper (*Religion, the Reformation, and Social Change* [London, 1967]) when he firmly rejects an approach "that holds unconscious demographic and economic forces in such awe that we learn little more about the human family than what it has in common with herding animals" (*When Fathers Ruled*, vii).

marriage has flourished.[15] Generally employing quantitative and statistical methodologies, historians have focused on long-term European marriage patterns in various areas, including age, social status, and other characteristics of marrying couples; the property transactions involved (principally dowry and inheritance); and the role and interests of parents, other relatives, and members of the community in the entire marriage procedure. Despite many differences in interests and interpretations, almost all of these scholars agree that the early modern period (fifteenth to eighteenth centuries) was a time of crucial transition in marital law and practice,[16] closely tied to the new economic and demographic forces of market capitalism.[17]

Without a doubt the most controversial theory in this respect has been the "great transformation" of European marriage and family proposed by Lawrence Stone and Edward Shorter.[18] While Stone prefers a more structuralist and elitist definition of the transformation than Shorter,[19]

[15] *Centuries of Childhood: A Social History of Family Life*, trans. Robert Baldick (New York, 1962). See historiographical overviews in Michael Anderson, *Approaches to the History of the Western Family, 1500–1914* (London, 1980); Richard Wall, "Introduction" in *Family Forms in Historic Europe*, ed. Robin Wall and Peter Laslett (Cambridge, 1982), 1–64; Michael Mitterauer and Reinhard Sieder, *From Patriarcy to Partnership: The European Family from the Middle Ages to the Present*, trans. Karla Oosterveen and Manfred Horzinger (Chicago, 1982), 178–226; and Barbara Diefendorf, "Family Culture, Renaissance Culture," *Renaissance Quarterly*, 40/4 (1987), 661–81.

[16] Alan MacFarlane (*Marriage and Love in England: Modes of Reproduction, 1300–1840* [New York, 1986]) identifies the beginning of the modern nuclear family in England with the onset of Malthusian restraint in marriage age and procreation, a development he places in the thirteenth century. Jack Goody (*The Development of Family and Marriage in Europe* [Cambridge, 1983]) attributes the breakdown of large kinship networks to a much earlier transformation during the fifth to eighth centuries and self-conscious ecclesiastical policies, aimed at bringing more land to the Church. Other historians differ on the exact point of transition but agree that it was most certainly not during the early modern period. See especially Ralph A. Houlbrooke, *The English Family, 1450–1700* (London, 1984).

[17] In this key respect, they echo recent neo-Weberian and Marxist connections of new religious forms and social structures with economic change. Cf. R. H. Hilton, ed., *The Transition from Feudalism to Capitalism* (London, 1978); S. Hoyer, *Reform, Reformation, Revolution* (Leipzig, 1980); O. Rammstedt, *Sekte und soziale Bewegung* (Cologne, 1966); P. M. Crew, *Calvinist Preaching and Iconoclasm in the Netherlands, 1544–69* (Cambridge, 1978).

[18] Lawrence Stone, *The Family, Sex and Marriage in England 1500–1800* (New York, 1977); Edward Shorter, *The Making of the Modern Family* (New York, 1975).

[19] Shorter's "great transformation" of the family from the "bad old days" is described generally and essentially engenders three "modern innovations": romantic love, domesticity, and maternal love. Since it involved the substitution of love for economic considerations in marriage, the first occurrence would have been among those least encumbered by property and preservation of social status – the poor. Stone, on the other hand, sets out with much more ambitious goals: "to chart and document, to analyse and explain, some massive shifts in world views and value

7

both argue that the economically induced change from a communal, or "open lineage," family structure to that of the modern nuclear family resulted in a dramatic transformation of marriage and family life in England, particularly in the innovative concepts of romantic love, domesticity, and maternal love. The early modern transformation of marriage and the family, Stone argues, was not an isolated event but merely one aspect of the greater social transformation of local, agrarian, kinship-based community (*Gemeinschaft*) to the larger, impersonal, capitalist society (*Gesellschaft*) of the modern West.[20]

In the midst of the heated debate stirred by such sweeping theories, some social historians have opted to set their sights somewhat more narrowly in examining changes in European marital practice. Focusing on the key element of the "great transformation" debate – the transition from extended to nuclear families in Europe – scholars such as John Hajnal, Peter Laslett, and André Burgière have attempted to define which European familial models apply where and when.[21] As a result, both the general applicability and chronology of Stone's and Shorter's theories have been widely criticized, with such criticisms casting similar

systems that occurred in England over a period of some three hundred years, from 1500 to 1800" (p. 3). The three phases which he subsequently discerns – Open Lineage (1450–1630), Restricted Patriarchial Nuclear Family (1550–1770), and Closed Domesticated Nuclear Family (1620–1800) – are all initiated by the propertied elite (see esp. 134ff.) and eventually trickle down to all parts of society.

John R. Gillis, *For Better, for Worse: British Marriages, 1600 to the Present* (New York, 1985), offers a subtler and more anthropologically inspired version of the same "transformation."

[20] Stone draws heavily on the "rise of individualism" tradition, most recently presented in Philippe Ariès and Georges Duby, eds., *Histoire de la vie privée*, especially vol. II: *Le Moyen Age*, ed. Georges Duby (Paris, 1986).

On the distinction between *Gemeinschaft* and *Gesellschaft*, see Chapter 5.

[21] Scholarship on family typology finds its roots in the works of several nineteenth-century European sociologists, most notably Frederick LePlay, *L'organisation de la famille selon le vrai modèle. . .* (Paris, 1875). LePlay introduced the theory of the modern nuclear ("unstable") family as the product of social decline, ultimately reaching fruition in the French Revolution.

Recent scholarship has seen a variety of typological theories, from a basic division between western Europe and everywhere else (J. Hajnal, "European Marriage Patterns in Perspective," in *Population in History*, ed. D. V. Glass and D. E. C. Eversley [London, 1965], 101ff; also "Two Kinds of Pre-industrial Household Formation System," in Wall, et al., *Family Forms in Historic Europe*, 65–104), to four major geographical groupings (western, middle western, mediterranean, eastern: Peter Laslett, *Family Life and Illicit Love in Earlier Generations* [Cambridge, 1977]), to three different types based on cohabitation, inheritance, and labor force need – nuclear, stem, and communitarian – in Andrée Burgière, "Pour une typologie des formes d'organisation domestique de l'Europe Moderne (XVIᶜ–XIXᶜ s.)," *Annales* 41 (1986), 639–55.

aspersions on any general "European" marriage pattern for the early modern period.[22]

Still others have chosen to examine more carefully changes in what they consider the most crucial component to understanding shifting marriage patterns – dowry and inheritance.[23] Some have taken a broader and more anthropological approach, demonstrating powerful connections between legal authority, social restrictions, religious ideology, and popular culture.[24] Research of this kind has especially contributed to related discussions of flexible "marriage strategies" among individuals and families of the period, recognizing a much broader variety of economic, social, and political factors in the choice to marry than the more general "transformation" or "familial model" theories suggest.

Nonetheless, for all the enormous progress made during the past thirty years in such previously unexplored aspects of European marriage development, this type of research also displays shortcomings. Most important – in direct contrast to the confessional formation approach –

---

22 In addition to their own misgivings on the early modern "beginning" of the nuclear family in England, MacFarlane (*Marriage and Love in England*, 3ff.) and Goody (*Family and Marriage in Europe*, 2ff.) express reservations (rare in Stone and Shorter) about the general applicability of English marital and familial patterns to all of Europe. Many historians agree that the search for a universal "European model" of marriage seems to have run its course. See especially the recent summary of family historiography in Tamara K. Hareven, "The History of the Family and the Complexity of Social Change," *American Historical Review* 96/1 (February 1991), 95–124; and David Sabean *Property, Production, and Family in Neckarhausen, 1700–1870* (Cambridge, 1990), 89–101, on historiographical attempts to define *Haus*.

23 See especially David Herlihy and Christiane Klapisch-Zuber, *Les toscans et leur familles: Une étude du catasto florentin de 1427* (Paris, 1978); Christiane Klapisch-Zuber, "'The Cruel Mother': Maternity, Widowhood, and Dowry in Florence in the Fourteenth and Fifteenth Centuries," in *Women, Family, and Ritual in Renaissance Italy*, trans. Lydia Cochrane (Chicago, 1985), 117–31; Christiane Klapisch-Zuber, "The Griselda Complex: Dowry and Marriage Gifts in the Quattrocento," in ibid., 213–46; Diane Owen Hughes, "From Brideprice to Dowry in Mediterranean Europe," *Journal of Family History* 3 (1978), 262–96; Stanley Chojnacki, "Dowries and Kinsmen in Early Renaissance Venice," *Journal of Interdisciplinary History* 4 (1975), 571–600; Jacques Lafon, *Les époux bordelais (1450–1550): Régimes matrimoniaux et mutations sociales* (Paris, 1972); and Goody, *Family and Marriage in Europe*. See also my discussion in Chapter 4.

24 John Bossy, "Blood and Baptism: Kinship, Community and Christianity in Western Europe from the Fourteenth to the Seventeenth Centuries," in *Sanctity and Secularity: The Church and the World*, ed. D. Baker (Cambridge, 1973); Natalie Zemon Davis, "Ghost, Kin, and Progeny: Some Features of Family Life in Early Modern France," *Daedalus* 106/2 (1977), 87–114; André Burgière, "Le rituel du mariage en France: Pratiques ecclésiastiques et pratiques populaires (XVIe–XVIIIe s.)," *Annales* 33 (1978), 637–49; Christiane Klapisch-Zuber, "Zacharias, or the Ousting of the Father: The Rites of Marriage in Tuscany from Giotto to the Council of Trent," in *Women, Family, and Ritual*, 178–212; Barbara Diefendorf, "Widowhood and Remarriage in Sixteenth-Century Paris," *Journal of Family History* 7/4 (1982), 379–95.

the roles of religious reformers in such long-term change are often handled in an overtly mechanistic and even dismissive manner. While many scholars reject as reductionist the sweeping formulations of Shorter, Stone, and Ariès, more specialized researchers rarely cast more than a cursory glance at contemporary religious and legal developments.[25] Once again we confront the same problem of historiographical perspective described in the first approach but in this case resulting in the opposite kind of imbalance, asking historians of marriage to choose between all-embracing theoretical structures and narrow, exclusively demographic or economic monographs.

This book seeks to combine the best of both approaches, fairly assessing the social effects of both revolutionary and evolutionary changes on marriage in sixteenth-century Germany. Beyond differences in sources and methods, the greatest obstacle to a balanced evaluation of the Reformation and marriage has been the inevitable teleological perspective of the modern investigator. Whether one adopts a Protestant Whig approach, such as Ozment, or the more negative view of Ariès, early modern changes in marriage are invariably assessed in light of their modern results. Indeed, the choice of a revolutionary or an evolutionary interpretation of marital change often appears a less important factor than the historian's own disposition toward the end product of such changes: either progressive interpretations of Protestantism and the modern State or antimodern revisionism and emphasis on the misogynist and other oppressive aspects of the same governmental and religious institutions.[26] Obviously, such personal evaluations represent the very essence of historical scholarship and neither could nor should be eliminated. Still, the question of the Reformation's immediate impact on Western marriage does require a different approach, one as free as possible from the knowledge of what ultimately follows.

---

[25] Cf., for example, the casual aside of Jean-Louis Flandrin in an otherwise well-considered treatment of family, marriage, and sexuality, in which he suggests a link between an early rise in contraception in France (a full century before the rest of Europe) and Jansenism and/or the "dechristianization" of Europe; See *Families in Former Times: Kinship, Household, and Sexuality,* trans. Richard Southern (Cambridge, 1979), 238ff. Even the cleverest connection of European developments in religion and marriage proposed by Goody supposes much greater unity in doctrine and effectiveness in enforcement than most medieval scholars would consider possible.

[26] Cf. similar complaints about family historians "overvaluing the present" in Goody, *Family and Marriage in Europe,* 2; and a related observation by Herlihy that "the medieval family has become the negative stereotype against which later families are compared, in order to show the alleged benefits of modernization" (*Medieval Households* [Cambridge, Mass., 1985], 112).

As a result, in evaluating the social impact of the Reformation on marriage, the perspective I have chosen is that of sixteenth-century reformers themselves, examining the nature, origin, and effect of their marriage reforms. I am aware of some risks to this approach, especially an overemphasis of the elite-popular distinction in early modern society, but I believe the advantages far outweigh potential dangers. First, the purported goals of sixteenth-century reformers provide fair and historically detached criteria for evaluating the success or failure of subsequent reforms. Second, this approach builds on the strongest primary sources of the period, namely those of legal and religious elites, and exploits these records' concentration on matters of obvious concern to the same reforming religious and secular elites. Third and most important, if we then examine these marriage reforms in both their short-term (ca. 1555–1619) and long-term (ca. twelfth–seventeenth century) contexts, we will be able to establish a historiographical balance that allows us to distinguish both individual agency and collective social evolution.

This combination of short-term and long-term perspectives has no precedent in the study of marriage and the Reformation. It offers, however, many insights on the question of religious reform and the social change in general. At first glance, the Reformation's revolutionary transformation of marriage appears irrefutable. Both traditional law and theology were indeed publicly refuted by reformers who proposed marriage as a superior religious ideal to celibacy, introduced divorce and remarriage, and initiated the secularization of marital law and jurisdiction. This portrait, however, misrepresents the very goals of reformers themselves. For when we begin to analyze the origins as well as the nature of such reforms, we immediately realize that the agendas of sixteenth-century Protestants and Catholics in fact both represented the intersection of two much older and more evolutionary reforms, one by ecclesiastical authorities since the twelfth century, the other by governmental leaders since the fifteenth century. Moreover, only when we understand the nature of these two long-term reforms of marriage, can we truly appreciate the goals, means, and results of their sixteenth-century intersection.

The book consequently is divided into two successive inquiries, dealing with the nature and origins of sixteenth-century marriage reforms (Part I) and their social impact (Part II). In Part I, we explore the apparent universal similarity in goals and methods among its proponents.

Introduction

Secular or religious, Protestant or Catholic, all reformers shared a remarkably similar view of not only the religious and social ideal of marriage but of the institutional means to implement such an ideal. In Chapter 1 we examine the common obsession of sixteenth-century reformers with selfish young people and other promiscuous individuals who placed themselves above "society" and formed various illicit liasons. Both Protestants and Catholics agreed that marriage represented a crucial connection between the public and private spheres and shared the perception of a dangerous new individualism at work, particularly in the marriages of minors and sexual morality as a whole. All marriage reformers also responded with the same solution: ostensibly a restoration of traditional paternal authority but simultaneously an attempt to redefine "society" in terms of Church and State with rulers and pastors as the paternalistic heads. Not surprisingly, reforming jurists and theologians also chose similar means to implement their visions, namely replacement of divisive local and oral traditions with the authority and uniform marital standards of the early modern Church and State.

This description of sixteenth-century marriage reformers is broadly compatible with the general early modern social transformation of Ariès and Stone, particularly in new division of public (Church and State) and private. It also concurs with much of the Reformation research indirectly inspired by writings of Norbert Elias and Michel Foucault,[27] and directly influenced by theories of "social disciplining" developed by Gerhard Oestreich.[28] Such interpretations stress the transformational role of social elites, particularly lawyers and theologians, in asserting new definitions of "society" and authority. For most of these scholars, the goals

---

[27] See especially Michel Foucault, *Discipline and Punish: The Birth of Prison*, trans. Alan Sheridan (New York, 1978), and Norbert Elias, *The Civilizing Process* (New York, 1978). For theories of acculturation, see Peter Burke, *Popular Culture in Early Modern Europe* (New York, 1978); Jean Delumeau, *Le peché et la peur: La culpabisation en occident (XIIIᶜ–XVIIIᶜ siècles)* (Paris, 1983); and Robert Muchembled, *Popular Culture and Elite Culture in France, 1400–1750* (Baton Rouge, 1985).

[28] Gerhard Oestreich, *Neostoicism and the Early Modern State* (Cambridge, 1982). See also criticisms of this approach in Heinz Schilling, "'Geschichte der Sünde' oder 'Geschichte des Verbrechens'? Überlegungen zur Gesellschaftsgeschichte der frühneuzeitlichen Kirchenzucht," *Jahrbuch des italienisch-deutschen historischen Instituts in Trient* 18 (1986), especially 173–78; and Stefan Breuer, "Sozialdisziplinierung. Probleme aund Problemverlagerungen eines Konzeptes bei Max Weber, Gerhard Oestreich und Michel Foucault," in *Soziale Sicherheit und soziale Disziplinierung*, ed. Christoph Sachße and Florian Tennstedt (Frankfurt a.M., 1986), 45–69; and a later elaboration in Winfried Schulze and Brigitta Oesterich, "G. Oestreichs Begriff 'Sozialdisziplinierung in der Frühen Neuzeit,'" *Zeitschrift für Historische Forschung* 14 (1987), 256–302.

and methods of Protestant and Catholic elites were, in this respect, practically identical – a theme of common "confessionalization," which has been most thoroughly developed by Wolfgang Reinhard and Heinz Schilling.[29] Building on earlier observations from Weber to Stone, Schilling in particular has stressed the importance of this confessionalization process for early modern statebuilding and the significant enhancement of central governmental authority as a consequence. More recently, other historians have focused on the role of gender and the strengthening of patriarchy in the elite transformation of early modern society.[30] Like many of those mentioned previously, these scholars place economic and demographic changes at the heart of such a transformation, but include women among those groups that are subsequently oppressed.

Beyond my chief disagreement on the oft-accelerated rate of social transformation, my differences with the "civilizing" and "confessionalizing" approaches are minor. I remain disinclined toward ι. more sinister and cynical characterizations of such "cultural elites," and rather more sympathetic to Ozment's portrayals of genuinely concerned and well-intentioned secular and ecclesiastical reformers. I am also uneasy with primarily economic explanations for what are usually more traditionally inspired and thus – from a capitalist viewpoint – inefficient reform ideas. And although the issue of gender clearly influenced all aspects of marriage reform, I am not entirely convinced of Roper's argument that "gender relations . . . were at the crux of the Reformation itself."[31]

To understand the origins of this common sixteenth-century emphasis on moral and legal reform of marriage among Protestant and Catho-

---

29 Wolfgang Reinhard, "Zwang zuf Konfessionalisierung? Prolegomena zu einer Theorie des konfessionellen Zeitalters," *Zeitschrift für Historische Forschung* 10 (1983), 257–77. Heinz Schilling, *Konfessionskonflikt und Staatsbildung: Eine Fallstudie über das Verhältnis von religiösem und sozialem Wandel in der Frühneuzeit am Beispiel der Grafschaft Lippe* (Gütersloh, 1981); or the same argument summarized in "The Reformation and the Rise of the Early Modern State," in *Luther and the Modern State in Germany*, ed. James Tracy (Kirksville, Mo., 1986), 21–30. See also Tracy's introduction in the same volume (9–19) on the historiography of the Lutheran Reformation and statebuilding.

30 For Germany, see especially Martha Howell, *Women, Production, and Patriarchy in Late Medieval Cities* (Chicago, 1986); Merry Wiesner, *Working Women in Renaissance Germany* (New Brunswick, N. J., 1986); Lyndal Roper, *The Holy Household: Women and Morals in Reformation Augsburg* (Oxford, 1989); and Lyndal Roper, "'Willie' und 'Ehre': Sexualität, Sprache und Macht in Augsburger Kriminalprozessen," in *Wandel der Geschlechterbeziehungen zu Beginn der Neuzeit*, ed. Heidi Wunder and Christina Vanja (Frankfurt a.M., 1991), 180–97.

31 *Holy Household*, 5. This issue will be discussed more fully in the next two chapters.

lic elites, Chapters 2 and 3 examine the long-term basis for this similarity, namely, the two very gradual and overlapping transformations of marriage that formed it: one religious and ideological, the other secular and bureaucratic. The religious reformation of marriage (Chapter 2) represented in effect a centuries-long process dating back at least to the scholastic reformers of the twelfth century. Their twofold goal of ensuring both a holy, indissoluble, and consensual definition of the conjugal bond as well as securing the Church's role in legal validation was adopted virtually unaltered by Catholic and Protestant reformers of the sixteenth century. Despite frequent rhetoric to the contrary, the reformed marriage doctrines of both confessions remained remarkably similar and faithful to the traditional ideology they jointly inherited. The true focus of Protestant and Catholic marriage reform was not traditional standards and ideals but their legal enforcement.

This overwhelming concern with stricter legal and moral enforcement during the sixteenth century reflected the area of overlap with the second reformation of marriage – that of the State (Chapter 3). Like their religious counterparts, governmental reformers of marriage also maintained a fundamentally conservative interest in ensuring both marital stability and their own authority in enforcement. Unlike ecclesiastical leaders, though, secular rulers were unable to exercise full judicial authority because of the jurisdictional implications of the twelfth-century sacramental definition. Not until secular courts and bureaucracies were more developed in the fifteenth century did these rulers begin to challenge openly ecclesiastical legal authority over marriage. The sixteenth-century secular reformation of marriage, then, also belonged to a centuries-long process, but one in this instance nearer to its beginning. Whereas the contemporary religious reformation in most ways represented the apex of ecclesiastical influence over marriage, the simultaneous bureaucratic expansion of State authority over marriage marked the starting demise of ecclesiastical legal juridsiction. Still, only in those German states with more developed bureaucracies, such as Swiss and imperial cities, was any kind of legal centralization possible or even desirable; in territorial states, the full transferal of legal jurisdiction and authority associated with the absolutist state remained far away.

This version of long-term institutional transformation also finds scholarly support in various quarters, most obviously in Duby's work on the gradual acculturation of the ecclesiastical model of marriage among the French nobility during the High Middle Ages.[32] More recently, a student of Elias, Michael Schroeter, has set out to apply Duby's model to late medieval Germany, describing the general social transformation from *Gemeinschaft* ("community") to *Gesellschaft* ("society") as reflected in marriage. Unfortunately, Schroeter's study fluctuates between over-estimating the role of both Church and State in this transformation of marriage and alternately displaying a pronounced antipathy to relying on any legal or other "official" documents from the same two institutions.[33] Consequently, I find my approach and conclusions in this section closer to those of John Bossy, particularly in terms of the gradual social and institutional change that he associates with the decline of local commu-nal and familial authority during the late medieval and early modern periods.[34]

Part II addresses the immediate social impact of these two uneven long-term reforms and their sixteenth-century Protestant and Catholic formulations. Here, the two main foci of sixteenth-century reform – the wedding procedure (Chapter 4) and marital discipline (Chapter 5) – provide the points of reference for our assessment. Once again, our understanding of the intersection of a mature ecclesiastical reform (uni-form high moral standards) with an underdeveloped bureaucratic in-volvement (inadequate means of enforcement) helps explain the com-mon result among all confessions, namely, the continuing local authority in both the moral and legal aspects of marriage. Although the medieval Christian ideal of holy, consensual, and indissoluble marriage appears to have been firmly established in popular perception by this time, newer objectives – such as greater legal uniformity and especially sexual disci-

---

[32] See Georges Duby, *Medieval Marriage: Two Models from Twelfth-Century France*, trans. Elborg Forster (Baltimore, 1978), especially 17ff. on this thesis.

[33] *"Wo zwei zusammenkommen in rechter Ehe . . ."*; *Sozio-und psychogenetische Studien über Eheschlie-ßungsvorgänge vom 12. bis 15. Jahrhunderts* (Frankfurt a.M., 1985). Schroeter states very early that his perspective is sociological rather than historical, castigating legal historians in particular for their overreliance on legal sources that fail to capture "ein wircklichkeitsnäheres Bild der ehelichen Beziehung" and instead promulgate "die Fiktion identischer Formen von Eheschließungen" during the late Middle Ages (vii, 11). His disregard and occassionally con-tempt for "juristiche Details," however, as at least one unfavorable review points out (Johannes Fried, *Historische Zeitschrift* 242 [1986], 681–84) consistently undermines his attempts to estab-lish institutional coercion by Church and State in replacing traditional parental authority in marriage. Since his argument in fact turns out to be more historical than sociological, official documentation and literary supplements – rather than the reverse – would have provided the more convincing case.

[34] See especially *Christianity in the West, 1400–1700* (Oxford, 1985).

pline – proved hard to achieve, particularly in view of persisting local custom and authority.

My interpretation of the Reformation's limited social impact clearly reinforces the conclusions of Gerald Strauss and other historians who have questioned the "success" of Protestant reforms. It also deepens our understanding of the relationship of religious and legal reforms of marriage to actual practice. Historians of Germany long maintained an undisputed lead in this area, but currently lag far behind English and French scholars in utilizing legal records to address the issue of social impact.[35] Like Ingram and Carlson for England, I find no evidence of significantly changed views of marriage and family in late sixteenth-century society, and similarly conclude that – with the notable exception of the married ministry of Lutherans and Calvinists – confessional differences in general appear to have much less important than bureaucratic ones in terms of social impact. The sixteenth century witnessed no immediate triumph of governmental or ecclesiastical authority over marriage, and certainly none of extreme usurpations or transformations assumed by some authors.[36] On the other hand, Protestant reformers did succeed in planting at least two seeds of legal and ideological innovation – divorce and elimination of the celibate religious ideal – which by

[35] The marriage Reformations of Strasbourg and the Swiss cities received the earliest attention. See especially François Wendel, *Le mariage à Strasbourg à l'epoque de la Réforme, 1520–1692* (Strasbourg, 1928); Walther Köhler, *Zürcher Ehegericht and Genfer Konsistorium*, 2 vols. (Leipzig, 1933–42); and Adrian Staehlin, *Die Einführung der Ehescheidung in Basel zur Zeit der Reformation* (Basel, 1957). Research on the rest of German-speaking Europe, however, has been slow in developing. See R. Weigand, "Die Rechtsprechung des Regensburger Gerichts in Ehesachen unter besonderer Berücksichtigung der bedringten Eheschliessung nach Gerichtsbüchern aus dem Ende des 15. Jahrhunderts," *Archiv für katholisches Kirchenrecht* 137 (1968), 403–63; Klaus Lindner, "Courtship and the Courts: Marriage and Law in Southern Germany, 1350–1550" (Th. D. diss., Harvard University, 1988); and Safley, *Let No Man Put Asunder.*

For England: Richard Wunderli, *London Church Courts on the Eve of the Reformation* (Cambridge, Mass. 1981); Martin Ingram, *Church Courts, Sex, and Marriage in England, 1570–1640* (London, 1987); Erik Josef Carlson, "Marriage and the English Reformation" (Ph. D. diss., Harvard University, 1987).

For France: Anne Lefebvre-Teillard, *Les Officialités à la Veille du Concile de Trente* (Paris, 1973); Beatrice Gottlieb, "Getting Married in Pre-Reformation Europe: The Doctrine of Clandestine Marriage and Court Cases in Fifteenth-Century Champagne" (Ph. D. diss., Columbia University, 1974); Alain Lottin et al., *La désunion du couple sous l'ancien régime: L'exemple du Nord* (Paris, 1985); and on French Switzerland, Jeffery Watt, *The Making of Modern Marriage: Matrimonial Control and the Rise of Sentiment in Neuchâtel, 1550–1800* (Ithaca, N. Y., 1992).

[36] Cf. Christopher Lasch, *Haven in a Heartless World: The Family Besieged* (New York, 1977); Ferdinand Mount, *The Subversive Family: An Alternative History of Love and Marriage* (London, 1981). Cf. also Ariès's ominous conclusion to *Centuries of Childhood:* "The concept of the family, the concept of class, and perhaps elsewhere the concept of race, appear as manifestations of the same intolerance towards variety, the same insistence on uniformity" (415).

the beginning of the next century played increasingly important roles in the gradual social process of confessionalization. The implications of both findings for evolutionary and revolutionary interpretations of the Reformation are discussed more fully in the book's conclusion.

The geographical perspective

The geographical scope of the following study is German-speaking Europe as a whole, or the Holy Roman Empire and Swiss Confederation, together comprising more than 250 independent states during the sixteenth century. For the purposes of confessional comparison, I focus – especially in Part II – on three secular states from the Rhineland Palatinate (or Palatinate, for short), located in west central Germany along the Rhine border with France: the Palatine-Electorate (Calvinist after 1560), the Prince-Bishopric of Speyer (Catholic throughout the period), and the imperial city of Speyer (officially Lutheran after the Augsburg Peace of 1555). (See Figure 1.) All three played key roles in German secular and ecclesiastical politics of the sixteenth century, all three shared roughly the same customary and official regulation of marriage before the Reformation, and, most important, all three represented ostensibly different confessional approaches to marriage reform.

The Palatine-Electorate was by far the most politically, economically, and militarily significant of the three. From the beginning of the Wittelbachs' six-century rule of the territory in 1214, the Counts-Palatine continually expanded both the boundaries and political clout of their strategically located principality. With the Golden Bull of 1348, the Count-Palatine was recognized as one of seven hereditary electors of the Holy Roman Emperor, and by the time of Ruprecht III's partition among his four sons in 1410, the Palatine-Electorate was one of the richest and most influential states in all of Germany.[37] Even after the major political setback of the expansionist Bavarian Succession War of 1503–5, Elector Philip's resources remained impressive: about 1,800 square miles of territory, including thirty-seven castles, twenty-four towns, thirty-four

---

[37] Cf. the excellent historical overview of Henry J. Cohn, *The Government of the Rhine Palatinate in the Fifteenth Century* (Oxford, 1965), 2ff. Ruprecht's main possessions on the Rhine and electorship went to Ludwig III; the Upper Palatinate, or Oberpfalz, to Johann; lands west of Ludwig's (Zweibrücken) to Stefan; and lands east of Ludwig's (Mosbach) to Otto. Cohn provides a helpful genealogical chart on p. 20, indicating changes in dynastic lines in 1559 (to Simmern-Zweibrücken) and 1648 (to Neuberg-Zweibrücken).

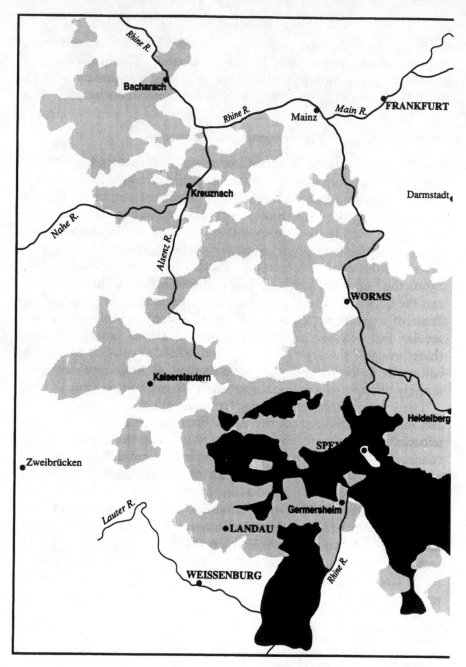

Figure 1. The Rhineland Palatinate and Holy Roman Empire, ca. 1600.

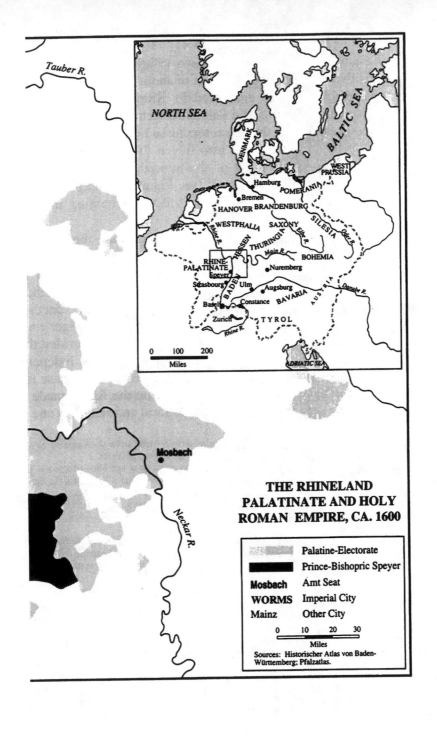

Tauber R.

NORTH SEA

BALTIC SEA

DENMARK

WEST PRUSSIA

Hamburg

Bremen
POMERANIA

HANOVER BRANDENBURG

WESTPHALIA
Rhine R.
SAXONY
Elbe R.
SILESIA
Oder R.

THURINGIA

HESSEN
Main R.
BOHEMIA

RHINE-
PALATINATE
Speyer
BADEN
Nuremberg

Strasbourg
Ulm
Augsburg
AUSTRIA
Danube R.

Basel
Constance
BAVARIA

Zurich
TYROL

Rhine R.

0   100   200
Miles

ADRIATIC SEA

Mosbach

Neckar R.

THE RHINELAND
PALATINATE AND HOLY
ROMAN EMPIRE, CA. 1600

	Palatine-Electorate
	Prince-Bishopric Speyer
Mosbach	Amt Seat
WORMS	Imperial City
Mainz	Other City

0   10   20   30
Miles

Sources: Historischer Atlas von Baden-
Württemberg; Pfalzatlas.

agricultural estates, and all or part of 450 villages.[38] Considered in combination with an estimated population of about 200,000 to 300,000 and the considerable revenue generated by Rhine tolls alone,[39] the political and economic might of the Palatine-Electorate made its rulers powerful figures well beyond their own territorial boundaries. Administratively, the Electorate was divided into fifteen districts, or Ämter, of varying size and importance. Most of the judicial evidence in Part II comes from the Oberamt of Bacharach (see Figure 1), comprising the city of Bacharach and three surrounding valleys, containing in total about 1,300 inhabitants in 1600.[40]

Considerably smaller both in area and population, the Prince-Bishopric of Speyer (ca. 800 square miles with a population of ca. 20,000)[41] and imperial city of Speyer (with a population of 7,000 to 8,000)[42] were forced to rely on military and political protection from their powerful neighbor throughout most of the late Middle Ages.[43] Nonetheless, the bishops' concurrent spiritual jurisdiction over a much larger area, combined with a strong imperial presence from 1527 on,[44] provided the Prince-Bishopric with a larger degree of legal and political independence than size alone might indicate. This was even more the case for the imperial city of Speyer, whose ideal location on the Rhine made it not only an economic crossroads but also a political and religious one –

[38] Volker Press, *Calvinismus und Territorialstaat. Regierung und Zentralbehörden der Kurpfalz, 1559–1619* (Stuttgart, 1970), 168ff.; Cohn, *The Government of the Rhine Palatinate*, 4.

[39] Cohn (*The Government of the Rhine Palatinate*, 4) sets the population at 150,000–200,000 in the fifteenth century and 300,000 by the end of the eighteenth century. Vogler (I:vii) sets the figure during his study (1555–1619) at 300,000–400,000, although without supplying his source. See also H. Fliedner, *Die Rheinzölle der Kurpfalz am Mittelrhein, in Bacharach und Kaub* (Trier, 1910).

[40] Heinz Schüler, *Die Konventsprotokolle der reformierten Klasse Bacharach, 1587–1620* (Cologne, 1977), 9–10.

[41] Based on analysis by Lawrence Duggan, *Bishop and Chapter: The Governance of the Bishopric of Speyer to 1552* (New Brunswick. N. J., 1978), 194–95, of the 1530 episcopal census, indicating a total of 28,240 persons living within the Prince-Bishopric, 8,245 of them subjects of the Elector, emperor, or others.

[42] Based on population counts of 7,000 in 1500, 7,950 in 1565, 7,814 in 1586, and ca. 8,000 in 1592, in Willi Alter, "Von der Konradinischen Rachtung bis fum letzten Reichstag in Speyer, 1420/22–1570," GStSp I:478, 534, 555; N. Ohler, "Alltag in einer Zeit des Friedens, 1570–1620," in GStSp I:584.

[43] The protectorate union (*Schutzvertrag*) between the Prince-Bishop and the Elector in 1365 was merely the first in a long series lasting well into the sixteenth century. Duggan, *Bishop and Chapter*, 111ff.

[44] From 1527 until the destruction of the city in 1689, both the *Reichsregiment* and *Reichskammergericht* were based in the city of Speyer, maintaining permanent staffs of at least 600–700, and providing the Catholic emperor with a strong foothold in mostly Protestant territory. Alter, in GStSp I:505, 515; Ohler, in GStSp I: 583–84.

seat to frequent imperial diets, with three times as many urban diets as any other German city of the fifteenth and sixteenth centuries.[45]

The Reformation came early to the Palatinate but was slow to gain official recognition. Martin Bucer, Michael Diller, Anton Eberhardt, and others brought the Evangelical faith to cities such as Speyer and Weissenburg in the early 1520s. Yet despite overwhelming Lutheran populations in both cities by 1540, magistrates remained too politically insecure to proclaim official conversion before 1555.[46] At that time, under the protection of the then Lutheran Palatine-Electorate and the newly signed Peace of Augsburg, all but one of the imperial cities in the diocese of Speyer officially embraced the Evangelical faith.[47] By the time of Elector Friedrich III's conversion to Calvinism around 1560, over two-thirds of the dioceses of Speyer and Worms had been lost to Protestantism, partly due to the inaction of Speyer's Bishop Marquad and partly to the aggressive evangelism of neighboring states.[48]

The principal time-frame of Part II, from the Peace of Augsburg until the beginning of the Thirty Years' War (1555–1619), was a period of intense religious and legal rivalry in the Palatinate. With the arrival of the Jesuit Peter Canisius in Speyer in 1567 and elections of an outspoken, reforming vicar-general (Beatus Moses) and like-minded bishop (Eberhard) in 1571 and 1582, respectively, the Catholic response to Protestant gains was well underway.[49] At the same time, secular and religious authorities of the Electorate and city of Speyer had already begun the process of moral and legal reform within their jurisdictions that would distinguish them from neighbori g Catholics. While the Cal-

[45] Thirty-nine of seventy-eight urban diets from 1471–1585, listed in Thomas Brady, *Turning Swiss* (Cambridge, 1985), 231–34.

[46] See O. R. Landsmann, *Wissembourg. Un siècle de son histoire, 1480–1590* (Rixheim, 1903), 6ff., 124ff., 136; Richard Raubenheimer, "Martin Bucer und sein humanistischen Speyerer Freunde," *Blätter für pfälzische Kirchengeschichte und religiöse Volkskunde* 32/1–2 (1965), 1–52. Alter in *GStSp* I: 485ff.; Ohler in *GStSp* I:578.

[47] Only Weilderstadt, in Württemberg, remained Catholic (Stamer III:49).

[48] Much of Marquad's failure to respond to the Protestant offensive has been attributed to his close personal relations with Elector Friedrich and Johannes Casimir, as well as possible Protestant sympathies. Volker Press, "Das Hochstift Speyer in Reich des späten Mittelalters und der frühen Neuzeit–Portrait eines geistlichen Staates," in *Oberrheinische Studien* (Karlsruhe, 1985), 262–63; Stamer II:325, III:14, 22–24, 41.

[49] Stamer III:65ff., 132–35, 209ff. See also the less engaged and more critical Hans Ammerich, "Formen und Wege der Katholischen Reform in den Diözesen Speyer und Straßburg: Klerusreform und Seelsorgereform," in *Oberrheinische Studien*, ed. Volker Press et al., vol. 6 (Karlsruhe, 1983) 291–327; and Marc Forster, *The Couter-Reformation in the Villages: Religion and Reform in the Bishopric of Speyer, 1560–1720* (Ithaca, N.Y., 1992).

vinist electors struggled on the stage of international politics, reformers such as Zacharius Ursinus, Caspar Olevianus, Thomas Erastus, and Christoph Ehem attempted to transform life within the Electorate into the more godly society inspired by their faith.[50] By 1618, the often provocative methods and alliances of the same culminated in a devastating war that cost the "Winter King" Friedrich V his electorship and realm – and a good number of his subjects their lives. Our study, however, ends before the religious reforms of all three Palatine states are overwhelmed by more immediate concerns of war "contributions" and sheer physical survival.

[50] On politics, see especially the brief overview of C.-P. Clasen, *The Palatinate in European History, 1559–1660* (Oxford, 1963). Among the many studies of Protestantism in the Palatinate, see especially Press, *Calvinismus und Territorialstaat;* Vogler, Henry J. Cohn, "The Territorial Princes in Germany's Second Reformation, 1559–1622," in *International Calvinism, 1541–1715,* ed. Menna Prestwick, (Oxford, 1985); *Controversy and Conciliation: The Reformation and the Palatinate, 1559–1583,* ed. Derk Visser (Allison Park, Pa., 1986); and most recently, *Geschichte der Kurplalz,* vol. II *(Neuzeit),* ed. Meinrad Schaab (Stuttgart, 1992).

Part I

The nature and origins of sixteenth-century marriage reform

I

Marriage reform and reformers

> All orders of human society derive from the first estate, matrimony, which was instituted by God Himself. On this origin and foundation stand all the other estates, communities and associations of men. . . . From the management of the household, which we call *oeconomia*, comes the administration of a government, a state being nothing more than a proliferation of households.
>
> Justin Göbler, *The Law-Mirror* (1559)[1]

> The estate of marriage is the spring from which all authority originates and flows.
>
> Georg Spalatin, *Fourteen grounds that should deservedly move everyone to esteem and respect the estate of marriage* (1531)[2]

At the beginning of the sixteenth century in Germany, the institution of marriage seemed to many contemporaries to be under a state of siege. The growing proliferation of tracts and dialogues satirizing the sorry state of the institution has led many historians to the same conclusion.[3] Sexual promiscuity, according to critics, ran rampant in all areas of society, making a mockery of the Church's traditional teachings on both marriage and celibacy. Whether ecclesiastical leaders and courts were

---

[1] *Der Rechten Spiegel* . . . (Frankfurt a.M., 1558), xiiii[a-b], translated in Strauss, *Luther's House of Learning*, 118.

[2] *Vierzehen ursachen/ die billich yederman bewegen sollen/ den Ehestand lieb und hoch zuhaben und achten* (Erfurt, 1531), 2[a].

[3] Based on the work of the Rabelaisian scholar Abel Lefranc, LeBras asserts, "On peut dire que de 1450 ou environ aux années qui virent le commencement de la Réforme le mariage apparaît comme une institution fortement battue en brèche." ("La doctrine du mariage," in *DTC* 9:2224). Ozment agrees that the perception of a marriage "crisis" was widespread and, though he overwhelmingly identifies such "defenders of the estate of marriage" as Protestant and proto-Protestant, he concedes that "concern for the estate of marriage was not confined to the ranks of Protestants and humanists" (*When Fathers Ruled*, 1–9). See also Waldemar Kawerau, *Die Reformation und die Ehe. Ein Beitrag zur Kulturgeschichte des 16. Jahrhunderts* (Halle, 1892), 4ff.

unwilling or unable to stop the marital chaos provided a subject of much debate among the new reformers of marriage. The detrimental effects on the dignity of the estate of marriage, meanwhile, seemed obvious to many observers:

> The estate of marriage . . . is so wickedly abused, despised, and degraded as a wretched and contemptible estate that even the young people shrink from it when they see how strange things are, saying, "It takes a lot to set up housekeeping," . . . for many it is nowadays a great horror, and among children a burden.[4]

Compared with the dramatic religious and political transformations of the times, marriage reform might be assumed a peripheral concern among secular and religious authorities. In fact, it stood by implication at the heart of almost every major legal, religious, and social reform of the period. Marriage and the household, as many early modern scholars have noted, served not only as the models for all social order, but as its fundamental building blocks as well.[5] Luther called marriage "the mother of all earthly laws," and Calvin agreed that the "inviolable law" of the estate provided the basis for all social order.[6] Erasmus Alberus summarized the relationship between private and public order succinctly:

> A wise and virtuous piece of advice:
> many pious burghers living without vice
> are the strongest walls of all against any disaster,
> protecting a city better than those of stone and plaster.[7]

---

[4] Leonard Culman, *Jungen gesellen, Jungkfrauwen und Witwen* (Magdeburg, 1534) A3ᵃ, D6ᵇ, cited in Ozment, *When Fathers Ruled*, 185, n. 13.

[5] Joy D. Wiltenburg, for instance, characterizes the household and family as the "model for the proper ordering of both sexual and social hierarchies" (*Disorderly Women and Female Power in the Street Literature of Early Modern England and Germany* [Charlottesville, Va., 1992], 77).

[6] Luther: *Grosser Kathechismus* (1529), *WA* 30/I:152; and sermon at wedding of Gmund von Lindenau in Merseberg (1545), *WA* 49:297: "es ist der eltist stand unter allen der gantzen welt, ja, alle andere komen aus dem her." Calvin: Commentaries Matt. 19:4–7, Gen. 2:24–27. On the pervasive sixteenth-century theme of the connection between good and disciplined *Oeconomia* or *Haushaltung* and social order, see also Strauss (*Luther's House of Learning*, 117ff.), Ozment (*When Fathers Ruled*, 8ff.), and Julius Hoffman, *Die 'Hausväterliteratur' und die 'Predigten über den christlichen Hausstand': Lehre vom Hause und Bildung für das häusliche Leben in 16., 17., und 18. Jahrhundert* (Weinheim, 1959), 5–33 (on ancient and medieval traditions of *Ökonomik, Agrarlehre*, and *Haustafeln*).

[7] "Ein weiser tugentreicher Rath / Vil frommer Burger in der staat / Die aller stercksten mawern sind / keyn besser Rinckmawren ich find." Erasmus Alberus, *Das Ehebuchlein* (Strasbourg, 1539), Dii.

Marriage reform and reformers

The elementary linkage of marital, familial, and social order in fact constituted a ubiquitous theme in all sixteenth-century literature. Generally most authors came to the same laudatory conclusion reached by Melanchthon in his discourse on the fourth commandment: "What a fine and useful thing it is, this admirable association of people linked in their several groupings, namely wedlock, civic assembly, government, justice, law and good discipline."[8] Though hardly new to the Greco-Roman tradition,[9] this hierarchical view of social order enjoyed unprecedented literary popularity and influence at all levels during the sixteenth century.

Disintegration of marriage and the family, consequently, was frequently linked to crises simultaneously confronting religious and political authorities during the "long sixteenth century" (roughly 1450–1620). The apparent similarity to modern scholarly assessments of the period, however, belies a crucial difference. Whereas modern historians look to the breakdown of early modern communal, ecclesiastical, and other large institutional authorities for explanations,[10] sixteenth-century critics consistently diagnosed the central problem at the level of the household. Early Lutheran reformers blamed the Church and its laws, later reformers (Catholics as well as Protestant) stressed individual moral degeneration, but the urgent need for action remained undisputed.

Marital and social disorder

Complaints about marital disorder made up only part of the virtual deluge of publications on marriage that followed the advent of the printing press in Europe. Until the Reformation, in fact, publications calling for legal and religious reform of the institution were far outnumbered by more traditional panegyrics and satires. We shall have occasion to treat this literature in the next chapter. For now, it is enough to observe that these two genres had a long history in Western culture and that they followed literary conventions and conceits that were established long before the Reformation era.

---

8 *Cathechismus* (1543); translated in Strauss, *Luther's House of Learning,* 239.
9 Cf. Gordon J. Schochet, *The Authoritarian Family and Political Attitudes in Seventeenth-Century England,* 2nd rev. ed. (Oxford, 1988), especially 18ff.; and fifteenth-century humanist idealizations of the *paterfamilias* in Herlihy, *Medieval Households,* 115–17.
10 See, for instance, the extensive bibliography on authority and *Herrschaft* in Thomas Robisheaux, *Rural Society and the Search for Order in Early Modern Germany* (Cambridge, 1989), 274ff.

The third genre, comprising works calling for legal and spiritual reform, was largely an innovation of the sixteenth century. In these writings, early Protestant polemicists attacked the Church's handling of
marriage as unjust and immoral.[11] Most often, writers focused on the
person of the pope and on the institutional ills resulting from his "false"
teachings. In particular these critics decried what they considered the
two worst violations of the natural social order: the marriage of minors
without their parents' consent or knowledge; and the pandemic sexual
promiscuity and marital discord, which threatened the very fiber of
marriage as an institution. And what was the ultimate source of this
contemporary breakdown in marital order? For those Lutheran reformers who attempted to answer this perennial question, the culprits
seemed obvious: the Canon law of marriage in general and the doctrine
of clerical celibacy in particular.

Nothing more clearly illustrated the crisis of patriarchal authority for
sixteenth-century Protestants than the specter of clandestine marriages
among minors. Combining both outright defiance of paternal authority
with perceptions of official Church indifference or even avarice, these
illicit unions provided the symbolic whipping boy of all sixteenth-century
marriage reformers. The origins of popular resentment may be traced
back at least to the twelfth century and the Church's formal assumption
of exclusive legal jurisdiction over marriage. Many laymen (and some
clerics) clearly resented having the undeniably social institution of marriage subjected to the authority of religious celibates. More seriously,
most apparently continued to consider the legal definitions and procedures introduced by ecclesiastical courts as "foreign" at best and socially
subversive at worst.

Sixteenth-century critics excoriated the accumulated Canon law of
marriage as confusing, inequitable, impractical, arbitrary, and easily
abused. Enforcement, by comparison, was supposedly even worse – sporadic, ineffective, and often corrupt. In one of his earliest public indictments of the Canon law of marriage, Luther captured the essence of
most contemporary criticism on the issue: "The pope [has made] mar-

---

[11] For the most interesting discussion of this literature, see Ozment's *When Fathers Ruled*, especially chap. 1. Most of the pamphlets discussed by Ozment are available, as most of those
discussed here, in the Tübingen Flugschriften Microfiche collection of Köhler (see Appendix
and the list of primary sources in the Bibliography).

riage a sacrament, free yet caught and entangled in countless strings."[12] In other words, the existing legal system made it both too easy and too difficult to contract marriage: "Too easy" in the overly simple consensual basis for validity; "too difficult" because of the network of impediments and legalisms constructed to counter such license. In both instances, the basis for complaints was Canon law's recognition of simple vows of consent between the marrying couple as the sole requirement for a legitimate and binding union. With marital validity based on their word alone, critics claimed, disobedient minors or unscrupulous philanderers could freely enter or leave a marriage without a hitch, even as many honest and upright couples remained hindered from marrying by the legal maze of impediments and the cost of obtaining dispensations from them. For many religious reformers, these disparities merely indicated the general insensitivity of the canonical system to the true social nature of marriage. For historians, these two foremost grounds of complaint against ecclesiastical control of marriage speak volumes on the perceived chasm between what many early modern observers thought marital law and enforcement were and what they ought to have been.

Clandestine marriages among minors, if many contemporary pamphleteers may be believed, were pandemic in Europe during the late fifteenth and early sixteenth centuries. Pre-Reformation court evidence during the late fifteenth and early sixteenth centuries remains less conclusive on actual frequency,[13] but the general opposition to such illicit unions clearly crossed all cultural, social, and religious boundaries. By the time of the Reformation, the stereotype of strong-minded, disobedient children marrying against their parents' wishes (and with disastrous consequences) had become a well-established topos of most European literature; the fifteenth-century legend of Romeo and Juliet is only the best-known example.[14] Protestant and Catholic reformers as diverse as More, Erasmus, Brenz, and Zwingli harshly condemned such

---

[12] Luther, "Misuse of the Mass" (1521), *LW* 36:213. On clandestine marriage, see especially "Von Ehesachen" (1530), *WA* 30/III:205–24. For a fuller discussion of Luther's writings on marriage, see Chapter 2.

[13] Although some modern scholars have accepted such polemic estimates at face value (cf. Ozment, *When Fathers Ruled*, 1–2, 25–31, 49), actual evidence of such illicit but valid unions is notoriously difficult to come by. See Chapter 4, for my comments on different judicial interpretations of "clandestine marriage."

[14] Other earlier and contemporary examples include Troilus and Criseyde, Aucassia and Nicolette, Tristam and Isolde, and John Webster's *Duchess of Malfi*.

private and secret marriages as diabolically inspired.[15] Jean de Coras subscribed to the French royal tradition of equating clandestine marriage with rape, and the otherwise permissive Rabelais argued for the right of a father to kill the clandestine husband of his daughter.[16]

Even more distressing to many early sixteenth-century observers was the apparent ineffectiveness of civil and ecclesiastical prohibitions of these unions and the relative ease with which such a marriage could be contracted. Most critics concurred with Luther's diagnosis that the main culprit was clearly the "fool's game" (*Narrenspiel*) of the *verba de presenti* and *de futuro* formulas, both representing medieval canonical attempts to bridge the gap between the worldly marriage contract and the sacramental definition of twelfth-century theologians.[17] From the time ecclesiastical courts had assumed exclusive legal jurisdiction over questions of marital validity in the twelfth century, the wording of the marriage vow itself had assumed central importance of all related litigation. Simple consent of the marrying couple alone, given in the present tense (i. e., "I take you"), sufficed to make the union valid; vows exchanged, on the other hand, in the future tense (i.e., "I will marry you") required consummation for validity, but still no additional rituals, publicity, or – most upsetting to sixteenth-century critics – parental approval. Worse yet, they claimed, the more subsequent canonists struggled to minimize the disparity between sacrament and contract, the more chaotic matters got, resulting in a variety of social and moral problems as bad as or worse than clandestine marriage. An early Evangelical tract by Hans Schwalb in 1521 could find no socially redeeming value whatsoever in the entire canonical system of marriage:

If a young man enters into conversation with a young woman, there

---

[15] Thomas More, *Utopia*, trans. and ed. H. V. S. Ogden (Arlington Heights, Ill., 1949), 58–59; Telle, *Erasme*, 350, 359; Johannes Brenz, *Wie yn Ehesachen* (Wittenberg, 1531), B 4ᵃ; Ozment, *When Fathers Ruled*, 28–29.

[16] Jean de Coras, *Des mariages clandestinement et irreverement contractés* (Toulouse, 1557); François Rabelais, *Tiers livre*, especially chap. 48, in *Oeuvres complètes*, ed. Guy Demerson (Paris, 1973), 355–557. For Rabelais, "perfection of filial duty of Christian morality lies in placing everything to do with marriage in the hands of one's father" (M. A. Screech, *The Rabelaisian Marriage* [London, 1958], 50–51).

[17] "Von Ehesachen" (1530), *WA* 30/III:211. According to LeBras, it was the imprecise consensual definition of the twelfth-century canonists itself that made Church law and doctrine vulnerable: "Une définition insuffisante des rapports entre le contrat et le sacrament fera le jeu des adversaires de la puisssance ecclésiastique. Et par ailleurs, les exagérations poétiques des panégyristes de l'ordre conjugal n'ouvrent-elles point souvent la voie aux contempteurs du célibat?" See "La doctrine du mariage," in *DTC* 9:2223; and my discussion in Chapter 2.

[Church authorities] are, warning that the man must drop his lord's work and make a [marriage] contract with the woman before the monkey's tail of an Official. From this comes great perjury and scandal. They proceed to question the woman's reputation with their oaths, interrogating and prosecuting her on her own conscience, as well as other shameful acts that I will not speak of here – all in the name of feminine propriety and upright character.[18]

For Luther, the problems themselves defied simple exposition: "Everything is in such dire confusion that one does not know where to begin, how far to go, and where to leave off."[19] Erasmus concurred that canonical marriage law contained too many artificial and useless legal subtleties, all largely due to the inadequacy of the consensual definition of the sacrament.[20]

Most disturbing to both reformers, however, was the recurrent theme of "abandon and confusion" among those lay people subjected to such a removed and impractical marriage law.[21] That ecclesiastical authorities could continue to tolerate this ever-growing gap between Canon law and real social need could only be attributed to ignorance, indifference, or greed. In the eyes of Luther and most early Protestants, the foremost indicator of the last motive was the existing system of impediments and dispensations.

By the time of the Reformation, the canonical tradition of marriage impediments had developed into a complex legal field in its own right. The "Angelic Summa" of fifteenth-century casuist Angelo Carletti di Chivasso, for example (retitled by an outraged Luther "The More Than Diabolic Summa"), listed eighteen impediments to marriage, each exhaustively defined in other parts of the canonical literature.[22] Most of these, however, could be dispensed by ecclesiastical authorities, usually for a small sum, and therein lay even more potent seeds of popular resentment.

---

[18] *Beklagung eines Laien, genannt Hans Schwalb über viel Mißbräuche christlichen Lebens* (1521), in *Flugschriften der frühen Reformationsbewegung, 1518–24*, ed. Adolf Laube, Annerose Schneider, and Sigrid Loos (Vaduz, 1983), I:64. Cf. the striking similarity to grievance no. 69 in the 1521 *Beschwerden der deutscher Nation*, quoted in Friedberg, *Das Recht der Eheschliessung*, 163.

[19] "Babylonian Captivity" (1520), *LW* 36:97.

[20] Telle, *Erasme*, 211–12.

[21] Erasmus, quoted in Pierre Bels, *Le mariage des protestants français jusqu'en 1685* (Paris, 1968), 59, 92. "A lack of realism and of charity" is how Ozment characterizes Luther's perception of the Canon law of marriage (*When Fathers Ruled*, 46).

[22] "Babylonian Captivity" (1520), *LW* 36:96–97. On marital impediments, see also my discussion in Chapter 2.

For most polemicists, the only possible motivation of ecclesiastical authorities in creating and maintaining such a system was sheer avarice. In addition to charging for the various dispensations (most commonly for cases of third- or fourth-degree consanguinity), bishops and officials made money from all related marital litigation, such as dissolution and separation cases. Outraged by such abuses, reformers attacked both the law and its enforcement with a brutality rivaled only by related anticlerical tracts on concubinage and simony.[23] Luther castigated Church legal authorities as "[sellers] of vulvas and genitals – merchandise indeed most worthy of such merchants, grown altogether filthy and obscene through greed and godlessness."[24] As far as he could see, the only purpose of creating the "snares" of impediments was to "catch" money – sentiments echoed by Johann Brenz: "Perhaps [the pope] had his eye on money and filling the coffers, and for that reason forbade certain degrees, so that they could be dissolved again if one had the money."[25]

Diocesan courts, or officialities, were also frequently included in indictments of existing marriage law enforcement. Hans Sachs, in his famous "Wittenberger Nightingale," complains:

Whoever holds goods with unjust cause
him they relieve of it without pause,
then hand a letter of guilt and fine
and take a guilder for their effort and time.
The number of these blackguards is n'er dwindling
– to me it's all just romanist swindling.
Look to the bishops for even more sport
and how marriage is treated in all of their courts,
with notaries, Officials, and what's more,
with summons, scribes, bailiffs, and others in store;
how maids and youths are cleaned out to a flaw,
all by their phony ecclesiastical law;
while they rip the married estate to shreds,
taking both money and more in its stead.[26]

---

[23] Cf. discussion of anticlerical pamphlet literature in Steven Ozment, "Pamphlet Literature of the German Reformation," in Ozment, *Reformation Europe*, 91ff.

[24] "Babylonian Captivity" (1520), *LW* 36:97.

[25] Brenz, *Wie yn Ehesachen*, E1ª.

[26] ". . . Wer unrecht guot hat in seim gwalt / dem helffen sy es ab gar bald / Auch gebens brieff für schuld und peyn, / da legt man in zü gulden ein. / Der schalckstrick sein so mancherley / Das heyst mir römisch schinterey / Für baß mercket von den bischoffen / wie is zü gee an iren höffen / mit notary, officiellen / mit citatz schreybern und pedellen / an irem falsch geystlichen

Most ominously, as in criticisms of the canonical definition of marriage, opponents of ecclesiastical enforcement went beyond issues of financial and legal abuse to challenge the very authority of the tradition that had produced such abhorrences. In his "Comparison of the Most Holy Lord and Father the Pope to Jesus," Heinrich von Kettenbach confronts the sacramentalization of marriage itself:

> *Christ's apostle Paul speaks in Eph. V:* It is a great and holy mystery in Christ and his Church, whom he has taken as his bride.

> *Pope and his apostates:* You should understand this word as the marriage between a man and woman, from which I have devised a sacrament. The universities [*hohenn schule*] may not say otherwise since they are my soldiers and scullery servants. Oh it brings much money![27]

The humanist and later/Protestant charge of a mistranslation of Ephesians 5:32 is discussed in the next chapter, but the accusation of purposeful, mercenary manipulation by Church authorities deserves notice here.

In short, opposition to the Church's handling of marriage encompassed a variety of anticlerical, anti-Roman law, and occasionally antinomian tendencies. Yet whatever the degree of antipathy toward the ruling Church establishment, one common denominator emerged: popular perception of an ever widening gap between marriage in law and in practice. Protestants and Catholics of the sixteenth century would fervently debate where reform was most needed, but none would discount the existence of such a gap, nor its detrimental effects on the holy estate of matrimony.

If the Church's legal definition of marriage stirred some resentment of clerical authority, its doctrinal definition of the "sacrament" eventually forced the long-standing tension between celibate and married religious ideals into an even more violent confrontation. The celibate ideal, critics argued, not only degraded marriage as a second-class institution in doctrine, but also consistently undermined it in practice as well by put-

---

recht / Wie man da schindet mayd und knecht / auch wie man do züreyß die ee / und nimmet gelt und anders mee . . ." Hans Sachs, *Wittenbergische Nachtigall* (1523), in Laube, et al. *Flugschriften*, II:597–98.

    Cf. similar complaints of ecclesiastical court corruption by Luther ("Von Ehesachen" [1530] *WA* 30/III:205–06, 209ff.), Calvin (*Institutes* IV.v.5ff.), and in the Palatine-Electorate's 1563 marriage court ordinance (*EKO* 293).

[27] Heinrich von Kettenbach, *Vergleichung des allerheiligsten Herrn und Vater des Papsts gegen Jesus* (1523), in *Flugschriften aus der ersten Jahren der Reformation*, ed. Otto Clemen, III/1 (Halle, 1907), 141; see also 135–36, nos. 13, 18.

ting spiritual leaders in unnatural, unbearable, and thus hypocritical situations. Despite the repeated efforts of many fifteenth and sixteenth-century bishops to remedy the apparently high incidence of clerical concubinage and adultery, enforcement of clerical celibacy remained undeniably sporadic at best. Most bishops and their chapters appeared to contemporaries unable or unwilling even to address the question. Once again, critics raised the accusation of institutionalized greed and corruption, citing as proof the "whore" and "cradle" taxes collected by many bishops from clerics in their diocese with concubines or illegitimate children.[28] And once again, as in the issue of ecclesiastical control of marriage, the effects of such alleged corruption reverberated in every part of society.

The most common complaint against the celibate rule was that it consistently produced more sexual incontinence and anarchy than it prevented. In addition to the usual problems of priests' concubines and illegitimate children, the irresistible sexual urge of celibate clerics, critics argued, often induced both them and their paramours to commit increasingly greater sins to satisfy both their lusts and need for secrecy. The old topos of the confessor as seducer, for example, resurfaced as a favorite of sixteenth-century polemicists:

> Virgins are miraculously impregnated by the spirit of the confessors. It has been established in sealed cloisters where the water hole stays open. Oh God, the most beautiful, most honorable, most virtuous are trapped in the confessional and often abducted. . . . The reputable women and maidens who come to the confessional pure and pious often become heartless, godless, dishonorable, and unscrupulous whores, [for] they have in their hearts – secretly and grievously – been stolen, betrayed, and sold.[29]

---

28 Cf. the typical accusations of episcopal corruption in Hanns Kolb, *Ein Reformation notturftig in der Christenheit mit den pfaffen und iren magten* (n.d.), and Sebastian Meyer, *Ernstliche Ermahnung Hugos von Landenberg* (1522), in Clemen, *Flugschriften aus der ersten Jahren der Reformation* IV/7 (Leipzig, 1911), 305ff. Though insufficient official documentation makes verification difficult, collection of the much decried *Hurenzins* (whore tax) and *Wigenzins* (cradle tax) undoubtedly varied from diocese to diocese. Constance Bishop Hugo von Landenberg, for instance, was credited with an annual (pre-Reformation) income of 6,000–7,500 gulden from collection of the *Hurenzins* within his diocese. A. Störmann, *Die städtischen Gravamina gegen den Klerus am Ausgang des Mittelalters und in der Reformationszeit* (Münster, 1916), 260ff. and 286ff.; August Franzen, *Zölibat und Priesterehe in der Auseinandersetzung der Reformationszeit und der katholischen Reform des 16. Jahrhunderts* (Münster, 1969), 92ff. There is no evidence, on the other hand, of this practice in Speyer during the same period (see my discussion in Chapter 5).

29 Heinrich von Kettenbach, *Ein new Apologia . . .* (1523), in Clemen, *Flugschriften*, I/1 (1907), 161. Cf. *Die deutsche Vigilie*, in Clemen, *Flugschriften*, I/2 (1908), 140–41.

Others accused clerics of open lechery, confident of inaction or, at most, wrist slapping by their superiors:

> Then when it comes to sin and delight,
> within reach to soothe his appetite:
> lovely, tender maidens and virgins pure,
> which he likes to follow up with a nice, cool beer.[30]

More sympathetic observers, usually clerics themselves, recounted the trials and tribulations of celibate life that led to such abuses. In "The Lamentations of seven pious but disconsolate priests whom no one can comfort" (1521), one unhappy cleric relates his own unsuccessful attempts to conquer the sexual urge, resulting in masturbation, wet dreams, lechery (including an affair with the wife of a friend), and eventually a concubine who bears him seventeen children in twenty years. Though tolerated by his bishop (because of the "whore tax") and his parishioners ("like stableboys accustomed to dung"), the pastor himself is continuously tormented by his own conscience, regretting the moral harm done his flock almost as much as that done his own soul:

> Thus am I entangled: on the one hand, I cannot live without a wife; on the other, I am not permitted a wife. Thus, I am forced to live a publicly disgraceful life, to the shame of my soul and honor and to the damnation of many who have taken offense at me [i.e., who refuse to receive sacraments from his hands]. How shall I preach about chastity and promiscuity, adultery, and knavish behavior, when my whore goes to church and about the streets and my bastards sit before my eyes? How shall I read the Mass under such circumstances?[31]

The image of the conscientious cleric tortured by his or her own religious vows proved an effective polemical tool among early Evangelicals. Luther's own attacks on the inhumanity of the celibate ideal are well known,[32] but he also actively sought out and published sympathetic stories from conflicted clerics. The memoirs of Florentina of Ober Weimar, for instance, tell of her ostracism and persecution by fellow

---

30 ". . . Dann was zü frevel und wollust sich / thüt schrecken [probably strecken] gibt er miltigklich / schön frewlein zart und meydlein jung / darauff schmeckt im ain küler trunck." Anonymous, *Ein neues Gedicht . . .* , in Laube, et al. *Flugschriften*, II:1317.
31 Johann Eberlin von Günzburg, *Syben frumm aber trostlos pfaffen klagen ire not* (1521), translation in Steven Ozment, "The Social History of the Reformation: What Can We Learn from the Pamphlets?" in *Flugschriften als Massenmedium der Reformationszeit; Beiträge zum Tübinger Symposion 1980*, ed. H.-J. Köhler (Stuttgart, 1981), 192–93.
32 See Chapter 2.

nuns (including being flogged and put in leg irons) when she confessed her own inner struggles with the celibate ideal.[33] Erasmus sympathetically concurred with those who found the solitary life "sad and more suited to animals than humans, rendering a man more often crazy than pious."[34] Perhaps the most effectively despairing image, though, is achieved in Eberlin's companion pamphlet to "The Lamentations of seven pious but disconsolate priests":

> There is no greater unhappiness than the daily gnawing and restlessness of one's own conscience, making all joy empty for the person, all comfort sad, all sweetness bitter. And so, as consolation, he often acts against his own conscience, whereupon the human temperament becomes dull and blunt, the heart hard, and respectability recedes. At the same time, the person also becomes uncivil and inhuman, with the spirit of compunction [*spiritus compunctionis*] often tacked onto that – such a blindness that he even hates his own well-being, begrudging all that is good, and loving his own misfortune.[35]

If the effects of the celibate ideal were disastrous for the clergy and priesthood in general, the direct and indirect impact on the institution of marriage, according to the critics, was even more destructive. The very "impossibility" and "inanity" of celibate vows, according to Erasmus, rendered all clerics, in conscience if not in action, hypocritical, causing in turn the mockery and "ruin of [true] Christian piety."[36] Entrusted with guiding the laity in word and deed, such hypocritical teachers instead professed obedience to a separate, higher set of Christian standards, which in reality was no more attainable for them than for their "inferior" married parishioners. The subsequent harm done to both marriage and the priesthood by such false spiritual models was far worse than that of any unbeliever, thus earning clerics Erasmus's derisive appelations of "barbarians, monkeys, asses, hypocrites, philistines, phar-

---

33 "Wie schmählich/schämlich/lesterlich und hönisch ich da von [the abbess] und andern aussgericht / ist nicht vor frümen lewtten zu reden oder zu schreyben." *Ain geschichte wie Got ainer Erbarn closter Junckfrawen aussgeholffen hatt* (Wittenberg, 1524), B 3ª. Cf. discussion of this work and the Protestant topos of "liberating" nuns in Ozment, *When Fathers Ruled*, 9–25.

34 Telle, *Erasme*, 76.

35 Johann Eberlin von Günzburg, *Der frummen pfaffen trost. Ein getrewer glaubhaffter underricht unnd antwort uff der siben trostlossen pfaffen klage . . .* (1521), cited in Ozment, "What Can We Learn from the Pamphlets?" 193–94. Cf. similar contemporary arguments and examples in Franzen, *Zölibat und Priesterehe*, 47–52.

36 From a letter to Roger Servetus (1514) in Telle, *Erasme*, 55. Cf. also 88–96, on the impossibility of celibacy vows.

isees, scribes, publicans, Essenes, sycophants, pseudo-apostles, pseudo-prophets, demons," and in general "Judaic."[37]

At a more basic level, the perception of a hypocritical double standard among self-avowed religious leaders called into question the very ideal of a "religious" life. Among the "Complaints" of Hans Schwalb:

> If a married man sleeps with another woman, one of them must leave the city. But our squires, the worthy clergy [*herren priester*], forcefully seize the wives and daughters of pious townsmen and peasants, holding them against God, honor, and law. Is that a "spiritual" [*geistlich*] life? It's better called a carnal [*flaischlich*] life if one admits it both publicly and in the confessional. Why are such pastors – and it is not an isolated case but many – not excommunicated? This is a fine example for us poor, ignorant peasants. Such examples teach me adultery, knavery, and heresy. These are our [spiritual] models, pastors, healers, shepherds who so amicably come before us. Did Christ also behave this way I'd like to know?![38]

As in attacks on the Church's sacramentalization of marriage, it was a short (though significant) step for such listings of abuses to go straight to the source – traditional ecclesiastical authority. In most cases critics found it severely lacking, in both scriptural justification and common sense.

> *Christ:* Whoever wishes to embrace chastity and is so endowed by God may do so; I allow every man to enter into matrimony. Mt. 19 [v. 11]

> *Pope:* I want all monks and nuns to take vows of chastity, whether they keep them or not. My clerics and priests should not have lawful wives but may disgrace three or four maidens as whores, carry on with married women, and practice sodomy; this I will not forbid them since my bishops – just like any other pimps – reap a great profit from the yearly tax.[39]

---

[37] The sweeping characterization of "Judaic" was the ultimate insult for Erasmus, and one frequently applied by him to priestly celibacy. Ibid., 81ff., 133, 150, etc.

[38] *Beclagung*, 64. Schwalb adds that "Sy reden die wort woll auß, aber sy bedeütten uns nicht, waz dar in zü thon sey. . . . Dann leychtvertige wort oder werck, wie sy seind, so geben sy doch ander leütten böse beyspyl, böse leer, raytzen den menschen zu sunde" (ibid., 67). Some laymen, according to an anonymous pamphlet of 1523, actually tried to use such immoral clerical practices to justify their own adultery: "darumb dass die / ain gaystlichs klaydt antragen / Eebruch offentlich treyben / und andere laster mer." See *Ayn kurtzlich Antwort ainer Ordens schwester / irem natürlichen bruder Cartheüser ordens zugeschickt / uber seine Christliche/ und Evangelische lere und ermanung* (Nuremberg, 1523), A 3[b].

[39] Heinrich von Kettenbach, *Vergleichung* . . . , in Clemen, *Flugschriften*, III/1 (1907), 137–38.

An anonymous pamphlet of the same year puts the evangelical challenge to the celibate ideal even more succinctly:

> . . . to punish the entrance into marriage [of priests]
> don't lie us blind with papist foolery.
> If you want to punish, punish by the scripture.
> If you can't, leave such papist poison.[40]

ʰHow could anyone, went the argument, respect the institution of marriage while such inventions of "human stupidity" continued to undermine the conflicting sacramental definition both in teaching and in practice? Not only were there discrepancies between Church teachings and enforcement of sacramental marriage and clerical celibacy, but there were contradictions within the teachings themselves. Wrote one early Evangelical pamphleteer:

> In the Old and New Testaments, the people were enjoined to take up the married life. In our time, however, they can do nothing but praise virginity and denigrate the estate of marriage, afraid of the trouble and work, fear and suffering therein. Such a burden no one undertakes gladly, and thus everyone avoids and flees from marriage. Our clergy, in particular, vigorously protect themselves against it, for it is said of them that they want to be married [but] are afraid that their knavish life will no longer be permitted should they enter into annoying marriage.[41]

Whether the problem lay in doctrine, law, or enforcement, sixteenth-century critics could agree on one thing: The Church's authority over marriage was in jeopardy.

Reordering marriage and society

On the surface, Protestant repudiation of traditional marriage authority appears comprehensive. Attacks on Canon law, Church courts, and clerical celibacy seemingly leave little room for either legal or theological continuity in the reforms to follow. In fact, though, their guiding idealizations of marriage reflected well-established theological topoi from at least the time of Saint Augustine. Perhaps more surprising, Protestant

---

[40] [Ulrich Sitzinger], *Ein getrewe vermanung* (Speyer: 1523), A 1ᵇ.
[41] Thomas Stör, *Der Ehelich standt von got mit gebenedeyung auffgesetzt / soll umb schwärhait wegen der seltzsamen gaben der Junckfrawshafft yederman frey sein / und niemant verboten werden* Nuremberg, (1524), A 4ᵇ.

attempts to realize this ideal made extensive use of the same canonical legal tradition so vehemently condemned in popular literature.

The explanation for this apparent contradiction lies in the true nature of all sixteenth-century marriage reform, namely, improvement of enforcement rather than rejection of legal and theological heritage. In this respect, three important innovations distinguished these new marriage reformers from their medieval predecessors. The first was a typically Protestant merging of the secular and the religious into a new, common standard for all Christians. Whereas all previous marriage reforms had been largely the province of clerical initiative, sixteenth-century reforms included lay jurists and moralists as well. The second was a new confidence in legal coercion as an effective means of reform, simultaneously endowing the State with a new moral authority and the Church with a new power of enforcement. Earlier reforms had focused exclusively on individual reform; sixteenth-century reforms aimed for institutional and legal reform as well. Finally, such reforms were inevitably accompanied by a more general and gradual ideological transformation of traditional paternal control over marriage to include both the Church and the State as well. The source of all three innovations was the same, namely, the background of sixteenth-century marriage reformers themselves.

Lawyers and theologians made up the core of sixteenth-century marriage reformers, reordering marriage and society according to their shared interpretation of patriarchal stability. Their common educational background imbued them with respect for the written word as well as reverence for its ordering power over society, whether as religious doctrine or as secular law. Their increasingly prestigious positions in German society in turn gave them confidence in their own abilities to implement the word in reordering marriage and society. Finally, their close ties to the leaders of various emerging early modern states provided what seemed to many the most effective means to enact such reforms. The result was a largely legal response to the problems of sixteenth-century marriage, with new paternalistic roles for the Church and the State.

Expanded governmental and ecclesiastical authority over marriage, of course, required some ideological support. For sixteenth-century marriage reformers, this meant building on the well-established Western tradition of strong paternal authority. Consequently, the well-known head of the household, or *Hausvater*, was joined in sixteenth-century rhetoric by two other paternal authority figures – the *Landesvater* (political ruler) and the *Gottesvater* (God the Father) – thus representing what Luther and other Protestant reformers considered "the three orders of Christian society": *ecclesia* (Church), *politica* (State), and *oeconomia* (household).[42]

All three patriarchal figures made extensive use of the biblical support for paternal authority in general. Genesis, Psalms, Proverbs, and Ecclesiasticus, for instance, all praised the love and companionship resulting in a strong marriage and family, but they also made abundantly clear the indispensible inequities of that familial society.[43] Like the kings and patriarchs of ancient Israel, the *Hausvater* possessed an authority that was both divinely ordained and inviolable; those who would undermine it risked the wrath of the *Gottesvater* himself.[44] Obedient submission by his wife and children was similarly scripturally sanctioned, the former as punishment for Eve's sin, the latter as the fourth commandment handed down to Moses.[45] Nor was this patriarchal model repudiated by the New Testament; as Paul's letters, particularly 1 Corinthians 11, explicitly reaffirm, "Man is not made from woman, but woman from man, and man was not created for the sake of woman, but woman for the sake of man."[46] An early evangelical treatise of 1524 described the chain of command prosaically: "For it is written, the head of the wife is the husband, the head of the husband is Christ, and the head of Christ is God," concluding "there is no nobler, greater authority on earth than

---

[42] Luther: "Ein Sermon von dem Sakrament der Taufe" (1519), *WA* 2:734, also *WA* 36:504–5; Calvin: Commentaries Gen. 2:18. For a fuller treatment, see Reinhard Schwarz, "Ecclesia, oeconomia, politia. Sozialgeschichte und fundamentalethische Aspekte der protestantischen Drei-Stände-Theorie," in *Protestantismus und Neuzeit*, ed. Horst Renz and Friedrich-Wilhelm Graf (Gütersloh, 1984), 78–88.

[43] See especially Adam Schubert, *Der Sieman / Das ist Wider den Hausteuffell* (Weissenfels, 1564), in Ria Stambaugh, *Teufelbücher in Auswahl*, (Berlin, 1970–80) II:271–307, and Andreas Musculus, *Wider den Eheteuffel* (Frankfurt, 1556; also in Stambaugh, *Teufelbücher*, IV: 94–96), on their exegetic praise of marriage and the family.

[44] Schubert, *Hausteuffell*, in Stambaugh, *Teufelbücher*, especially II:244–45; also Hoffman, *Hausväterliteratur*, 92ff.

[45] Wifely subservience as a punishment for Eve's sin was a frequently cited scriptural justification among proponents of strong patriarchal authority. See, for instance, *Zwey Schöne Newe Lieder / wie man ain Braut ansingen soll* (Straubing, [1560s]), cited in Wiltenburg, *Disorderly Women*, 74ff; also Schubert, *Hausteuffell*, in Stambaugh, *Teufelbücher*, II:241–43.
On the new emphasis of sixteenth-century Protestants on the fourth commandment (fifth, by Calvinist reckoning), see Bossy, *Christianity in the West*, 116ff.

[46] Schubert, *Hausteuffell*, in Stambaugh, *Teufelbücher* II:243. Other Pauline and New Testament citations included Col. 3:19–4:1, 1 Tim. 5, 1 Titus 2, 1 Pet. 2–3, and Eph. 5:22-6:9. See also Florian Daul, *Tanzteufel: Das ist / wider den leichtfertigen / unverschempten Welt tanz / und sonderlich wider die Gotts zucht und ehvergessene Nachttenze* (Frankfurt a. M., 1567), in Stambaugh, *Teufelbücher*, II: 97.

that of parents over their children, since they have both spiritual and worldly authority over them."[47]

Again, the ideal of the strong *paterfamilias* as a remedy to marital and social disorders was certainly not an innovation of the sixteenth century. Rather the traditional theme was transformed in a distinctly early modern adaptation of the patriarchal ideal to the expanding social roles of Church and especially State. By the time of the Reformation, for instance, the ancient ideological identification of the authority of the head of the household with that of the head of government had become so commonplace in popular literature that the terms themselves – *Hausvater* and *Landesvater* – appeared virtually interchangeable at times. Lyndal Roper, for instance, has remarked on the "obsession" of Augsburg magistrates with tracing such crimes as prostitution back to improper parental guidance, and both she and Merry Wiesner emphasize the paternalistic tone and language of almost all German municipal legislation of the period.[48] Thomas Robisheaux and Kristen Zapalac have noted similar increases in references to "fatherly love" among the counts of Hohenlohe and the magistrates of Regensburg, respectively.[49] Perhaps the most striking evidence, though, of this virtually indiscriminate mixing of political and familial metaphors comes from the popular religious reform literature of the period. In his *Against the Marriage-Devil*, first published in 1556, Andreas Musculus makes frequent use of both symbols of patriarchal order: "Thus it is well and justly said that it is as great and difficult an art, requiring as much leadership and skill, to rule a wife as a tiny country"; and later, "for it is in the 'house-regiment' as in worldly government . . . just as there can be only one sun in the sky, so too only one lord and ruler . . . two lords in one land, two fools in one house; neither can endure for long."[50]

As with images of *Hausvater* and *Landesvater*, artistic and literary ref-

---

[47] Caspar Gütell, *Ueber den Evangelion Johannis* . . . (Zwickau, 1524), 4ᵃ, 7ᵇ.

[48] A 1537 Augsburg ordinance, for example, speaks of "die vorgeenden Vätterlichen Ermanungen," and "und hat ein Erbar Rat die Straffen und / Censuren so Vätterlich / mildt und träglich Gesetzt." Roper, *Holy Household*, 68–69, 115ff.; Wiesner, *Working Women*, 6ff., 190ff. See also Schochet, *The Authoritarian Family*, especially 30ff.

[49] Robisheaux (*Rural Society*, 164–74) cites several instances of the counts of Hohenlohe referring to themselves as the *Hausväter* of their realms, and Kristin Zapalac (*"In His Image and Likeness"*: *Political Iconography and Religious Change in Regensburg, 1500–1600* [Ithaca, N.Y. 1990], 135–66) notes a similar sixteenth-century increase of paternal language and imagery concerning the magistracy of Regensburg in both wills and official decrees.

[50] Musculus, *Wider den Eeteuffel* in Stambaugh, *Teufelbücher*, IV:120, 123–24.

erences to the *Gottesvater* apparently also increased dramatically in the early sixteenth century.[51] Similar to familial and governmental counterparts, the image of God as the "top father" (*oberste Hausvater*) represented an amalgam of "severity, justice, watchful anxiety, and infinitely caring solicitude."[52] Some theologians, such as Johann Spangenberg, stressed the consoling aspects of the analogy: "For if God is our father, we are his beloved children, and I know that my heavenly father will use me as graciously as a *Hausvater* treats his beloved child."[53] Calvin reversed the compliment, noting that because God is called "father," there is "something divine in every father."[54] At the same time, the ever present threat of paternal punishment lent both force and permanence to divine commands and wishes:

> All pious children should know God's will
> to be their father and protector from ill;
> the bad ones, though, he turns away
> and gobbles them up on the Judgement Day.[55]

The three pillars of early modern society – *Hausvater, Landesvater,* and *Gottesvater* – represented more than an abstract chain of command; they embodied the best hopes of religious and secular reformers in restoring a disintegrating social order at three concentric levels. Similarly, the personal ideal of the *Hausvater* offered more than an ideological metaphor for these reformers; it provided the practical model for their solutions to current marital chaos. For early Lutheran reformers, the symbiosis of theological and political authority seemed both natural and – at least initially – uncomplicated. Theologians at the University of Rostock who spoke to the Mecklenburg dukes of "government as our common father" might have been courting favor but, more likely, were simply typical adherents of a profound and enduring Lutheran trust in existing

---

[51] Zapalac (*In His Image and Likeness*, 67ff.) notes an apparent increase in both artistic emphasis on paternal representations of God and explicit references to God the Father in Regensburg wills from 1500 to 1600.

[52] Hoffmann, *Hausväterliteratur*, 95ff., 134–35; Strauss, *Luther's House of Learning*, 122.

[53] *Der gros Catechismus und Kinder Lere D. Martin Lutheri . . .* (Wittenberg, 1551; preface dated 1541), Lvii[a–b], translated in Strauss, *Luther's House of Learning*, 121.

[54] Calvin, *Institutes* II.viii.35. Cf. also contemporary references to the father as *Hausbischoff, Hausprediger,* and *Gottes Werckzeug* (Hoffmann, *Hausväterliteratur*, 98, 134).

[55] "Got wil der frommen kinderlein / Beschützer und ir Vater sein / Die bösen aber wil er nicht / Er frist sie auff der Sünden gicht." Based on translation of Theocritus from the Greek in Andreas Hoppenrod, *Wider den Hurenteufel* (Eisleben, 1565), in Stambaugh, *Teufelbücher*, II:229–30.

political authority.[56] Jurist theologians such as Melanchthon were especially enthusiastic supporters of a strong government role, again effectively combining the social authority of *Hausvater, Landesvater,* and *Gottesvater:*

> We have two objects in mind as we learn to give honor to those to whom it is due under [the fourth] commandment. One is that we must respect our parents, magistrates, and teachers in their persons; the other is that we must revere the political order itself, for it has been created by God to help us keep our burger society safe, sound, and in good working condition.[57]

Catechistical literature, as Strauss has remarked, likewise made particularly frequent and effective use of the child–subject analogy, though rarely with the succinctness of Caspar Huberinus's social formulation: "God has divided mankind into parents and magistrates who dispose and command, and children and subjects who submit."[58]

Unlike his medieval predecessors, though, the magistrate or prince of the sixteenth century was now increasingly presented – like his household counterpart – as the *source* of authority as well as its instrument of enforcement. The German word "authority" itself (*Obrigkeit*), as Roper and Zapalac have pointed out, was no longer applied to the community as a whole but exclusively to the ruling governmental body.[59] Paternal concern had become paternalistic regulation, making the divisions between governors and governed both more defined and less permeable. Clearly, this process of statebuilding legitimization (or "oligarchization,"[60] as some scholars have termed it) was already well underway in

---

56 From a 1556 memorandum, quoted in Strauss, *Luther's House of Learning,* 313, n. 53. Luther's position from at least the Peasants' War on was fairly representative of his followers. See especially Eric Gritsch, "Luther and the State: Post-Reformation Ramifications," in Tracy, *Luther and the Modern State in Germany,* 49–50; also Zapalac, *In His Image and Likeness,* 151–53, and my discussion in Chapter 3.

57 *Cathechismus, das ist ein kinderlehre Herren Philippi Melanchthonis aus dem Latein ins Deutsche gebracht durch Caspar Bruschen* (Nuremberg, 1543); translated in Strauss, *Luther's House of Learning,* 239. Cf. similar arguments by Calvin in *Institutes* II.vii.35ff.

58 *Spiegel der Hauszucht* (Nuremberg, 1565), Aiiii[v], in Strauss, *Luther's House of Learning,* 241. Calvin considered such obedience a universal rule (*Institutes* II.viii.35–38, IV.xx.32).

59 Roper describes the transformation in Augsburg as a "gradual shift in the center of political gravity" from the guilds to the council. Roper, *Holy Household,* 69, 73ff.; Zapalac, *In His Image and Likeness,* 135–66, especially 142ff.

60 For theories of "Oligarchisierung," see especially Eberhard Naujoks, *Obrigkeitsgedanke, Zunftverfassung und Reformation: Studien zur Verfassungsgeschichte von Ulm, Esslingen und Schwäbisch Gmünd* (Stuttgart, 1958); Heinrich Bornkamm, "Die Frage der Obrigkeit im Reforma-

most states before the Reformation, but the theological reinforcement of reformers was surely welcomed by secular officials.

Sixteenth-century marriage reform, then, was both patriarchal and paternalistic, both traditional and modern. Again, the key to understanding this typically early modern amalgam lies in the background and goals of the very architects behind such social transformation, namely, jurists and theologians. Male and predominantly bourgeois leaders in a profoundly conservative society, these proponents of reform at the same time represented the most educated and most ambitious elements of the same society.[61] Most, if not all, of the newly Protestant territorial states mantained executive councils composed exclusively of these two types of professionals, both of whom played instrumental roles in the drafting of all new Protestant legislation. Reformed theologians and ministers of the Palatine-Electorate, for example, actively participated in matters of State while .pious jurists such as Dr. Christoph Ehem (later the Elector's director of foreign policy) shaped marital and other religious ordinances.[62] Most important, these pillars of the establishment shared a remarkably similar vision of restored marital and social order. Layman

tionszeitalter," in *Das Jahrhundert der Reformation. Gestalten und Kräfte,* 2nd ed. (Göttingen, 1961), 291–315; and Hans-Christoph Rublack, "Grundwerte in der Reichstadt im Spätmittelalter und in der frühen Neuzeit," in *Literatur in der Stadt, Bedingungen und Beispiele städtischer Literatur des 15. bis 17. Jahrhunderts,* ed. Horst Brunner (Göppingen, 1982), 9–36.

[61] On the formation and character of these early modern bourgeois elites, see G. Franz, ed., *Beamtentum und Pfarrerstand, 1400–1800* (Limburg, 1972); Thomas A. Brady, Jr., *Ruling Class, Regime, and Reformation at Strasbourg, 1520–55* (Leiden, 1978); H. Diederiks and H. Schilling, eds., *Bürgerliche Eliten in den Niederlanden und in Nordwestdeutschland; Studien zur Sozialgeschichte des europäischen Bürgertums im Mittelalter und in der Neuzeit* (Cologne, 1985); Volker Press, "Stadt und territoriale Konfessionsbildung," in *Kirche und gesellschaftlicher Wandel in deutschen und niederländischen Städten der werdenden Neuzeit,* ed. Franz Petri (Cologne, 1980), 251–96; Walter Bernhardt, *Die Zentralbehörden des Herzogtums Württemberg und ihre Beamten, 1520–1629* (Stuttgart, 1972–73), 77–107, on the social background and education of Württemberg bureaucrats; also Hsia, *Social Discipline in the Reformation,* especially 15ff., 174–82, and the bibliographical notes on 191–92 and 211–12.

On the emergence of lawyers as a social class in early modern Germany, see Gerald Strauss, *Law, Resistance, and the State: The Opposition to Roman Law in Reformation Germany* (Princeton, 1986), 165–70; and William Bouwsma, "Lawyers and Early Modern Culture," *American Historical Review* 78/2 (1973), 303–27.

The most comprehensive work on early Protestant clerical elites remains Bernard Vogler, *Le clergé protestante rhénan au siècle de la réforme (1555–1619)* (Paris, 1976). See also Bernhard Klaus, "Soziale Herkunft und theologische Ausbildung lutherischer Pfarrer der reformatorischen Frühzeit," *Zeitschrift für Kirchengeschichte* 80 (1969), 22–49; and Hans-Christoph Rublack, "'Der wohlgeplagte Priester': Vom Selbstverständnis lutherischer Geistlichkeit in Zeitalter der Orthodoxie," *Zeitschrift für Historische Forschung* 16 (1989), 1–30.

[62] Clasen, *Palatinate,* 13–15. See also the biography of a Palatine official: F. H. Schubert, *Ludwig Camerarius, 1573–1651: Eine Biographie* (Munich, 1955); and my discussion in Chapter 3.

or cleric, Protestant or Catholic, the solution was the same: greater paternalistic authority to enforce "discipline" (*Zucht*) and "order" (*Ordnung*) at all levels of society.[63]

Some historians have argued that this marks the point at which religious and secular reformers went their separate ways, reiterating the distinction made by the Lutheran reformer Mobianus between the inward discipline sought by ministers and the outward discipline enforced by magistrates.[64] Certainly the question deserves some consideration. First and foremost, we confront the obvious apocalyptic fervor of the early Reformation, which – as Robin Barnes has convincingly demonstrated – continued well into the seventeenth century among many German Lutherans.[65] Indeed, the author of the 1567 *Dance-Devil's* conviction that he was living in "the last and worst times of the world"[66] was not uncommon among many late sixteenth-century marriage reform authors. Calvinists, too, remained generally pessimistic about social change, guided no doubt by the Genevan reformer's conviction that "the world grows worse as it grows older."[67] Moreover, as other scholarly critics of "social reform" have stressed, the foremost goal of all religious reformers was not social amelioration but individual redemption, a kind of reform only God could create through His Word and the Holy Spirit.[68] "Thus," according to Barnes, "public morality and civil obedience were reflections of individual humility and repentance; the real concern was salvation."[69]

Undoubtedly institutional reform represented an "implicit paradox" among religious reformers of apocalyptic conviction. Lutheran and Calvinist doctrines of radical Original Sin and total reliance on divine grace

---

[63] Cf. historiographical overview on Zucht and Ordnung (especially among Calvinists) in Paul Münch, *Zucht und Ordnung. Reformierte Kirchenverfassungen im 16. und 17. Jahrhundert (Nassau-Dillenburg, Kurpfalz, Hessen-Kassel)* (Stuttgart, 1978), 16–19 also 183–89. Schilling in fact considers what he calls the "turn toward life" or "third use of the law" to be more characteristic of the Second (Reformed) Reformation; see *Religion, Political Culture and the Emergence of Early Modern Society* (Leiden, 1992), 272ff.

[64] Cf. Strauss, *Luther's House of Learning*, 236ff.

[65] Robin Barnes, *Prophecy and Gnosis: Apocalypticism in the Wake of the Lutheran Reformation* (Stanford, 1988), passim, esp. 256ff.

[66] Florian Daul, *Tantzteuffel* (1567), in Stambaugh, *Teufelbücher*, II:64.

[67] *Commentaries* Dan. 2:31–35; also *Institutes* III.iv.19 on the current "unhappy age," and discussion in William Bouwsma, *John Calvin: A Sixteenth-Century Portrait* (Oxford, 1988), 81–85.

[68] See especially Heiko Oberman's explicit criticism of studies such as Gerald Strauss's *Luther's House of Learning*: "Martin Luther: Vorläufer der Reformation," in *Verifikationen: Festschrift für Gerhard Ebeling zum 70. Geburtstag*, ed. E. Jürgel et al. (Tübingen, 1982), 93ff.

[69] Barnes, *Prophecy and Gnosis*, 69.

created yet another.[70] Yet the fact remains that most religious reformers of the sixteenth century not only supported marital and other institutional reforms but actively participated in their implementation. Again we return to the common backgrounds and attitudes of university-education secular and religious reformers and their "tightly woven social network of office, property, prestige, influence, and power."[71] Given the social prominence of both groups and the many mutual interests engendered by such authority, their common reliance on legal reform should not really surprise us. After all, as Gerald Strauss has pointed out, the very word *reformatio* always "carried associations of law and jurisdiction and, inevitably, of the controversies raging around these."[72] All of the major Protestant reformers, he notes, made heavy use of legal terms and imagery in their religious writings (e.g., "judge," "orderly law," "appeal") and well before the Reformation many German secular authorities had conversely appropriated the scene of the Last Judgment for their own courtrooms.[73] Moreover, whatever their individual opinions of the Last Days, sixteenth-century clerics and jurists agreed that human nature remained, in the words of the magistrates of Augsburg, "unfortunately more inclined to evil than to good."[74] Consequently they required coercion ("discipline") and guidance ("order") at every turn. As God's representatives in the patriarchal chain of authority, pastors and magistrates felt compelled – especially from the 1530s on – to provide such guidance and coercion to what Melanchthon called "the stupid people" and Luther simply "the mob."[75] Their combined paternalistic response – termed "social control" by some historians and "acculturation" by oth-

---

[70] Cf. Strauss's conclusions on this aspect of Lutheran educational reforms: "Torn between their trust in the molding power of education and their admission that the alteration of men's nature was a task beyond human strength, they strove for success in their endeavors while conceding the likelihood of defeat" (*Luther's House of Learning*, 300). Roper (*Holy Household*, 168) notes the same contradictory impulses among the Lutheran magistrates of Augsburg.

[71] Gerald Strauss, "Comment on 'Jewish Magic' and 'The Devil and the German People'" in *Religion and Culture in the Renaissance and Reformation*, ed. Steven Ozment (Kirksville, Mo., 1989), 130. Cf. Roper, *Holy Household*, 76–82, on the composition of Augsburg's discipline courts and marriage judges.

[72] Strauss, *Law*, 52.

[73] Ibid., 194–95, 240ff. See also Luther's references to Moses as an *Amtman* and the Mosaic Code as the Jews' *Sachsenspiegel* (207, 212).

[74] Roper, *Holy Household*, 57.

[75] "*Das dumme volck*" in "Epitome renovatae ecclesiasticae doctrinae" (1524) in *Melanchthons Werke in Auswahl*, ed. Robert Stupperich (Gütersloh, 1951), I:184; "*der Pöfel*" in "Wochen predigten über Johannis 16–20" (1528), *WA* 28:246–47; *WA Tischreden* 2:314, no. 2982. Cf. other references by Melanchthon to the "crazy mob" (*tolle pöfel*), "crude mass" (*hoc vulgus nostrum*) and "Lord Everyman" (*Herr Omnes*) in Strauss, *Luther's House of Learning*, 6ff.

46

ers[76] – merely represented the fulfillment of their divinely ordained duties as "fathers" to the rest of society.

Sixteenth-century marriage reform, as we are about to see, clearly typified this new combination of patriarchal objectives and paternalistic methods. True to their cultural and social ideals, secular and religious authorities interpreted current problems with marriage in paternalistic terms: Either the proper standard for behavior ("order") was not clearly taught, or it was not properly enforced ("discipline"). Their agenda for reform was similarly representative of their educational background: rationalization or standardization of all marital doctrine and law; publicizing and indoctrination of the same theological and legal standards; effective prevention and punishment of all transgressions against the standards. In a series of reforms that fused religious and secular authority behind one standard, private morality became public policy and the immoral became the criminal.

The resulting marriage reforms were far from identical. Even within a highly organized Protestant state, such as the Reformed Palatine-Electorate, it would be misleading to speak of any unified "program" or "policy" of marriage reform. Still, the legal and paternalistic nature of the sixteenth-century search for greater uniformity in practice did lead all reformers to some similar conclusions, despite important confessional and political differences. All, for instance, agreed that both the current law and enforcement of marital standards and sexual discipline required some revision. Their respective solutions, as we shall see, ranged from cosmetic to substantial legal, doctrinal, and bureaucratic changes. Protestant reformers of marital doctrine made several initial attempts to return to a purely biblical standard, yet they eventually ended up with a model based overwhelmingly on medieval canonical principles. Secular attempts at improved marital law enforcement likewise led German Protestant and Catholic political leaders to strikingly similar ends, though this time based more on their common bureaucratic limitations and failures than their success. The basis for this similarity is the subject of the next two chapters.

---

[76] See the discussion of this issue in the Introduction.

2

Marriage and the Church:
The ideological reformation

For this reason, a man must leave his father and mother and be joined to his wife, and the two will become one body. This sacrament has many implications; but I am saying it applied to Christ and the Church.

Vulgate version of Eph. 5:31–33

Not only is marriage regarded as a sacrament without the least warrant of Scripture, but the very ordinances which extol it as a sacrament have turned it into a farce.

Martin Luther, The Babylonian Captivity of the Church (1519)[1]

Since the time of the early Church Fathers, the Western Church's teaching on marriage had been characterized by a pronounced duality of Christian ideals. On the one hand, marriage was a holy and indissoluble *sacramentum,* an intrinsically positive act. On the other, marriage was a *remedium* for the ravages of sinful lust and fornication – an inferior, albeit legitimate, option to the preferred state of celibacy and total chastity. Many historians have oversimplified the history of this doctrinal ambivalence by supposing the total dominance of the remedial concept of marriage before the Reformation and a complete reversal of emphasis among sixteenth-century Protestants.[2] For these scholars, Luther's characterization of marriage as "an outward, worldly thing" in combina-

---

[1] *LW,* 36:92.
[2] Brundage, for instance, perceives a sharp divergence in the sixteenth century between Protestant and Catholic beliefs on "the aims and purposes of human sexuality" and marriage. Unlike their traditional Catholic counterparts, he argues, predominantly Protestant societies after the Reformation preferred to leave "many issues relating to marital sex and contraception to the conscience of the individual, rather than trying to enact norms on these matters into law" (*Law, Sex, and Christian Society,* 574–5). Ozment (*When Fathers Ruled,* 3ff.) portrays a similar contract between the confessions.

tion with the many other Protestant attacks on clerical celibacy and the entire canonical system represented a progressive and – at least initially – comprehensive rejection of the remedial definition of marriage. The Catholic Tridentine reform, by contrast, was characterized by a conservative, even reactionary, reaffirmation of the same medieval tradition, both in ideal and practice. In truth, the remarkable continuity in doctrines of both marriage and celibacy throughout the sixteenth-century – despite confessional, legal, and political differences – suggests a very different transformation.

Long before the Reformation, the ambivalent heritage of the early Church's marriage teachings experienced a much more significant transformation. During the scholarly renaissance of the twelfth century, Canon lawyers and theologians attempted to systematize marriage doctrine in theory and in practice. The result was a legal definition of marriage as sacramental, indissoluble, and consensual, to be exclusively adjudicated by ecclesiastical courts. In doctrine, marriage was also exalted as a *sacramentum*, but "not as highly" as the superior state of celibacy (because of the former's remedial character) – thus the apparently innovative emphasis on the power and permanence of the couple's vows was also qualified.

In the sixteenth century, complaints about the same theological and legal system produced by the first reformation triggered a second and much more modest ideological reformation. Here, despite many apparent differences between Protestant and Catholic revisions of marriage theology and law, the substance of the twelfth century's reforms survived largely intact. Though Protestants appeared to reject both the sacramental and remedial characterizations of marriage, their reforms – like those of Catholic contemporaries – actually represented the final reception of a holy, indissoluble, and consensual ideal of marriage. With the important exception of a newly instituted married ministry among Lutherans and Calvinists, most Protestant theologians focused less on doctrinal revisions than on more effective implementation of the same.

This chapter examines the ideological transformation begun with the theological and legal reforms of the twelfth century and culminating in the final Protestant and Catholic revisions of the sixteenth century. Though we will carefully explore the important doctrinal differences among the confessions, our discussion of this process will nonetheless emphasize their overwhelming similarities in all aspects of marriage ideology. The practical significance of this religious and legal conservatism will then be addressed more fully in the following chapter's examination of legal and bureaucratic reforms.

The formation of Christian marriage doctrine and law

Despite multiple references to the institution of marriage in both the Old and New Testaments,[3] the early Church Fathers never reached any doctrinal consensus on the role and nature of Christian marriage. Still, by the fourth century, two general currents of opinion were discernible.[4] One, most clearly articulated by Saint Augustine, defended the marriage of Christians as a holy and edifying act, the *sacramentum* already mentioned. In his many works on marriage and related issues, Augustine identified a "triple good" (*triplex bonum*) resulting from the conjugal bond: procreation (*proles*), fidelity (*fides*), and sacrament (*sacramentum*).[5] Of the three, it was this last, the characterization of marriage as a sacrament (based largely on the Vulgate translation of Ephesians 5:32)[6], that would exert by far the most theological and legal influence in the centuries to follow.

"Why is Christian marriage an unbreakable bond, unlike that of pagans?" he asked; "[because] Christian marriage is a *sacramentum*, that is a symbol of stability."[7] In his "sacramental" definition, Augustine combined both the traditional "goods" of social stability – legal offspring and fidelity between spouses – with less clearly defined but equally tangible

---

[3] In the Old Testament, see especially Gen. 1:26ff., 2:18ff., and 3:1ff.; in the New Testament, Matt. 5:27ff.; Mark 10:2ff.; John 2:1ff.; and especially the epistles of Paul: Rom. 7:2; 1 Cor. 7:1ff.; Eph. 5:22ff.; Col. 3:10; Gal. 5:16ff.; and 1 Pet. 3:1. There are, of course, many other references to sexuality, marriage, and the family, but these represent the most frequently cited in theological writings.

[4] On the early patristic writers and marriage, see especially Peter Brown, *The Body and Society: Men, Women, and Sexual Renunciation in Early Christianity* (New York, 1988); and the exhaustive survey of Brundage, *Law, Sex, and Christian Society*, 62–76; as well as John T. Noonan, *Contraception: A History of Its Treatment by the Catholic Theologians and Canonists* (Cambridge, Mass. 1965), 56ff.; and L. Godefroy, "Le mariage au temps des Pères," in *DTC* 9:2078–87.

[5] Cf., for example, *De bono coniugali* (*CSEL* 41:227): "Haec omnia bona sunt propter quae nuptiae bonae sunt, proles, fides, sacramentum." The most important works of Augustine on marriage and celibacy include *De continentia* (*CSEL* 41:139–83), *De bono coniugali* (*CSEL* 41:185–231), *De sancta virginitate* (*CSEL* 41:233–302), *De bono viduitatis* (*CSEL* 41:303–43), *De adulterinis coniugiis*, libri I and II (*CSEL* 41: 345–410), *De nuptis et consupiscentia* (*CSEL* 42:211–310); also Brundage, *Law, Sex, and Christian Society*, 80–93; Noonan, *Contraception*, 126ff.

[6] "Sacramentum hoc magnam ist, ego autem dico Christo in Ecclesia." *De bono coniugali* (*CSEL* 41:227). See L. Godefroy, "Le mariage dans l'Ecriture Sainte," in *DTC* 9:2070–71.

[7] *De bono coniugali* (*CSEL* 41:196–7).

spiritual benefits of such a union. The notion of the indissolubility of marriage had been preached often among early Christians but it was first with Augustine's literal application of Ephesians 5:32 and especially the analogy of the permanent bond between Christ and His Church that such a view was given greater theological authority.[8] Most significant, both the spiritual and the social "goods" were inexorably bound to this notion of permanence and indissolubility. Yet when it came to the very maintenance of this union, Augustine confronted a major obstacle to total endorsement of marriage as a holy ideal of choice, namely, the intrusion of sexual desire and lust.[9]

While he consistently maintained that another of marriage's sacramental effects was to provide a legitimate outlet (*remedium*) for such urges, Augustine could never quite absolve the conjugal act of all sinful overtones. Nor could he therefore defend it as being equally as sanctified and as much a part of the City of God as complete sexual abstinence.[10] This characterization of marriage as an inferior estate in fact typified all of the early Fathers, gaining even greater currency as the ascetic, celibate ideal grew in popularity among subsequent Church leaders and theologians. Ambrose and Jerome, in particular, went much further than Augustine in their exaltation of the celibate state over the necessary, worldly compromise of marriage. "Any man who loves his wife excessively is an adulterer," warned Jerome, at the same time exclaiming, "Marriages fill the earth; virginity [fills] heaven."[11] The growing enthusiasm for clerical celibacy and monasticism likewise transformed definitions of marriage and the priesthood alike. Already bishops were prohibited from remarrying after the death of their spouses, and with the Theodosian Code (420) enforced chastity was extended to

---

[8] Augustine was undoubtedly influenced in this interpretation by the strong views of his mentor Ambrose on the subject, particularly in the latter's *Comment. in epist. ad Ephes. V:32* (*CSEL* 3:513). Cf. also Esmein I:64–65, 68; and Godefroy, "Le mariage dans l'Ecriture Sainte," in *DTC* 9:2066–67; Godefroy, "Le mariage au temps des Pères," in *DTC* 9:2105–9.

[9] Godefroy, "Le mariage au temps des Pères," in *DTC* 9:2095; Brundage, *Law, Sex, and Christian Society*, 89–93; Noonan, *Contraception*, 129ff.

[10] *De civitate Dei contra Paganos* (*CSEL* 40–41).

[11] "Nuptiae terram replent, virginitas paradisam." (*Adversus Jovinianum*), quoted in Godefroy, "Le mariage au temps des Pères," in *DTC* 9:2091. Jerome's exhaltation of virginity was echoed by most of the early Latin and Greek fathers. See, for example, Ambrose's *De virginibus, De viduis, De virginitate,* and *De exhortatione virginitatis,* discussed in Godefroy, "Le mariage au temps des Pères," in *DTC* 9:2087–93.

　　See also Brown, *Body and Society,* 76–82; and Brundage, *Law, Sex, and Christian Society,* 80–82, on Tertullian.

include living first wives and families, absolutely forbidding any cohabitation after investiture as bishop.[12]

By the time of the legal and theological renaissance of the twelfth century, the marriage doctrine of the Fathers had undergone a subtle but significant transformation. The sacramental aspect of Augustine's *triplex bonum* was almost universally accepted by scholars, but the theological as well as legal implications of such a classification had by now become staggering by comparison.[13] Most significantly, since the Carolingian era, theologians, jurists, and, above all, bishops had increasingly interpreted this sacramental definition as providing justification for total ecclesiastical jurisdiction over all legal matters relating to marriage. The practical obstacles to effective enforcement of such a jurisdiction remained formidable. Nonetheless, by the beginning of the Gregorian Reform's aggressive legal expansionism, most secular authorities had accepted, at least in principle, the Church's jurisdiction over the sacraments, including marriage.[14] With this concession, theologians and other scholars were now in a position to do what even Augustine could not have hoped for in the Christianized Roman Empire: translate the Church's doctrine of marriage into law and thereby into practice.

The vast potential for such a religious reformation of society was not lost on the canonists of the twelfth century. Up until that point, the marriage laws of the Church had for the most part consisted of "separate, juxtaposed – and occasionally contradictory – rules," chiefly regarding consanguinity impediments, and were sporadically enforced at

---

[12] The prohibition against remarriage of bishops was based on 1 Tim. 3:2ff. and gradually, beginning with the Apostolic Constitutions (ca. 420), extended to include all members of the clergy.

Complete clerical celibacy, on the other hand, while widely backed by most of the Greek and Latin fathers as well as various councils (esp. canon 33 of the Council of Elvira, ca. 300, and the Roman Council of 386), was much less universally accepted or enforced in the early Church. E. Vancandard, "Célibat ecclésiastique," in *DTC* 2:2069–81; Godefroy, "Le mariage au temps des Pères," in *DTC* 9:2096–2101; also B. Köttig, *Die Priesterehe in der alten Kirche* (Münster, 1968).

[13] The most specific and widely cited references to marriage as a sacrament during this period were those of the Council of Verona (1184), a 1210 profession of faith by Innocent III, Lateran IV (1215), and the unified Greek (1274). The first explicit mention of the definitive seven sacraments, though, did not come until the Council of Florence in 1433.

Consensus on the theological and legal implication of *sacramentum*, moreover, was still not universal during the eleventh and twelfth centuries. See R. Naz, "Mariage en droit occidental," in *DDC* 6:750ff.; LeBras, "La doctrine du mariage," in *DTC* 9:2123ff., especially 2196–2201; Esmein I:153–56; Brundage, *Law, Sex, and Christian Society*, 176–228, especially 187ff.

[14] LeBras, "La doctrine du mariage," in *DTC* 9:2123; Brundage, *Law, Sex, and Christian Society*, 223ff., 319–23; and my discussion in Chapter 3.

that.[15] The very prospect of a coherent and comprehensive Canon law of marriage that was at the same time theologically and practically sound clearly excited many of the greatest legal minds of the time, most notably Gratian (died 1159?) and Peter Lombard (ca. 1100–60). In their respective legal compilations, the *Decretum* and the *Sentences*,[16] we find not only the most influential and widely imitated canonical formulations of marriage, but also the clearest and boldest attempts at such a union of marriage doctrine and practice.

Before attempting to translate Christian marriage theory into practice, both Gratian and Peter Lombard were faced with the problematic dual ideals of the *sacramentum* and the *remedium*. By the time of the Gregorian Reform and its efforts to enforce clerical celibacy at all levels,[17] the bias of many theologians and jurists against marriage was already well established. Most of the twelfth-century canonists, including Gratian and Lombard, shared such reservations about the carnal lust still present in marriage, and some even went so far as to propose the unconsummated and therefore "perfect" union of Mary and Joseph as a model.[18] Numer-

---

[15] Esmein I:108. On the lack of theological and legal unity in the Church's teachings on marriage during this time, see also LeBras, "La doctrine du mariage," in *DTC* 9:2124–34. The controversial argument of Goody, *Family and Marriage in Europe*, assumes a much more uniform and consistent application of impediments of consanguinity by the Church in order to minimize the potential for heirs and gain more property for itself in the process.

[16] For the relevant passages on marriage, see *CIC*, Gratian, *Decretum*, causae 27–36; Lombard, *Sententiarum*, 4.27.2–5, 4.28.3. The most comprehensive surveys of canonical marriage law during this period are Freisen, *Geschichte des kanonischen Eherechtes bis zum Verfall der Glossenliteratur;* Dauvillier, *Le mariage dans le droit classique de l'Eglise, depuis le Décret de Gratian (1140) jusqu'à Mort de Clement V (1314);* and Brundage, *Law, Sex, and Christian Society*, especially 229–324, on Gratian, Peter Lombard, and the early Decretists.

[17] According to Erler, Gregory VIII's campaign to enforce clerical celibacy included legal pressures from below (delegitimizing all children of priests as *irregulares ex defectu natalium*, with no legal rights whatsoever) and above (doctrinal revision). Adalbert Erler, *Kirchenrecht*, 5th ed. (Munich, 1983), 23–24; also Brundage, *Law, Sex, and Christian Soceity*, 214–28.

[18] For most canonists, all sexual pleasure was sinful, and thus as a group they remained "restrained in their enthusiasm for marriage as an institution." See James Brundage, "Carnal Delight: Canonistic Theories of Sexuality," in *Proceedings of the Fifth International Congress of Medieval Canon Law*, ed. Stephan Kuttner et al. (Vatican City, 1980), 361–85. Cf. marriage writings of Ivo of Chartres, discussed in Georges Duby, *The Knight, the Lady, and the Priest: The Making of Modern Marriage in Medieval France*, trans. Barbara Bray (New York, 1983), 161–85; also Esmein I:80–90; Noonan, *Contraception*, 255ff.; LeBras, "La doctrine du mariage," in *DTC* 9:218off.; the monograph M. Müller, *Die Lehre des heiligen Augustinus von der Paradiesehe und ihre Auswirkung in der Sexualethik des 12. und 13. Jahrhunderts bis Thomas von Aquin* (Regensburg, 1954); and H. J. F. Reinhardt, *Die Ehelehre der Schule des Anselms von Laon. Eine theologische und kirchengeschichtliche Untersuchung zu den Ehetexten der frühen Pariser Schule der 12. Jahrhunderts* (Münster, 1974).
The "unconsummated love" and chaste ideals of the canonists find interesting secular parallels, as some historians have pointed out, in the "courtly love" literature of this period and

ous conciliar statutes, culminating in those of Lateran IV (1215), reinforced the position that marriage, even as a *remedium*, remained a course of second choice for Christians and therefore to be avoided at all costs by those intending to be spiritual leaders.[19]

Ironically, the very success of an extreme ascetic ideal, chiefly among dualist heretics, prompted many of these same canonists to come to the defense of marriage.[20] Both Gratian and Lombard perceived the exclusive elevation of celibacy and consequential neglect of marital practice as responsible for widespread denigration of the sacrament among heretics and orthodox believers alike. Their response was to take Augustine's *triplex bonum* and remedial benefits of marriage even further, emphasizing the cultivation, by parenthood and affinity, of the sentiments of charity and love, as well as "the reconciliation of enemies, beauty, and riches."[21] Both canonists also clearly recognized the indispensable political significance of marriage among medieval aristocrats,[22] yet at the same time they endeavored to emphasize and develop the spiritual nature and potential of the *sacramentum*, particularly by elevating it beyond a predominantly economic or political function. With little exaggeration, nothing less than a total religious reformation of marriage and society was their goal, with Canon law and ecclesiastical jurisdiction as the means.

In redefining marriage along more "sacramental" lines, canonists were forced to consider the great mass of local marital customs that currently prevailed throughout Europe. Generally speaking, the marital joining had evolved locally into a series of acts and rituals, usually in-

---

following. Charles Donahue, Jr., "The Policy of Alexander III's Consent Theory of Marriage," in *Proceedings of the Fourth International Congress of Medieval Canon Law*, ed. S. Kuttner (Vatican City, 1975), 278; Noonan, *Contraception*, 181–83, 195–96.

19 See especially Synod of Pisa (1135), canon 1; Lateran II (1139), canon 7; Synod of Reims (1148); and the clearest statement in the *Summa Theologica* of Aquinas, III, q. 53, a. 3. Vancandard, "Célibat ecclésiastique," in *DTC* 2:2087; Naz, "Mariage en droit occidental," in *DDC* 6:750–56, 781; also Thomas N. Tentler, *Sin and Confession on the Eve of the Reformation* (Princeton, 1977), 166ff.

20 LeBras argues that Cathar attacks on marriage provided the main motivation behind the twelfth-century "defense" of the institution ("La doctrine du mariage," in *DTC* 9:2139, 2173, 2180, 2220). Noonan (*Contraception*, 221–44) concurs.

21 Esmein I:89. Noonan remarks that the concept of marriage for love was in some ways very innovative of twelfth- and thirteenth-century canonists (*Contraception*, 255–6). Cf. R. Weigand, "Liebe und Ehe bei den Dekretisten des 12. Jahrhunderts," in *Love and Marriage in the Twelfth Century*, ed. W. Van Hoecke and A. Welkenhuysen (Louvain, 1981), especially 41–58.

22 See especially the aristocratic model of marriage confronting clerical reformers as described in Duby, *The Knight, the Lady, and the Priest*, xix, 18ff.

cluding betrothal, or engagement (reflecting the recognition and approval of the family and community); consent of the couple; sexual intercourse (*copula carnalis*), marking the completion of the marriage; and nuptial blessing by the bishop or parish priest, symbolizing approval of the Church.[23] With the writing of Gratian and Lombard, these elements and their proper sequence were examined and analyzed in their relationship to the actual sacrament.

Although in agreement on the holy and indissoluble nature of marriage, Gratian and Lombard remained divided on the question of which of these four elements were essential to the validity (but not licity, or propriety) of the sacrament.[24] Gratian, foremost spokesman of the Bolognese school, maintained that consent between the two parties did not make a valid and indissoluble marriage until consummated by subsequent sexual union.[25] Lombard, supported by the Masters of Paris, argued that words of present consent (*verba de presenti*) alone made a valid marriage.[26] The eventual resolution of this theological and legal dispute would shape the entire Canon law of marriage for centuries to come. Almost equally as significant, though, was the matter-of-fact exclusion of all other traditional elements of the marital act in the canonists' definitions, especially familial and ecclesiastical approval.

Again, the legal rationale of Gratian and Peter Lombard must be tied

---

23 Although, according to Canon law, the benediction was supposed to occur before consummation, the concept was slow to penetrate popular practice. Esmein I:97–106. See also Chapters 3 and 4.

24 R. Naz, "Divorce," in *DDC* 4:1315ff.; Naz, "Mariage en droit occidental," in *DDC* 6:744ff.; Heinrich Portmann, *Wesen und Unauflösigkeit der Ehe in der kirchlichen Wissenschaft und Gesetzgebung des 11. und 12. Jahrhunderts. Ein Beitrag zur kirchlichen Rechtsgeschichte* (Emsdetten, 1938).
   On the distinction between validity and licity of a marriage: "*Mariage valide et licite*. Mariage dans la conclusion duquel ont été respectées ensemble les prohibitions des empêchements dirimants [i.e., those of Canon law, regarding the validity, such as consanguinity and affinity] et celles des empêchements prohibitifs [i.e., those restrictions of secular and ecclesiastical authorities regarding the "propriety" of the marriage, such as requirements for publicity and parental approval]. Le mariage est dit valide mais illicite lorsque seuls les empêchements prohibants n'ont pas été observeés" (Naz, "Marriage en droit occidental," in *DDC* 6:742). See also my comments in Chapter 4 on valid but illicit clandestine marriage.

25 The distinction Gratian makes is between a marriage initiated through vows of any kind (*coniugium initiatum*) and one that has been "completed," and therefore validated, through consummantion (*coniugium ratum*). According to Esmein, Gratian bases his argument on a nonexistent passage he attributes to Saint Augustine, and an obscure fragment of Leon of Rusticus. Esmein I:95, 99: Le Bras, "La doctrine du mariage," in *DTC* 9:2149–51; Naz, "Mariage en droit occidental," in *DDC* 6:741ff.; and Brundage, *Law, Sex, and Christian Society*, 236ff. Cf. also Willibald Plöchl, *Das Eherecht des Magisters Gratianus* (Leipzig, 1935).

26 Esmein I:119; LeBras, "La doctrine du mariage," in *DTC* 9:2151–53.

to their ambitious reformation of the role of marriage in society. As a sacrament, they argued, marriage must by definition be made freely available to all, and dependent only on the consent of the participants for its efficacy. Both canonists opposed, therefore, the forced marriage of children; for Gratian, such coercion was even a further argument in favor of requiring consummation, and therefore sexual maturity, for validity.[27]

The same logic held for the requirement of familial approval. Peter Lombard was the first to argue that parental consent was not necessary for the validity of the sacrament of marriage. Even Gratian, who expressly opposed marriages against the wishes of parents, conceded that such marriages were nonetheless valid and indissoluble.[28] Both recognized the social role of marriage intrinsic to Augustine's *triplex bonum*, but at the same time proposed a return in practice to the Roman consensual basis of marriage, which they considered more appropriate to a sacrament. Typically, as Esmein notes, neither of these or subsequent canonists made much of a distinction between the civil contract and sacrament of marriage. In their eyes, the very sacramental definition of marriage and all of its legal implications rendered such a distinction meaningless.[29] Still, the precise legal definition of this consensual and indissoluble union continued to divide twelfth-century reformers of marriage. In the midst of the ongoing Paris–Bologna dispute, ambiguous and conflicting local secular ordinances on marriage formalities, and an increased amount of marriage litigation in Church courts, some definitive ruling was clearly in order. This, at least, was the understanding of Pope Alexander III (1159–81), who attempted to resolve the confusion during his pontificate.

Alexander, a celebrated jurist himself, eventually decided on a compromise between the Parisian and Bolognese definitions of marriage, but only after a long and arduous evolution of policy.[30] His final decision

---

[27] Since Ivo of Chartres (1040–1116), the official minimum age of Church law had been set at seven. Article #55 of the *Schwabenspiegel*, however, recognized the higher minimum set by Alexander III of fourteen for boys and twelve for girls. Esmein I:150–51, 156.

[28] Esmein I:114, 158; LeBras, "La doctrine du mariage," in *DTC* 9:2151–53.

[29] Esmein I:80, 156–59; LeBras, "La doctrine du mariage," in *DTC* 9:2182ff.; Naz, "Mariage en droit occidental," in *DDC* 6:746–48.

[30] Donahue describes the evolution of Alexander III's thought on marriage as beginning with the then current standard of both *de futuro* and *de presenti* vows as valid, changing to Gratian's argument that consummation of either was necessary, then to a subtle distinction between *de futuro* and *de presenti* vows, with solemnities necessary for the latter, before finally deciding on the compromise between the two that became Church doctrine. Donahue, "Alexander III's Consent Theory," 253ff. Cf. Brundage, *Law, Sex, and Christian Society*, 325ff.

accepted Peter Lombard's argument that words of present consent alone formed a valid marriage (*consensus nudus facit nuptum*), but also that a betrothal, or promise to marry (*verba de futuro*), was generally made valid and indissoluble by subsequent sexual intercourse.[31] The personal intentions of Alexander III remain debatable[32] but the legal implications of his actions were quickly evident and far-reaching.

The foremost was that it made a valid marriage possible without any formalities or consent other than that of the marrying couple. This not only eliminated the restrictive element of parental consent present even in Roman law, but dispensed with the traditional betrothal and public banns as essential to the marriage act.[33] Although many general and local restrictions continued to define the licity of a marriage with various formalities and possible civil and ecclesiastical punishments, the judicial standard for validity of a marriage remained established in the decrees of Alexander III, that is *verba de presenti*.

Satisfying both the communal and the more individualistic, sacramental goals of the reformers thus often involved maintaining a precarious balance, best described by Michael Sheehan as "a steady insistence on the publicity of marriage that completely overshadowed the quiet admission that such publicity was not essential to the union."[34] Such a policy had been successfully implemented at a local level in England and France during Alexander's reign, and it was generally adopted by the Church at Lateran IV (1215). Canon 51 of this council required three public banns, two witnesses, and marriage solemnization in the parish church or at very least by the parish priest (*in facie ecclesiae*) – all other vows were clandestine and illicit (though still valid).[35] Such require-

---

31 Donahue, "Alexander III's Consent Theory," 251–56; Esmein I:127–33; LeBras, "La doctrine du mariage," in *DTC* 9:2154–59.
32 Donahue takes as his thesis that "Alexander's rules on the formation of marriage constitute a conscious and at least partially successful attempt to use canon law to influence the course of social development" ("Alexander III's Consent Theory," 235). Esmein concurs, identifying the two major goals of the Canon law of marriage from Alexander on as to establish as much equality as possibility between the couple and to assure maintenance of communal life and conjugal duty (Esmein I:302). The success of such attempts is discussed more at length in subsequent chapters.
33 Esmein I:153; Naz, "Mariage en droit occidental," in *DDC* 6:752.
34 Michael Sheehan, "Theory and Practice in the Conciliar Legislation and Diocesan Statutes of Medieval England," *Medieval Studies* 40 (1978), 459.
35 Esmein I:28. Cf. 1215 decree of Innocent III prohibiting clandestine marriage and requiring all unions "to be publicly proclaimed in the churches by the priests, allowing a suitable time within which anyone who can and wishes to may bring forward a legitimate impediment" (*CIC* Gregory IX, Liber extravagantium decretalium, 4.3.3). On the implementation of this policy in Germany, see Chapter 4.

ments did not revoke Alexander's definition. Rather, they provided a disciplinary check against the marital anarchy some secular and ecclesiastical authorities feared, reaffirming the social role of marriage in face of its new sacramental definition.

If secular authorities were frustrated by the sacramental definition of marriage that ecclesiastical jurisdiction had imposed on them, many canonists and Church judges shared their annoyance. By theological definition, only personal eligibility for the sacrament could be restricted (i.e., impediments), and even here the consensual and indissoluble definition proved highly inflexible.[36] The decretalists and other subsequent canonists could elaborate and further delineate the early formulas of *verba de presenti* and *verba de futuro*, refine the list of impediments, or make procedural changes for marital litigation. The holy, indissoluble, and consensual definition of validity, however, was itself beyond modification by any authority.[37]

The twelfth-century reformation of marriage was replete with paradoxes. While attempting to elevate and sanctify marriage, canonists made it so readily accessible as to engender, at least potentially, a variety of abuses and disputes. While assuming a much more active role in marital legislation and litigation, ecclesiastical authorities also made their task more difficult by the radical deformalizing of the entire validating marriage act. Perhaps most significant, despite their defense of the positive social role of marriage, canonists elevated the individual choice of the marrying couple above any familial or communal approval, placing, in the words of Donahue, "tremendous trust in human choice."[38]

---

[36] "[The Church] ne peut en changer ni la matière ni la forme en tant qu'elles ont été fixées par Jésus-Christ, mais elle peut determiner quelles personnes sont capables de recevoir ce sacrament" (Naz, "Mariage en droit occidental," in *DDC* 6:752–4).

[37] As the early court formulas for defining *verba de presenti* and *verba de futuro* became inadequate, many new constructions and elaborations appeared. Marriage vows, for instance, eventually could be exchanged by signs (for the deaf and dumb), by letter (in absence), and with some conditions attached. In addition, various rules on admission of testimony (the usual source of proof) were accumulated, chiefly to curb the potential for perjured evidence. Esmein I:166–70; Richard Helmholz, *Marriage Litigation in Medieval England* (London, 1974), 31–48, 71; Erler, *Kirchenrecht*, 28–30; LeBras, "La doctrine du mariage," in *DTC* 9:2162ff.; Brundage, *Law, Sex, and Christian Society*, 346ff.
  On impediments, see Esmein I:203ff. and my subsequent discussion in this chapter.

[38] Donahue, "Alexander III's Consent Theory," 277. Cf. similar conclusions of Raymond Decker, "Institutional Authority versus Personal Responsibility in the Marriage Sections of Gratian's *A Concordance of Discordant Canons*," *Jurist* 32 (1972), 51–65.

Concurrent Church endorsement of several legitimizing formalities may have temporarily obscured, but not eliminated, the disjunction between the sacramental ideal of the canonists and traditional social values. As Sheehan writes:

> However much theologians and canonists stressed the importance of the social controls and supports of marriage, they had launched a new set of ideas whereby marriage would be considered from the point of view of the couple rather than that of the extended family.[39]

One need not accept the degree of radical innovation or successful popular reception that Sheehan suggests to appreciate the unique and momentous nature of the attempt. In fact, there is no better testimony to the "loftiness" of the twelfth-century reformers' ambitions for marriage than the very criticisms leveled against their entire canonical system by religious reformers of another, much later century.

The Protestant ideal of marriage

Reformers of the sixteenth century viewed themselves as the liberators of marriage from a disdainful theological tradition. Yet praise for the estate of marriage, as even most Protestant Whig historians must admit, constituted a prominent theme of German tracts and pamphlets well before the onset of the Reformation.[40] Beyond repeating the traditional *triplex bonum* of Augustine, many fifteenth- and early sixteenth-century writers lauded marriage as a holy estate "recommended [first] by Nature, then by scripture, and finally by the example of the saints."[41] In contrast to the derogatory caricatures of contemporary satirists, Gabriel Biel considered marriage not just a sacrament among the others, but

---

39 Michael Sheehan, "The Formation and Stability of Marriage in the Fourteenth Century: Evidence of an Ely Register," *Medieval Studies* 33 (1971), 229. Cf. similar conclusion of Rudolf Weigand in "Kirchenrechtliche Bestimmungen mit möglicher Bedeutung für die Bevölkerungsentwicklung," *Saeculum* 39/2 (1988), 173–83.

40 Ozment concedes that "humanists and Protestants were not the first to defend the estate of marriage" (*When Fathers Ruled*, 6), and Kawerau (*Die Reformation und die Ehe*, 64) agrees that sixteenth-century literature praising marriage "war allerdings nichts neues."

    Cf. other pre-Reformation writings praising marriage discussed in Falk, *Die Ehe am Ausgang des Mittelalters* (Freibourg, 1908), 22ff.; Kawerau, *Die Reformation und die Ehe*, 64–67; Noonan, *Contraception*, 304ff.; Wendel, *Le mariage*, 21ff.; Duby, *The Knight, the Lady, and the Priest*, 211–26; and Yost, "Changing Attitudes toward Married Life in Civic and Christian Humanism," *Occasional Papers of the American Society for Reformation Research* 1 (1977), 153ff.

41 Nicolas [de Blony], *Sermones de tempore et de sanctis* (Strasbourg, 1494), xix (sermon for first Sunday after octave of Epiphany).

"the most excellent and first of all by the moment and place of its institution and by the signification and efficacy of its end."[42] Probably the most famous advocate of the married estate during the fifteenth century was Albrecht von Eyb who, in his frequently reprinted "Marriage Booklet," extended the benefits of the conjugal union far beyond the couple themselves:

> In short, marriage is thus an honorable . . . useful, [and] beneficial thing: through it, land, field, and house are built, multiplied, and sustained; many disputes, severe wars and enmities stilled and laid aside; good friends and relatives made among strangers; and the entire human race perpetuated.[43]

Yet although sixteenth-century German Protestants and Catholics alike were heirs to this literary tradition, Protestant writes were unquestionably the most prolific in its continuance. Evangelical and Reformed pamphlets, tracts, poems, and plays all preached the marital fruits of love, fidelity, and procreation, with the most important product being the personal and social stability praise by Eyb.[44] All of the major sixteenth-century Protestant reformers wrote at one time or another on the Christian ideal of marriage and the related subject of clerical celibacy.[45] Like their Catholic predecessors and contemporaries, most directly addressed the current problems of clandestine marriage and sexual immo-

---

[42] Gabriel Biel, *Sermones dominicales* (Hagenau, 1510), xixff. Biel, it should be noted, still professed a personal preference for celibacy.

[43] Albrecht von Eyb, "Ob einem mannen sey zu nemmen ein eelichs weyb oder nicht," in *Ehebüchlein* (Nuremberg, 1472; facsimile: Wiesbaden, 1966), 80–1.

[44] See my subsequent discussion in this chapter.

[45] Luther wrote and preached extensively on marriage throughout his career, though, as noted by Dieterich (37), "zwar ergeben Luthers Lehren von der Ehe kein lückenloses System." His major works on the subject include *Ein sermon von dem ehelichen Standt* (1519), *WA* 2:162–71; *De captivitate Babylonica eclesiae praeludium* (1520), *WA* 6:484–573, especially 550–60; *Vom ehelichen Leben* (1522), *WA* 10/II:267–304; *Dass Eltern die Kinder zur Ehe nicht zwingen noch hindern und die Kinder ohne der Eltern Willen sich nicht verloben sollen* (1524), *WA* 15:155–69; *Von Ehesachen* (1530), *WA* 30/III:198–248; and his final word on the subject, *Predigt vom Ehestand* (1545), *WA* 49:797–805.

The writings of other major sixteenth-century reformers on celibacy and marriage are too numerous to list here, but among the most influential were Ulrich Zwingli, *Die Ordnungen und erkandnussen wie hinfür zu Zürich in der Statt über Eelich sachen gericht sol werden* (Zurich, 1525); Johannes Bugenhagen, *De coniugio episcoporum* (Wittenberg, 1525), and *Vom Ehebruch und Heimlichen Weglaufen* (Wittenberg, 1541); Brenz, *Wie yn Ehesachen;* Phillip Melanchthon, *Defensio coniugii sacerdotum* (Wittenberg, 1539); Heinrich Bullinger, *Der christliche Ehestand* (Zurich, 1540); John Calvin, *Commentaries* on 1 Cor. 7:37 (1546) and Eph. 5:22–6 (1548), as well as various parts of the *Institutes;* and Martin Bucer, *De Regno Christi* (Basel, 1550), especially book II, chap. 15–47.

rality. What most distinguished the new Evangelical reformers, though, was their attempted resolution of the traditional *remedium–sacramentum* dilemma of marriage. For Luther and others, the current denigration of marriage (particularly among young people) and of the priesthood both emanated from the same source – the "unnatural" celibate ideal. According to them, the natural sexual drive rendered celibacy tortuous or hypocritical for clerics yet also tainted marriage as "unspiritual" and inferior for its willing surrender to the carnal appetite.

Their solution was dramatically simple, though not a little ironic: desacramentalizing marriage and the priesthood in order to raise the prestige and holiness of both estates. Heiko Oberman has suggested in his biography of Luther that this Protestant alteration marked the dramatic transformation of an ascetic and otherworldly Christianity into a religion of this world and its demands.[46] Certainly the decline of religious celibacy among Protestants deserves such commemoration, but its replacement by a new or different Protestant marital ideal appears to have been a much more gradual and subtler process. Lutheran and Calvinist theologians not only continued to define marriage in terms of the traditional *triplex bonum*, but consistently resisted total rejection of the ascetic ideal. Even as they relieved priests of "unrealistic" expectations, reformers incorporated the celibate ideal's language of "good works" in their defenses of marriage. The balance between *remedium* and *sacramentum* undoubtedly shifted among Protestants but only slowly and reluctantly.

The formation of a distinctive Protestant ideal of marriage thus entailed two distinct and successive feats of varying complexity; abolition of the celibate religious ideal and elevation of marriage in its place. The first, refutation of celibacy, drew on three typically Protestant sources: scripture, the doctrine of *sola fide* justification, and practical experience. The undisputed leader in the scripturally based refutation of the celibate ideal was Erasmus of Rotterdam. Jesus, he argued, neither commanded celibacy nor disapproved of those who were married, such as his apostles. Where, then was the scriptural basis for such a teaching? Nowhere, he concluded, and in a detailed exegesis on virginity and celibacy, the humanist proceeded to demonstrate that vows of chastity are contrary to

---

[46] *Luther: Man between God and the Devil*, trans. Eileen Walliser-Schwarzbart (New York, 1989), 272.

the laws and commandments of God, Christ, Moses, and all other scriptural authorities.[47] Erasmus's scriptural argument was quickly incorporated into the criticisms of other reform-minded Catholics and Evangelicals – particularly Karlstadt and Luther – who also resented the unbiblical denigration of all estates other than celibacy as "unfortunate" or "unholy" (*unselig*). Paul's advice to the Corinthians, for instance, was clarified by Caspar Güttel: "St. Paul did not want to tie anyone to virginity. It was for this reason he himself said: 'I tell this to help you, not to put a leash around your necks'."[48]

The traditional treatment of virginity as a sanctifying good work likewise provided a ready target for early Evangelicals. For Luther, the very idea that a life of chastity in itself "earned" one a spot in heaven was reason enough to question the Church's teaching.[49] Erasmus viewed the entire ascetic ideal as a harmful relic of the Judaic conception of salvation, expected to produce rather than flow from supernatural powers, and favored its gradual retirement from practice.[50] Most important, stressed Luther, grace and faith – not works – made a Christian just, once again bringing to the forefront the ideal of a "religious" life and its relationship to salvation. Indeed, the immediate implications of *sola fide* justification for clerical celibacy were not difficult to fathom. If, as Geiler von Keiserberg, the most famous pre-Reformation preacher in Strasbourg claimed, "carnal integrity is not a virtue, nor even the essential part of a virtue,"[51] what then was the value and place of celibacy? Put more bluntly by Bernhard Rem: "If the life of the cloister were really as important as you presume, then we would all have to become monks and nuns."[52]

The final and probably most popularly accessible objection of Protestant reformers was the overwhelming "practical" obstacle to celibacy, namely, the irresistibility of the sexual urge. Luther estimated that at best one out of a thousand (later revised to one in a hundred thousand)

---

[47] Telle, *Erasme*, 3ff., 164, 177, 233–55. Cf. similar exegesis by Calvin in *Institutes* IV.xii.22ff. and *Commentaries* 1 Tim. 4:3 where he links opposition to marriage to the early heresies of Montanists, Encrantites, Tatianists, Manicheans, and later the Cathars.

[48] Gütell, *Ueber den Evangelion Johannis*, 3ª. The first notable Protestant assault on the celibate ideal was Karlstadt's *De Coelibatu, monachatu et vinditate* (Wittenberg, 1521).

[49] See Baranowski, *Luthers Lehre von der Ehe*, 13, 34–49; the same point is made in Bugenhagen, *De coniugio episcoporum*, Bᵇ.

[50] "Fateor quae publice recepta sunt perperam, paulatim sunt abroganda, quemadmodum Paulus abolevit Legem Mosaicam, sed tamen antiquanda sunt." Telle, *Erasme*, 23–41, 150.

[51] Geiler vaon Kaiserberg, *De arbore humana* (Strasbourg, 1514), lxxiii and lxxxi.

[52] Bernhard Rem, *Ain Sendtbrieff an ettlich closterfrawen zu sant Katherina und zu sant Niclas in Augsburg* (n.p., 1523), A 3ª⁻ᵇ, quoted in Ozment, *When Fathers Ruled*, 22.

could truly and joyfully lead a celibate life without any impure thoughts or actions.[53] The gift of chastity, according to Erasmus, was for the most part reserved to the angels,[54] a position shared by Calvin who considered clerical celibacy "a diabolical conspiracy" and "dangerous innovation." "Let no one cry out against me," the Genevan reformer added, "that with God's help he can do all things, for clearly this did not apply to chastity."[55] Their common point required little elaboration in popular evangelical polemic:

> To give up virginity is a bad thing, but burning is also trouble. That's why an unpleasant marriage is better than unpleasant chastity; better a sour and difficult marriage than a sour and difficult chastity. Thus it's better to be freed than burn. . . . After all, a priest is a man, God's creature and work, made to be fruitful and multiply like other people.[56]

As usual, though, Luther surpassed all in defining the argument in its bluntest terms: "Nature never lets up . . . we are all driven to the secret sin. To say it crudely but honestly, if it doesn't go into a woman, it goes into your shirt."[57]

So strong was this theme of natural urges (*Naturflüssen*) among the early reformers that many Catholic contemporaries and some historians have accused Luther and others of allowing their personal struggles with celibacy to cloud their theological reasoning on the subject.[58] Centuries

---

53 "Vom ehelichen Leben" (1522), *WA* 10/II:279; "Das siebente Kapitel S. Pauli zu den Corinthern" (1523), *WA* 12:115. See also Baranowski, *Luthers Lehre von der Ehe*, 54ff.

54 The distinction between virginity and celibacy was a key element in Erasmus's (unsuccessful) defense against censure by the Sorbonne in 1525. His position was that while virginity was still the most exalted of states (eulogized in his 1529 *Vidua Christiana*), it was possible only among angels, not men, and celibacy was thus an exercise in frustration and/or hypocrisy. "Non ego nunc loquor de iis Monachis quorum mores et mundus detestator, sed de his, quos vulgus miratur, non ut homines, sed ut angelos" (*Enchiridion*). Telle, *Erasme*, 132ff., 311ff., 319, 425.

55 *Institutes* II.viii.42. Calvin was responding specifically to Eck's 1541 *Enchiridion* on clerical celibacy. See also *Commentaries* 1 Tim. 4:3; *Institutes* IV.ix.14 and IV.xii.22–8.

56 Thomas Stör, *Der Ehelich stand* (1524), C1ᵃ–C2ᵃ. This argument is reiterated by Melanchthon in articles 23 and 27 of the *Augsburg Confession* and later in his *A very godly defense full of learning defending the marriage of Priests* (English trans., 1541; German original, Wittenberg, 1539), B4ᵇ–C2ᵃ. Melanchthon especially relies on 1 Cor. 7, Heb. 13, and 1 Tim. 4.

57 "Wider den falsch genannten geistlichen Stand" (1522), *WA* 102:156, translated in Strauss, *Luther's House of Learning*, 103. Strauss reminds us that such sexual explicitness was common in sixteenth-century literature, even in sermons.

58 The accusation is old though not always confessional in origin. Catholic contemporaries, of course, attacked the character and motivation of all major Protestant reformers in this area; cf. especially Joachim von der Heyden, *Ein Sendtbrieff Kethen von Bhore Luthers vormeynthem eheweybe sampt eynem geschenck freuntlicher meynung tzuvorfertigt* (Leipzig, 1528). Beginning in the nineteenth century, however, scholars of both confessions began to subject theological pro-

of tradition had proved, Catholic polemicists argued, that sexual abstinence *was* possible, and it was an insult to all those chaste saints as well as long-separated but faithful married persons to maintain otherwise. The Church's teachings on celibacy and marriage allowed each person to choose the estate most suited to his or her abilities; the only possible individuals with an interest in denying God's ability to bestow such gifts were those with a predilection to whoring.[59] As the Council of Trent admonished skeptics, "God does not refuse that gift [chastity] to those who ask for it rightly, neither does he suffer us to be tempted above that which we are able."[60] Marriage did provide a necessary and sanctifying *remedium* to sinful urges but that did not eliminate the possibility or superiority of total chastity.[61]

Protestant demolition of the celibate religious ideal, however, apparently required little elaboration for popular acceptance. The same cannot be said of its proposed successor as the ideal Christian estate. Protestant difficulties in establishing marriage as the new "spiritual" ideal have even led some historians to suggest that the "elevation" of marriage by reformers was merely the only alternative left them after the celibate ideal had been throughly discredited.[62] Obviously this explana-

nouncements of Luther and others to closer biographically based scrutiny. E. Friedberg (*Studien und Skizzen zur Geschichte der Reformation* [Schoffennhausen, 1846], 67ff.) was among the first to theorize that Luther's attack on celibacy was almost entirely based on personal experience, forcing him to sacrifice his intellectual convictions for practical necessity. Baranowski (*Luthers Lehre von der Ehe*, 49ff.) concurs that the sexual urge "war für Luther eine wichtige, wir können ruhig sagen: die wichtigste Instanz im Kampfe gegen den Cölibat, das stärkste Motiv für Anpreisung er Ehe." Modern psychohistorical approches (cf. the highly controversial Erik Erikson, *Young Man Luther* [New York, 1958]) have, if anything, only further exacerbated the division among scholars.

59 This was a frequent accusation among Catholic propagandists, including Thomas More, who in his *Dialogue Concerning Heresies* (ca. 1530), rejected his friend Erasmus's attacks on a celibate priesthood (Carlson, "Marriage and the English Reformation." 158–59). See also Johannes Lansberg, *Eyn schöne underrichtung was die recht Ewangelisch geystlicheit sy / und was man von den Clöstern halten soll* (Cologne, 1528), E4a; and Peter Canisius, *Catholischer Cathechismus* (Cologne, 1563), Nvii–Pii.

60 From canon 9 of the "Doctrine of the Sacrament of Marriage" (*Tametsi*), in *Canons and Decrees of the Council of Trent*, ed. H. J. Schroeder (St. Louis, 1941), 182.

61 See canons 6 and 10 of *Tametsi*, which clearly reaffirm that virginity and celibacy are superior to marriage, and that such vows supercede and dissolve any *unconsummated* marriage vows. Schroeder, *Council of Trent*, 181–82.

62 Baranowski, *Luthers Lehre von der Ehe*, 10. Josef Mausbach (*Die katholische Moral, ihre Methoden, Grundsätze und Aufgâben*, 2nd ed. [Cologne, 1902], 118) takes the opposite approach to the didactic relationship between the two ideals: "mit Anerkennung des Bessern wird das Gegenteil als böse hingestellt . . . wer sieht in der höheren Wertschätzung des Gottes eine Verachtung des Silbers, wer in Vorliebe für die Rose eine Geringschätzung anderer Blumen – diese Vergleiche kammen schon bei den Kirchenvätern vor . . ."

tion oversimplifies, but it does at least correctly identify the greatest challenges to a new Protestant ideal for marriage. The inherent sexual drive of all humans provided a foundation for marriage as the most natural state but still on a largely remedial basis. Very few reformers were able to absolve even marital sex of all sinful aspects and the vast majority thus hesitated to issue unqualified endorsements of the estate. The "worldliness" of marriage that Oberman perceives as radically innovative of Protestantism in fact troubled many sixteenth-century reformers greatly, particularly in view of their perception of the world as Satan's realm. Like their twelfth-century predecessors, they found the combination of spiritual and worldly characteristics of marriage a difficult theological balance. Unlike scholastic marriage reformers, however, they decided on the exact opposite solution: desacramentalization.

Theological attacks on the sacramentality of marriage cut right to the heart of traditional doctrine. "Nowhere in all of Holy Scriptures," writes Luther in the *Babylonian Captivity,* "is this word *sacramentum* employed in the sense in which we use the term; it has an entirely different meaning."[63] How else, Calvin concurred, could one explain such an absurd dogma that "affirm[ed] that in the sacrament the grace of the Holy Spirit is conferred [and] taught copulation to be a sacrament [yet] denied that the Holy Spirit is ever present in copulation?"[64] Luther and Calvin were in fact expanding upon a popular humanist argument most recently revived by Erasmus in his 1516 edition of the New Testament. According to Erasmus, not only had the original Greek of the pivotal Ephesians 5:32 been mistranslated in the Vulgate as *sacramentum* instead of *mysterium,* but the entire sacramental construction and all of its implications had been fabricated by Durandus of Saint Pourcain and later twelfth-century canonists. What was the special sign, where was the source of grace, he asked, and if marriage was truly a sacrament, why deny it to clerics?[65] Moreover, if the metaphorical use of marriage in Ephesians rendered it a sacrament, then the Bible contained hundreds of other such "sacraments" (including burglary, Calvin mischievously

---

[63] "Babylonian Captivity," *LW* 36:93.
[64] *Institutes* IV.xix.36.
[65] Erasmus's contribution was actually a systematic exegesis of an already long-extant philological and theological debate among scholars, also discussed in Jacques Lefevre d'Etaple's *Epistole divi Pauli . . .* (Paris, 1517), 39ff. Reaction among most of Erasmus's French colleagues, however, was considerably cooler, ultimately resulting in the 1525 censure of his marriage writings by the Sorbonne. Telle, *Erasme,* 257–92, especially 260–68; Bels, *Le mariage des protestants français,* 33.

added, since the Lord comes "like a thief in the night").[66] The Sorbonne's 1525 censure of Erasmus's writings on the subject only further encouraged Protestant sympathizers, particularly in Germany, where the "more appropriate" *mysterium* became *Geheimnuß* and the chief scriptural basis for the sacramentality of marriage thereby evaporated.

Protestant theologians now faced the extremely delicate task of eliminating the theological "errors" of the Catholic sacramental system while still preserving the sanctity of the married estate. Frequent confusion over Luther's well-known characterizations of marriage as "a worldly thing" clearly illustrates the difficulty in conveying what was actually a much more nuanced synthesis of the profane and the sacred. For Luther, as well as the majority of subsequent Evangelical and Reformed theologians, marriage in fact represented a divinely ordained institution that was secular only in a post-Lapsarian sense. And even though this "noblest" estate's place in the divine order had been altered by Adam and Eve's sin, Luther believed that "since it is based on God's word . . . it should also be treated as spiritual."[67] Calvin also considered marriage to have predated the Fall, and thus only "worldly" in its remedial purpose thereafter.[68] The difference between subsequent sixteenth-century Protestant description of marriage as "divinely ordained," "blessed," and "holy" and traditional Catholic characterizations consequently remained a subtle one.[69] Even Calvin's carefully worded definition of "an exterior ceremony ordained by God for confirming some promise"[70] suggests the elusiveness of such a distinction for most believers.

To complicate matters further almost all of the reformers themselves

---

[66] *Institutes* IV.xix.34–46. "Anyone who would classify such similitudes with the sacraments," he added, "ought to be sent to a mental hospital."

[67] *Traubüchlein* (1529), *WA* 30/III:75. See also "Das siebente Kapitel S. Paul zu den Corintern (1523), *WA* 12:105; and "Auslegung des sechsten Gebots.," in *Deutsch Catechismus* (1529), *WA* 30/I:162. Luther also termed marriage *institutio Dei, Dei ordinatio in creatione*, and *sanctum coniugium* (Dieterich 34ff.).

[68] Like Augustine, Calvin believed that sexual intercourse became lustful only after the Fall, and thus was only accidentally remedial. It was, rather, a "good" and "holy" "foedus Dei, quia excellet supra omnes humanos contractus," but still not a sacrament. *Institutes* II.viii.41; also IV.xix.34–36 on worldly metaphors for marriage; and Josef Bohatec, *Budé und Calvin: Studien zur Gedankenwelt des französischen Frühhumanismus* (Graz, 1950), 652ff.

[69] Cf. Bucer's description of "holy ordinance" of marriage in *De Regno Christi* (1550), in *Opera Latina*, ed. François Wendel (Paris, 1955), XV:152ff., 209; also Dieter Schwab, *Grundlagen und Gestalt der staatlichen Ehegesetzgebung in der Neuzeit bis Zimm Beginn des 19 Jahrhunderts* (Bielefeld, 1967), 110ff., on similar mixture among all sixteenth-century theologians and jurists.

[70] Joseph Faurey, "Le droit écclésiastique matrimonial des calvinistes français" (Ph.D. diss., Paris, 1910), 54; Bels, *Le mariage des protestants français*, 21.

expressed traditional reservations about unqualified elevation of marriage as a spiritual ideal. Despite – or perhaps because of – their repeated affirmations of the sexual drive, most Protestant theologians refused both to absolve marital sex of all sin and to dismiss or condemn chastity altogether. Only Bucer completely rejected the sinfulness of sex within marriage, and even Luther – who considered the act "God's Word and work" – restricted his approval to intercourse for procreative purposes.[71] The remainder, like Calvin, continued to rank the remedial aspect of marriage as the most important of the traditional *triplex bonum*.[72] Sexual attraction within marriage was both natural and necessary, Calvin conceded, but no one should confuse this lustful post-Lapsarian version with its sinless predecessor in the Garden of Eden. Rather, marriage – like prostitution – should remind humans of their fallen nature and of the truly spiritual state to which they aspire.[73] In fact,

> [so] that [husbands] may not complacently take delight in the goods of marriage, [God] either causes them to be troubled by the depravity of their wives or humbles them by evil offspring or afflicts them with bereavement.[74]

Given such strong ascetic continuity, the continuing influence of the celibate ideal among Protestants is perhaps not surprising. Many first-generation reformers quoted Paul's admonition to remain in one's cur-

---

71 *De Regno Christi* in *Opera Latina* XV:232; "Christliche Schrift an W. Reisenbusch sich in den ehelichen Stand zu begeben" (1525), *WA* 18:275. Later in his career, Luther acknowledged that there could be "keyn ehepflicht on sund geschickt" (cf. "Ein Predigt vom Ehestand" [1545], *WA* 49:797–805). See also Baranowski, *Luthers Lehre von der Ehe*, 10, 19–21, 49ff.
   The only other contemporary theological advocates of marital sex for pleasure alone were two fifteenth-century Parisian masters, Martin LeMaistre and John Major. See Noonan, *Contraception*, 323ff., and Tentler, *Sin and Confession*, 185–86.

72 Though fluctuating on this earlier, Calvin eventually decided that procreation was a consequence of marriage (*Commentaries* Gen. 1:28) and that marriage's function as medicine (*Commentaries* Matt. 19:10), or "remedium incontientine" (*Institutes* II.viii.43), was most important. Cf. the almost universal acceptance of the traditional teaching on sinful aspects of sexual intercourse within marriage among all sixteenth-century religious leaders, Protestant and Catholic, as well as their almost identically worded emphasis on the fundamentally remedial nature of marriage: Erasmus (Telle, *Erasme*, 417); Francis Lambert of Avignon (Wendel, *Le mariage*, 44); and others (Dieterich 78–80; Phillips, *Divorce*, 87ff.; Brundage, *Law, Sex, and Christian Society*, 555–56; Ozment, *When Fathers Ruled*, 10ff.; Noonan, *Contraception*, 353, 503–9).

73 *Commentaries* Deut. 23:12–17. While he recognized the usefulness of sexual attraction within marriage – as in the instance of Jacob and Rachel (*Commentaries* Gen. 29:18–131) – Calvin was still shocked by the sexual appetite of a seventy-year-old remarrying widow in his congregation (1540 letter to Nicolas Parent, cited in Bouwsma, *Calvin*, 53) and – like Ambrose – admonished husbands not to be "paillae" of their own wives (*Institutes* II.viii.44).

74 *Institutes* III.ix.1.

rent state, maintaining that God respected marriage as much as chastity, and that both vows were sacred to Him.[75] Virginity, Calvin stressed, "is a virtue not to be despised," yet "let every man abstain only so long as he is fit to observe celibacy."[76] Even the otherwise exceptional Bucer agreed that "he does best who himself stays out of marriage."[77] The Lutheran "liberation" of nuns and subsequent overflow of unmarried women into the marriage market similarly forced some secular Protestant authorities into the compromising position of maintaining several convents and abbeys well into the seventeenth century, sometimes euphemistically redubbing them "educational centers" (*Ausbildungsstätte*).[78] Perhaps the most revealingly traditional statement of all, though, comes from the Augsburg Confession of 1530: "And yet we do not equate marriage with virginity; just as for instance [to be given] the gift of prophecy is preferable to eloquence . . . so the gift of virginity is superior to marriage."[79] The distinction remains crucial to understanding the key difference of Protestant marriage teaching from Catholic tradition. Chastity was still preferable in the abstract to any sexual activity, in or out of wedlock; in the concrete, however, that governed this life, the physical impossibility or at least improbability of such a life demanded the more practical ideal of marriage.

With this less than wholehearted endorsement, Protestant reformers

---

[75] Erasmus and Luther in particular had difficulty renouncing their own vows of celibacy (Telle, *Erasme*, 73ff., 197ff.; Baranowski, *Luthers Lehre von der Ehe*, 32ff.). As Luther wrote to Melanchthon (9 September 1521), "Obsecro, an non obscurissime hoc dicis, nonne sic dicis ac si velis: ideo non stare votum, quia impossibile est impleri? Et hac ratione etiam divina praecepta solvenda concedas" (*WA* Briefwechsel 3:222). Cf. popularization of the same status quo endorsement in Gütell, *Ueber den Evangelion Johnannis*, 3^vff.

[76] *Institutes* II.viii.42–43.

[77] Letter of 28 April 1524 to Odile von Berckheim: "der auss der ehe bleibt der schafft in selb das besst der gebrandt würdt und also in dei ehe kuumpt, der holt auck sein nutz davon . . . der aber der eh gefreyet ist vnd wurdt erst vmb der bruder wil hen ein knecht, der sucht allein das sein nit, der ist in der lieb der volkumest, nemlich so meniglich weyss, wie furderlich es ist zu allem guten" (*Correspondence de Martin Bucer*, ed. Jean Rott [Leiden, 1979], I:240).

[78] On the continuation of monasteries among sixteenth-century Lutherans, see H. C. Erik Midelfort, "Protestant Monastery? A Reformation Hospital in Hesse," in *Reformation Principle and Practice: Essays in Honour of A. G. Dickens*, ed. Peter N. Brooks (London, 1980), 71–94; Merry Wiesner, "Ideology Meets the Empire: Reformed Convents and the Reformation," in *Germania Illustrata: Essays on Early Modern Germany Presented to Gerald Strauss*, ed. Susan C. Karant-Nunn and Andrew C. Fix (Kirksville, Mo. 1992), 181–95; and Roper, *Holy Household*, 206ff.

[79] "Neque tamen aequamus coniugio virginitatem; sicut enim donum dono praestat prophetia praestat eloquentiae . . . ita virginitatis donum est praestantior coniugio" (*Confessio Augustana*, cited in Falk, *Die Ehe am Ausgang*, 38). This position is still apparent in the next generation of Lutheran ministers; cf. Johannes Mathesius's *Vom Ehestand und Hauswesen* (Nüremberg, 1564), discussed in Susan C. Karant-Nunn, "Kinder, Küche, Kirche," in Karant-Nunn and Fix, *Germania Illustrata*, 127ff.

and theologians thus set about the task of filling the ideological void left by the removal of an impractical, unreachable religious ideal. Most early Evangelical tracts consequently portrayed the married estate as bringing about all those benefits claimed by celibate clerics: discipline, fidelity, chastity, charity, and so forth. Even the "good work" argument of greater sacrifice and burden under the celibate rule proved adaptable to marriage. Married couples who raised God-fearing children, Luther insisted, performed "a better and nobler good work than all monks and nuns."[80] After listening to a cleric's litany of complaints on the hardships of the celibate life, the Evangelical baker and hero of Hans Sachs's "Conversation about the Illusory Works of the Cloistered" remained similarly unsympathetic:

> I have to work with my servants the entire day, eat poorly and often barely get to bed before Matins, at which time my children begin singing Matins to me. I have a much harder station [*ordnen*] than you do.[81]

Clerics, he argues, live protected from the "taxes, rents, and other burdens" of married life, a point that the Catholic confessor in "Conversation of a Mother with Her Daughter" attempts to use to his advantage in convincing the young Evangelical heroine Barbeli to enter the cloister:

> Shield yourself from the poor, married life
> which has nothing to offer but suffering and strife;
> it's also not so worthy nor high of an estate
> to be assured warm welcome by God within his gates.[82]

Yet despite reformers' adaptation of traditional language and imagery for marriage as a religious ideal, it is doubtful that marriage was quickly accepted as the "spiritual" and "holy" equivalent of the abandoned medieval celibacy. The same experiential basis for the abandonment of the celibate ideal cut both ways, often resulting in skepticism and confusion over Luther's alternate characterization of marriage as "a spiritual estate." Again, the subtlety of theologians' dual-nature definition of marriage was no doubt lost on many who knew from experience the very worldliness of married life. Parodies and even vilifications of the married

80 "Ein Predigt vom Ehestand" (1545), *WA* 49:802.
81 Hans Sachs, *Eyn gesprech von den Schweinwercken der Gaistlichen* . . . (1524), 7, cited in Ozment, "What Can We Learn from the Pamphlets?" 191.
82 "... hut dich vor dem armen eelichen statt // der nüt denn ellend und iamer hatt // so ist er ouch nit so wirdig unnd hoch // vorkummen / angenem vor got das sinn doch." Anonymous, *Ein gesprech / vonn einer müter // mit ir tochter* . . . (1526), Av^b–Avi^b.

life were more frequent in later sixteenth-century drama than before the Reformation. Evangelical leaders pleaded with readers to have faith that, despite the many bad spouses and bad marriages, "marriage is [still] a thousand times more good than bad."[83] Calvin and Bucer likewise emphasized that it was such sacrifices, suffering, and service (i.e., the Lutheran "marriage cross") that made an often "bestial" (*vihisch*) married life virtuous and pleasing to God.[84] At least one Protestant apologist, though, could not keep his pessimism from showing, even in a panegyric:

> Better are bad times without sin
> Than good ones to be sinful in;
> the cross must be endured.
> Time here is short
> But long the joy
> That Christ has us assured.[85]

In such instances, we cannot not help but be struck by the pervading apprehension common to all reformers that many worthwhile ideals have been unintentionally uprooted along with deleterious ones. Once again we confront the pervasive fear of social disorder and the fundamentally conservative nature of Protestant marriage reform. By now, though, marriage represents not only a preferable religious ideal but the only defense against the licentious anarchy following celibacy's precipitous decline. Erasmus Alberus repeats the advice of the ancient Roman Metellus Numidicus on the subject:

> If we could be freed from our wives, we would be overtaken by lust. Since it has been so decreed by Nature that we cannot be with them without desire, then we must rise above such lust and for the sake of propagation of the race gladly accept the baseness of women.[86]

If "a pagan who knew nothing of God's word" recognized this, Alberus writes, how much more valued should marriage be in Christian society.

---

[83] Erasmus Alberus, *Das Ehebüchlein*, Ei; cf. the similarly defensive tone of Musculus, *Wider den Eeteufel*, in Stambaugh, *Teufelbücher*, V:95–96; also Strauss, *Luther's House of Learning*, 116ff., on this general tendency among Lutheran apologists.

[84] Calvin sermon 19 on 1 Tim. 2:13–15; Bucer, "Von der Ehe und Ehescheidung," unpublished manuscript cited by Herman Selderhuis, "Martin Bucer und die Ehe," in *Martin Bucer and Sixteenth Century Europe* (Leiden, 1993), 178–79. See also Justus Menius, *Oeconomia Christiana* (Wittenberg, 1519), G6ᵇ, on "voly möye unde arbeides / sorge unde angstes" of marriage, and Hoffmann, *Hausväterliteratur*, 110, on popular Lutheran themes of *Ehecreutz* and *Gottes Academia*.

[85] Anonymous, *Ein lied vom Ehestand* (n.p., n.d.), translated in Wiltenburg, *Disorderly Women*, 75.

[86] Erasmus Alberus, *Das Ehebüchlein*, Div.

The reasoning, tone, and language all recall the magisterial themes of social order and discipline. References to the spiritual nature and benefits of marriage on the other hand remain secondary, again suggesting the "alternative" origin of Protestant "elevation" of marriage proposed by Baranowski: "The more [Luther] combatted celibacy and vows, the more strongly he had to emphasize and elevate marriage in contrast."[87]

The idea of marriage as a divine ordinance certainly carried special appeal for Luther and Calvin, perhaps accounting for their strikingly traditional descriptions of spousal relations. Although both vehemently rejected the overtly misogynist strains of most scholastic theology, neither reformer was willing or able to part with its vision of "natural" social order. As part of that order, marriage represented a divinely ordained means for humans to balance their duties with their desires, their natures with their functions. Calvin, in particular, marveled at the inherent order in God's providential division of humanity into two genders, each with its own nature and corollary social role.[88] Both he and Luther, in fact, considered the couple (not the family) as the smallest natural unit of society – in some senses, and innovative enhancement of the twelfth-century ideal of marriage.

Idealizations of companionate marriage, however, hardly signaled the beginning of a new attitude toward marital authority and women that some historians have proposed.[89] In fact, all major Protestant reformers except Bucer ranked mutual love and fidelity last among the *triplex bonum* of marriage.[90] Their theological pronouncements on the nature of this mutual love likewise reinforced rather than redefined spousal relations. Like their Catholic contemporaries, Protestant reformers recognized the spiritual equality of men and women in matters of salva-

---

[87] Baranowski, *Luthers Lehre von der Ehe*, 10, and cf. a similar point by Karant-Nunn in "Kinder, Küche, Kirche," 136ff.

[88] *Commentaries* Gen. 2:18.

[89] Cf. arguments for "ein neues sittliches Ideal" (Kawerau, *Die Reformation und die Ehe*, 3ff.), the reformers' "liberation" of nuns from cloisters as a reaction "against the age's antifeminism" (Ozment, *When Fathers Ruled*, 1ff.), Lutheran reversal of medieval misogynist tendencies (Elizabeth Ahme, "Wertung und Bedeutung der Frau bei Martin Luther," *Luther* 35 [1964], 61–68), and general sexual enlightenment in Roland Bainton, *Women of the Reformation in Germany and Italy* (Minneapolis, 1971). See also a more moderate version of this interpretation in Gerta Scharffenorth, "'Im Geiste Freunde Werden': Mann und Frau im Glauben Martin Luthers," in Wunder and Vanja, *Wandel der Geschlechterbeziehungen*, 97–108.

[90] *De Regno Christi*, in *Opera Latina* XV:209. Bucer actually ranked the remedial aspect fourth in importance, after cohabitation, mutual affection, and holiness.

tion,[91] but also the worldly inequities that separated the genders in social function and authority. A wife, Luther concluded, by reason of her physical, mental, and emotional nature, was clearly intended by God to be the submissive half in a marriage:

> The female body is not strong – it cannot bear arms, etc. – and the spirit is even weaker; according to the normal course of events, it follows [that] if only the Lord had joined together defiance or gentleness, woman is half-child. Let everyone who takes a wife know that he is the guardian of a child. . . . She is thus a wild animal; you recognize her weakness of mind.[92]

Calvin, too, considered every man "by privilege of Nature" superior to every woman and quoted the oft-repeated excerpt from 1 Corinthians comparing the wife and her husband to the body and its head.[93] Certainly both reformers strongly opposed any tyrannical behavior on the part of a husband, yet the scriptural basis for his authority remained indisputable. Just as the natural human sexual drive made marriage necessary, the natural physical and mental limitations of women made submission to their husbands inevitable.

The case, then, for ideological continuity in Protestant definitions of marriage itself appears overwhelming. We need only consider the archetypically traditional pronouncement of Luther, late in his career:

> [Thus] the true definition is: marriage is a divine and legitimate union of a husband and woman in the hope of offspring [*prolis*] or at least the avoidance of fornication and sin for the sake of the glory of God. The greatest end is to obey God and avoid sin, to invoke God, pray, love, educate offspring to the glory of God, live with one's wife in fear of the Lord, and bear the cross. And if no offspring result, then you, wife, should still live content and avoid wandering desires.[94]

[91] Cf. Dennis Doherty, *The Sexual Doctrine of Cardinal Cajetan* (Regensburg, 1966), 257ff.

[92] "Predigt am 2. Sonntag nach Ephiphanias" on 1 Pet. 3:7 (1524), *WA* 15:419–20.

[93] *Commentaries* 1 Cor. 7:3-7; *Commentaries* 1 Tim. 2:11–15, 5:13; as well as sermon on Deut. 23:24–5, 24:1–4, 1 Cor. 7:24, and Eph. 5:22–6 (*Corpus Reformatorum* (Berlin/Leipzig/Zurich, 1834–), 29:149ff., 49:721ff., 52:739). See also Jane Dempsey Douglass, *Women, Freedom, and Calvin* (Philadelphia, 1985), especially 42–65; and Biéler, *L'homme et la femme*, 148ff.
   Cf. similar sentiments of Bucer: "Das ist aber das recht ganntz ennde der eh, das die ehleüt in aller lieb und drew einander dienen, das weib des mans gehülffe und fleisch, der man des weibs haupt und heyland seye" ("Von der Ehe," 12ᵃ, cited in Wendel, *Le mariage, 45–46*).

[94] "Vorlesungen über a. Mose" (1535–45), *WA* 43:310. See also earlier "Ein Sermon von dem ehelichen Stand" (1519), *WA* 2:168–69.

Such conservatism does not discount the many eloquent and often touching Protestant elegies to marriage as either insignificant or irrelevant.[95] It merely illustrates that the true Protestant innovation was less in theology and imagery of marriage and much more in the elimination of the rival religious ideal of celibacy. It was no coincidence that far more Evangelical tracts and pamphlets during the first half of the sixteenth century focused on the discrediting of the celibate ideal and the abolition of a divided set of religious standards than on marriage itself. The chief difference from Catholic tradition – and it was a significant one – was that for the vast majority of Protestants, marriage was no longer second choice for the pious Christian but the only choice. The same human weakness that made the *remedium* necessary in the first place simultaneously rendered celibacy virtually impossible; Scripture, Original Sin, and especially experience made no other conclusion possible.[96]

By the second half of the sixteenth century, Protestant polemic on marriage had shifted from defending the estate against the Catholic celibate ideal to popularizing the received definition. In Germany this resulted in the creation of two new literary genres, both overwhelmingly dominated by Lutherans.[97] The first, comprising sermons and other pedagogical publications on marriage and the family, was known as the *Hausväterliteratur*, or household literature.[98] Its subjects included the

---

[95] Cf., for instance, Luther's own conjugal ideal: "dye eheliche liebe, das ist eyn brawt liebe, die brinnet wie das fewer und sucht nicht mehr, dan das eeliche gemahl, dye spricht: Ich will nit das deyne, ich will widder golt noch sylber, widder dysz noch das, ich will dich selb haben, ich wils gantz oder nichts haben." "Ein Sermon von dem ehelichen Stand," (ibid.), *WA* 2:167.

[96] In this respect, I agree with Ozment's assesment that "both experience and belief had set Protestants unalterably against the celibate life." (*When Fathers Ruled*, 24–25).

[97] Hoffman found "keine volkstümlichen, geschlossenen Hauslehren" amoung German Catholics (*Hausväterliteratur*, 215, n. 65).

[98] The household literature of Protestants from the sixteenth to eighteenth centuries has gradually received more attention from early modern historians. The standard work on the subject, Hoffmann's *Hausväterliteratur*, has been supplemented by Otto Brunner, "Das 'Ganze Haus' und die alteuropäische Ökonomik," in *Neue Wege der Sozialgeschichte*, ed. O. Brunner (Göttingen, 1968), 33–61; and Gotthardt Frühsorge, *Der politische Körper. Zum Begriff des Politischen im 17. Jahrhundert und in Romanen Christian Weises* (Stuttgart, 1974), especially 59ff. See also recent American examinations of the *Hausväterliteratur* in Miller, "Marriage: Lutheran Views of Marriage and the Family"; Eileen Dugan, "Images of Marriage and the Family Life in Nördlingen: Moral Preaching and Devotional Literature, 1589–1712" (Ph.D. diss., Ohio State University, 1988); Karant–Nunn, "Kinder, Küche, Kirche," 121–40; and especially Ozment, *When Fathers Ruled*, chaps. 2 and 4.

For the English equivalent of the *Hausväterliteratur*, see Susan Dwyer Amussen, *An Ordered Society: Gender and Class in Early Modern England* (Oxford, 1988), 35–66.

Figure 2. The spectrum of popular literature on marriage among sixteenth-century Protestants: (a) an early evangelical treatise against clerical celibacy.

proper relationship between a husband and a wife accompanied by several scriptural passages in praise of the estate of marriage (see Figure 2b). In almost all instances, the "papist evil" of clerical celibacy received little or no mention, placing the focus on the practical realization of the Protestant marital ideal. Theological definitions remained accordingly brief and highly traditional, as in the most popular and influential work on the subject, Cyrius Spangenberg's 1570 collection of sixty-six sermons entitled "The Marriage Mirror":

> The estate of marriage is a bringing together or union of a man and a woman, through God's word, with the consent of both, who are to conge-

Figure 2. (b) one of the first examples of the *Hausväterliteratur*, a 1528 treatise by Justus Menius (Bibliothek der Germanischen Museum).

Figure 2. (c) a satirical woodcut on frivolous love vows (ca. 1550).

Der Sieman/das ist
wider den
Hausteuffell.
Wie die bösen Weiber ihre
frome Menner / vnd wie die bösen
Leichtfertigen buben/ ihre frome Weiber
plagen/ Sampt einer vormanung aus H-
Schrifft vnd schönen Historien / wie sich
frome Eheleurt gegen einander ver-
halten sollen/ Nützlich vnd
lustig zu lesen/beschrie-
ben Durch/

Adamum Schubartum.

Figure 2. (d) *The Siemann, or Against the House-Devil*, a 1564 polemic against "bad wives" and household strife (Stambaugh, Teufelbücher, II: 237).

nially and honorably live with one another until death, avoid sin, and bear fruit.[99]

Some authors did attempt to enliven doctrinal pronouncements with colorful excerpts or even theatrical dramatizations,[100] but otherwise resisted any substantive revision of the message. Most importantly, as inventories of Lutheran and Calvinist libraries in the Palatinate demonstrate, such works clearly helped shape the intellectual views and presumably sermons of local pastors on the subject of marriage.[101]

The other kind of marriage literature emerging after 1550 embodied a darker and more pessimistic side of sixteenth-century Protestantism. The *Teufelbücher*, or devil books, also largely represented revised sermons by Lutheran ministers, but covered a wider spectrum of moral and social disorders, all attributable to diabolic influence.[102] Whereas authors of the *Hausväterliteratur* stressed the positive examples of a successful marriage and household, the wildly popular *Teufelbücher*[103] focused on Satan as the sworn enemy of the divinely ordained institutions of marriage and the family. Andreas Musculus, author of the extremely successful *Against the Marriage-Devil*, identified eight specific plans of attack the devil employed to undermine a successful marriage, most of

---

99 Cyriakus Spangenberg, *Ehespiegel* (Strasbourg, 1570), 3a. Cf. Dieterich 75ff., on similar continuity among all other major reformers, and Hoffmann, *Hausväterliteratur* 89ff., 107ff., on the same in popular literature.

100 Cf. discussion of Paul Rebhun's plays on Susannah in Susan C. Karant-Nunn, "The Transmission of Luther's Teachings on Women and Matrimony: The Case of Zwichau," *Archiv für Reformationsgeschichte* 77 (1986), 42ff.; also Kawerau, *Die Reformation und die Ehe*, 67–74. For pedagogical examples, see Strauss, *Luther's House of Learning*, especially chap. 3.

101 In addition to important works by Luther, Melanchthon, Bugenhagen, and Calvin, the *Ehespiegel* of Spangenberg was found in 16 of 56 Lutheran pastoral libraries in Zweibrücken (1580–85) and 6 of 54 Reformed collections (1609). Vogler, *Le clergé rhénan*, 240ff.

102 Sigmund Feyrabend collected twenty *Teufelbücher* in his *Theatrum Diabolorum* (Frankfurt, 1569); many of these have since been republished in Stambaugh, *Teufelbücher*. See Max Osborn, *Die Teufelliteratur des XVI. Jahrhunderts* (Berlin, 1893); Heinrich Grimm, "Die deutschen 'Teufelbücher' des 16. Jahrhunderts: Ihre Rolle im Buchwesen und ihre Bedeutung," *Archiv für Geschichte des Buchwesens* 16 (1959), 1733–90; Bernhard Ochse, "Die Teufelliteratur zwischen Brant und Luther" (Ph.D. diss., Freie Universität Berlin, 1961); Keith L. Roos, *The Devil in Sixteenth-Century German Literature: The Teufelbücher* (Bern, 1972); and Rainer Alsheimer, "Katalog protestantischer Teufelserzählungen," in *Volkererzählungen und Reformation: Ein Handbuch zur Tradierung und Funktion von Erzählstoffen und Erzählliteratur im Protestantismus*, ed. Wofgang Brücker (Berlin, 1974), 417–519.

103 Roos estimates that at least 250,000 *Teufelbücher* of all kinds were circulating in Germany during the second half of the sixteenth century (*The Devil in Sixteenth-Century Literature*, 108–9). One of the most popular, Musculus's *Wider den Eeteufel*, underwent ten editions during 1556–68 alone (Stambaugh, *Teufelbücher*, IV:273).

them playing on the couple's own carnal weaknesses.[104] Similar to the pope of earlier reform literature, Satan especially enjoyed twisting God's Word to suit his own purposes. Invariably, the chief target of both villians' attacks was the patriarchal household, where they attempted to invert all "natural" relationships of authority and obedience, setting wife against husband, child against parent.

This perversion and inversion of the authority relations between husband and wife in fact represented the most recurrent theme of all late sixteenth-century Protestant publications on marriage. As Joy Wiltenburg has noted, "In a society where power is a masculine trait, the exercise of power by women is a threatening usurpation, an expression of the disorderly forces besetting a carefully constructed society."[105] The almost pathological fear of "masterless" women "living under their own smoke" is evident in all German literature of the period, even yielding a new brand of misogynist literature that instructed husbands on wife beating.[106] From the days of Eden, wrote reformers, Satan had endeavored to set married couples against one another, forever tempting wives to subvert their husband's God-given authority over them. The stereotypical shrewish, domineering wife (*böse Weib*) and the humiliated, henpecked husband (*Siemann*, or "she-man") were surely among the

---

[104] Musculus, *Wider den Eheteufel*, in Stambaugh, *Teufelbücher*, IV:85ff.

[105] Wiltenburg also notes that German literature of the period was generally much more concerned about female lust for power than sexual lust (*Disorderly Women*, 141–42, 206–7, 255ff.). Her examination of contemporary English literature, on the other hand, reveals the exact opposite emphasis, perhaps accounting for England's reputation among Germans as a "woman's paradise," where wives continually beat and dominated their husbands (Cf. Amussen, *An Ordered Society*, 48–50). See also Maria Müller, "Naturwesen Mann. Zur Dialektik von Herrschaft und Knechtschaft in Eheleben der frühen Neuzeit," in Wunder and Vanja, *Wandel der Geschlechterbeziehungen*, 43–68.

Scholarship on sixteenth-century women, religious reform, and the patriarchal family has recently grown at a phenomenal rate. In addition to those studies already mentioned, see Jane Dempsey Douglass, "Women and the Continental Reformation," in *Religion and Sexism*, ed. Rosemary Rudford Ruether (New York, 1974), 292–318; Natalie Zemon Davis, "City Women and Religious Change," in *A Sampler of Women's Studies*, ed. Dorothy McGuigan (Ann Arbor, Mich. 1973); Allison Coudert, "The Myth of the Improved Status of Protestant Women: The Case of the Witchcraze," in *The Politics of Gender in Early Modern Europe*, ed. Jean R. Brink et al. (Kirksville, Mo., 1989), 61–89; and especially the recent historiographical overview of Merry Wiesner on women and the Reformation, "Women's Response to the Reformation," in *The German People and the Reformation*, ed. R. Po-Chia Hsia (Ithaca, N.Y., 1988), 148–71.

[106] The most famous is probably Hans Sachs's *Die Zwölff Eygenschafft eines boßhaffligen weybs* (Nuremberg, 1553). See discussion of this genre in Wiltenburg, *Disorderly Women*, 108ff.; as well as *Ob die Wieber Menschen seyn, oder nicht?*, ed. Elisabeth Gössman (Munich, 1988), and Douglas, *Women, Freedom, and Calvin*, 66–107, on the *querelle des femmes*.

most recurrent figures of all early modern literature, alternately serving as an occasion for amusement or admonition to permissive husbands (see Figure 2d).[107] Possibly based on an apocryphal story of a henpecked Simon Peter at the wedding of Cana (hence also a pun on the apostle's name), the *Siemann* topos was particularly popular with marriage reformers, who widely applied the label to such notables as Adam ("the first *Siemann*"), Socrates, various kings and princes, and virtually any man who exhibited too much public deference to his wife's opinion. In a relatively moderate tract, *The Siemann, or Against the Household-Devil*, Adam Schubert combined a humorous and vivid account of one husband's fistfight and eventual killing of the *Siemann* figure with scriptural, classical, and proverbial warnings of the disastrous consequences of female domination of the household. All of Germany is under siege by "the tyrant *Siemann*," he laments, "and there are now some well-known places that the lord *Siemann* has entered with several thousand horses and set up camp."[108]

Female readers of the *Hausväterliteratur* and *Teufelbücher* were usually presented with two models for wives, one diabolic and the other divine. The inverted nature of the two was both obvious and literal, in both cases emphasizing the same scriptural-patriarchal ideal of the wife. Positive examples of humility, modesty, and, above all, obedience were held up as role models; negative examples provided corollary proof of God's punishment of proud and domineering women.[109] The *Household-Devil*, for instance, praised the pious examples of Sarah, Elizabeth, Mary, Mary Magdelene, and Tabitha, while condemning the wicked examples of Jezabelle, Athalia, and Queen Baalim, all punished by God for their

---

[107] *Die verkehrte Welt* of a women sexually dominating a man was an especially popular humorous theme (cf. Wiltenburg, *Disorderly Women*, 107ff., 155ff.); also Natalie Zemon Davis, "Women on Top," in *Society and Culture in Early Modern France* (Stanford, 1975), 124–51. On the *böse Weib* topos, see Elfriede Moser-Rath, "Das streitsüchtige Eheweib: Erzählformen des 17. Jahrhunderts zum Schwanktyp ATh 1365," *Rheinisches Jahrbuch für Volkskunde* 10 (1959), 40–50; Franz Brietzmann, *Die böse Frau in der deutschen Literatur des Mittelalters* (Berlin, 1912); Rudolf Schmidt, *Die Frau in der deutschen Literatur des 16. Jahrhunderts* (Strasbourg, 1917); Hoffmann, *Hausväterliteratur*, 115–20; and Kawerau, *Die Reformation und die Ehe*, 42–63.

[108] Schubert, *Hausteuffel*, in Stambaugh, *Teufelbücher*, II:244, 252.

[109] Niclaus Schmidt, for instance, in his *Zehen Tuefeln* directly contrasted the ten devils of the bad, disorderly wife – godless, proud, disobedient, quarrelsome, shameless, drunken, unchaste, murderous, thieving, and *unfreundlich* (in the familial sense) – with ten contrary virtues of the good wife. *Von den Zehen Tuefeln oder Lastern / Damit die Bösen unartigen Weiber besessen sind* (Leipzig, 1557), in Stambaugh, *Teufelbücher*, II:309–56. See also discussion in Ozment, *When Fathers Ruled*, 63–70.

willful pride.[110] As the Evangelical "good" wife scolds her "bad" sister in the anonymous dialogue *Of Bad Wives:*

> Be as patient as Leah, as friendly as Ruth, as faithful to your man as David's wife Michal; be as sensible as Abigail, as moderate as Judith, as meek as Hester, as chaste as Susanna, and as obedient to your husband as Rebecca. Just as Christ is the head and lord of the congregation [so should your husband be to you].[111]

Male readers were likewise admonished to conform to scriptural injunctions or suffer the consequences. Their authority as husbands, like that as fathers, represented a responsibility as much as a privilege; not only was the God-fearing husband bound to resist himself the temptations of Satan, but to protect his wife and children from them as well. Even Hans Sachs, one of the most virulent satirists of shrewish wives, suggested that slothful and violent husbands, particularly those who abandoned their financial obligations, carried most of the blame for failed marriages and broken homes.[112] The author of *Against the Whoring-Devil* concurred that "thus it is often the husband himself who is the cause of the wife's infidelity and shame," adding:

> Pay close attention to your wife,
> that God's Word molds and shapes her life;
> keep her at home inside your house
> and throw all would-be lovers out;
> see that she's enough work to incur
> and all desires will flee from her.[113]

---

110 Schubert, *Hausteuffell*, in Stambaugh, *Teufelbücher, II:285–87).* Wiltenburg (*Disorderly Women,* 161-62) notes that Judith was also a favorite model of sixteenth-century German writer, possibly because of her application of natural feminine wiles (and thus power) to a noble end, that is, the beheading of Holofernes. The book of Ecclesiasticus (eventually declared apocryphal by Protestants) was especially popular with marriage reformers, particularly chapters 25 and 26 on good and bad wives (cf. *Wider den Eeteufel,* V:96; *Hausteufell,* II:307; and *Zehn Teufel,* II:311; all in Stambaugh, *Teufelbücher).*

111 Anonymous, *Der bösen Weiber . . .* (Frankfurt a.M., ca. 1535), Aiii^{v}ff. The concluding admonition is based on Eph. 5:22–23.

112 Hans Sachs, *Der Lose Mann* (Nuremberg, 1556), in *Sämtliche Fabeln und Schwänke von Hans Sachs,* ed. Edmund Goetze (Halle: Max Niemayer, 1893), I:454–58. Cf. similar point by Johann Freder (1510–62) who also strongly criticized the misogynist excesses of Sachs and other fellow Lutherans: Scott Hendrix, "Christianizing Domestic Relations: Women and Marriage in Johann Freder's *Dialogus dem Ehestand zu Ehren," Sixteenth Century Journal* 23 (1992), 251–66. See also Hoffmann, *Hausväterliteratur,* 102–4.

113 "Also ist offt ein Mann selbst ursach das sein Weib trawlos und zu schanden wird . . . Hab vleissig achtung auff den weib / Zu Gottes wort mit ernst sie treib / Behalt sie heim in deinem

The loving husband, according to Andreas Musculus, should always view his wife as "the prettiest, most beautiful, and most pious of all women," and have eyes only for her – for both their sakes.[114] Satan remained the chief antagonist at work, but he could only succeed with some negligence on the part of the *Hausvater.*

The exasperation and even despair of the *Hausväterliteratur* and *Teufelbücher* should not be interpreted as indicating a total failure in Protestant attempts to establish marriage as a spiritual estate. The problem of balancing its remedial and sacred aspects had troubled Church theologians since the time of the Fathers; eliminating the celibate ideal merely accentuated the traditionally ambiguous nature of Christian marriage. Rather, where Lutheran and Calvinist reformers most distinguished themselves from their Catholic contemporaries was much less in their words than in their deeds. For while Catholic clerics such as Loyola praised but also avoided the sacrament of matrimony, Luther and all of the first-generation Protestant reformers (except Melanchthon) had publicly embraced the estate and taken wives by 1525. While both Protestant and Catholic authors struggled to convey the spiritual dignity of marriage, married Lutheran and Calvinist ministers provided living examples of the same conviction. As many Protestant reformers discovered, brief reflections on the spiritual benefits of their own marriages gave them far more credibility with their parishioners than volumes of scriptural or theological expositions.

Not surprisingly, the reintroduction of clerical marriage in the 1520s was not without negative consequences. Melanchthon, in particular, realized the dangerous polemical potential of Luther's 1525 marriage to Katharina von Bora, but was overruled (and subsequently uninvited to the wedding) by his mentor.[115] Indeed, subsequent Catholic accusations of sexual depravity among marrying clerics were legion, ironically relying on the same images of lecherous priests and nuns that Protestant pamphleteers had used to discredit clerical celibacy. Some focused on the uncomfortable and potentially disastrous blurring of lay and clerical divisions in society if priests married. In an early response to Luther's call for a "priesthood of all believers," a dumbfounded Hieronymus

---

Hauss / Las junge Buler alle draus / Schaff das sie möge arbeit han / Wird ir der kützen wol vergahn." Hoppenrod, *Hurenteuffel,* in Stambaugh, *Teufelbücher,* II:192.

[114] Musculus, *Wider den Eeteufel,* in Stambaugh, *Teufelbücher,* V:105–6.

[115] Oberman, *Luther,* 181–82; also Richard Fridenthal, *Luther* (London, 1970), 431ff.

Emser confided that "one even finds fools who, in addition to spiritual benefices and goods, also want to have wives, [so that] all become priests and no one wants to work anymore."[116] A much later writer raised practical problems of another kind, clearly appealing to the common perception of gossiping wives:

> Who then would want to entrust something to a married priest that wouldn't be found out by his wife or the entire neighborhood? What if the priest's wife – as is often the case – is somewhat jealous, and because of that – as is customary with women – begins to act crazy? What would happen if such a priest had bad, disobedient children; how then could he advise others on their children?[117]

Protestant reformers, though, possessed a powerful polemical tool in the person of the married minister and they knew it. It was quickly evident, moreover, that their success in conveying the spirituality of marriage hinged as much on the personal character and reputation of the local pastor and his wife as his knowledge of official doctrine. Their behavior, consequently, was the focus of constant scrutiny and surveillance,[118] but also the site of their greatest success in establishing a new spiritual ideal of marriage. By the end of the sixteenth century, the Protestant *Pfarrhaus* had become a well-established and influential ideological institution in Germany.[119] Catholic reformers could match Lutheran and Calvinist recruitment, training, and disciplining of their respective clerics, but not the living spiritual authority that married ministers lent to the institution of marriage itself. The Protestant ideal of

116 Response of Hieronymus Emser to Luther's *Babylonian Captivity*, quoted in Kawerau, *Die Reformation und die Ehe*, 13–14. See also Eck's *De celibatu clericorum* (1525).
117 Aegidius Albertinus, *Hauspolizei* (Munich, 1602), quoted in Kawerau, *Die Reformation und die Ehe*, 39. Cf. a similar point in a contemporary English pamphlet quoted by Carlson ("Marriage and the English Reformation," 153) that people should trust a priest's wife "the day that pigs grow wings."
118 Cf. Bacharach consistory's questioning of wives of the local pastor and schoolmaster "wegen vorgebrachter Uneynigkeite" – that is, lodging three "frembde loße Menner" during the schoolmaster's absence (27 July 1592; Schüler, *Die Konventsprotokolle*, 70). Five years later the widow of the then deceased schoolmaster was again summoned on account of similar rulers (27 April 1597; ibid., 96).
119 Cf. Luise Schorn-Schütte, "'Gefährtin' und 'Mitregentin': Zur Sozialgeschichte der evangelischen Pfarrfrau in der Frühen Neuzeit," in Wunder and Vanja, *Wandel der Geschlechterbeziehungen*, 109–53; Hartmut Lehmann, "'Das ewige Haus': Das lutherische Pfarrhaus im Wandel der Zeiten," in *"Gott kumm mir zu hilf": Martin Luther in der Zeitenwende*, ed. Hans Look (Berlin, 1985), 177–200; Manfred Köhler, "Über die soziale Bedeutung des protestantischen Pfarrhauses in Deutschland" (Diss. phil. masch., Heidelberg, 1952), esp. 145ff.; and my discussion in Chapter 5.

marriage had at last found its most successful medium, yielding – at least in the instance of clergy – "a sharp division of confessional cultures."[120]

Protestant and Catholic legal revisions

Despite theological conservatism, the legal implications resulting from Protestant doctrinal revisions of marriage remained potentially revolutionary.[121] One of the most obvious to members of all confessions was the immediate result of desacramentalizing marriage, namely, transfer of legal jurisdiction from ecclesiastical to secular authority. The degree to which religious reformers were cognizant of or motivated by such an end result remains unclear. Initially, at least, many early reformers believed that Scripture, Christian love, and at most pastoral guidance would suffice to resolve any marital questions or disputes among Evangelicals.[122] As the need for greater institutional organization became apparent, most religious leaders still favored a slightly modified version of the existing system, with princes and other secular authorities acting only in the temporary capacity of "emergency bishops."[123]

Luther apparently considered the jurisdictional implications of the worldly definition self-evident:

> Since weddings and marriages are worldly affairs, we clerics and ministers should not control or govern any aspect of them, but leave them to the manners and customs of each respective city and land.[124]

Yet except for Bucer and Melanchthon,[125] he stood alone as an advocate of complete secularization of marriage jurisdiction – a position that Luther admits was based more on practical necessity than theological or

---

[120] Schorn-Schütte, "Gefährtin und Mitregentin," 117.
[121] For the most complete overviews of sixteenth-seventeenth century Protestant marriage law, see Dieterich; and Schwab, *Grundlagen und Gestalt.* Cf. also Paul Hinschius, *Das Kirchenrecht der Katholiken und Protestanten in Deutschland,* 6 vols. (Berlin, 1869–95); Hans Christian Dietrich, *Evangelisches Ehescheidungsrecht nach den Bestimmungen der deutschen Kirchenrechts des 16. Jahrhunderts* (Erlangen, 1892); Faurey, "Le droit écclésiastique matrimonial des Calvinistes français"; Manfred Erle, *Die Ehe im Naturrecht des 17. Jahrhunderts. Ein Beitrag zu den geistesgeschichtlichen Grundlagen des modernen Eherechts* (Göttingen, 1952), 190ff.; Friedrich Abert Hauber, *Württembergisches Eherecht der Evangelischen* (Stuttgart, 1858).
[122] Dieterich 76ff.; and my comments in Chapter 3.
[123] Melanchthon suggested the ambiguous title *defensor coniugii* for secular authorities, reminiscent of the *defensor vinculi* of Canon law (Dieterich 78–83, 86ff.).
[124] Introduction to the *Großer Katechismus* (1529), *WA* 30/III:25ff.
[125] Dieterich 41ff., 86; Wendel, *Le mariage,* 50.

political inspiration. Pastors and theologians, he feared, were "drowning in the water of worldly affairs," leading him to cry out in frustration: "I want us to be free of marriage matters . . . this belongs to the magistracy."[126] As in elimination of the celibate ideal, the single-minded and spontaneous concern with the ungodly and unscriptural took precedence; the practical and legal consequences of desacramentalizing marriage (discussed in Chapter 3) remained for most religious reformers a secondary matter.

Redefining the indissoluble nature of marriage involved subtler legalist reasoning. Once again, though, revision focused not on the theology itself but on the legal enforcement of its ideal. The marriage bond was indeed a *vinculum insolubile*, affirmed all major Protestant reformers;[127] it was the existing canonical system that was at fault, undermining rather than reinforcing this ideal in practice. Only a legal interpretation and application founded on Scripture and practical experience could effectively close the gap between theory and practice, a legal interpretation theoretically freed from centuries of canonical and papal tradition.

The canonical impediment system, harshly attacked from all sides, was the first part of the indissoluble definition to be put to the scriptural test. Most early Evangelicals initially proposed basing the entire marriage impediment system on Mosaic prohibitions, particularly Leviticus 18. The practical limitations of the relevant passages, however, and the need for extensive interpretation soon became apparent. Once again, reformers were presented with an opportunity – comparable with that of their twelfth-century predecessors – that might have resulted in a radical reformation of the entire marriage legal system; the fact that it did not is just one more sign of their conservatism.

Rather, most theologians and jurists chose to treat impediments as "indifferent" matters, rejecting only those restrictions explicitly in conflict with Scripture and otherwise rely on the discretion of the pastor or secular authority involved. Like their canonical predecessors, all reformers accepted Leviticus's second-degree prohibition as absolute and indispensable. Many (including Luther, Melanchthon, and Osiander) also favored maintenance of the canonical third-degree limitation, while

---

126 "Von Ehesachen" (1530), *WA* 30/III:206, also 246ff. Tischreden no. 3980 (1538), *WA* TR 4:52ff.
127 "Auch den evangelischen Juristen der Reformationszeit ist die Unauflöslichkeit der Ehe selbstverständlich" (Dieterich 49ff., 103ff., 142).

others, most notably Brenz and Calvin, even proposed keeping the traditional fourth-degree prohibition.[128] Similarly, on the subject of affinity
restrictions, few Protestant leaders eliminated all traditional impediments, and none but Luther mentioned reform of "public honesty" and
"illegitimate affinity."[129] Only Bucer favored a radical reduction of the
entire list to two (impotence and the rare call to celibacy),[130] and even
then the traditional character of both of these belies the more radical
reformation that might have been.

Forbidden degrees of consanguinity had in fact already returned to
the fourth degree in the 1533 diet of the Swiss Confederation (Zurich,
Bern, Basel, Schaffenhaussen, and Saint Gallen participating), with
many other cities and principalities following suit.[131] Köhler attributes
the Confederation's return to canonical consanguinity standards in 1533
to immediate Catholic political pressure, but throughout the rest of the
century in Protestant Germany the unmistakable trend remained a return to the previous canonical standards. Some Protestant marriage
codes, such as those of Zurich and Strasbourg, maintained the forbidden degree of consanguinity at the third or even second level, and
eliminated affinity prohibitions altogether. Others, most notably Geneva
and the Duchy of Württemberg, never deviated from the Canon law
definition of either in the first place (at the urging of Calvin and Brenz,
respectively). By the end of the sixteenth century, the only canonical
impediments unanimously rejected by Protestant jurists and marriage
codes were those of spiritual affinity and public honesty (both simultaneously redefined by the Council of Trent and frequently dispensed in
Catholic areas).[132] Impediments of affinity in general were limited to the
second degree and consanguinity to the third, with the remainder of
pre-Reformation restrictions (condition, person, etc.) preserved intact.[133]

---

[128] Dieterich 97–101; Telle, *Erasme*, 391–404.
[129] Luther lampooned both as "Eyn lautter narrn werchkund alfentzen nur umbs gelts willen und
die gewissen tzu verwyrren entrichtet" ("Von Ehesachen" [1530], *WA* 30/III:246). See also
Dieterich 61–68, 97ff.; Schwab, *Grundlagen*, 229–31; and Esmein I:203ff.
[130] Wendel, *Le mariage*, 46.
[131] Kö I:82; II:248–59, 283, 635.
[132] See my subsequent discussion in this chapter.
[133] Dieterich 97–101, 134–41, 157–62, 205ff., 214–26. The 1563 marriage ordinance or the
Palatine-Elector was similarly conservative in the matter, maintaining both prohibitions of
third-degree consanguinity and third degree of affinity. While the ordinance noted that natural
law only prohibited marriage within the first degree of affinity (sister-in-law, son-in-law, etc.),

The other major focus of the indissolubility reform, divorce, likewise spawned less of a major deviation than might at first seem the case. At issue were the traditional canonical definitions of indissolubility and *divortium*, the latter more accurately translated as "annulment" because – on the grounds of an existing impediment – the marriage bond had never been properly (and therefore indissolubly) formed.[134] Protestant "introduction" of divorce was in fact an extension of *divortium* to the very few scripturally backed instances where valid marriages could be dissolved by the subsequent actions of one or both of the spouses. Adultery, for instance, considered both a spiritual as well as a criminal offense, had been long acknowledged by ecclesiastical authorities to be disruptive to marriage and society in general. It could not, however, be considered a preexisting impediment and therefore could not dissolve the conjugal bond. According to Protestant critics, though, the canonical alternative of legal separation (*divortium quoad torum et mensam*) punished the innocent party more than the guilty one, forcing him or her to choose between the loneliness (and many sexual temptations) of a single, separated life and the company of his or her children (and unfaithful spouse).[135] In the words of the Zurich marriage judges in 1532: "Only separating from bed and table . . . makes no sense, since sharing of bed and table are the main reasons for marriage."[136] As in Protestant condemnation of celibacy, only stable marriages provided the necessary *remedium* to the sexual urges that otherwise led single and lonely individuals into sin.

The Protestant solution was to return to an application of *divortium* in the old sense of the early Church.[137] Just as certain impediments pre-

---

it allowed that secular leaders might restrict such unions up to the third degree. As in the instance of third degree of consanguinity, the power of dispensation was reserved to the elector's *iuriconsulti* and *eerichter.* 1563 *EO; EKO* 244. See also 1556 *EO* (*EKO* 224) and 1563 *EGO* (*EKO* 305ff. 312–13).

[134] Cf. Naz, "Divorce," in *DDC* 4:1315ff.

[135] Telle, *Erasme,* 211–16. Erasmus's position, which Telle judges "naive" on the legal consequences, was that a marriage formed by consent should be able to be dissolved *ex consensu.*

[136] Kö I:138.

[137] On the original and later Christian legal definitions of "divorce," see Naz, "Divorce," in *DDC* 4:1315ff; also Ludwig Aemilius Richter, *Beiträge Zur Geschichte des Ehescheidungsrechts in der evangelischen Kirche* (Berlin, 1858); Adolf von Scheurl, "Luther über die Ehescheidung," *Sammlung kirchenrechtlicher Abhandlungen* 4. Abt. (Erlangen, 1873), 463–500; Anneliese Sprengler, "Um eine schriftgemäße Behandlung des Problems der Trauung Geschiedener," *Zeitschrift für evangelisches Kirchenrecht* 3/1 (1953–54), 163–6; and the impressive survey of Phillips, *Putting Asunder.*

vented a marriage bond from ever forming, so certain offenses prevented such a bond from being maintained. Most of the offenses – especially adultery – were already punished by ecclesiastical authorities with separation, but the indissolubility of the marriage bond as defined by Canon law prevented remarriage of the innocent party. Based on scriptural justification (Matt. 19:9; 1 Cor. 7:13) and pastoral experiences, Protestant reformers simply argued that crimes such as adultery rendered the guilty party spiritually dead. Thus, as in physical death, the marriage bond was dissolved and the innocent spouse was free to remarry and avoid the temptations of life alone.[138] The marital bond, affirmed the Palatine-Elector's marriage ordinance, remained "indissoluble"; however, whereas Canon law had recognized certain instances for divorce but prohibited remarriage, divine law expressly named two cases in which remarriage was permitted.[139] Only cases of adultery and malicious desertion possessed sufficient scriptural justification for most reformers; all others were to be handled in the traditional, canonical manner – reconciliation or forced separation without remarriage.[140]

The same theological reasoning was applied, though with less unanimity, to other potential grounds for divorce. After adultery, malicious desertion was the most often cited source of marital disruption among Protestant religious leaders and theologians, again based on the sexual temptation to which the abandoned spouse was subjected. Still, many reformers expressed concern at the potential for judicial abuse in this area, intentional or otherwise, and thus provided strict guidelines and waiting periods to establish the validity of such claims.[141] In the instance

[138] The converse effect was that, as spiritually dead, the guilty spouse was universally prohibited from remarrying (Dieterich 69ff., 103ff.). Matt. 19:1–9 (also Mark 10:11–12; Luke 16:18) provided the scriptural basis for divorce in the case of adultery, while the so-called Pauline privilege (1 Cor. 7:12–16) was occasionally extended to include not just apostasy but malicious desertion as well.

[139] 1556 *EO; EKO* 224. Cf. also 1563 *EGO; EKO* 318ff. Significantly, in both kinds of cases – adultery and malicious desertion – the ordinances make repeated references to imperial and even canonical legal precedents.

[140] Even in the century following the Reformation there was very little support among Protestant jurists for admitting any other grounds for divorce than these, which were themselves reserved as the *ultima ratio* in marital disputes. See Chapter 5; also Hans Gert Hesse, *Evangelisches Ehescheidungsrecht in Deutschland* (Bonn, 1960); Dieterich 142–46, 234ff.; A.-P. Hecker, "Ehescheidungsprozeß," in *HRG* 1:843; A. Villien, "Divorce," in *DTC* 4:1455ff.; and Schwab, *Grundlagen*, 240–45.

[141] Bugenhagen distinguished between three types of abandonment: friendly (the spouse has left with the knowledge of the other and will return); angry; and owing to religious differences. All reformers rejected remarriage for the first type (especially concerning the great number of men

of runaway wives, for example, Bucer required the husband to make sure she wasn't visiting friends or relatives, and only after he had searched "for some time" was his petition to be considered, "since a man in such cases cannot hold out as long as a woman."[142] The abandoned wife, on the other hand, like the ever patient and faithful Griselda of legend, was expected to show more fortitude, yet at the same time was kept under constant surveillance.[143] Reformed Geneva extended the mandatory waiting period beyond the canonical seven years to ten years, and even then prohibited the abandoned wife from remarrying if authorities harbored any suspicions that her spouse had been imprisoned or "hindered by some other mishap."[144]

Apprehension about making divorce too free or common appears in all of the reformers' writings. The "modern" concept of divorce by mutual consent espoused by More's Utopians[145] was probably as alien to sixteenth-century sensibilities as had been the Christian model of marriage to their Germanic forebears. Only Luther and Brenz favored divorce because of neglect of marital duty, or what might be termed irreconcilable differences,[146] yet these same two reformers, it should be noted, remained so vehemently opposed to divorce in general that they

off on military campaigns) unless death could be established or until after the end of the usual five-year waiting period (Bucer proposed reducing the time to two to four years, rather than the canonical seven years). Abandonment of the second and third types was only considered grounds for divorce if all attempts at reconciliation or locating the spouse failed (after at least a year). *Vom Ehebruch* (Wittenberg, 1541), 1ᵇff.; also Dieterich 71–73, 105ff.; and Ozment, *When Fathers Ruled*, 90. Cf. similar language of Luther in "Von Ehesachen" (1530), *WA* 30/III:242–44.

142 Cf. *De Regno Christi*, lex 7, Liber II: chap. 23ff., in *Opera Latina*, XV:169ff.; also Kö II:432. See application of this principle in 1565 Strasbourg code (Wendel, *Le mariage*, 199). Bucer did suggest, however, reducing the waiting period for an abandoned wife to two to four years. Cf. similar double standard among the canonists: Brundage, *Law, Sex, and Christian Society*, 201.

143 On similar literary topoi of the faithful wife, see Falk, *Die Ehe am Ausgang des Mittelalters*, 44ff., and my discussion in Chapter 5.

144 *The Register of the Company of Pastors of Geneva in the Time of Calvin*, trans. and ed. Philip Edgcumbe Hughes (Grand Rapids, Mich., 1966), 78. See also Calvin's Comments on Genesis (*Commentaries* I:239, 551) for similar caution against rash divorce.

Basel, on the other hand, followed the traditional Germanic *Echtedingsfrist* of three public summons and then a wait of six weeks and three days (Staehlin, *Ehescheidung*, 114).

145 T. More, *Utopia*, trans. Paul Turner (London, 1965), 104. More's vague and idealistic proposition (when one party is guilty of "intolerably bad behavior") is reminiscent of a similar proposition by his longtime friend, Erasmus. See Emile Telle, "Marriage and Divorce on the Isle of Utopia – Utopian Reverberations with Erasmus of Rotterdam," *Erasmus of Rotterdam Society Yearbook* 8 (1988), 91–117.

146 Dieterich 72, 106. Bugenhagen also leaned toward this position but could find no scriptural justification for it (*Vom Ehebruch*, N4ᵇ).

both professed preference of bigamy.[147] Even Bucer, who inverted Matthew 19:6 to create the justification, "What God has not joined together, man may put asunder," opposed any divorce by mutual consent unless absolute irreconcilability had been proved over a long period of time.[148] In this he echoed all the reformers, who repeatedly encouraged sincere and prolonged attempts at reconciliation by the couple and the pastor before making any separation final.[149]

Despite all its conservative reluctance, Protestant reinterpretation of the legal implication of indissolubility had many far-reaching effects. Revision of the impediment system as well as the reintroduction – albeit severely limited – of divorce and remarriage cannot be dismissed lightly. Still, the defensive and cautious tone of most reformers' pronouncements on the subject, often in response to attacks within their own ranks,[150] should also not be ignored. It would be difficult to characterize their overwhelming concern with sexual order and discipline as "progressive," yet this has all too often been the case among scholars of the Reformation when referring to the reintroduction of divorce.[151] The right of the innocent spouse to remarry in the few separation cases discussed was rarely proposed or defended by any Protestant reformer

---

[147] Luther's famous advise to Philip of Hesse, however, appears to have been an isolated and, in all likelihood, politically motivated episode. He later adopted the traditional interpretation that permission of polygamy had been limited to ancient times (*Auslegung des ersten Buches Moses* [1535–45], *WA* 42:231–33, 488, 578, 43:137ff.) and, like Brenz (*Wie yn Ehesachen*, F2bff. and H2aff.) and Calvin (sermon on 1 Tim.; *Corpus Reformatorum*, 53:245–46), considered all contemporary polygamy, such as that of the Munsterites, as godless and contrary to Scripture. See also Willi Rockwell, *Die Doppelehe des Landgrafen Philipp von Hessen* (Marburg, 1904); Hastings Eells, *The Attitude of Martin Bucer toward the Bigamy of Philip of Hesse* (New Haven, 1924); Geoffrey Bullough, "Polygamy among the Reformers," in *Renaissance and Modern Essays Presented to Vivian de Sola Piato in Celebration of His Seventieth Birthday*, ed. G. R. Hibbard (London, 1966) 5–23; Oberman, *Luther*, 283–87; and Dieterich 50, 80, 104.

[148] And only, Bucer added, where "den selten on ehebrecherisch gemüt begeret würdt," and both are tempted to bigamy. Kö II:428ff.; Ozment, *When Fathers Ruled*, 63, 86–87; Wendel, *Le mariage*, 154ff. The language and argument are very close to that of Erasmus, especially in the latter's long note (42) to 1 Cor. 7:39 in his translation of the New Testament (Telle, *Erasme*, 205ff.).

[149] Bugenhagen argued that such attempts at reconciliation were comparable with a "resurrection" of the spiritually dead and the beginning of a "new" marriage for the troubled couple (*Vom Ehebruch*, M4ªff.).

[150] Cf. attacks on Bucer by Erasmus Sarcerius (*Von Ursprung, angang, und kerkommen des Heyligen Ehestandts* [Frankfurt, 1553]) and by Théodor de Beza (*Tractio de repudiis et divortiis* [Geneva, 1569]) on Bucer for admitting divorce too easily.

[151] "While it cannot be claimed that Protestants were unique in achieving loving marriages, their new marriage laws, especially those that recognized for the first time a mutual right to divorce and remarriage, became the most emphatic statement of the ideal of sharing, companionable marriage in the sixteenth century" (Ozment, *When Fathers Ruled*, 99).

without reference to the interests of social order and discipline coming before those of the individual(s) concerned. Divorce was not, as these writers repeatedly emphasized, a ready option for a spouse to dissolve unhappy or restrictive bonds but rather the legal recognition of an already irreparable breach, posing a threat to the innocent spouse, household, and community at large.

Finally, we turn to the most seemingly radical yet thoroughly conservative legal reform of the canonical marriage definition: consensualism. Widespread consternation over clandestine marriages already discussed led many Protestant reformers to a fundamental reconsideration of the entire consensual basis for the validity of a marriage. For most of these, the threat posed to Christian society by easy and collusive marriages, especially of disobedient minors, represented a far more serious practical and moral concern than the supposed freedom and sacredness of vows represented by a purely consensual legal foundation, denounced by Bucer as

> that supremely godless dogma that the compact of matrimony made verbally by the contracting parties, as they say, binds at once, if only those who contract are of the age of puberty, and that such a pact is not invalidated if it is made without the knowledge or consent of the parents, out of blind love and desire of the flesh, and for the most part out of the deviousness of seducers and the wantonness of the seduced.[152]

The issue, Bucer stressed, was not the rights of marrying children, but those of the parents, relatives, and communities who nurtured them and had their own stakes in ensuring prudent and successful marriages. Unlike discussions of either sacramentality or indissolubility, it seemed, the twelfth-century insistence on a purely consensual legal basis for marriage left no room for Protestant revision or adaptation; either consent was the sole basis or it was not.[153]

Yet once again, and in the most ingenious manner of all, Protestant reformers managed to synthesize theological tradition and immediate practical demands into a harmonious legal redefinition. Consent, they

---

[152] *De regno Christi*, quoted and translated in Ozment, *When Fathers Ruled*, 29. Cf. similar sentiments of Luther in "Von der Ehesachen" (1530), *WA* 30/III:207–14.

[153] Lebras considers the struggle against clandestine marriage, "l'un des chapitres les plus curieux . . . de l'histoire du mariage," adding that "la clandestinité ne pouvait être exclue que par une réforme profonde du mariage, car elle était dans la logique d'une doctrine qui spiritualise au plus haut point l'union conjugale" ("La doctrine du mariage," in *DTC* 9:2223).

decided, remained the basis of a valid marriage, but it had to be extended to include not just the couple but their parents and community as well. Most legal requirements for public approval (three successive public banns, witnesses, Church blessing, etc.) were actually the same as those first imposed by Lateran IV for licity of a marriage and later also made mandatory by the Council of Trent.[154] The role of the couple's consent in the ceremony and in the marriage's validity remained unchanged. The most significant legal difference was that, in desacramentalizing marriage, Protestants were now able to legislate on a union's validity as well, resulting in a wave of new ordinances in Protestant lands annulling marriages between minors without their parents' permission.[155]

At the same time, both the theological and legal traditions of consensualism (even including the much-reviled *verba de praesenti* and *de futuro*) were preserved largely intact, including frequent admonitions by reformers that parents not use the legal revision to force their children into unwanted marriages.[156] Free and mutual consent continued to be recognized by all sixteenth-century Lutheran and Calvinist jurists as the irrefutable legal basis of every valid marriage. Although legal reformers differed on additional public requirements for legitimacy and some popular perception of betrothal as sufficient for validity persisted, none disputed the ultimate authority of the marrying individuals to accept or reject a proposed union or the value of Canon law in making such determinations.[157]

In sum, Protestant revision of the holy, indissoluble, and consensual legal definition of marriage reflected the same overwhelming concern with social order and, thus, continuity evident in theological reforms. Indeed, in terms of radical social reformation, the reformers of the twelfth century displayed much more ambition both in scope and devia-

---

[154] Helmut Coing, *Europäisches Privatrecht* (Munich, 1985), I:229–31; Dieterich 93–94, 121–22, 153, 185–88; Schwab, *Grundlagen*, 231–34: Friedberg, *Das Recht der Eheschliessung*, 227ff.

[155] Dieterich 56ff., 93ff.; and see my Chapter 4.

[156] Although only Monner followed Melanchthon's total acceptance of the canonical distinction between *sponsalia de presenti* and *sponsalia de futuro* (cf. *De coniugio* [Wittenberg, 1551], 37ff.), all other sixteenth-century Protestant jurists continued to consider all consummated *de futuro* vows as binding and indissoluble. Dieterich 121–22; and see my Chapter 4.

[157] In the Electorate, see 1563 *EO* (*EKO* 280–81) and 1563 *EGO* (295ff.); cf. examples of Zurich (Kö I:93-103), Ulm (Kö II:49–50), Nuremberg (Harvey, "Nürnberg Marriage Laws," 48–60; note that *Trauung* was not *required* until 1537), and Strasbourg (Wendel, *Le mariage*, 94ff.; Kö II:435ff.). See also Dieterich 123–26, 154–55, 200–1; and my comments in Chapter 4.

tion from tradition than any of their Protestant detractors. Instead, Lutheran and Calvinist changes in legal jurisdiction, impediments, divorce, and validity of clandestine vows were typified by their very conservative determination to make the existing theological and legal traditions work. Theirs were reforms of practice rather than ideal, of law enforcement rather than moral and social standards. In this respect, the parallels to Catholic marriage reform are both obvious and instructive.

For Catholic reformers, especially those of the Council of Trent, the solution to current social and legal disorder in marriage was also better and more comprehensive enforcement, but not at the expense of any of the theological or legal traditions they inherited. The root of abuses of celibacy was not Church teachings, but laxness in enforcing those teachings.[158] Similarly, it was the practice, not the substance, of the Church's marriage law that cried out for reform. Some historians have accused Catholic leaders of being handcuffed and restrained from more serious reform by their reliance on tradition, others of jealously protecting their own authority and power over marriage with every defense possible.[159] Ironically, though, it was this same emphasis on theological continuity that resulted in so many similarities to the marriage reforms of their evangelically inspired contemporaries.

Some prominent theological and legal differences between Catholics and Protestants still remained, of course. At the Council of Trent's first session discussing the sacraments (3 March 1547), the representatives unanimously reaffirmed that marriage was not a secular affair but a sacrament of Jesus Christ and the Church: at the same time they refuted Protestant allowance of divorce and remarriage, while defending the Church's right to lay down impediments.[160] Most Church leaders would probably have agreed with Cardinal Cajetan's qualification that marriage was "essentially a sexual union" and not sacramental *simpliciter*, and

---

158 Cf. Chap. 7 and 8 of *Tametsi*, calling on help from the secular arm in enforcing laws against concubinage, bigamy, and adultery. Schroeder, *Council of Trent*, 188; also Franzen, *Zölibat und Prieterehe*, 52–63 on relevant imperial and territorial diets; and my discussion in Chapter 5.

159 Safley, for instance, concludes "Limited by its established, inspired tradition and doctrine, the Catholic Church could not answer in kind but was forced to react, strengthening its institutions and substituting discipline and order for reform and change" (*Let No Man Put Asunder,*, 195).

160 Cf. *Tametsi* on sacramentality (canon 1), indissolubility (canons 5, 7, and 8) and legal powers of the Church (canons 3, 4, 11, 12). Schroeder, *Council of Trent*, 180–82; Hubert Jedin, *Crisis and Closure of the Council of Trent*, trans. N. D. Smith (London, 1967), 141; Esmein II:151; Lebras, "La doctrine du mariage," in *DTC* 9:2229.

93

indeed the council voted that *sacramentum* and *mysterium* were in this sense theologically interchangeable.[161] On the issue of ecclesiastical authority, however, the delegates remained firm. In deference to secular complaints, the council did make some revision of canonical regulations, especially concerning impediments of affinity,[162] but it steadfastly refused to give princes and magistrates the kind of blanket powers of enforcement that Protestant theologians had granted their secular authorities. Only marital property and criminal marriage cases belonged to the magistracy; the rest, by Scripture and tradition, remained ecclesiastical matters.[163] Yet just as the issue of clerical abuse of celibacy had threatened lay acceptance of that theological tradition, so a social problem of equally drastic proportions challenged the credibility of all ecclesiastical jurisdiction over marriage – the problem of clandestine marriage.

The political obstacles involved in finding a practical and, at the same time, theologically sound remedy to clandestine marriage were enormous. Although questions of sacramentality and indissolubility were never seriously disputed among Catholics, the definition of consensualism and the more specific and seemingly unsophisticated issue of clandestine marriage were so explosive as to be postponed until the very last year of the council (1563).[164] The volatile nature of the debates on clandestinity and the tenuous nature of their resolution in the decree *Tametsi* recall the same pervasive Protestant concern to reorder marriage along the lines of parental, communal, and governmental concerns, only in this instance from completely within the Church and its traditions.

---

[161] Lebras, "La doctrine du mariage," in *DTC* 9:2229; Dieterich 70–82; Doherty, *The Sexual Doctrine of Cardinal Cajetan,* 235–37, 243. The council actually cited the same scriptural passages used by Protestants (Gen. 2:23ff.; Matt. 19:4ff.; Mark 10:6ff.; and Eph. 5:31) to reinforce the sacramental definition. Schroeder, *Council of Trent,* 180.

[162] The impediments of *publica honestas* and *affinitas illegitima* were reduced to within the first and second degree respectively, but not, as Luther had sought, eliminated completely. Chapters 3 and 4 of *Tametsi* in Schroeder, *Council of Trent,* 186.

[163] Though chapters 7 and 8 rely on help from the secular arm in criminal marriage matters, all marital validity cases remained exclusively within ecclesiastical jurisdiction (canon 12). Schroeder, *Council of Trent,* 182, 188. See also Schwab, *Grundlagen,* 70–80; and my Chapter 3 on secular and ecclesiastical jurisdiction over criminal marriage matters.

[164] For a highly detailed account of the debates on clandestine marriage, see R. Lettmann, *Die Diskussion über klandestinen Ehen und die Einführung einer zur Gültigkeit verpflichtenden Eheschliessungsform auf dem Konzil von Trent* (Münster, 1967). Cf. also Jean Bernhard, "Le décret *Tametsi* du Concile de Trente: Triomphe du consensualisme matrimonial ou l'institution de la forme solennelle du mariage," *Revue de droit cononique* 30 (1980), 209–33; Jedin, *Crisis and Closure,* 155ff.; Esmein II:155ff.

The result was a sacramental definition unchanged in theory, but irreversibly altered in practice by the compromises that ensued.

Hubert Jedin, the eminent Tridentine scholar, summarizes the theological issue at stake:

> Did the Church's power over the form of the sacrament extend so far that it could declare the mutual consent of the partners to marry – and this consent formed an essential part of the marriage – null and void if it did not satisfy certain conditions?[165]

The few theologians at the council, in keeping with the canonical tradition of the twelfth century, asserted most vehemently that this was theologically untenable.[166] In direct opposition, the French and Spanish delegations, led by the cardinal of Lorraine and the Jesuit Laynez (Loyola's successor as superior general), insisted that the marriages of minors without parental consent be denied canonical validity.[167] The arguments presented for increased familial control of the sacrament were often identical to those of Protestant reformers,[168] allowing speculation as to the profundity of these same delegates' theological comprehension or commitment in their previous affirmation of marriage as sacramental. Clearly, some legates, such as Hosius and Simonetta, recognized both the theological and political consequences such a concession would bear, consequences already visible in Henri II's marriage edict of 1556.[169] Marriage, in the eyes of these theologians, had to be protected as a free and indissoluble sacrament of the Church, just as Jesus Christ had instituted it and their scholastic predecessors had defined it. ·

---

[165] The first subcommittee, composed of six Spaniards, four Frenchmen, three Italians, and two Portuguese, met thirty-six times from 9 February, to 22 March 1563 to consider two heretical articles: "Matrimonium non esse sacramentum a Deo institutum, sed ab hominibus in Ecclesiam invectum, nec habere promissionem gratiae"; and "Parentes posse irritare matrimonia clandestina, nec esse vera matrimonia, quae sic contrahuntur, expedireque, ut in Ecclesia hujus modi in futurum irritentur." Jedin, *Crisis and Closure*, 142; Lebras, "La doctrine du mariage," in *DTC* 9:2234.

[166] Esmein II:157–59; Jedin, *Crisis and Closure*, 143, Lebras, "La doctrine du mariage," in *DTC* 9:2234ff.

[167] Cf. the monograph by Johannes Wahl, *Die Stellung der Spanier zu dem Problem der klandestinen Ehen in den Verhandlungen auf dem Konzil von Trient* (Bonn, 1958); also Jules Basdevant, "Des rapports de l'Eglise et de l'Etat dans la legislation du mariage du Concile de Trente" (Ph.D. diss., Paris, 1900), 24ff.; and Jedin, *Crisis and Closure*, 143.

[168] Basdevant ("Des rapports de l'Eglise," 5–6) makes special note of the many similarities between the two confessions in both reasoning and language.

[169] Jedin, *Crisis and Closure*, 143; Esmein II:201ff.; James Traer, *Marriage and the Family in 18th Century France* (Ithaca, N.Y., 1980), 33.

The first three general debates on clandestinity (24–31 July, 7–23 August, 26–27 October 1563) ended deadlocked amid exceptionally emotional appeals. Every draft of a compromise decree contained, at the insistence of the French and Spanish delegations, great stress on parental consent, and was therefore opposed by all who thought this position theologically untenable.[170] Several other compromises were proposed, including invalidation of clandestine marriage under the existing impediment of "violence" in consent. Because some feared that such a decree would also, however, annul all past and present "clandestine" marriages, and make all the offspring of such unions illegitimate, the proposal was rejected. Every attempt by those in favor of increased requirements for publicity and control was resisted by the significant minority who felt this in violation of the professed *ad honestatem, non ad necesitatem* of sacramental marriage.[171] After a violent between-sessions dispute in the house of Cardinal Morone, the disheartened peacemaker lamented, "We dispersed in greater disunity and confusion than when we had come together."[172]

Finally, in the November session of 1563, a compromise was reached, yielding the decree *Tametsi*. In a concession to the minority, the requirement of parental consent was dropped. Still, the decree lamented the "grave sins which arise from clandestine marriage," and acknowledged the inefficacy of existing ecclesiastical prohibitions. As a result, the council made the formal regulations of Lateran IV – that is, publication of banns and the presence of a priest and at least two witnesses at the ceremony, – now necessary for the *validity* of a marriage.[173] As an additional control, the council adopted the Lutheran practice of requiring marriage (and birth) registers in all parishes.[174]

Although the publicity requirement remained theologically indefensible, its political value was uncontested and considered by many sufficient justification for a less serious deviation from Church tradition. In fact, the council allowed for dispensation and exceptions to the require-

---

[170] Esmein II:155ff.; Lebras, "La doctrine du mariage," in *DTC* 9:2237ff.
[171] Esmein I:78, II:159–61.
[172] Jedin, *Crisis and Closure*, 143; Lebras, "La doctrine du mariage," in *DTC* 9:2241.
[173] Jedin, *Crisis and Closure*, 142; Esmein II:165ff. In addition to the publicity requirements, chapter 1 of *Tametsi* called for *ipso jure* suspension of any priest other than the couple's pastor who performed such a ceremony. Schroeder, *Council of Trent*, 183–85.
[174] Chapter 1 of *Tametsi*, Schroeder, *Council of Trent*, 185. In practice, however, this requirement was only sporadically followed before the seventeenth century. See my Chapter 4.

ment at the discretion of the local bishop, and continued to insist, despite great pressure, that secular rulers resist the great temptation to take such authority into their own hands (as French monarchs already had).[175] Amid the extraordinary outcries of Catholics and Protestants for more regulation and formalization of marriage, the Council of Trent maintained a compromised but firm resistance in favor of the traditional, sacramental, and consensual definition of matrimony.

The swing toward more secular control of marriage, however, was almost as well underway among Catholics as it was among Protestants. In this respect, the council's reluctant imposition of human regulations on marriage spoke much louder than all of its sacramental decrees. As for most Protestants, the chief focus of Catholic marriage reformers was the reestablishment of ignored public controls; for most of the latter, the concessions of the Council of Trent did not go nearly far enough. *Tametsi* was never accepted in France (where the clandestine marriages of minors continued to be considered *rapt de séduction*),[176] and inconsistently applied throughout Germany and most of Catholic Europe.[177] As

---

175 Cf. chapter 9 of *Tametsi:* "Worldly inclinations and desires very often so blind the mental vision of temporal lords and magistrates, that by threats and ill usage they compel men and women who live under their jurisdiction, especially the rich or those who expect a large inheritance, to contract marriage against their will with those whom these lords of magistrates propose to them. Wherefore, since it is something singularly execrable to violate the freedom of matrimony, and equally execrable that injustice should come from those from whom justice is expected, the holy council commands all, of whatever rank, dignity and profession they may be, under penalty of anathema to be incurred *ipso facto*, that they do not in any manner whatever, directly or indirectly, compel their subjects or any others whomsoever in any way that will hinder them from contracting marriage freely" (Schroeder, *Council of Trent*, 189).

176 Following Henri II's Edict of 1556, which set the ages of independence at thirty and twenty-five (for men and women respectively), Henri III issued the *Ordonnances de Blois* (1579). Using the same disinheritance punishments of 1556, the new edict required four witnesses (instead of two), no dispensation from the public banns, absolute necessity of priest's presence at actual exchange of vows (required by Trent), prosecution for rape of any priest marrying minors without consent of their parents, and general invalidation of all marriage not thus conducted. As this was distinctly royal legislation and not a ratification of Church law, Pope Gregory XIII urged Henri to rescind his edict and accept the decrees of Trent. Cardinal Pithou responded for the king, claiming all that Henri decreed was in accordance with Church law and his own competence and authority. See Victor Martin, *Le gallicanisme et la réforme catholique: Essai historique sur l'introduction des décrets du Concile de Trente (1563–1615)* (Paris, 1919), esp. 166ff. Cf. also Traer, *Marriage Law and the Family*, 33ff.; Pierre Taillandier, "Le mariage des protestants français sous l'Ancien Régime" (J. D. diss., Poitiers, 1919), 53ff.;"Marriage civil," in *DDC* 6:735–36; Schwab, *Grundlagen*, 203–8; Basdevant, "Des rapports de l'Eglise," 64–65; and Sarah Hanley, "Engendering the State: Family Formation and State Building in Early Modern France," *French Historical Studies* 16/1 (1989), 4–27.

177 For acceptance and enforcement of Tridentine marriage decrees in Catholic Germany, see

the fathers of Trent soon discovered, preserving doctrinal unity throughout Catholic Europe was one thing, and a tenuous one at that; preserving the Church's officially exclusive legal jurisdiction over marriage, especially amid overwhelming secular pressures, was quite another. Already compromised by a myriad of secular as well as ecclesiastical controls, the free and individual sacrament of Alexander III – if it had ever truly been realized – appeared well on the way to becoming a paper fiction.

Protestants and Catholics did not always come up with the same answers, but they were invariably asking the same question: How do we preserve and promote both the spiritual and social character of marriage? Despite polemical rhetoric to the contrary, all religious reformers of marriage from the twelfth century on were concerned with this same basic objective. To portray Protestant and Catholic doctrinal responses as ideologically opposed clearly misrepresents the very nature of all sixteenth-century reform. All reformers recognized the problems and abuses surrounding marriage in their times and, moreover, all shared a remarkably similar vision of the ideal being defiled. Where they differed was on the translation of this ideal into practice and even here legal and theological tradition prevailed.

Perhaps the most persuasive evidence of this common continuity is the striking similarity, by the end of the sixteenth century, between Protestant and Catholic marriage codes. In the Palatinate, a comparison of the Calvinist Elector's marriage ordinance of 1556 (revised in 1563 and 1578) and its Catholic counterpart issued by the Prince-Bishop of Speyer in 1582 renders the close resemblance immediately apparent.[178] Significantly, both begin by addressing themselves to the paramount concern of all sixteenth-century marriage legislation, namely the "disor-

Hermann Conrad, "Das Tridentische Konzil und die Entwicklung des kirchlichen und weltlichen Eherechts," in *Das Weltkonzil von Trient, sein Werden und Wirken*, ed. Georg Schreiber (Freiburg, 1951), 297–324, and my discussion in Chapters 4 and 5. On Spain, Portugal, Poland, and Latin America, see Friedberg, *Das Recht der Eheschliessung*, 127ff.; and Schwab, *Grundlagen*, 194–221.

[178] The elector's *EO* was the work of jurist and later chancellor Christoph Ehem (1528–92), borrowing heavily from the Württemberg marriage ordinance of 1557. *EKO* 36–37; E. Fabian, "Christoph von Ehem," *Neue Deutsche Biographie* 4 (1959), 4:342; Press, *Calvinismus und Territorialstaat*, 25 130–34, 213ff.

Bishop Eberhard's introduction of Trent's *Tametsi* on 3 July 1582 was his first reform act after coronation earlier that year. It was reissued by his successor, Christoph von Sötern, on 15 July 1614. Ammerich, "Formen und Wedge der katholischen Reform," 295ff.

ders, troubles, crimes, . . . and confusion" resulting from clandestine marriages of minors, entered into "out of pure high-spiritedness, thoughtlessness, falsity, and deceit, as well as now and then through seduction by gifts and promises, or else through ignorance."[179] Both decry the harm done to the holy, "divinely instituted," and "indissoluble" estate of matrimony by such sham marriages and prescribe the traditional canonical formula of publicity: Those marriages not conducted in such orderly and regulated fashion were automatically invalidated by both.[180] Any and all disputes regarding the validity of a marriage were not to be handled by the pastor or families but by the respective marriage court or consistory.[181] Similarly, all criminal marriage matters were to be referred to the local secular authority (e.g., bailiff or town council) alone.[182]

The divergences that remained – namely on sacramentality, divorce, and forbidden degrees of affinity and consanguinity – cannot be ignored, but even bearing these in mind, the fundamental agreement in purpose between the two ordinances is striking. The sixteenth-century reform of marriage law, despite all early efforts by Protestant theologians, remained in essence just that – a legal, and not religious, re-

---

[179] Prince-bishop of Speyer ordinance: "Daß unß nun mehrmaln von anfang unserer Regierung, underandern onordnungen, mangel und gebrechen vielfeltige lagen furkommen. Welcher maßen ein zeit hero auß den heimlichen verborgenen vermahelshafften und winkelehen, allerhand shedlich mißbreuch, deßgleichen so mal beschwerliche mißverstand und oneinigkeit, mit groste unheil und Zerruttlichen onwesen aller Christlichenn lieb und shuldigen gehorsamb Zwishen den eltern und kindern, alß Zwishen den hinderrugkt verknipften personen selbst . . . " (GLA 67/426 32ʳ; *Collectio* II:385). Cf. predecessor ordinances for Weissenburg (1577) and Joehlingen and Wäschbach (1580) (GLA 61/10945, 423; Landsmann, *Wissembourg,* 170) and reasons cited for renewal of episcopal ordinance in 1614 (*Sammlung* 36–37).
   Elector of Palatinate ordinance: " . . . Und aber in solchem eheversprechen dise ergerliche und schädliche leichfertigkeit bey vilen ungehorsamen kindern, so noch under dem gewalt irer eltern sein, täglicchen gespürt und befunden wirdet, das sich dieselbige kinder one irer eltern vorwissen, rath und bewilligung auß lauterem mutwillen, leichfertigkeyt, falsch und betrug, auch bißweilen durch schänkungen und verheissungen oder sonst durch unwissenheyt verführet, mit anderen ehelich verloben, versprechen und verheuraten . . . " (*EKO* 280; cf. 221ff.). See also my discussion in Chapter 4.
[180] *EKO* 221, 224. Cf. the two ordinances on publicity requirements: approval of parents if minor (*EKO* 281; *Collectio* II 386–87), three banns announced on consecutive Sundays at church (*EKO* 284; *Collectio* II:387), minimum of two or three witnesses (*EKO* 282–84; *Collectio* II:387), and necessity of Church blessing by own pastor (*EKO* 282–84; *Collectio* II:387–89). Cf. also requirements for examination of the engaged couple by local pastor, to screen for possible impediments and to question both on their faith (LAS A1/1753, 110–11; Stamer III:118). See also my comments in Chapter 4.
[181] *EKO* 277; *Collectio* II:390.
[182] *EKO* 283–86 (also Press, *Calvinismus und Territorialstaat,* 43); *Collectio* II:391; and see my Chapter 3.

form, carried out by trained jurists.[183] Protestant reformers' scriptural interpretations exerted more than a slight influence on subsequent marriage codes, but even in the most outstanding examples of this – divorce and the invalidation of clandestine marriages – the interests of Protestant magistrates essentially mirrored those of their Catholic counterparts: correction of abuses and disorders in the marriage law with as much legal continuity as possible.[184] Moreover, as we have seen, the success of this or any other social reform invariably returned to the issue of effective legal enforcement, the fundamental supposition shared by all sixteenth-century complaints of sexual immorality and legal laxity in the control of marriage.

[183] Wendel agrees that the very differences in Protestant and Catholic marriage doctrines themselves were based less on religious divisions than "l'infinie variété de leur application aux besoins de la pratique." Though this characterization probably does not give adequate shrift to the doctrinal limitations for Catholic magistrates confronting the same "needs," it is probably fair to conclude that "la législation protestante du mariage est surtout née de ces besoins et que les théories des théologiens n'ont eu qu'une influence secondaire" (Wendel, *Le mariage*, 178).

[184] On the strong similarity between sixteenth-century Protestant and Catholic marital law, cf. the conclusions of Kö I:2–3, 442–543; Esmein I:34; Wendel, *Le mariage*, 177; Coing, *Europäisches Privatrecht*, 224–25; Harvey, "Nürnberg Marriage Laws," 254ff.; Safley, *Let No Man Put Asunder*, 38: Dieterich, 82.

While all recognize that reformed marriage law was only slightly modified Canon law, only Köhler argues (Kö II:443) that the changes represented a "notwendige und grundsätzliche" transformation of the same. For France, Pierre Bels (*Le mariage des protestants français*, 184, 193ff.) even goes so far as to note that French Reformed marriage law and practice were much closer to Canon law than French royal (and Catholic) legislation.

3

Marriage and the state:
The bureaucratic reformation

No one can deny that marriage is something exterior and worldly, like clothing, food, a house, the court, and subject to secular authority as demonstrated in the constitutions proclaimed by the emperors.

> Martin Luther, *On Marriage Matters* (1530)[1]

If anyone says that matrimonial causes do not belong to ecclesiastical judges, let him be anathema.

> Council of Trent, session 24, *Doctrine on the Sacrament of Matrimony*, canon 12 (1563)[2]

State enforcement in marriage neither began nor dramatically changed as a result of the Protestant Reformation. Its association with sixteenth-century religious reform, however, has become commonplace in most accounts of the period largely because of the influential writings of one brilliant nineteenth-century legal historian. In his classic study of the Canon law of marriage, Adhémar Esmein described a cycle in European marriage authority during the past two millennia that began with secular enforcement of Roman law, was followed in the Middle Ages by a period of ecclesiastical legal jurisdiction, and ultimately – beginning with the Reformation – returned to a "secular" marriage law and enforcement at the hands of the modern State.[3] Since the first publication of this work in 1891, this general schema of European marriage jurisdiction has attained the status of unquestioned orthodoxy. Even the most recent historical and legal studies continue to characterize the sixteenth century

---

1 "Von Ehesachen" (1530) *WA* 30/III:205.
2 Schroeder, *Council of Trent*, 182.
3 Esmein I:3–4.

and the Reformation as the "secularizing" turning point of marital law and jurisdiction in Germany and other Protestant countries.[4]

Unfortunately, as with many other monumental nineteenth-century historical works, Esmein's overly literal interpretation of an extremely limited and narrow set of sources has in some key respects distorted the reality.[5] First, his initial period of "Roman law" was throughout most of the continent actually one of familial and local control of marriage, governed primarily by unwritten customary law. Second, the Canon law and ecclesiastical courts introduced in the twelfth and thirteenth centuries did not immediately replace such traditional marriage controls but, rather, coexisted in a divided marriage jurisdiction well into the sixteenth century. Third, and most important for our study, the legal and jurisdictional changes in marriage during the sixteenth century arose much less from confessional or even secular–ecclesiastical divisions than this long-standing conflict of authority between local custom and codified Roman and Canon laws.

These notable revisions rest in turn on a critique of three crucial assumptions in Esmein's model. First, we must reconsider the definition of "marital" litigation itself. Until now, all scholarly discussion of the subject has been limited to those disputes involving the formation and validity of the marriage bond alone, cases that, for convenience, we will call "validity disputes": disputed vows, multiple vows, permanent or temporary separation of spouses, annulment, divorce with remarriage, and so on. This indeed was the type of litigation that ecclesiastical authorities had in mind when they claimed exclusive marital jurisdiction, hence Esmein's definition. Yet, as all judicial authorities as well as the distinguished French scholar were well aware, there were many other kinds of cases involving other important aspects of marriage. By far the

---

[4] Some of these emphasize the expansive nature of the early modern state; see especially Safley, *Let No Man Put Asunder*, and Hermann Rebel, *Peasant Classes: The Bureaucratization of Property and Family Relations under Early Habsburg Absolutism, 1511–1636* (Princeton, 1983). Others, such as Marc Raeff, conversely stress the overall decline in the Church's legal role and its more general withdrawal, "voluntary or forced," from such vital realms of social and cultural life as education and the care of the poor, creating "a vacuum quickly filled by the territorial state and its ordinances"; see *The Well-Ordered Police State: Social and Institutional Change through Law in the Germanies and Russia, 1600–1800* (New Haven, 1983), 16–17.

[5] Much of this historical generalizing of course has to do with the natural bias of extant sources for the medieval period, such as ecclesiastical legal codes, decrees, and charters. Cf. historiographical overview in the Introduction.

most prevalent of these were disputes over dowries, prenuptial contracts, and separation of marital goods – cases we may call "marital property" disputes. A third significant general area was that of "criminal" marriage law and litigation: moral offenses relating to marriage, such as adultery, fornication, concubinage, bigamy, clandestine marriage, abandonment, and abuse. Although these three terms themselves would have been foreign to jurists and litigants of the times, the judicial distinctions implicit in each certainly would not. Consequently, equating "marital litigation" with validity disputes alone obviously distorts the experience of medieval courts and litigants with marriage.

The second revision of Esmein's thesis concerns a related question, namely, the fundamental distinction between secular (*weltliche*) and ecclesiastical (*geistliche*) jurisdiction in all medieval and early modern litigation. By the twelfth century in most of Europe, all legal matters, including marital ones, were theoretically placed into one of these two categories and handled by the appropriate judicial authority. Although most scholars since Esmein have readily acknowledged the traditionally private nature of marriage before the thirteenth century in Germany, they have also too readily accepted the Church's exclusive legal jurisdiction thereafter as a fait accompli. Consequently, any explanation of sixteenth-century changes in marriage jurisdiction must hinge on adaptation or rejection of an extensive and total ecclesiastical control over all aspects of marriage law. Yet, actual marital jurisdiction, especially over the previously unconsidered criminal and property cases, never constituted an exclusively ecclesiastical matter. Despite all jurisdictional advances achieved by the Church during the Middle Ages, there is no evidence that ecclesiastical authorities ever achieved *or intended* more than a split jurisdiction in marriage control.[6] Even with the medieval Church's success in reestablishing (at least in theory) the Carolingian division of jurisdiction, secular authorities remained very active in

---

[6] This is strongly disputed by Jack Goody, who argues that from the early Middle Ages on, the Church purposefully and persistently attempted to enhance its own economic power by extending its controls over marriage and the family as far as possible, especially in its regulation of consanguinity (*Family and Marriage in Europe*, esp. 134–56). As Brundage (*Law, Sex, and Christian Society*, 606–7) points out, however, this thesis "is only partly consistent with the evidence." Adoption did apparently decline dramatically during this period, but official measures against illegitimate children came, if at all, from secular authorities; the Church made very few attempts itself to restrict either lay or clerical concubinage and other threats to its supposedly overriding economic strategy of accumulating property for itself.

marriage-related legislation and litigation, often overlapping (as in the instances of prince-bishops[7]) or even directly competing (as in city-states) with ecclesiastical authorities.

The third and final modification of Esmein's "secularization" thesis concerns the important judicial conflict ignored in his exclusive concentration on validity disputes and the judicial organ that adjudicated them. When other kinds of marital litigation are also considered, not only the secular–ecclesiastical distinction becomes more blurred, but the nature of judicial authority itself is called into question. For all marital cases other than those examined by Esmein, "lower," or local, jurisdiction rather than "higher," or territorial, jurisdiction was the norm.[8] The principal transition, then, from medieval to early modern marital jurisdiction was not one from an ecclesiastical territorial court to a secular one, but from a variety of local and territorial "courts" to fewer, more centralized institutions of mixed secular and ecclesiastical nature. Just as emphatically, there was no sudden shift originating with the Reformation but a very gradual expansion of the territorial State's authority, beginning in the fifteenth century and continuing, among Catholics as well as Protestants, well into the eighteenth and nineteenth centuries. Full secularization and centralization of marital legal authority were indeed the ultimate results in Germany, but certainly not during the time of the Reformation.

This chapter examines the early stages of that transformation in three roughly chronological sections: the nature of marital jurisdiction during the Middle Ages in Germany, including the establishment and growth of ecclesiastical courts from the twelfth to the fourteenth centuries; the growth of municipal and territorial state bureaucracies during the fifteenth and early sixteenth centuries, accompanied by increasing competition with ecclesiastical courts in all areas of marital litigation; and the

---

[7] Many bishops, known as prince-bishops, were also secular lords who exercised both kinds of jurisdiction within their respective realms. The secular realm of the prince-bishop rarely corresponded exactly to the boundaries of his spiritual realm (the diocese), as in the case of Speyer. This was further complicated by the frequent use before the thirteenth century of bishop's *klein-* or *untervogte*, functionaries common to all secular lords, to handle both secular and "spiritual" matters, often indiscriminately. Riedner I, 7; Justus Hashagen, "Zur Charakteristik der geistlichen Gerichtsbarkeit vornehmlich im späteren Mittelalter," *Zeitschrift der Savigny-Stiftung für Rechtsgeschichte, Kanonistische Abteilung* 6 (1916), 245.
[8] Karl Siegfried Bader, *Studien zur Reschtsgeschichte des mittelalterlichen Dorfes*, vol. I: *Das mittelalterliche Dorf als Friedens- und Rechtsbereich* (Weimar, 1957), 180ff.; Heinrich Mitteis, *Deutsche Reschtsgeschichte*, 18th ed. (Munich, 1988), 192–94.

roles of Church and State in the jurisdictional breaks and "new" marital jurisdictions that resulted after the agreements of the Peace of Augsburg. After consideration of all three phases in the early transformation of the State's role in marriage, we will then return briefly to propose a modified version of Esmein's model.

Marriage jurisdiction during the Middle Ages

The control of marriage among Germanic peoples had been left largely, as it had been among the Romans, to the family and immediate kinship group.[9] Establishment of the marriage contract, exchange of property, and divorce or punishment for adultery and other marital offenses all took place within such closed circles, with little or no reference to or intervention by any state or ecclesiastical authority. The early Christian Church consistently taught some restrictive rules on marriage (chiefly concerning consanguinity) but, even after toleration, it could not touch the laws of the empire or those of local custom.[10] With the fall of Rome, Church influence grew even more tenuous, relying on the strength of a dispersed variety of local rulers and consequently allowing customary marriage practice to prevail in most areas. Thus, though expressly forbidden by ecclesiastical authorities since at least the Council of Carthage (406), a kind of divorce by mutual consent continued to thrive with little opposition in most of western Europe well into the eleventh century. Consequently, Church leaders focused their reform efforts more on eliminating the most excessive barbarian practices, such as *Frauenraub* (a Germanic custom of marriage by force, literally kidnapping the bride) and enforcing consanguinity and affinity prohibitions.[11] Beginning in sixth-century Gaul, priestly blessing of a marriage gradually became

---

9 Some early medieval Germanic codes do frequently mention marriage, but generally depend on members of the kinship group for enforcement. On importance of the clan (*Sippe*) in early Germanic marriage law, see P. Mikat, "Ehe," in *HRG* 1:81off. On the Roman law of marriage, see Percy E. Corbett, *The Roman Law of Marriage* (Oxford, 1930).

10 Esmein I:4–7. Again, cf. the arguments of Goody, who supposes a much stronger and unified ecclesiastical enforcement of consanguinity impediments during this period (*Development of the Family*, 134ff).

11 Though the laws of Constantine had reacted strongly against divorce and remarriage, the practice was never abolished and continued to be permitted in the empire, even in the Justinian code. In France such divorce required mutual consent, but in Germany the husband's right to set aside his wife remained intact at least until the tenth century and possibly later in some areas. Esmein I:5, 11, 19. On the early medieval Church's battle against *Frauenraub*, see Mikat, " Ehe," in HRG 1:825ff.

customary but never necessary, in ecclesiastical or local law, for the marriage's validity.[12]

The first major attempt to establish greater secular and ecclesiastical authority over marriage practice in the Germanic lands came, as might be expected, during the Carolingian era. Here a system of approximate legislative and judicial duality was erected in which almost every imperial district and official had their ecclesiastical counterparts, from the count and his bishop to the bailiff (*Schultheiß*) and archdeacon.[13] Theoretically, rivalries between the two spheres were checked by the different jurisdictions assigned them, with all marriage validity disputes usually conceded to the bishop and his functionaries (albeit in their capacity as servants of the Carolingian emperor, who reserved jurisdiction in this area into the tenth century).[14] Even within such relatively well-defined boundaries, however, enforcement remained inconsistent and jurisdictional disputes were widespread. The synodal courts of bishops and their archdeacons continued to expand their jurisdiction to include not only arguably "spiritual" crimes, such as adultery and illicit marriage, but various "secular" ones as well, including negligent homicide and use of false weights and measurements. Similar abuses occurred on the secular side, ultimately resulting in an almost total breakdown of Charlemagne's dual network of courts and offices within fifty years of his death, with a similar fate for any systematic marriage controls.[15]

The Carolingian division of marital jurisdiction was not restored until the twelfth century. By then, most secular rulers in western Europe had accepted – at least in principle – the preeminence of ecclesiastical authority in both marriage law and enforcement. Matters generally con-

---

[12] Esmein I:9–14; Mikat, "Ehe," in *HRG* 1:818, 825; D. Schwab, "Heiratserlaubnis," in *HRG* 2:66-67.

[13] The bishop's realm corresponded exactly to that of the count, as did the court of the archdeacon to the lower court of the *Zentgraf* and *Schultheiß*. Riedner I, 4–5; Esmein I:16ff.

[14] Despite the application of *sacramentum* to marriage by Hincmar of Reims (died 882), there is no mention whatsoever of marriage as a sacrament in the later theological or juridical sense of the word, even in the false capitularies or pseudo-Isodoran decretals (ninth century)–a classification that would have put it incontestably under the Church's jurisdiction *de ratione rerum*. F. L. Cross, *The Oxford Dictionary of the Christian Church*, 2nd ed. (London, 1974), 889ff., on "Matrimony"; Esmein I:16; P. Fournier, *Les Officialités au Moyen Age* (Paris, 188), xi; Riedner I, 6.

[15] Esmein argues that the dual jurisdiction of Church and State over marriage probably disappeared in the mid-tenth century in Italy and roughly the same time in France, while somewhat later in Germany, though it should be noted that this is limited to validity disputes only and not the property aspects of marriage control and litigation, which had always remained chiefly within the secular realm. Esmein I:27–31; also Riedner I, 6ff.

sidered within the secular realm by this time included both criminal marital matters (such as adultery, concubinage, prostitution, incest) and all marital property disputes. Ecclesiastical jurisdiction, on the other hand, which reached its apex during this same period, comprised all matters considered "spiritual" or "ecclesiastical" either by reason of person (*de ratione personarum*) or of subject matter (*de ratione rerum*).[16] Marriage, generally counted among the sacraments at least since the twelfth century,[17] was thus officially included under ecclesiastical jurisdiction *de ratione rerum,* with limited involvement in criminal marriage matters. For Esmein, this legal concession marked the end of the Church's practical limitation to a "purely disciplinary" and reactive jurisdiction and the dawning of the "classical age" of Canon law and ecclesiastical courts.[18]

Yet as Richard Helmholz suggests of medieval England, it is probably a "wasted effort" to attempt to determine exactly when Church courts reestablished "exclusive" marital jurisdiction in Germany.[19] Because the early medieval Church never sought nor achieved complete control over all marriage practice, it is also misleading. Again the limitations of most previous scholars to questions of marital validity must be borne in mind. While acceptance of the Church's proper jurisdiction in this area generally spread throughout Europe during the tenth to twelfth centuries, ecclesiastical claims over criminal marriage matters, such as adultery, received much less universal recognition, even in principle.[20] More important, as we will also see in the medieval confrontation between customary and Canon law, the principal concern of marriage control during this period was much less competition between existing secular and ecclesiastical court systems than a concerted effort by all authorities to ensure "that ordinary marriage disputes went to any court at all."[21]

---

[16] *De ratione personarum* included all members of the clergy but also extended to certain other qualified persons if they so requested, such as crusaders, scholars, travelers, *personae miserabiles* (widows, orphans, paupers), and in some cases Jews. Ecclesiastical jurisdiction *de ratione rerum* included administration of sacraments, vows, ecclesiastical censures, elections, and all matters regarding benefices. W. Trusen, "Die Gelehrte Gerichtsbarkeit der Kirche," in *HQL* I:483–86; Fournier, *Les Officialités,* 12–13, 65, 79, 82–84; W. Trusen, "Offizialat," in *HRG* 2:1216.

[17] See my discussion in Chapters 2 and 3.

[18] Esmein I:11, 31, 153–56.

[19] Helmholz, *Marriage Litigation,* 5; also Coing, *Europäisches Privatrecht,* I:100ff.

[20] R. Lieberwirth ("Ehebruch," in *HRG* 1:837) claims as late as the thirteenth century in Germany, and even then it was at best shared with secular authorities in practice. See also Schwab, *Grundlagen,* 15–32.

[21] Helmholz, *Marriage Litigation,* 4–5.

Undoubtedly the most significant development in this respect was the spread of a new institution during the thirteenth century, namely, the *Officialatus*, or bishop's court. Its sole judge, the Official (*Officialis*) held full responsibility for enforcing the bishop's ecclesiastical jurisdiction, including questions of marital validity and occasionally morality. The term *Officialis* first appeared in England and France in the late twelfth century.[22] The first appearance of a seal for the new court, or *Officialatus*, suggests that the courts originated a little later in the western dioceses of Germany and slowly spread eastward over the period of the next century, reaching Mainz in 1221, Speyer in 1237, and Worms in 1243.[23] Papal endorsement of the Official and his court was also forthcoming, including indirect references to such a court in Lateran IV documents on ecclesiastical trials (1215), the *Romana ecclesia* of Innocent IV (1246), and the *Liber Sextus* (1298).[24]

The Official's judicial authority stemmed from that of the bishop, in the latter's capacity as supreme legal authority with *potestas ordinaria* for his diocese.[25] He was appointed directly by the bishop and could be replaced at any time. His jurisdiction was mandated (*iurisdictio mandata*, not *propria*) and was of two types: general (*officialis principalis*) or subject-specific (*officialis foranis*). Although some dioceses began with more than one *officialis principalis*, by the end of the thirteenth century (1272 in Speyer), there was in general one per diocese and two per archdiocese.[26] The bishop reserved the right to intervene and judge person-

---

[22] Before 1170 in Canterbury, and about 1170 in Rouen (Fournier, *Les Officialités*, 4–5).

[23] First appearances of the new *Officialatus* seal included Mainz (1210/21), Speyer (1237), Worms (1243), Strasbourg (1248), Cologne (1252), Constance (1253), Lausanne (1260), Augsburg (1264), Basel (1265), Münster (1265), Chur (1273), Würzburg (1275), Eichstätt (1281), Hildesheim (1291), Magdeburg (1295), Halberstadt (1297), Paderborn (1309), Osnabrück (1325), Minden (1326), Bremen (1329), and Merseburg (1330), with the exception of only a cathedral chapter *Officialatus* in Bamberg (1344). Trusen, "Offizialat," in *HRG* 2:1214–15; Ingeborg Johanek, "Geistlicher Richter und geistliches Gericht im spätmittelalterlichen Bistum Eichstätt" (Ph.D. diss., Universität Würzburg, 1981), 3–5; Trusen, "Die Gelehrte Gerichtsbarkeit," in *HQL* I:467–73.
  The actual term first used in Speyer was the general *Officiatus*, with the narrower sense of the word (the bishop's ecclesiastical judge) apparently well-known by the end of the thirteenth century. Riedner I, 23–24.

[24] Lateran IV uses the terms *coadiutores* and *cooperatores* of the bishop in reference to ecclesiastical judges. Trusen, "Offizialat," in *HRG* 2:1215; Johanek, "Geistlicher Richter," 1.

[25] This power included *potestas ordinis* (also *iura pontificalia*), *potestas magisterii*, and *potestas iurisdictionis*. Hinschius, *Das Kirchenrecht der Katholiken und Protestanten in Deutschland*, II:40, sec. 79.

[26] There were many exceptions to this rule, however, including the diocese of Speyer, which, despite an agreement between the bishop and archdeacons in 1357 acknowledging one Official

ally in serious cases (e.g., heresy, murder of a cleric, physical assault on a cleric), but the authority of the Official generally remained sovereign.[27] All appeals, thanks to a ruling by Innocent III at the behest of the bishops, went not to the pope but rather to the archbishop, an option that appears to have been rarely exercised in marriage cases.[28]

The Official's jurisdiction over marital validity cases does appear to have been generally recognized by secular territorial rulers (at least from the thirteenth century on). Although it is difficult to establish this development with any certainty, it is worth noting that in medieval France, for instance, there is not one recorded challenge of ecclesiastical control of marriage.[29] Conflicts between the bishop's court and secular courts, especially on criminal and inheritance matters, constituted a constant fixture throughout medieval Europe, but jurisdiction over marital validity was rarely, if ever, the focus of such disputes.

Rather, especially in episcopal towns, the opposite kind of legal aggression appears to have been the case. In the city of Speyer, for instance, a papal privilege of 1260 brushed aside the town's citizens' imperial privileges of 1111 and 1182 and unilaterally granted the bishop's Official full legal jurisdiction within the city.[30] The assumption of "vol-

---

(the bishop's) for the entire diocese (see nn. 40–42), continued to also host a rival *Officialatus* operated by the cathedral chapter. See Fournier, *Les Officialités*, 15–19, 21; Riedner I, 39.

   The competence of the *officialis foranis*, or delegated judge, was limited either by subject (usually marriage) or region (part of a diocese). This practice does not appear to have been as widespread in medieval Germany as it was in France. See Fournier, *Les Officialités*, 13–14; Nikolaus Hilling, *Die Offiziale der Bischöfe von Halberstadt im Mittelalter* (Stuttgart, 1911), 3, 90–91; Trusen, in *HQL* I:480–81. Although Riedner (I, 71) notes some sporadic use of such delegated judges with ad hoc authority in the diocese of Speyer, there is nothing to suggest that this was even a major factor in marriage litigation.

27 After 1272 in Speyer, for instance, all bishops took an oath at their consecrations not to alter the Official's verdict. Riedner I, 98.

28 The appeal process was an extremely expensive and time-consuming one for all involved, both in ecclesiastical as well as secular courts, and therefore officially discouraged in most cases. Still, occasionally some marriage validity cases were permitted to be appealed, such as a 1510 complaint of defloration and suit for marriage against Heinrich Cluet, a Speyer cleric, in which the plaintiff, Florian Hensel, not satisfied with the Speyer Official's eight-gulden fine without marriage, appealed to the archbishop (result unknown). See GLA 67/417, 99ᵛ–100ᵛ; Riedner II, no. 86, 258–59. See also Hilling, *Die Offiziale*, 56; Riedner I, 14; Trusen, "Offizialat," in *HRG* 2:1216; and cf. Stamer II:76, on appeals in the diocese of Speyer to the archbishop of Mainz in general.

29 A 1205 decision of Philip Augustus of France gave women the option of taking dowry disputes to ecclesiastical or royal courts, a compromise generally accepted by the Church. Fournier, *Les Officialités*, 80–83, also 94–127; and Lieberwirth, "Ehebruch," in *HRG* 1:837, for Germany.

30 Duggan, *Bishop and Chapter*, 96; Riedner I, 7, 12, 62, 64. On the practice of *freiwillige* jurisdic-

untary" secular jurisdiction by bishops in episcopal cities was an old tradition, in Speyer dating back at least to a 969 privilege of Otto the Great. Although repeatedly challenged by the town council in the thirteenth century, the bishop of Speyer continued to maintain the upper hand during this period. In a typical agreement arbitrated by representatives of Pope Celestine V in 1294, the town's citizens agreed to submit to the *Officialatus* as long as the bishop did not establish any more judges outside the city. The criminal ordinances of 1314 and 1328 restored much criminal jurisdiction to the city's own court, but as late as the end of the fourteenth century the bishop's Official still handled one-half of all criminal cases within the city.[31]

The real challenge to the bishop's marriage jurisdiction, rather, came from within his own house. As Fournier aptly puts it, "at no time did the bishop possess absolute power within his diocese."[32] Nowhere is this more apparent than in the bishop's struggle with his archdeacons and their chapters over judicial supremacy in ecclesiastical matters.

References to archdeacons as "the eyes and hands" of the bishop date back to the early Church. Their responsibilities included diocesan discipline since the seventh century, and visitations and other administrative duties at least since Carolingian times.[33] With the growth of parishes and, consequently, dioceses, one archdeacon became several, each responsible for a different geographical area of the diocese. The number of archdeacons per diocese varied with size of the diocese and other factors. The diocese of Speyer, for example, comprised four arch-

---

tion, see Nikolaus Hilling, "Die Bedeutung der iurisdictio voluntaria und involuntaria im römischen Recht und im kanonischen Recht des Mittelalters und der Neuzeit," *Archiv für katholisches Kirchenrecht* 105 (1925), 449–73; also Karl Hofmann, *Die freiwillige Gerichtsbarkeit im kanonischen Recht* (Paderborn, 1929).

[31] Theodor Harster, *Das Strafrecht der freien Reichsstadt Speier in Theorie und Praxis* (Breslau, 1900), 104. Harster's sources for this claim, however, are unclear.

Use of the *Officialatus* for notarial purposes of all kinds was also widespread in many dioceses, such as Halberstadt, throughout the fifteenth century. In Strasbourg, the bishop's court was long the only notarial court in the city and, even after the city became Protestant in the sixteenth century, continued to act as the official municipal Notariat. See Hilling, *Die Offiziale*, 110–14; Hashagen, "Zur Characteristik der geistlichen Gerichtsbarkeit," 223–24.

[32] Fournier, *Les Officialités*, xvii; Hashagen, "Zur Characteristik der geistlichen Gerichtsbarkeit," 223–24.

[33] "Oculus et manus episcopi" (Trusen, in *HQL* I:482); Eugen Baumgartner, *Geschichte und Recht des Archidiakonates der oberrheinischen Bistümer mit Einschluss von Mainz und Würzburg* (Stuttgart, 1907), 5, 8–9. See also Jörg Müller-Volbehr, *Die geistliche Gerichte in den Braunschweig-Wolfenbüttelschen Landen* (Göttingen, 1973), 22–31.

deaconeries, as did the diocese of Worms, whereas the larger diocese of Constance maintained ten archdeacons.[34]

As the power of the archdeacons grew over the centuries, they gradually gained independent administrative positions from the bishop.[35] Beginning in the twelfth century, many archdeacons attempted to maintain separate administrative and judicial competencies parallel to those of the bishop. As a result, several archdeacons, including those of the dioceses of Speyer and Worms, began to judge marriage cases themselves or appointed their own Officials to judge these and other ecclesiastical matters.[36]

Relationships between bishops and their archdeacons regarding marriage clearly varied considerably from diocese to diocese. In dioceses such as Worms, Eichstätt, Bamberg, and particularly Constance, shared jurisdiction over marriage matters remained a well-established and undisputed tradition among archdeacons and their Officials well into the sixteenth century.[37] Indeed, in large dioceses such as Constance, this type of judicial delegation was almost unavoidable; even if bishops wanted to maintain exclusive jurisdiction – as in Mainz – the geographical distances alone made it virtually unenforceable.[38]

In other dioceses, however, jurisdictional competition between the

[34] Baumgartner, *Geschichte und Recht des Archidiakonates*, 82, 90–91, 136; Ernst Voltmer, "Von der Bischofsstadt zur Reichstadt: Speyer im Hoch- und Spätmittelalter (10. bis 15, Jahrhundert)," in *GStSp* I:265.

[35] This process generally peaked in the thirteenth century in France and Germany. Fournier, *Les Officialités*, xxv. For Speyer see Stamer II:43; F. X. Glasschröder,, "Das Archidiakonat in der Diözese Speier im Mittelalter," *Archivalische Zeitschrift* n.s.10 (1902), 114–54.

[36] Stamer II:43; Riedner I, 39–42; Fournier, *Les Officialités*, 8, 16; and cf. Baumgartner, *Geschichte und Recht des Archidiakonates*, 95; also Müler-Volbehr, *Die geistliche Gerichte*, 129–36.

[37] Johanek finds no evidence of any struggle whatsoever between the bishops and archdeacons of Eichstätt during the entire period, similar to Wunderli's conclusion for late medieval London, that despite ambiguous boundaries between Church courts, "there is amazingly no hint of strife between archdeacons and the Bishop's (lower) commisary court." Wunderli, *London Church Courts on the Eve of the Reformation*, 16; Johanek, "Geistlicher Richter," 57. See also Heinrich Straub, *Die geistliche Gerichtsbarkeit des Domdekans im Alten Bistum Bamberg von den Anfängen bis zum Ende des 16. Jahrhunderts* (Munich, 1957), 62, 81, 115ff.; Baumgartner, *Geschichte und Recht des Archidiakonates*, 87–88; Harvey, "Nürnberg Marriage Laws," 77.

[38] Since 1310, for instance, the bishops of Mainz forbade archdeacons to handle marriage cases but there appear to have been no attempts to enforce this jurisdiction before the sixteenth century. Georg May, *Die geistliche Gerichtsbarkeit des Erzbischofs von Mainz in Thüringen des späten Mittelalters* (Leipzig, 1956), 9, 154.
Maintaining episcopal jurisdiction vis-à-vis archdeacons was especially difficult in rural and mountainous areas throughout Europe (Fournier, *Les Officialités*, 61) and Hilling even proposes that in northern Germany much of the original purpose in establishing the bishop's *Officialatus* was to resist the archdeacons' expanding administrative and judicial powers (Hilling, *Die Offiziale*, 58).

bishop's Official and the archdeacons was often unremittingly intense.[39] By the end of the thirteenth century in Speyer, not only did each of the four archdeacons maintain his own Official, but the cathedral chapter even demanded a permanent seat on the bishop's *Officialatus* as well as the chapter's own exemption from any such court's jurisdiction.[40] The first condition met with irregular compliance at best from the bishop; the second was rejected outright. Finally, the ongoing jurisdictional dispute between the bishop and archdeacons from 1296 to 1300 was resolved by the archbishop of Mainz, acting as intermediary.[41] A later agreement (1357) established one Official – the bishop's – as the sole judge for all ecclesiastical cases within the diocese of Speyer, but this was never effectively implemented.[42] Thus, two competing Officials, the bishop's and the cathedral chapter's, continued to operate their respective courts into the sixteenth century, and synodal records of the same period indicate continued disregard of the 1357 treaty's provisions on marriage jurisdiction among the other archdeacons as well.

Despite its problems, the marital validity jurisdiction achieved by the bishop's *Officialatus* represented a remarkable degree of centralization by medieval standards. Legal authority in marital property and criminal cases, on the other hand, remained more typically diffuse. Gerald Strauss has described the dispersed court "'system'" of late medieval and early modern Germany as "well fitted to a society of such varied political complexion and such contentious habits . . . [reflecting] the needs and peculiarities of the country's diverse regions and cultures."[43] Like questions of betrothal and vows, marital property and morality cases had a long and deep tradition of familial and local control accord-

---

[39] Cf. examples of Hildesheim, Halberstadt, and Würzburg; J. Krieg, *Der Kampf der Bischöfe gegen die Archidiakone in Bistum Würzburg* (Stuttgart, 1914); Müller-Volbehr, *Die geistliche Gerichte*, 218–22.

[40] Duggan, *Bishop and Chapter*, 60. The sources are not clear as to whether this 1294 demand of the archdeacons implied a return to the collegial system of judges, which had been abolished in Speyer in 1272 according to Riedner (I, 39).

[41] In the final draft of the agreement, the archdeacons pledged obedience to the bishop, and promised not to hinder anyone from going to the bishop's Official or synod or to hinder his visitations, benefices, dispensations, and so forth. Significantly, the oath also precluded any outside secular intervention on the side of the archdeacons: ". . . gegen Urteile und Verfügen des Bischofs nie und nimmer die Hilfe des weltlichen Armes in Anspruch zu nehmen" (Baumgartner, *Geschichte und Recht des Archidiakonates*, 89).

[42] Riedner I, 67–68, and my subsequent discussion in this chapter.

[43] Strauss, *Law*, 120.

ing to customary law. Unlike validity disputes, however, these matters were not generally considered part of the bishop's marriage jurisdiction and were thus generally unaffected by the new diocesan courts of the thirteenth century.[44]

Legal authority at the local level, whether secular or ecclesiastical, represented a hybrid of two distinct judicial traditions. The first was the consensual justice of the village commune (*Gemeinde*) typified by reliance on elders or jurors, oaths, oath helping, and banishment. The other was the unilateral authority of a single representative of the territorial Church or State, either at the district level, involving the bailiff (*Amtman* or *Vogt*) or archdeacon, or at the village level, involving the headmaster (*Schultheiss*), mayor (*Burgermeister*), or pastor. Together, the representatives of the community and of the lord enforced the legal traditions and customs of the locality.

Despite the variety of institutional forms,[45] most local courts were essentially of two kinds. The first kind was a secular jury court, presided over by the local headman, bailiff, or mayor.[46] In the Palatine-Electorate, for example, the local bailiff exercised all criminal jurisdiction, though up until the reign of Ludwig V (1508–44) always in conjunction with the *Landschrieber* (chief financial officer of the *Amt*). In the Prince-Bishopric of Speyer, such cases were also handled by the bishop's bailiffs and occasionally, though improperly, some ecclesiastical authorities as well. This representative of the territorial lord was himself usually drawn from

---

[44] While presumably more of these offenses were being handled by some kind of public authority by the High Middle Ages, evidence of official punishment for adultery before the fifteenth century is rare. The first such recorded case Köhler can locate is in Ulm in 1380 (Kö II:3), and the earliest I have found are from 1382–83 in Nuremburg (Werner Schultheiss, ed., *Satzungsbücher und Satzbuch der Reichstadt Nürnberg im 14. Jahrhundert* [Nuremberg, 1965], nos. 811, 837, 840, 860). A case might be made for the continuing practice of private punishment, especially since both the *Tötungsrecht* and *Rachtbefügnis* of a cuckolded husband are still present as late as the *Bambergensis* (1507) and the *Carolina* (1532), but judging from indirect evidence of public punishment and execution for sexual offenses (cf. the example of Strasbourg; Kö II:359ff.), the issue is most probably one of insufficient documentation from the earlier period rather than lack of official involvement in prosecution and punishment. See also John H. Langbein, *Prosecuting Crime in the Renaissance: England, Germany, France* (Cambridge, Mass., 1974), 144ff.

[45] See Bader, *Rechtsgeschichte*, II:99ff. and 342–63, on the many different forms of the medieval *Dorfgericht* or *iudicum villae*, and Bader I:169ff. on the related *Elter-* or *Zaungerichte*. See also F. Battenberg, "Schöffen, Schöffengericht," in *HRG* 4:1463–69.

[46] On the judicial and police authority of the *Schultheiss* and *Amtman* in medieval Germany, see Richard Schroeder, *Lehrbuch des deutschen Rechtsgeschichte* (Leipzig, 1889), 583ff., and Bader, *Rechtsgeschichte*, II:298ff. On the monopolization of these local offices by the village *meliores, seniores,* or *elteste,* see Bader II:285ff.

the local patriciate, as were without exception the jurors (usually either seven or twelve in number), frequently representing the various guilds. Procedure and punishment were determined by local custom as interpreted by the jurors; the role of the presiding judge remained purely administrative. Although any individual could summon another before the court, most town and some villages maintained permanent informants or accusers (*Rügen;* hence the usual court name of *Rügegerichte*) to watch over the property and morals of the community.[47] Unless specially convened, the courts met infrequently in the country (two or three times yearly) and somewhat more often in cities. Their jurisdiction included all except the largest marital property disputes and all acts of criminal violence, including rape and domestic violence.[48]

Few of the imperial or Swiss cities had any more-developed police or standing judicial organs before the late fourteenth century.[49] Speyer was no exception. In the thirteenth century, criminal and property issues were decided by four members of the town council in monthly rotation (*Monatsrichter*); not until 1380 were standing judges (known as the *Vierrichter* from 1429 on) appointed with one-year terms.[50] The court handled a wide variety of offenses described in the criminal codes issued by the town council, including prostitution, unnatural sexual intercourse (incest, homosexuality, bestiality), and other moral crimes.[51] Cases of concubinage and adultery, though generally considered "crimes against God" and consequently sent to the city's lay synod, were still decided, however, by a jury of the twelve magistrates and punished by the same.

[47] On the structure and general criminal jurisdiction of rural *Rüggerichte* and other lower courts, see Schroeder, *Lehrbuch*, 558f.; W. Sellert, "Rügegericht, Rügeverfahren," in *HRG* 4:1202–5; and Bader *Rechtsgeschichte*, II:309–10, n. 213, for variations. On the use of *Rügegerichte* in maintaining communal norms and mores, see K. S. Kramer, "Rügebräuche," in *HRG* 4:1198; and Bader, *Rechtsgeschichte*, II:300ff., on *Heimburgen*.

[48] Cf. customaries of Pellenz (fourteenth century), Herbizheim (1458), and Trappstädt (1527). Grimm II:22, III:894, VI:626.

[49] Cf. structure and jurisdiction of fourteenth-century municipal courts of Zurich; Susanna Burghartz, *Leib, Ehre, und Gut: Deliquenz in Zürich Ende des 14. Jahrhunderts* (Zurich, 1990), 31ff.

[50] Also known as "die Vier an dem Gericht," in 1436 the court changed back to the rotation system before reverting again to the standing one-year terms in 1443. Harster, *Strafrecht*, 7–13; Alter, in *GStSp* I:384–85, 455.

[51] Speyer criminal code of 1314, with major revisions in 1328 and 1435. Alter, in *GStSp* I:386. This kind of criminal marriage jurisdiction is typical among German cities, though in Speyer, as in Landau, the city court handled only noncapital crimes (*frevel*) and never maintained a professional executioner. Johann-Georg Lehmann, *Urkundliche Geschichte der ehemaliges freien Reichstadt und jetzigen Bundesfestung Landau in der Pfalz* (Landau, 1851), 103ff.; Harster, *Strafrecht*, 7, 13.

This ecclesiastical synod – whether archidiaconal or lay – represented the second kind of local court, concerned mainly with moral issues, including those related to marriage.[52] The language of the thirteenth-century *Schwabenspiegel* typified the vague nature of marriage jurisdiction guaranteed the Church,[53] a tenuous situation well evident in the frequent disputes over borderline and related issues. Inheritance and marital property cases had long been conceded to the secular arm, but in the ambiguous area of "public morality," local ecclesiastical authorities actively competed with secular courts and authorities for jurisdiction.[54] Secular authorities, for instance, generally reserved the right to judge all adulterers caught in the act, as well as to execute all punishments, pecuniary or corporal.[55] By the late Middle Ages, many large cities even employed professional "morals police" (*Sittenpolizei*) with extensive ex officio powers in this area.[56] Ecclesiastical synods, however, continued to predominate in sexual and moral offenses, including adultery, abandonment, concubinage, prostitution, all kinds of fornication, abduction, unnatural sexual acts, and singing obscene or blasphemous songs.[57]

The tradition of calling episcopal and archidiaconal synods to judge moral offenses dated back at least to Carolingian times. Then, the

---

52 Also called *synodus, synodus laicalis/parochialis, Kanzelgericht*, or even simply *Rügegericht*. H.-J. Becker, "Sendgericht," in *HRG* 4:1630; Müller-Volbehr, *Die geistliche Gerichte*, 22–31.

53 The *Schwabenspiegel* on marriage jurisdiction: "diz ist umbe eine ê und daz suln richten geistliche richte, unde so ez an den lip gat, so suln es richten geistliche richter." in Kö I:185. In other marital-related matters, however, such as adultery, Bader also notes considerable confusion or at least inconsistency on questions of jurisdiction (Bader, *Rechtsgeschichte*, II:358–63).

54 In addition to the long-standing Carolinigian tradition in this respect, Alexander III, the chief architect of the medieval Church's marital law, also recognized secular jurisdiction over property disputes. Carlson, "Marriage and the English Reformation," 93ff. See also the example of Bern in Kö I:318.

55 Not until later, in the fifteenth and sixteenth centuries, were diocesan courts strong enough to also claim adultery as part of their proper jurisdiction per se, and even then with mixed results. Fournier, *Les Officialités*, 124. Cf. also Harvey, "Nürnberg Marriage Laws," 115; and my subsequent discussion in this chapter.

56 On the development of municipal criminal jurisdiction in general during this period, cf. Schroeder, *Lehrbuch*, 588ff.; Richard Allen, "Crime and Punishment in Sixteenth-Century Reutlingen," (Ph.D. diss., University of Virginia, 1980), 60ff.; Richard Van Dülmen, *Theater des Schreckens: Gerichtspraxis und Strafrituale in der frühen Neuzeit* (Munich, 1985), 8ff.

57 Cf. 1488 customary juror instruction from Dürkheim (diocese of Speyer), especially questions 15 and 16 on concubinage and adultery. Albert M. Koeniger, *Quellen zur Geschichte der Sendgerichte in Deutschland* (Munich, 1910), 172; also Müller-Volbehr, *Die geistliche Gerichte*, 71–72.
    The notable exception, of course, was any kind of morals or criminal case involving a member of the clergy which, *de ratione personarum*, belonged to the proper jurisdiction of the *Officialatus*. Fournier, *Les Officialités*, 284–86; and on the general jurisdiction of these synods, see Albert M. Koeniger, *Die Sendgerichte in Deutschland*, vol. I (no other volumes published) (Munich, 1907), 130–35; Baumgartner, *Geschichte und Recht des Archidiakonates*, 156.

bishop was obliged to travel at least once a year to the cathedral of his diocese and hold synodal court on all matters within his spiritual jurisdiction. Similar practices developed among the archdeacons, only in this instance with almost universal support and approval of their bishops.[58] The convening of synods appears to have been much more regular in Germany than in France, though probably only once or twice a year rather than the three annual synods called for in the thirteenth-century *Sachsenspiegel.*[59] Unlike many other areas of ecclesiastical jurisdiction, adjudication of sexual and marital offenses appears to have been unaffected by the introduction of the *Officialatus* in the thirteenth century.[60] Indeed, if anything, the expansion of the bishop's judicial powers only reinforced the need for such local ecclesiastical courts to screen out lesser matters.

The remarkable durability of the lay synod is perhaps best accounted for by its deft meshing of ecclesiastical and local secular authority, even in its combination of clerical and lay personnel. In most instances, both the jurors or informants (called *Kirchengeschwörne*, or churchwardens) were the same as those of the local secular court.[61] The annual lay synod of the city of Speyer, for example, consisted of a jury of the twelve city councillors (here presided over by the cathedral provost or his Official), judging cases brought to the court by forty-five oath holders – thirty-three guild members, and twelve pastors from the city's parishes.[62] In fact, except for the presiding clerical judge and "ecclesiastical" nature of the litigation, these so-called "lay synods" were virtually indistinguishable from local secular courts, even convening on the same

---

58 From the eighth to eleventh centuries, this power was mandated to the archdeacons by the bishop, but from the end of this period until the Council of Trent, most archdeacons maintained their own proper jurisdiction in this area. Koeniger, *Die Sendgerichte*; Riedner I, 4–6; and Baumgartner, *Geschichte und Recht des Archidiakonates*, 147.

59 Müller-Volbehr finds evidence of two yearly meetings in the dioceses of Halberstadt, Paderborn, Münster, and Verden, but believes that the yearly synods of Speyer were probably typical of most German dioceses (*Die geistliche Gerichte*, 89). See also Baumgartner, *Geschichte und Recht des Archidiakonates*, 147–55; Stamer II:262ff. Fournier, *Les Officialités*, 285–86; Harster, 179; Schroeder, *Lehrbuch*, 571–73.

60 Riedner (I, 101) maintains that throughout the thirteenth century in the diocese of Speyer, the majority of "spiritual" crimes, including marital ones, continued to be judged and punished by the synods rather than the *Officialatus*.

61 Bader, *Rechtsgeschichte*, II:184–95, 207ff. Note, however, the major exception to this tendency in many eastern German dioceses (Müller-Volbehr, *Die geistliche Gerichte*, 98, 122–28).

62 Walther Kohl, "Das Laiensendgericht in der mittelalterlichen Stadt Speyer" (J.D. diss. [masch.], Mainz, 1951), especially 1–7, on the organization and workings of the synod; also Stamer II:44, 261–62; Harster, 15–16.

traditional Germanic day of assembly (*Dingtag*).[63] Like their secular counterparts, these ecclesiastical *Rügegerichte* decided cases by traditional Germanic procedure, not by Canon law. Thus, accusation by official informants, collegial judges or jurors, oath helping, and other customs characterized both kinds of local courts. Moreover, this joint jurisdiction of secular and ecclesiastical authorities in matters considered public morality continued into the sixteenth century.[64]

The influence of medieval territorial rulers – secular or ecclesiastical – thus remained extremely restricted in most legal and judicial matters. Certainly the creation of diocesan courts in the thirteenth century significantly improved the bishop's control of marital validity jurisdiction, but even here, as we have seen, the authority of locally based archdeacons represented a serious rival. Leaders at the village or municipal level exerted even more direct influence over the resolution of most legal disputes, including marital property and criminal cases. Most important, these local authorities, whether bailiff or pastor, were themselves usually drawn from the community they served.[65] Both their legal standards and procedures, as reflected in ecclesiastical as well as secular courts, remained invariably customary in nature. The legal involvement of their respective lords was more at the level of visible authority and domination than direct legislative or judicial influence. Thus, though the legal structures and procedures of these local institutions remained crude and

---

63 The term "lay synod," in fact, is used mainly to distinguish such lower courts from those synods that dealt exclusively with clerical cases. In many cases, the division between lay and clerical synods was roughly contemporary with the introduction of the *Officialatus*. Up until the thirteenth century, the episcopal synod of the diocese of Speyer, for instance, had been presided over by a mixture of laymen and clergy, and dealt with a variety of ecclesiastical issues. By the early fifteenth century, however, its jurors had become exclusively clerical, as had, to a large degree, its agenda. See Franz Haffner, *Die kirchlichen Reformbemühungen des Speyerer Bischofs Matthias von Rammung in vortridentinischer Zeit (1464–78)* (Speyer, 1961), 198–99, and Stamer II:261–63 on some continuing criminal marriage litigation, mainly concerning adultery, in the episcopal synod.

64 Cf. 1492 synodal ordinance of Speyer (StAS 369/43) discussed in detail in Kohl, "Das Laiensendgericht," 23ff., and the continuing jurisdiction of the court on matters of sexual morality until the controversy of 1556; also synodal ordinances of Plarig (1512) and Rokenberg (1505), fairly typical representations of the substance of such customaries (Grimm IV:440–41, 611–14). For a discussion of the highly ritualized convening procedures of such synods, see Müller-Volbehr, *Die geistliche Gerichte*, 90ff.

Cf. also use in some cities, such as Nuremberg, of secular *Schöffenämte* in place of lay synods, though identical in structure, personnel, and procedure with the latter. Harvey, "Nürnberg Marriage Laws," 121–31. Secular–ecclesiastical distinctions were further obscured by the active role of Speyer's magistrates in enforcing verdicts of the lay synod in criminal marriage matters (e.g., the 1376 expulsion of four citizens' concubines from the city; Harster, 187–90).

65 Bader, *Rechtsgeschichte*, II:98, 211, 299ff.

inefficient compared with those of diocesan courts, their grasp on public morality and property matters was firm, even from within such "ecclesiastical" institutions as the lay synod. Until more effective territorial control was sought, let alone achieved, legal authority in most issues concerning marriage would remain defined by this type of local particularism and communal control.

Expansion of state bureaucracies and jurisdictions

The struggle over marriage jurisdiction in Germany from the early fifteenth century on is a story of gradual and apparently purposeful judicial expansion by a variety of secular authorities, both at the territorial and the municipal level. Most legal authority remained locally concentrated, but secular rulers were able to make some inroads through their chosen representatives, the *Amtleute* and *Schultheisse* in territorial states, and municipal criminal courts in imperial and Swiss cities. Most episcopal jurisdictions, on the other hand, while still preserving exclusive jurisdiction over marital validity disputes, declined in integrity, particularly in other marriage-related and "spiritual" matters.

Why did territorial princes and city-states continue to expand and solidify their jurisdictions while most bishops were barely able to preserve theirs? More to the focus of our study, why did these otherwise aggressive secular polities apparently draw the line at ecclesiastical jurisdiction over marriage? The answer to both questions lies in the very nature of late medieval and early modern legal and judicial hegemony.

Contrary to the ambitious absolutist designs of a later era, "state-building" during the fifteenth and sixteenth centuries was an extremely gradual and reactive process. Most successful judicial expansion, in fact, depended on the needs and preferences of litigants as much as those of secular authorities. The limited authority and power of early modern princes, as Thomas Robisheaux has remarked,

> followed not simply from the poorly developed structures of princely authority and domination in the countryside, but also from the fact that power rested, to a degree still not fully understood, on villagers sharing in the process of their domination.[66]

Territorial rulers, consequently, encouraged but usually did not require the choice of their courts and officials over ecclesiastical rivals. Except for

[66] Robisheaux, *Rural Society*, 10.

a handful of more aggressive and developed Swiss and imperial cities, most secular authorities thus avoided direct confrontation with Church courts over a marital jurisdiction they were hardly capable of assuming.

Not that secular rulers were not consciously seeking to expand their own legal roles – quite the contrary. Judicial hegemony was viewed by medieval and early modern rulers as a key measure of political domination, or *Herrschaft*.[67] Jurisdictional rivalry, consequently, remained a constant feature of the period, pitting all judicial institutions, secular and ecclesiastical, against each other in almost all areas of law. In marital jurisdiction, as in all litigation, success was defined by two criteria: legislative consolidation, or codification; and jurisdictional consolidation and preservation. Comparison of secular and ecclesiastical accomplishments in these two areas provides the best illustration of their diverging fortunes in marital jurisdiction during this period.

The single most important legal development for marriage during the Middle Ages was undoubtedly the codification and introduction of Canon law in western Europe. After the establishment of ecclesiastical courts and jurisdiction during the thirteenth century, all marital validity disputes fell under the direct governance of Canon law and the indirect influence of its Roman components. How deeply either Canon or Roman law penetrated common perception and practice, however, is a question less easily resolved,[68] especially since their main opponent was

---

[67] On the concept of *Herrschaft*, and especially *Gerichtsherrschaft*, see Dietrich Hilger, "Herrschaft," in *Geschichtliche Grundbegriffe: Historisches Lexikon zur politisch-sozialen Sprache in Deutschland*, ed. Otto Brunner et al. (Stuttgart, 1982), 3:1–102; D. Willoweit, "Die Entwicklung und Verwaltung der spätmittelalterlichen Landesherrschaft," in *Deutsche Verwaltungsgeschichte*, ed. Kurt Jeserich et al., vol. I (Stuttgart, 1983), 66ff.; David Sabean, *Power in the Blood: Popular Culture and Village Discourse in Early Modern Germany* (Cambridge, 1984), 20–28; Volker Press, "Herrschaft, Landschaft und 'Gemeiner Mann' in Oberdeutschland vom 15. bis zum 19. Jahrhundert," *Zeitschrift für die Geschichte des Oberrheins* 123 (1975), 169–214; and bibliographies in Heinrich Mitteis and Heinz Lieberich, eds., *Deutsche Rechtsgeschichte*, 18th ed. (Munich, 1988), 259–62, and Robisheaux, *Rural Society*, 274ff.

[68] The issue of when and to what degree Canon and Roman legal concepts and procedures were absorbed into German society is a well-debated one, with an immense bibliography. The most recent and comprehensive synthesis of the huge mass of literature on "the reception" of Roman law is in a bibliographical series edited by Helmut Coing: *Handbuch der Quellen und Literatur der neueren europäischen Privatrechtsgeschichte*, vol. I: *Mittelalter: 1100–1500* (Munich, 1973); vol. II: *Neurere Zeit: 1500–1800*, pt. 1, *Wissenschaft* (Munich, 1977); and pt. 2, *Gesetzgebung und Rechtsprechung* (Munich, 1976). See especially H. Coing, "Die Juristische Fakultät und Ihr Lehrprogram," I:25–35, and his bibliography on the spread of Roman law; also Alfred Söllner, "Die Literatur zum gemeinen und partikularen Recht in Deutschland, Österreich, den Niederlanden und der Schweiz, II, pt. 1:501–614; and Mitteis, *Deutsche Rechtsgeschichte*, 321–

customary, and therefore usually unwritten, law. Even later written municipal and territorial codifications, although obviously at least inspired by Roman and canonical models, continued to proclaim customary, rather than canonical, legal principles and definitions regarding marriage. Some understanding, then, of these deeply rooted traditional marriage controls is obviously necessary before the impact and effectiveness of Canon law and later secular codifications can be assessed.

The concept of a common *ius germanicum*, written or unwritten, is, as Helmut Coing has pointed out, largely an invention of eighteenth-century scholarship.[69] Throughout the Middle Ages there were probably as many different local customs (*consuetudines particularum*) governing betrothal and especially marriage property in Germany as there were villages. As late as the fifteenth century, for instance, subjects of the Elector of the Palatinate continued to observe different dowry laws on either side of the Rhine.[70] The substance of these medieval customary marriage laws remains largely a matter of inference and reconstruction, usually based on much later written versions. In Germany, for instance, the practice of recording previously oral custom (according to the local jurors) peaked everywhere west of the Elbe during the fifteenth and sixteenth centuries. The subject of these customaries, or *Weistümer*,[71]

---

31. Among the most important works on the subject: Georg von Below, *Die Ursachen der Rezeption des römischen Rechts in Deutschland* (Munich, 1905; reprint: Aalen, 1964); Helmut Coing, *Die Rezeption des römischen Rechts in Frankfurt am Main* (Frankfurt a.M., 1962); W. Trusen, *Anfänge des gelehrten Rechts in Deutschland* (Wiesbaden, 1962); Wolfgang Kunkel, "Das römische Recht am Vorabend der Rezeption," *Studi Koschaker* 1 (Milan, 1964), 1ff.; and Strauss, *Law*.

For a series of lectures on the Palatinate, see O. Karlowa, *Über die Reception des römischen Rechts in Deutschland, mit besondern Rücksicht auf der Churpfalz* (Heidelberg, 1878).

69 Even in speaking only of general regional customs (*consuetudines generalarum*), it is impossible to establish common acceptance or application of such customs. Cf. Coing, *Europäisches Privatrecht* 106ff., 114.

70 Coing, *Europäisches Privatrecht* 112; Cohn, *The Government of the Rhine Palatinate*, 121.

71 The origins of *Weistümer* (also called *Oeffnungen, Sprachen*, and, in Saxony, *Ordele*) can be traced back to the medieval practice of *Landfrieden*, or territorial peace pacts, with the first recorded imperial example that of Henry IV in 1103. About the same time several local authorities convened special meetings (*Weisungen*) to establish jurisdictional boundaries and record other oral customs (Bader, *Rechtsgeschichte*, II:335ff.). See the pioneering collection of Jacob Grimm ed., *Weisthümer*, 7 vols. (Göttingen, 1840–78; reprint: 1957); and the more recent work, Peter Blickle, ed. *Deutsche ländliche Rechtsquellen; Probleme und Wege der Weistumsforschung* (Stuttgart, 1977). See also Gerhard Köbler, *Das Recht im frühen Mittelalter. Untersuchungen zu Herkunft und Inhalt frühmittelalterlicher Rechtsbegriffe im deutschen Sprachgebiet* (Cologne, 1971); D. Werkmüller, *Über Aufkommen und Verbreitung der Weistümer nach der Sammlung von Jacob Grimm* (Berlin, 1972); G. Buchola, "Landrechtsbücher," in *HRG* 2:1536; and the bibliography in Mitteis and Lieberich, *Deutsche Rechtsgeschichte*, 224-28, 299–300.

varied considerably, but usually concerned tithes, seigneurial rights, jurisdictional boundaries, and customs regarding marital property and inheritance. Punishment in criminal marital questions such as adultery were also occasionally mentioned, but more frequently were left to the few existing criminal codes of the period, particularly the *Sachsenspiegel* (1221–24; most influential in northern Germany and parts of Poland and Bohemia) and the *Schwabenspiegel* (1275–76; most authoritative in the south, including the Palatinate).[72]

The other kind of secular law was statutory, which by its very nature was written and innovative. Statutory laws could be issued by territorial rulers, such as the Elector of the Palatinate or Prince-Bishop of Speyer, as well as by cities, such as the imperial city of Speyer. In principle, they did not compete with or invalidate either Canon or customary law but were intended as specific supplements along the same lines. Swiss and imperial cities were especially active in this type of legislation[73] but surviving sources of this nature are unfortunately scarce before the fifteenth century, particulary for statutes touching on marriage. The only relevant ordinances for the city of Speyer, for instance, are those establishing a permanent criminal court in the thirteenth century and subsequent criminal codes (including adultery punishments) for the court in 1314 and 1328.[74]

Before the advent of ecclesiastical jurisdiction over marriage, local custom – together with occasional supplementary written statutes – encompassed all aspects of marriage practice and control, from betrothal

For examplary *Weistümer* of the Palatinate, see the incomplete W. Weizsäcker, *Pfälzische Weistümer* (Speyer, 1957–68); also F. Zimmermann, *Die Weistümer und der Ausbau der Landeshoheit in der Kurpfalz* (Berlin, 1937).

72 For the most authoritative versions, see the editions of the *Monumenta Germaniae Historica, Fontes Iuris Germanici Antiqui, Nova Series*, ed. Karl August Eckhardt, including the *Sachsenspiegel* (no. 1; Munich, 1933, reprint: 1973); and *Schwabenspiegel* (nos. 4–6; Munich, 1960–64). In addition to the most influential *Sachsenspiegel* were the supplementary *Richtsteig* and *Sächsische Weichbild*, as well as the less influential *Deutschenspiegel* of Augsburg (1274–75). The *Schwabenspiegel*, was not so called until much later (1609), and was simply referred to as the *Kaiserrecht*, with the appearance of the fourteenth-century *Frankenspiegel* amended to the *großen Kaiserrecht* to distinguish it from the newcomer. Otto Stobbe, *Geschichte der Deutschen Rechtsquellen* (1860; reprint: 1965), I:288-355; A. Wolf, "Die Gesetzgebung der entstehen den Territorialstaaten Römisch-deutsches Reich," in *HQL*, II:588-91; Schroeder, *Lehrbuch*, 620-31.

73 Cf. seven articles on weddings and *Eheschließung* formalities in two fourteenth-century legal codifications of Zurich (Burghartz, *Leib, Ehre, Gut*, 41ff., esp. 46–47).

74 Cf. 67 articles of Speyer's 1328 criminal code (especially on adultery and parental consent) cited in Georg Christoph Lehmann, *Chronica Der Freyen Reichstadt Speier . . .*, expanded by J. M. Fuchs, (Frankfurt, 1711), 845; Mone, "Beiträge zur Geschichte des Eherechts," 62ff.; Harster, *Strafrecht*, 7–10; Voltmer, in *GStSp* I:324ff; Alter, in *GStSp* I:386. On medieval municipal law in general, see Schroeder, *Lehrbuch*, 635–51.

and dowry to remarriage of widow(er)s. Preserving such traditional controls after the thirteenth century involved some conflicts, at least in principle, with the new, ruling Canon law. Chief among these was Canon law's recognition of the marrying couple's consent alone as requisite to a valid marriage. Although never directly challenged by secular authorities, the canonical definition of a "free and individual" act was consistently interpreted and defined by customary and statutory laws upholding this traditional familial and seigneurial control through fines and other punishments. Statutes and ordinances requiring parental approval for "minors" probably represent the oldest written laws issued by German secular rulers and magistrates for marriage. They differed only in the age of independence for a child and the punishment for disobedience, the latter spanning from large fines to disinheritance to banishment. Seigneurial requirements of consent, though likewise ubiquitous, were often dispensable with a fine.[75]

The complaints of sixteenth-century marriage reformers notwithstanding, such inconsistencies between customary and Canon law did not pose serious challenges to ecclesiastical authority over marital validity. Rather, the much greater threat to local marriage customs during the late Middle Ages came from municipal and territorial authorities and the increasing volume of legislation on issues of marital property and criminal offenses. Clearly for these governmental leaders, the inconsistency and arbitrariness of various local customs on dowries and the joining of property represented serious obstacles to their ambitions of consolidation and even aggrandizement of their own legal hegemony. Inspired by traditional regional codes such as the *Sachsenspiegel* and, more significant, by the "law of the Empire" (as the Roman law of the German emperors was known), territorial and municipal rulers from the fifteenth century on issued wave upon wave of criminal codes and territorial ordinances (*Landesordnungen*) covering just such questions.[76]

[75] See my discussion in Chapter 4.
[76] The spread of codification and standardization in this area of marriage law was certainly a major concern of territorial rulers during the fifteenth and sixteenth centuries, and the influence of regional Germanic codes such as the *Sachsenspiegel* (twenty-two editions from 1482–1599) and more significantly the "law of the Empire" (Roman law as reintroduced by the Holy Roman Emperors) was evident throughout, especially in southern and western Germany. See Romanized codes in Franz Beyerle, gen. ed., *Quellen zur neueren deutschen Privatrechtsgeschichte*, vol. I: *Landrechte*, ed. W. Kunkel (Weimar, 1935).
   On fifteenth-century codification, see Fritz Hartung, *Deutsche Verfassungsgeschichte vom 15. Jahrhundert bis zur Gegenwart*, 7th ed. (Stuttgart, 1959), 73–74; Coing, *Europäisches Privatrecht*,

The weakness of fifteenth-century governmental bureaucracies, however, combined with the general legal conservatism among rulers and ruled resulted in few changes where marriage was concerned. In questions of marital property, the path of least resistance was territorial generalization of local customs. In 1467, for instance, the Palatine Elector inquired of the town council of Heidelberg its customs for inheritance of marriage property without a marriage contract, then issued the council's response as an ordinance for the town of Mockmühl.[77] By contrast, more Romanized and "foreign" codifications, such as the inheritance laws of Elector Friedrich I for the Palatinate in 1472 and 1484, and of Speyer's Prince-Bishop Ludwig I in 1486, were – as the rulers themselves admitted – farther from popular practice and conceptions and thus more difficult to install and enforce.[78] Municipal codifications were even more consistently resistant of any "innovations" whatsoever of Roman law, particularly the alien concept of separate marital goods.[79]

The same legal inertia was even more evident in the two kinds of "morals" (*Sitten*) legislation dealing with marital issues during this period: those covering minor, or sumptuary, restrictions and those dealing with major criminal marital offenses, such as adultery, concubinage, and prostitution. Statutes and ordinances of the first variety often combined wedding ordinances with other prohibitions on swearing, excessive drinking, and overly luxurious clothing. Their contents included restrictions on the number of wedding guests permitted, which persons could not be invited (e.g., prostitutes or foreigners), what the guests and married

---

115; Stobbe, *Deutsche Rechtsquellen* II:207–78, 336ff.; P. Caroni, "Kodifikation," in *HRG* 2:907ff.; A. Laufs and K. P. Schroeder, "Landrecht," in *HRG* 2:1527ff.; and Strauss, *Law*, 76ff.

77 Cohn, *The Government of the Rhine Palatinate*, 177. This appears to have been a common method of customary consolidation. Cf. Rolf-Dieter Hess, *Familien- und Erbrecht im württembergischen Landrecht von 1555* (Stuttgart, 1968), 6–7.

78 Cohn, *The Government of the Rhine Palatinate*, 245; *Sammlung* 10; and cf. 1484 inheritance ordinance of the Elector, introducing *ius representaionis*, in Philipp W. L. Flad, *Specimen anecdoton iuris Palatini de successione ab intestato ante statutum Palatinum* (Heidelberg, 1743), 12–13. See Hess, *Familien- und Erbrecht*, 11–18, on similar resistance in Württemberg.

79 Communal marriage property (*Gütergemeinschaft*) was the norm throughout most of medieval Germany, Cf. marriage codes of Ulm (1382, 1423, 1463) (Kö II:4.) and my discussion in Chapter 4.
  For examples of Roman "infiltration" of municipal legislation, see the annotated versions of various legal "Reformations," published in the *Arbeiten zur Rechts- und Sprachwissenschaft* series, ed. Gerhard Köbler, including Nuremberg (no. 25; 1984), Worms (no. 27; 1985), and Freiburg im Breisgau (no. 28; 1985). See also Roderick Stinzing, *Geschichte der populären Literatur des römisch-kanonischen Rechts in Deutschland am Ende des 15. und Anfang des 16. Jahrhunderts* (Leipzig, 1867; reprint: Aalen, 1959), xvii–lii, on the role of "*halbgelehrten*" such as *Stadtschreiber* in the promulgation of Roman legal concepts during this period.

couple could wear, the value of presents to the couple, the time and place of the wedding feast, how much food, drink, and music were to be allowed.[80] Such "police" (*Polizei*) ordinances were widespread, especially in the cities, from the late fourteenth century on, as was secular legislation on major marital offenses such as adultery, concubinage, and prostitution. In almost every instance, however, both procedure and punishment remained highly traditional.[81] The Palatinate was typical in this respect, witnessing several territorial and municipal statutes completely in keeping with the criminal articles of the *Sachsen-* and *Schwabenspiegel*.[82]

This is not to suggest that Roman law had no direct influence whatsoever on German criminal marriage laws during this period. By the mid-fifteenth century, every German university not only provided classes in Roman law but maintained a full faculty on the subject.[83] Such instruction obviously had a tremendous impact on the same jurists who helped shape the form and substance of imperial, territorial, and even municipal criminal law throughout the fifteenth and early sixteenth centuries. As in property questions, many municipal and territorial leaders

[80] See for instance, the wedding ordinances of Zurich (1304); Nuremberg (1310, 1320, 1350, 1388); Ulm (fourteenth century); Strasbourg (1322, 1453); Bern (1389); Eßlingen (1392); Constance (1444); Isny (1452, 1461, 1480, 1485); Memmingen (1474, 1478). Burghartz, *Leib, Ehre, Gut* 234; Schultheiss, *Satzungsbücher*, 64, 66, 69, 78, 149, 150, 184, 192, 215, 236, 257–60; Kö I:309; II:3, 92, 124, 144–45, 206–7, 363; my comments in Chapter 4 on Protestant and Catholic continuation of such laws.

[81] The term *polizei* was first used in German law during 1476–95. Cf. the imperial city of Landau's ordinances of 1465 and 1487, with similar marriage sumptuary laws in the Palatine-Electorate in 1465 and 1475, and the Prince-Bishopric of Speyer in 1493. Lehmann, *Landau in der Pfalz* 103–4. Friedrich I first introduced sumptuary laws (including against concubinage) in Heidelberg and the *Amt* of Neustadt in 1465, before issuing the same ordinances for all of the Palatinate in 1475 (Cohn, *The Government of the Rhine Palatinate*, 244). The 1493 wedding ordinance of the Bishop Ludwig of Speyer also contained the traditional prohibitions (*Sammlung* 11). See also G. K. Schmelzeisen, "Polizeiordnungen," in *HRG* 3:1803–5; H. Meier, "Polizei," in *HRG* 3:1800–3.

[82] Cf. punishments of adultery, prostitution, and concubinage in Speyer municipal criminal codes of 1328 and 1435 (Franz Joseph Mone, "Beiträge zur Geschichte des Eherechts vom 13.–15. Jahrhundert (in Bayern, Hessen, Badden, Elsass, und der Schweiz)," *Zeitschrift für die Geschichte des Oberrheins* 19 [1866], 62ff.; Harster, *Strafrecht*, 191ff.) and local *Weistümer* in Prince-Bishopric and Palatine-Electorate (my Chapter 5).

[83] Fully trained jurists during this period were expected to hold degrees in both (JUD: *iuris utriusque doctor*). Subsequent application by legally trained city magistrates and territorial chancellors and advisors varied by location but overall was also quite significant, especially in criminal law and procedure, though, as we shall see, less so in criminal matters related to marriage. Otto Kimminich, *Deutsche Verfassungsgeschichte* (Frankfurt, 1970), 193–94; Coing, *Europäisches Privatrecht*, 12ff.; Strauss, *Law* 67ff., 123, 147ff. Also see Stobbe, *Deutsche Rechtsquellen*, II:9–142; H. Coing, "Die juristische Fakultät und ihr Lehrprogram," in *HQL* I:39–128 (1100–1500); II:3–102 (1500–1800); and Alfred Söllner, "Die Literatur zum gemeinen und partikularen Recht in Deutschland, Österreich, den Niederlanden und der Schweiz," in *HQL* I:501–614.

realized the great value of Roman law as an instrument of statebuilding in the fifteenth century,[84] and were able to incorporate some Roman precepts in their own criminal legislation.

Increased use throughout Germany, for instance, of the canonical inquisitorial process in favor of the traditional Germanic accusatorial and oath-helper procedure provides one obvious example of such influence. Despite some earlier historians' argument for the relatively late or independent development of the inquisitorial process in Germany, John Langbein has convincingly demonstrated that the new procedure's fifteenth-century spread was directly attributable to the influence of Church courts and Canon law.[85] Such influence occasionally also extended to other aspects of procedure, such as the equal right of a woman to bring suit for adultery, mentioned in both the *Bambergensis* (1507) and the later *Carolina* (1532).[86]

Still, there is too much evidence to the contrary to support the claim

84 Helmut Coing, *Römisches Recht in Deutschland* (Milan, 1964), especially 30–31; Walter Ulmann, *Medieval Foundations of Renaissance Humanism* (London, 1977), 37; Joseph R. Strayer, *Medieval Statecraft and the Perspectives of History* (Princeton, 1971), especially 251ff.; Perry Anderson, *Lineages of the Absolutist State* (London, 1974), 22ff.; Dietmar Willoweit, *Rechtsgrundlagen der Territorialgewalt. Landesobrigkeit, Herrschaftsrechte und Territorium in der Rechtswissenschaft der Neuzeit* (Cologne, 1975).

85 Langbein argues that the first major inquisitorial statutes in Germany – the *Maximilianischen Halgerichtsordnungen* (1499, 1506), *Wormser Reformatio* (1498), *Bambergensis* (1507), and ultimately the *Carolina* (1532) – were actually the culmination of much inquisitorial procedure already in practice throughout Germany, already evident by the mid-fifteenth century. Any thesis advocating the sudden reception of Roman law in Germany with these ordinances is thus highly questionable, particularly the arguments of Eberhard Schmidt (*Inquisitionsprozess und Rezeption. Studien zur Geschichte des Strafverfahrens in Deutschland vom 13. bis 16. Jahrhundert* [Leipzig, 1940]) that the inquisitorial procedure developed independently in Germany well before this time (even though Langbein does concede some routine use of the inquisitorial method as early as the thirteenth century). Rather, very gradual replacement of the traditional accusatorial and "oath-helper" procedure during these centuries appears the most likely scenario, generally stemming from, as Langbein emphasizes, the growing influence of lawyers and magistrates trained in Canon and Roman laws. Langbein, *Prosecuting Crime in the Renaissance*, 129ff. especially 138, 144–53, 158–209; also cf. bibliography in Mitteis and Lieberich, *Deutsche Rechtsgeschichte*, 304ff.

86 On the general influence of imperial criminal ordinances, see Josef Segall, *Geschichte und Strafrecht der Reichspolizeiordnungen von 1530, 1548, und 1577* (Breslau, 1914); and Langbein, *Prosecuting Crime in the Renaissance*, 158ff. On the effect of imperial codes on adultery in particular see Lieberwirth, "Ehebruch," in *HRG* 1:832ff.; Harvey, "Nürnberg Marriage Laws," 116–122, 189; and my discussion in Chapter 5.

For a discussion of the influence of the 1495 *Reichskammergerichtsordnung* on the Elector of the Palatinate's *Hofgerictsordnung* (1513), see Klaus Bender, "Die Hofgerichtsordnung Kurfüst Philipps für die Pfalgrafschaft bei Rhein" (Ph.D. diss., Mainz, 1967); and Press, *Calvinismus und Territorialstaat*, 17ff. Cf. Hieronymous Nopp, *Geschichte der Stadt und ehemaligen Reichsfestung Philippsburg* (Speyer, 1881), 81ff., on similar influence of Roman/canonical procedure on the prince-bishop of Speyer's *Hofgericht*.

that Roman law lost its outsider status during this period through the influence of the *Officialatus* and universities.[87] Resentment of "foreigners" (in most cases, actually German lawyers who had studied in foreign universities) and their foreign legal concepts ran high throughout the fifteenth and early sixteenth centuries, usually stemming from "tenacious localism" regarding customary laws.[88] Matters considered part of public morality were especially subject to such traditional attitudes and controls, and thus even more resistant to any "foreign" intrusions.[89] Certainly some canonical concepts, such as unrestricted vows of present consent between the couple alone as the sole basis for a valid marriage, were slow to penetrate local custom if at all. The equal legal status of the woman also appears to have been a "foreign" idea with little general support. Although it is true, for instance, that beginning late in the fourteenth century husbands could also be punished for adultery (a break with all German customs), the punishment was still usually much milder than that for married women.[90]

Overall, proponents of Roman and Canon laws during this period had to be satisfied with a foothold in ecclesiastical courts and a gradual and largely indirect influence on the courts' secular counterparts in related marital legislation. Most secular authorities appreciated the utilitarian advantages of such a codification, but the substance of the same and its

---

[87] Riedner I, 106–7; Adolf Laufs, *Rechtsentwicklungen in Deutschland*, 3rd ed. (Berlin, 1984), 41–69.

[88] Gerald Strauss stresses that in the late medieval and early modern frame of reference, "a person from a neighboring territory or city – especially one of the imperial cities – was an outsider" and "it was a man's roots in a place that made him a native," thus also subject to his locality's many customs. Strauss, *Law*, 28–29.

[89] Many German historians of the nineteenth century echoed their ancestors' resentment and even condemnation of the "foreign" Roman law as injurious to the moral and social fiber of the German people. One of the most prominent of these, Friedrich Karl von Savigny, set the tone of the debate by contrasting the natural customary legal system of the *Volk*, "originating in common morality and belief . . . , made by inner, anonymously active forces," with the artificial, politically motivated "academic jurisprudence [at the service of] the arbitrary power of a lawgiver." See *Vom Beruf unserer Zeit Für Gesetzgebung und Rechtswissenschaft* (Heidelberg, 1814), 14, cited in Strauss, *Law*, 57. For more on the nineteenth-century scholarly debate, see H. Kiefner, "Rezeption (privatrechtlich)," in *HRG* 4:982, and M. Stolleis, "Rezeption (Öffentlichrechtlich)," in *HRG* 4:984–91.

[90] In all early Indo-Germanic law, adultery was defined as sexual intercourse of a married woman with a man other than her husband. The reverse was not punished before the eighth century in Italy and the late fourteenth century in some German cities. On the comparative punishment of adultery for men and women, see Harster, 187ff. (Speyer), and Harvey, "Nürnberg Marriage Laws," 116 (Nuremberg); and my comments in Chapter 5. On the general legal status of women in Canon law versus medieval secular laws, see Coing, *Europäisches Privatrecht*, 26; Lieberwirth, "Ehebruch," in *HRG* 1:836–37.

definition of marriage remained foreign concepts in a society still ruled by the ancient and largely unwritten customs of its ancestors.

With a comprehensive legal code (Canon law) and a highly organized central court (the *Officialatus*), the fifteenth-century bishop appears to have held a considerable advantage over all jurisdictional rivals, secular or ecclesiastical. Once again, however, the independent officialties and synodal courts of his archdeacons often thwarted all episcopal ambitions of centralized authority. Even in those dioceses where the bishops had successfully reached agreements with the archdeacons and their chapters on "spiritual" jurisdiction, compliance was often another matter. The cathedral chapter in Speyer, for instance, despite fourteenth-century agreements to the contrary, continued to operate a rival standing *Officialatus* within the same city as the bishop's throughout this entire period. Repeated synodal admonitions against "rural deacons and courts as well as parish priests, rectors, and vicars . . . hearing matrimonial or other cases without proper authority" suggest similar abuses throughout the diocese.[91]

In addition to deciding marital validity cases and granting dispensations, the cathedral provost or his Official continued to preside over the city's lay synod, handing out punishments in criminal marriage matters as well.[92] By 1458 the active voluntary jurisdiction of the cathedral provost's *Officialatus* had become so extensive as to warrant a mandate from Emperor Friedrich III on behalf of the city of Speyer not to

---

91 The strict admonition of Bishop Rabanus in the Fall Synod of 1397 is typical: "Item prohibemus omnibus ruralibus Decanis & Camerariis nec non Ecclesiarum parochialium Rectoribus plebanis & vicariis, ne causas matrimoniales vel alias quarum cognicio ad eos non pertinet auctoritate propria audiant nisi ab illis, ad quorum Jurisdictionem seu cognicionem & Decisionem pertinent specialiter eis sint commisse decernenter injustos & inanes processus aliter habitos & habendos coram eis, volumus enim, ut cause omnes ad examen illorum ad quos earum cognicio & Decisio pertinet, remittantur Clandestina quoque matrimonia sub pena Excommunicacionis fieri prohibemus & per plebanos inhiberi sub eadem pena mandamus & precipimus ut fiant in facie Ecclesie publice juxta morem . . ." (*Collectio* I:5). See also episcopal synods of 1398 (Rabanus), 1464 and 1465 (Mathias), 1478 (Ludwig), 1508 and 1509 (Philip). *Collectio* I:9–10, 71–73; II:6, 149–50.
92 Such disciplinary powers in marriage were not unusual and, as noted previously, even traditional for archdeacons. Cf. example of Basel (Constance) Kö I:232, among others.
  It should be emphasized, though, that all verdicts were still those of the traditional lay jury of twelve (in Speyer the twelve city councillors) and merely pronounced by the authority of the presiding archdeacon or his Official. The procedure in other chapters of the diocese of Speyer is less clear, but presumably also customary in nature. Cf. 1506 adultery sentence by the Official of the cathedral provost in the lay synod (GLA 67/417, 172 ʳ⁻ᵛ; Glasschröder, "Das Archidiakonat in der Diözese Speier," 127); Stamer II:262; Baumgartner, *Geschichte und Recht des Archidiakonates*, 210.

infringe on the city's authority in secular matters.[93] Accusations of judicial encroachment by both sides in criminal marriage matters, with its vaguely defined boundaries, were even more frequent.

Although such judicial power sharing was frequently tolerated or even actively sought in some dioceses such as Worms and Eichstätt, the bishops of Speyer offered fervent – albeit sporadic – resistance. Unfortunately, their fifteenth-century campaigns to regain judicial supremacy in marital and all other areas of ecclesiastical jurisdiction failed miserably. The position of vicar-general, for instance, initially created to reinforce episcopal jurisdiction, quickly became still another independent rival for legal hegemony, even competing with the bishop's own *Officialatus*.[94] Meanwhile, archidiaconal courts, despite more agreements to the contrary, continued to hear cases of marital validity and morality claimed by the bishop. So great was the political independence of the archdeacons that the cathedral chapter of Speyer continued to defy openly the bishop's jurisdiction within his own city until the second half of the sixteenth century.[95] Whether such divisiveness in judicial authority led to "comparative shopping" among potential civil marriage litigants or – more important – frequent reversals of other courts' decisions remains an open question.[96]

What is clear is that the fifteenth and early sixteenth centuries were a time of intense competition between secular and ecclesiastical courts, in which the deciding factor in jurisdictional gray areas such as criminal marriage matters actually appears to have been whichever authority acted first. In the 1477 case of the wife of the city clerk of Sinsheim, for instance, it was the Prince-Bishop of Speyer's Official who punished the offender for her "immoral life-style," although the case rested properly within the jurisdiction of either the local lay synod or bailiff.[97] Here, as

---

[93] Mandate of 5 August 1458. StAS IA/331; also Riedner II, 69–70.

[94] Cf. the defense of acting Vicar-General Peter von Stein of the office's traditional marriage jurisdiction (Riedner II, no. 20, 91–96 [1467]) and a subsequent agreement with the bishop's Official on boundaries between the two in ecclesiastical jurisdiction (ibid., no. 21, 96–97).

[95] There is evidence of continuing operation of the archidiaconal *Officialatus* until at least the end of the Council of Trent, and possibly until the council's official adoption by the diocese of Speyer in the 1570s. See court ordinances of ca. 1540 and 1560 with references to "consistorum ecclesiasticorum spirensium" in GLA 67/486, 2–21 (Riedner II, no. 34, 143ff.); GLA 67/277, 8ᵛ–9ʳ (ibid., no. 40, 156ff.).

[96] Cf. Joel F. Harrington, "An Estate Pleasing to God and Man: Secular and Religious Reformation of Marriage in the Palatinate, 1555–1619" (Ph.D. diss., University of Michigan, 1989), 130–37, on the details of Bishop Mathias of Speyer's campaign to centralize judicial power.

[97] *Urkunde* 22, December 1477, GLA 43/239, cited in Richard Lossen, *Staat und Kirche in der Pfalz im Ausgang des Mittelalters* (Münster, 1907), 91.

always, though, local authorities – secular or ecclesiastical – maintained their undisputed edge in legal prosecution and enforcement. Here too, at the local level, the territorial State made the most significant advances in marriage jurisdiction.

Unlike bishops, secular rulers faced not only geographical limitations on their legal authority but legislative and institutional ones as well. As we have seen, even with the advent of territorial codifications, the lord's representative remained – like other communal leaders – primarily the executor of local laws and customs. Moreover, most princes continually encouraged local resolution of all but the most serious or costly disputes, even after the increasing creation of supreme courts (*Hofgerichte*) in the fifteenth century to replace the more irregular medieval assemblies (*Landtaidinge*).[98] The 1470 *Amtleute* ordinance of the Prince-Bishop of Speyer, for instance, typically encouraged as much decision making as possible at the local level ("and not to come to us all the time"). Local bailiffs were thus provided with wide-ranging jurisdiction in religious as well as secular matters, including the right of immediate punishment or execution "by drowning, beheading, the wheel, drawing and quartering, eye gauging, ear clipping, finger chopping, or whatever the law entails."[99]

Nonetheless, territorial rulers did achieve some advances during this period in expanding their judicial hegemony. As the political power and prestige of many fifteenth-century princes increased, so too did the judicial authority of their bailiffs. The subsequent increase in number of litigants (including clerics) who came to princely courts for decisions in turn adversely affected all other judicial authorities – especially those of the commune and the bishop. Bishops, of course, attempted various measures to preserve clerical immunity and traditional secular–ecclesiastical jurisdictional divisions, but apparently often in vain.[100]

---

[98] Otto Brunner, *Land und Herrschaft* (Darmstadts, 1965), 331–33, 360; William Wright, *Capitalism, the State, and the Lutheran Reformation* (Columbus, Ohio, 1983), 33; Mitteis and Lieberich, *Deutsche Rechtsgeschichte*, 267ff.

[99] *Sammlung* I:1–8; also the shorter 1483 version of Bishop Georg (*Sammlung* I:9–10). Typically, lower courts were expected to handle not only criminal cases, but all those involving less than a certain amount of money (e.g., twenty gulden), thus effectively protecting the higher court from an overwhelming caseload. Cf. 1524 Saxony *Hofgerichtsordnung* (Wright, *Capitalism, the State and the Lutheran Reformation*, 33).

[100] Such voluntary use of secular courts by clerics in general and by laypersons in spiritual matters, for instance, was expressly forbidden by the bishops of Speyer in the court reforms of 1466, 1479, and several other ordinances, including a 1478 prohibition by Ludwig (Lossen, *Staat und Kirche*, 87). See, for example, a typical certificate of special permission issued by the bishop of

The most immediately visible result was an apparent decline in all ecclesiastical jurisdiction throughout Germany during the late fifteenth and early sixteenth centuries. Powerful territorial states such as Würtemberg, Bavaria, Ernestine Saxony, and the Palatinate were especially aggressive and – by the estimate of many scholars – successful.[101] The many cases of open violation of clerical immunity by the Elector (including almost complete administration of all benefices by his *Amtleute* by 1499) confirm that the bishop of Speyer's spiritual jurisdiction was no exception.[102]

Not that bishops were completely innocent of similar judicial abuses, according to secular rulers.[103] A 1503 treaty between Elector Philip and Bishop Philip of Speyer, for example, contained the characteristic charges of judicial usurpation by each as well as resolutions by both rulers that ecclesiastical cases (unspecified) go to ecclesiastical courts and secular cases (likewise unspecified) go to secular courts.[104] Whether

Speyer to members of his clergy to avoid appearing before secular judges in 1515 (GLA 67/417, 164; Riedner II, no. 97, 276–277).

[101] Cohn on the Palatinate: "the jurisdiction of the princely courts expanded with the support of clerical litigants and without serious opposition from church courts, until it embraced nearly all ecclesiastical causes" (*The Government of the Rhine Palatinate*, 148). Lossen concurs, that in the Palatinate, "die geistliche Macht war im Sinken, die weltliche im Steigen, das zeigt sich hier [in cases of expanded secular jurisdiction] wie auf anderen Gebieten" (*Staat und Kirche*, 87).

Cf. Müller-Volbehr, *Die geistliche Gerichte*, 223–31, and the acts of German provincial synods from the late fourteenth century following the disregard of many secular rulers of the traditional secular–ecclesiastical boundaries (Hashagen, "Zur Characteristik der geistlichen Gerichtsbarkeit," 205, 229).

[102] Records of the Electors' violations of spiritual jurisdiction in the Palatinate during the fifteenth century are especially plentiful as witnessed by the case listings in Baumgartner, *Geschichte und Recht des Archidiakonates*, 168–81, and Lossen, *Staat und Kirche*, 188–93. Throughout Germany, ordinances such as the Elector's 1497 ordinance requiring of all benefice holders to take loyalty oaths to him were rampant, as was legal hegemony of all kinds (Cohn, *The Government of the Rhine Palatinate*, 140ff., especially 145–46, 202ff.; Duggan, *Bishop and Chapter*, 123; Lossen, *Staat und Kirche*, 27, 79–81, 185–87).

[103] As was the case for most ecclesiastical as well as secular courts, the *Officialatus* of the bishop frequently practiced voluntary jurisdiction in many secular matters, thus drawing countercharges to their own accusations of secular hegemony in ecclesiastical matters. Cf. examples of Brandenburg and Tirol (Hashagen, "Zur Characteristik der geistlichen Gerichtsbarkeit," 213–15; Halberstadt (Müller-Volbehr, *Die geistliche Gerichte*, 159–67), and Speyer (see nn. 30–31); also bibliography in Mitteis and Lieberich, *Deutsche Rechtsgschichte*, 259ff.

[104] HStAMü Abt. II/K. 398/1, I, 12ʳ–13ᵛ, 61ᵛ–62ʳ, 139ʳ⁻ᵛ. In this instance, the alleged usurpers were the Elector's *Amtleute* in Germersheim and the bishop's *Officialatus* in Neustadt.

Although treaties between secular powers – such as the Elector's 1459 pact with the king of Bohemia and 1460 agreement with the prince-archbishop of Mainz – repeatedly stipulated "geistliche Sachen vor geistlichen Gerichte," the area of disagreement in boundaries was ever expanding, especially in matters traditionally disputed by both, such as criminal marriage cases.

this terse resolution reflects the self-evident nature of jurisdictional boundaries or their purposeful ambiguity remains unclear.

By far the strongest advances into ecclesiastical and voluntary jurisdiction were achieved by the Swiss and imperial cities. The same pattern is evident in cities throughout German-speaking lands – namely, increased involvement by city magistrates and their auxiliaries in all areas of law enforcement, even greater than the previously discussed increase among territorial states. Almost all of the cities examined by Köhler witnessed a noticeable increase in the activity of their respective council and city courts in issues of public morality during this period, usually through special "morals police,"[105] and corresponding to the dramatic increase in all legislation already discussed.

Competition from municipal authorities in such traditionally secular marriage matters was, if not promoted, at least tolerated by rival ecclesiastical and territorial powers. Further inroads into marriage jurisdiction, especially that of the bishop, met with much greater resistance and even hostility. Most intolerable to bishops, jealous of their already threatened jurisdiction, was the gradual and often explicit legal usurpation by city magistrates in questions of marital validity. The well-established city court of Ulm originally handled all marriage matters within the city, including mandatory approval by the town council of all marriage contracts (1440 statute), enforcement of consanguinity and affinity restrictions, and punishment of broken vows. By the late fifteenth century, the city's frequent usurpation of the bishop's jurisdiction

See Karl Menzel, ed., "Regesten zur Geschichte Friedrichs I," in *Quellen zur Geschichte Friedrichs I. des Siegreichen Kurfürsten non der Pfalz*, part III, ed., Konrad Hoffman, (Munich, 1862; reprint: Munich, 1969), 310–311, 346–48.

Cf. also a 1509 treaty alternating appeals for cases involving subjects of both between the supreme courts of each (cited in Lossen, *Staat und Kirche*, 92), and provisions in a 1521 treaty governing the strict procedure by which a subject of the Elector may appeal to the bishop's *Officialatus*–"außgescheiden geistlich sachen als zehend, ee, wucher, und dergleichen beuren," already within the bishop's jurisdiction (GLA 67/277, 26–27; Riedner II, no. 33, 139–40).

105 Cf. the *Drei über Ehebruch* of Basel (protocols dating back to 1442), *Bettelherrn* of Ulm (originally for poor relief but later also police duties), and the frequent practice of guild police, such as *Die Elfer* in Memmingen (directed by two to five members of the town council), and the *Sibenzüchter* (since 1433) of Strasbourg (Kö II:3–6; 146–147, 236–237, 360). See also similar developments in Nuremberg (Harvey, "Nürnberg Marriage Laws," 143), Zurich (Kö I:5ff.), Saint Gallen (Kö I:387–89), Constance (Kö II:89–91), Bern (Kö I:309), Eßlingen (Kö II:125), Lindau (Kö II:183), Isny (Kö II:205).

Duties of Speyer's twenty *Scharwächter* (with two divisions, alternating day and night shifts), established in 1500, appear to have been limited to protection of property (against theft, fire, etc.); their role in moral matters in unclear. Alter, in *GStSp* I:444.

in this area provoked several complaints to the council "that such matters ought to be heard and settled by the ecclesiastical court at Constance."[106] Similarly, the city council of Zurich, though granted the right by the bishop to appoint a commissary for marriage cases in the city, also continued to expand its own jurisdiction. By 1511 its magistrates were judging all kinds of marital validity cases, prompting further complaints from the bishop of Constance that such actions were not only "against the spiritual privilege and ordinances of the Church," but harmful to the sacrament of marriage as well.[107] Open usurpation of this degree appears less widespread in other imperial cities, though general disputes over ecclesiastical jurisdiction within the city most certainly were not.

The political and judicial independence gained by the city of Speyer by the end of the thirteenth century, for instance, was never fully accepted by successors to the episcopal seat. As in the case of many other episcopal city councils and their bishops, jurisdictional struggles between the two were constant. Perhaps due to the bishops' recurring attempts to reconquer the city and the frequent complaints of judicial abuses on both sides, in 1456 the magistrates prohibited all citizens from appealing any of their decisions to one of the bishop's secular courts (especially that of the *Schultheiß* in the city). Three years later, they also appointed seven deputies to see that the prohibition was enforced and that the city's judicial sovereignty was maintained.[108] The bishop responded by emphatically forbidding all cases involving clerics or spiritual matters from going to the town council or its criminal court rather than to his *Officialatus*.[109]

---

[106] Kö II:1–6. The magistrates, however, remained undeterred in their program of judicial expansion, which culminated in still more rights gained from the bishop in the early sixteenth century, among them, concurrent jurisdiction (with the bishop) over defloration, the 1513 right to throw immoral priests into prison (though still judged by the bishop), and in 1519 the right to expel priests' concubines from the city.

[107] Kö I:5–17. The magistrates of Zurich were very slow (late fourteenth century) to recognize the bishop's exclusive jurisdiction over marriage, and even then continued to judge and punish cases of defloration, disputed and broken vows, and of course marriage property disputes (since 1487 all cases of the latter handled exclusively "durch die geswornen schetzer" of the magistrates). See also Burghartz, *Leib, Ehre und Gut*, 172–79.

See also secular inroads in Strasbourg (Kö II:354ff, 365–68) and Nuremberg (Harvey, "Nürnberg Marriage Laws," 74–77).

[108] Alter in *GStSp* I:397, 436, 459.

[109] Alter in *GStSp* I:436. Similar conflicts in Landau with the bishop of Speyer over ecclesiastical jurisdiction were addressed in the 1484 treaty with the local rent masters (*Steugeherren*). Hans Hess, "Gerichtswesen und Gerichtsordnungen der Stadt im Spätmittelalter und in der frühen Neuzeit," in *Landau in der Pfalz*, ed. H. Hess (Landau, 1974), 152; Duggan, *Bishop and Chapter*, 173–74.

Other cities – Ulm, Saint Gallen, and Zurich – adopted the more insidious strategy of forcing plaintiffs in unsuccessful appeals to the bishop of Constance's *Officialatus* to bear all costs, thus effectively scaring off all but the surest (or richest) plaintiffs. In 1499, the perpetually embattled episcopal Official of Constance complained that because of Zurich's 1495 statute, "hundreds and hundreds" who feared punishment for doubtful cases had been held back from going to his court, resulting in "considerable harm and detriment to the jurisdiction and authority of the laudable Church of Constance."[110]

As with territorial courts and authorities, the actual degree of the municipal usurpation of ecclesiastical jurisdiction in most instances can only be inferred from incomplete records.[111] Obviously, the creation in Zurich of a local commissary more susceptible to the town council's influence, or a papal alliance against the bishop (as in Ulm) strengthened the magistrates' position in deciding "ecclesiastical" cases.[112] The relative political strength and even physical distance of a city from the bishop likewise played a pivotal role in the latter enforcing his proper ecclesiastical jurisdiction, as in the case of Eßlingen's 1488 statute assuming jurisdiction over all clergy involved in secular cases.[113] Conversely, in many precariously situated cities, such as Speyer, any jurisdictional advances remained a significant political gamble.[114]

Thus despite frequent abuses of clerical immunity and other eccle-

---

[110] Kö I:11, 61. See also the 1502 complaint of the bishop to the Zurich city council that the city was acting as a court of appeal for decisions of the bishop's *Officialatus*.

[111] Though some of the city's *Achtbücher* from 1396–97 (StAS IA/694) and 1415–1510 (StAS IA/704) have survived, there are no complete records of the *Vierrichter* before 1576 or of lay synod proceedings whatsoever.

[112] In Zurich this was the case since 1502 (Kö I:12). In many cities, such as Bern, marital cases were handled by the archdeacon with the bishop's approval (Kö I:309). In Biberach, a commissary was appointed by the local Latin schoolteacher solely for taking depositions in episcopal cases (Kö II:225), an ad hoc position in Speyer and other dioceses (cf. GLA 67/417, 15; Riedner II, no. 89, 262–63).

Since 1488, the city of Ulm maintained the right to publish papal briefs and privileges without prior approval of the bishop of Constance, an arrangement indicative of papal restraints on the bishop's power through alliances with imperial cities within a respective diocese (Kö II:2ff.).

[113] Kö II:125. As Köhler remarks of a 1498 treaty between the bishop of Constance and city of Zurich defining ecclesiastical jurisdiction, what force could an imperially arbitrated agreement have "in einer unaufhaltsamen territorialstaatlichen Entwicklung gegenüber?" (Kö I:10–11).

[114] The political position of Speyer, as already discussed (see the Introduction), was especially tenuous, relying on frequent protective alliances with the Elector, such as the *Schutzvertrag* of 1488–1512. (Alter, in *GStSp* I:392, 441) See also E. Voltmer, *Reichstadt und Herrschaft: Zur Geschichte der Stadt Speyer im hohen und späten Mittelalter* (Trier, 1981).

siastical matters in both municipal and territorial courts, as well as repeated complaints about the bishop and his Official in petitions and resolutions of these secular authorities,[115] there is no direct evidence of extensive or even sporadic violation of the bishops' marriage jurisdiction outside of a few city-states. Nevertheless, the continually expanding scope of all other competing institutions had made its mark. Whether, as was the case for some dioceses,[116] the overall number of litigants in ecclesiastical courts declined is unclear; that the integrity and even necessity of all ecclesiastical legal institutions of the diocese, even the lay synod, came under fire is obvious. Most important for marital litigation of all kinds, the sheer growth in legal apparatus among secular authorities could only exacerbate the long-standing conflicts of sovereignty governing all legal jurisdiction. As all authorities struggled for judicial as well as political preeminence, the institutional pluralism confronting them would become increasingly intolerable.

The limitations of state expansion

By the early sixteenth century the trend toward greater secular control of marriage had reached new heights. In large dioceses such as Constance, the bishop's impotence in enforcing his proper ecclesiastical jurisdiction had resulted in de facto assumption of all marriage jurisdiction by many powerful Swiss and imperial cities well before 1520.[117] Yet for all their obvious usurpation in this area, secular authorities still appeared cautious, even reluctant to assume *officially* all marriage jurisdiction before the late 1520s and 1530s. In retrospect, these steps appear to be a logical

---

[115] The long history of antagonism between the city's citizens and clergy is especially evident in complaints from the 1512–13 guild uprising, which resulted in the reorganization of the city government (esp. StAS IA/20, no. 2). Although none of the articles challenged the sovereignty or jurisdiction of the town council in any respect, complaints against the clergy, especially concerning morality, and ecclesiastical jurisdiction (cf. articles 5–7 and 10–13) were numerous. Members of the city's clergy, in turn, were ordered by the cathedral chapter "to avoid all disputes with the citizens" during the resulting agreement's negotiation, and regarding ecclesiastical jurisdiction "by altem gebrauch und gemeynen rechten [zu verbleiben]" (15 February 1513; Manfred Krebs, *Die Protokolle des Speyerer Domkapitels, 1500–17* [Stuttgart, 1968–69], no. 3739). The resulting treaty in 1514 confirmed, for the time being, the bishop's traditional ecclesiastical jurisdiction (LAS F1/71).

[116] See Safley, *Let No Man Put Asunder*, especially 5off., on the *Officialatus* of Constance; and Hans Tütken, *Geschichte des Dorfes und Patrimonialgerichtes Geismar bis zur Gerichtsauflösung im Jahre 1839* (Göttingen, 1967), 85–86, 191ff., on pre-Reformation decline of local synods in the diocese of Mainz.

[117] Kö I:17–27; II:7–8.

completion of the expansion of their jurisdiction. Why then did they hesitate? And what eventually persuaded them to make the break complete and official?

Again, the reluctance on the part of the magistrates can be attributed largely to the general conservatism of their political goals.[118] Although most councils and courts of imperial and Swiss cities continued to practice aggressive judicial expansion in all areas (especially ecclesiastical), diplomatic considerations predisposed them toward gradual and unofficial – rather than radical and abrupt – aggrandizement of power. Rejection of the traditional and legitimate judicial (episcopal) and legal (canonical) authorities remained an obviously dangerous political step, particularly in the early 1520s, with potentially disastrous political consequences. Even the most devout of reformed magistrates were no doubt cognizant of this fact. It was no coincidence that when cities and territorial states did begin to break with episcopal jurisdiction, the most politically secure – Swiss and imperial cities – led the way.[119]

Even the many political advantages of complete local secular jurisdiction could not justify a radical rupture for most. Various magistrates had themselves argued the case for improved effectiveness in law enforcement as well as the elimination of "great expense, trouble, and labor"[120] involved in taking a case to the distant *Officialatus*, especially in larger dioceses, such as Constance. Yet for all these magistrates' aggrandizing ambitions, reform from within the system must have appeared a viable option, at least in the first years of reformed preaching. Throughout 1523, the members of the Swiss Confederation continued to appeal to the bishop of Constance to come to their cities for "marriage matters or other similar affairs," as a solution to the overwhelming costs of the existing system.[121] Indeed, as late as 1524, the religious reformers of Constance presented their city council with a series of proposed marriage reforms, stipulating that, if the bishop were willing to "proceed

---

[118] See Bernd Moeller, *Imperial Cities and the Reformation*, trans. H. C. E. Midelfort and M. Edwards (Durham, N.C., 1972), 61ff., on the humanist ideal of civic tranquility and the general conservativeness of German magistrates. See also Euan Cameron, *The European Reformation* (Oxford, 1991), 226–34; and my discussion in Chapter 1.

[119] Cf. Hans-Christoph Rublack, "Nördlingen zwischen Kaiser und Reformation," *Archiv für Reformationsgeschichte* 71 (1980), 113–33; and Robisheaux, *Rural Society*, 100ff., on the relatively late introduction of the Reformation in small territorial states.

[120] Kö I:1.

[121] Diet of 19 August 1523; Kö I:2. Again, note the late date. This plea is almost identical to one of the diet of 31 March 1500, and was often repeated in early Zurich protocols.

according to the laws of God's word rather than his own statutes," the city should continue to recognize his jurisdiction in such matters.[122]

Ultimately, it was the preaching and actions of reformed clerics that prompted the first official breaks with episcopal authority, later followed by other Protestant cities and territorial states. More than sporadic charges of moral corruption and abuse in marital litigation,[123] the canonical system's apparent deviations from biblical standards – particularly the forbidden degrees of consanguinity and affinity "created by the popes"[124] – left little room for compromise. At the most basic level, those magistrates who openly accepted the principle of *sola scriptura* were thus obliged by definition to reject all papal and episcopal as well as canonical authority unless or until the latter conformed absolutely to the reformed interpretation of Scripture – an unlikely scenario to most by 1525.[125] Whatever the political fallout, once a city or state decided to adopt officially this Evangelical principle of authority, assumption of all existing episcopal jurisdiction and ecclesiastical legal authority was a logical and necessary consequence.

At a more practical level, an official break was usually prompted by a more immediate effect of reformed preaching, namely, the specter of marital chaos. Because many reformed cities continued to recognize officially their bishops' marriage jurisdiction well into the late 1520s while at the same time de facto refuting his magisterial and pastoral authority, many potential marriage litigants were forced to turn to whatever ad hoc authorities they could find. Often, as in Nuremberg and Strasbourg, marriage litigants consulted their local reformed pastors for decisions based on "common lessons that we have received from [Jesus

---

122 Kö II:97–99. This ostensibly reconciliatory document of 6 December 1524, however, also contains the first recorded proposal of purely Evangelical marriage courts for all imperial and Swiss cities, presided over by "etlich geschriftverstendigen gortzförchtigen mennern . . ." and deciding all marriage cases "nach usswysung der haylgen götlichen geschrift . . ."

123 The brief characterization of previous practice in the Elector's 1563 *Ehegerichtsordnung* is both unusual and vague: ". . . bevorab bey den bäpstichen consistoriis gewesene ungestalten und mißbreuch nicht frunehmen noch volgen . . ." (*EKO* 293).

124 Cf. Palatinate *Kirchenordnung* of 1556, esp. *EKO* 215ff., and see my comments in Chapter 1.

125 Moeller ("Die Kirche in den evangelischen freien Städten Oberdeutschlands in Zeitalter der Reformation," *Zeitschrift für die Geschichte des Oberrheins*, n.s., 73 [1964], 155–56) notes that once the magistrates of a city decided to turn Lutheran, there existed "ein akuter Notstand der das Eingreifen der weltlichen Behörden nahelegen mochte; denn es hatte ja die alte Kirche immerhin einen Bereich des Lebens noch so gut wie vollständig unter ihrer Kontrolle und Judikatur gehabt, nähmlich Eheschließung und Ehescheidung, und es lag daher auf der Hand, daß man, wenn man sich von ihr lossagte, auch einen Ersatz für die kirchliche Ehegerichtsbarkeit schaffen mußte."

and the Apostles], judged by brotherly love."[126] In many cities, the town council or its criminal court attempted to fill the judicial void, but since these institutions had no official, legitimate authority, such a jurisdiction could not be legally enforced. In the time after most cities' break with episcopal jurisdiction, one of the following patterns emerged. Either the city experienced a period of legal chaos with no specified marriage authority or code (e.g., Nuremberg); the introduction of a new marriage court but no code (e.g., Geneva, Speyer); the combination of a new code with an already existing institution, such as a town council, municipal court, or supreme court (e.g., Augsburg); or, in some rare and generally later instances, the immediate creation of both a new marriage court and comprehensive code (e.g., Zurich) (see Table 1). The potential variance in legal standards and application alone was enough to concern any magistrate.[127] The increasing occurrence or even possibility of self-divorce (abandonment and remarriage) as well as other marital disorders, however, convinced even the most cautious of their number that governmental assumption of such jurisdiction represented the only means to preserve order and legal conformity in marriage practice.

On 1 May 1525, the city of Zurich became the first secular polity to break formally with its bishop's marriage jurisdiction.[128] Over the next half century all other Protestant Swiss and imperial cities as well as territorial states eventually followed suit, though along different patterns and with varying consequences. As Table 1 illustrates, in the majority of cities and territorial states, introduction of Protestant teaching and major religious reforms coincided closely (sometimes within months or even days) with the inevitable break with episcopal civil marriage authority.

---

[126] From an early instruction to Strasbourg pastors, quoted in Dietrerich 248ff.; Wendel, *Le mariage*, 73; Harvey, "Nürnberg Marriage Laws," 177–78; Hecker, "Ehescheidungsprozeß," in *HRG* 1:843; Kö I:173, 110; II:377–85, 539. Cf. a similar preference in the 1542 Reformation ordinance of Braunschweig, asking pastors to refer to the Superintendent only "wo sachen schwer und wichtig wären" (Müller-Volbehr, *Die geistliche Gerichte*, 251).

[127] A 1527 Visitation Instruction of the Elector of Saxony complained that "Nachdem sich auch viel ungeschicklikeiten ein zeitherr damit zugetragen, daz etzliche pfarrer und prediger in ehesachen mit scheiden und sunst leiderlich zuhandeln sich angemast." See Emil Sehling, *Evangelische Kirchenordnungen des XVI. Jahrhunderts* I (Kursachsen) (Leipzig, 1902), 142.

[128] On 25 February 1525, a commission of two nobles, two citizens, and four clerics (including Zwingli) had been established by the town council to study and make recommendations on marriage matters within the city, citing as ground, "zusprüchen und irrungen in eelichen sachen, darumb die parthyen für und für einandern gen Constentz oder andere frömde gericht geladet." The marriage court ordinance of 10 May was the result (Kö I:1). See also Küngolt Kilchenmann, *Die Organisation des zücherischen Ehegerichts zur Zeit Zwinglis* (Zurich, 1946), 11–19.

Table 1. *Protestant marriage law and jurisdictions*

Jurisdiction[a]	Rejection of clerical celibacy	Official jurisdictional break	Judicial organ[b] (yrs. after jurisdictional break)	1st complete marriage ordinance (yrs. after jurisdictional break)
Municipal				
Zurich (R)	1525	1525	1525;M (–)	1525[d] (–)
Nuremberg (E)	1524–25	1525[c]	1526;M (1)	1533 (8)
Lindau (R)	1524–25	1524[c]	ca. 1540;M (16)	1566 (42)
Bern (R)	1528	1525	1528;M (3)	1529 (4)
Saint Gallen (R)	1528	1526	1526;M (–)	1547 (19)
Constance (R)	1524	1527	1531;G (–)	1531[d] (4)
Strasbourg (R)	1524	1529[c]	1529;M (–)	1530[d] (1)
Ulm (E)	1531	1529[c]	1534;M (5)	1531 (2)
Basel (R)	1529	1529	1529;M (8)	1529[d] (–)
Memmingen (R)	1526	1528	1532;C(4)	1532/69 (4)
Augsburg (E)	1524	1537[c]	1537;M/G (–)	1537 (–)
Geneva (R)	1536	1536	1541;C (5)	1561 (25)
SPEYER (E)	1556	1556	1556;G/C (–)	Late 17th cent (100+)
Territorial				
Württemberg (E)	1524	ca. 1524	1525–26 M (–)	1536; 1553[d] (12;29)
East Prussia (E)	1525	1525	1525; M (–)	1539 (14)
Albertine Saxony (E)	1539	1539	1545; G/M (6)	1545 (6)
Hessia (E)	ca. 1528	1528	1567; C (39)	1572 (44)
Brandenburg (E)	1539–40	1539	1572–73; C (33)	1540/73 (–)
Palatinate (E/R)	1546	1556	1563; M/G (7)	1556/63 (–)

[a]E = Evangelical; R = Reformed
[b]M = separate marriage court; C = ecclesiastical consistory; G = existing governmental organ.
[c]Until Augsburg Interim (1548).
[d]Influential marriage code.
Sources: Kö I & II; EKO.

Even then, as in the instances of the Palatinate-Electorate and city of Speyer, there were occasionally gaps of several years between the two events.

Once again, we must consider the political and administrative advantages of continuing unofficial usurpation of episcopal jurisdiction, rather than risking the more dangerous open break. Both the Elector of the Palatinate and officials in other reformed cities and villages (including the city of Speyer) apparently adopted this casual attitude toward the bishop of Speyer's ecclesiastical jurisdiction. The Palatinate's Marriage Court Ordinance of 1563 begins its official assumption of jurisdiction with the preamble that the Elector had already long been involved in settling marriage disputes.[129] Protocols of the cathedral chapter of Speyer confirm repeated violations of the bishop's marriage jurisdiction by the Electors' *Vögte* and *Amtleute*, including "various cases of improper marriage dispensations" and general "rejection of ecclesiastical procedure."[130] Once Protestant polities felt politically secure enough to embrace fully the Evangelical faith, such an open jurisdictional break then became not only preferable but unavoidable. As for many others, the moment of opportunity for the city of Speyer and the Palatine-Electorate came with the Peace of Augsburg in 1555.

The Peace of Augsburg was originally formulated as an extension of the perpetual Land Truce of 1495, adding the formal choice of religious confession to the territorial rulers' traditional disciplinary powers.[131] The *ius reformandi* that resulted thus applied to Catholic as well as Protestant princes, and was not exclusively associated with the latter until the Peace of Westphalia in 1648.[132] Because marriage jurisdiction was never mentioned explicitly in the 1555 treaty, though, the issue

---

[129] "Nachdem sich in unserm chur- und furstentumb der pfaltzgraveschaft am Rhein nhun ein guete und lange zeit hero etlich viel sachen strittiger ehe und dergleichen zugetragen, auch heufiglich vorhanden, darin die partheyen mit unstadt und merglichem nachtayl aus mangel ordentlichen christlichen ehegerichts (dann unß an die bäptischen consistoria die partheyen kommen zu lassen beschwerlich) biß daher ufgehalten . . ." (*EKO* 290). Attacks by the Electors on all other aspects of ecclesiastical privilege have already been discussed.

[130] All disputed marriage vows, the chapter stresses to its own official, are to be decided by "den geistlichen Richter oder vicarien mit geistlichen Recht. . . ." See Krebs, *Die Protokolle des Speyerer Domkapitels*, especially nos. 5843, 5858, 5889 (all 1522); 6221 (1524); 6444 (1525); 6720 (1526); 7136 (1528); 8146, 8166 (1530). See also Stamer II:308ff.

[131] See B. von Bonin, *Die Praktische Bedeutung der* ius reformandi (1902; reprint: Amsterdam, 1962), 1ff., for the disciplinary aspect of *ius reformandi* and its origins in medieval *Vogteirecht*; also K. Brandi, *Der Augsburger Religionsfrieden vom 25. September 1555*, 2nd ed. (Göttingen, 1927).

[132] Von Bonin, *Die Praktische Bedeutung*, 11, 23ff.

continued to cause considerable confessional strife during the years leading up to the Thirty Years' War.

Ironically, legal apologists of each confession were forced to rely on justifications entirely contrary to their respective theologies. Catholic rulers, for instance, turned to the argument later propounded by the Jesuits Laymann and Forer, that marriage should not be considered a confessional matter but more of a governmental issue, such as tithes.[133] Lutheran apologists, on the other hand, necessarily downplayed their own *causa mixta* characterization and instead emphasized the spiritual nature of marriage, implicitly included, they insisted, in article 20 of the treaty, which suspended traditional episcopal jurisdiction in questions of "religion, faith, appointment of ministers, use of churches, ordinances, and ceremonies."[134] A 1559 decision of the imperial supreme court rejected the Protestant interpretation of article 20, but did recognize marriage as a matter of "religion and conscience" (rather than ceremony).[135] Still, Catholic bishops continued to fight all Lutheran claims of marital jurisdiction, prompting official complaints at the imperial diets of 1594 and again in 1598 and 1613. Until ultimately resolved by thirty years of bloody war, German marital jurisdiction remained a contest for survival of the politically fittest.

Elector Ottheinrich had already converted to Lutheranism in 1546 but did not fully introduce the Reformation in the Rhenish part of his realm until after the provisions of Augsburg had taken effect. Within one year of signing the treaty, he then assumed the full ecclesiastical jurisdiction guaranteed all evangelical rulers and established a separate marriage court at Heidelberg.[136] Shortly thereafter, his successor, the Calvinist Friedrich III, followed with the much more detailed marriage and marriage court ordinances of 1563.[137] Significantly, although the ordinance forbade all subjects of the Elector from taking any marriage case to the Catholic bishop's *Officialatus*, it conceded that as the Elector's

---

[133] *Pacis Compositio inter Principes et Ordines Imperii Romani Catholicos* . . . (Dillengen, 1629), a commentary on the Peace of Augsburg; Dieterich 252–53.

[134] Dieterich 251ff. Dieterich points out that the article 20 approach was not part of initial Protestant arguments for marital jurisdiction.

[135] "res spirituales conscientiaque." Dieterich 254–56.

[136] Cf. 1556 *Von den eesachen* (*EKO* 221–25); also introductory remarks of Goeters on 26. Although this brief ordinance mentions the Elector's *eerichtern*, there are no procedural or organizational guidelines provided until the 1563 *EGO*.

[137] Cf. 1563 *EO* (*EKO* 275–88); 1563 *EGO* (*EKO* 289–332) and introductory remarks of *EKO* 36–37.

advice and judgment had already been granted to many foreigners in such matters, he graciously extended the same privilege to his own subjects ("albeit with our knowledge") to appear before other "Christian" (i.e., Protestant) courts.[138]

In the same year, the city of Speyer, still wary of the large imperial presence within its walls, broke with the last remnant of episcopal jurisdiction there, the lay synod, citing a breach by the cathedral provost in its traditional convening procedure.[139] Shortly thereafter, the town council (whose members, not coincidentally, also composed the jurors of the synod) added that the punishments of the lay synod had been much too mild to ensure effective discipline.[140] Such legal maneuvers deceived no one, however, including the cathedral provost who responded, "if they didn't have this [legal] pretext, they would have invented another one so that nothing would come of the matter."[141] Further protests by the provost, appealing to the council's concerns about both law and moral order, met with the same indifference as previous appeals, as did a 1561 attempt to revive the synod.[142] After 1589, despite a still-pending protest in the imperial supreme court, the lay synod was never again mentioned by any authority.[143]

Municipal authorities were apparently more tolerant of ongoing com-

---

138 1563 *EGO*; *EKO* 292. Cf. the example of such cooperation among Evangelical courts in a letter from the magistrates of Speyer to the marriage court of Strasbourg (13 March 1596; StAS IB/23, Bd. 5, 7ᵛ–8ʳ).

139 Three weeks after provost Georg Göler von Ravensburg made the traditional public announcement of the synod, only eight or nine of thirty-three prospective church wardens showed up on the first morning of the synod, complaining that they too were "unlustig . . . den sendt zu besitzen und zu volbringen" since only the normal oathtaking procedure had been "ungleich." StAS 369/6, 43, cited in Kohl, "Das Laiensendgericht," 77.

140 "Seiner Herrschaft Vorfahren haben ja die Laster straffen helfen, sodaß die milden Strafen nit dem Dhomprobst allein Schimpf und Spott eingetragen haben. Es soll auch gedachter Syndicus erinnern lassen, das nit ein Leien Sendt ad poenam severam et sanguinis (welche der weltlichen oberkeit zu irrogieren zusteht und vorbehalten daran ein Erbar Rath nie kein eintragh geschehen) sondern ad solutionem cere vel pecuniae vel ad carceris poenam producirt werden soll" (StAS Fasz. 369/46, 66ʳ, cited in Kohl, "Das Laiensendgericht," 72).

141 Kohl, "Das Laiensendgericht," 78.

142 From the 1556 libel of the provost to the town council: "das exercitium synodi Laicalis nit ein blossen eusserlich ceremonien, sondern vast nottwendig sey, sonderlich zu diser Zeit, do sich allerlei erschrecklich irthums wider die Augspursschen Confession einreissen und erheben sampt anderen lastern, welchen allen möcht man füglich durch dis mittell entgegen kommen. . . . Item war, das solchen nit allein Verhutung, Abschaffung und Straff allerlei Sunds und Laster, sonder auch zu Pflanzung, Erhaltung und Mehrung christlicher Zucht und Furcht, gutter burgerlicher Ordnung und Pollizei auch aller ehrbar und Billichkeit gedient und gereicht habe" (StAS Fasz. 369/46, 37ᵛ, 86ᵛ, cited in Kohl, "Das Laiensendgericht," 54).

143 Alter, in *GStSP* I:546ff.; Kohl, "Das Laiensendgericht," 83.

petition from the bishop's *Officialatus* in nearby Udenheim, but eventually this vestige of episcopal authority over marriage too came under attack.[144] "Although the honorable Council has until now tolerated that its citizens and subjects have been summoned before the spiritual court in marriage matters," wrote the city's legal advocate, the council henceforth fully rejected all such pretended authority of the bishop and his courts.[145] Marital disputes, as other recent protests maintained,[146] clearly came under the heading of ecclesiastical jurisdiction as defined by the Peace of Augsburg; all present and previous efforts to deny the council such jurisdiction were in violation of the same treaty. Moreover, certain ungrounded provisions of "papist" marriage law – especially clerical celibacy, spiritual affinity, and fourth-degree consanguinity – made any concurrent jurisdiction, as suggested by the vicar-general, inconceivable.[147] Any summons or other orders or decisions of the *Officialatus* in marriage matters were likewise rejected as illicit and therefore "invalid."

The council's protest was personally delivered by two emissaries to the Prince-Bishop's Privy Council on 14 April 1598.[148] Not until 13 May did they receive a written response – the predictable one – to which the council immediately responded within two days, reiterating the same points and claims.[149] In the absence of actual court protocols, it is difficult to surmise the results of the war of paper that continued, except for noting the efforts of each to gain more powerful supporters. While the bishop petitioned the imperial supreme court to uphold his

---

[144] Despite occasional agreements between the city and bishop on other areas of criminal jurisdiction (cf. jurisdictional treaty of 4 July 1589; StAS IB/29, Bd. 9, 47ʳ–52ᵛ), ecclesiastical jurisdiction of all varieties was continually a source of dispute. Cf. GLA 61/10945, 81 (18 April 1578); GLA 61/10949, 56 (23 August 1589); StAS IB/22, 357ᵛ–360ʳ (16 March 1584); StAS IB/23, Bd. 4; StAS IB/6, Bd. 1, 448ʳ (1589); and especially the 1598 Zigler v. Zingermann cases that brought the dispute over marital litigation to a climactic head, discussed in Joel F. Harrington, "Reformation, Statebuilding, and the 'Secularization' of Marriage: Jurisdiction in the Palatinate, 1450–1619," *Fides et Historia* 22/3 (Fall 1990), 53–63.

[145] 22 March 1598; StAS IB/8, Bd. 2, 206ʳ–ᵛ.

[146] Cf. similar cases involving city's jurisdiction in disputed marriage vows: StAS IB/8, Bd. 2, 11ᵛ–13ʳ (8 May 1595); StAS IB/8, Bd. 2, 193ᵛ–194ʳ (12 January 1598).

[147] 12 April 1598; StAS IB/22, 595ʳ–596ᵛ. Cf. *Rat's* response to five-point complaint of the bishop (22 September 1597; StAS IB/8, Bd. 2, 164ᵛ–167ʳ), especially references to agreements with previous bishops and the uproar of other Protestant princes and magistrates on the same subject at the 1594 Regensburg *Reichstag*.

[148] *Ratsprotocol* of 14 April 1598 (StAS IB/6, Bd. 2, 20ᵛ); and StAS IB/22, 599ʳ–601ʳ.

[149] For the *Hofrat's* position, see StAS IB/22, 599ᵛ–600ʳ. For the town council's reply (15 May 1598): StAS IB/8, Bd. 2, 209ʳ–210ᵛ.

mandate, for instance, the city council sought out the protection of the Elector, each appealing to a confessional ally.[150] In the meantime, jurisdictional rivalries in all marriage-related areas continued among all three Palatine polities up to the Thirty Years' War, much as they had before the Reformation.[151]

The larger, external picture of marriage jurisdiction was thus less suddenly transformed during this time than might first appear the case. Clearly the creation of the already mentioned Protestant consistories and marriage courts significantly altered the map of marriage jurisdictions in Germany. The ensuing disputes and rivalries, however, continued much more along the traditional lines of sovereignty (as in criminal and property cases) rather than confessional distinctions. All territorial states, Catholic and Protestant alike, continued to exert their own judicial sovereignty as far as their respective political clout would allow them, with traditionally antagonistic relationships, such as between the city and Prince-Bishopric of Speyer, exacerbated but not substantially transformed by religious differences.

The ensuing struggle to shape new Protestant marriage laws and courts was initially characterized by often bitter conflicts between jurists trained in Roman and Canon laws and theologians and preachers with solely scripturally based agendas. One of the few fundamentals that theologians, jurists, and magistrates all agreed upon, however, was the need for one comprehensive and consistently applied standard for all marriage cases. Ironically, this same principle led them away from the myriad of customary and scriptural models and back to the Canon and Roman laws that many early Protestant reformers had rejected out of hand.

The origin of this perhaps surprising turn of events may be found in the very nature of sixteenth-century marriage reform, Catholic as well as Protestant – namely, deep concern with public order and law enforcement first, with as little actual legal revision and improvisation as

---

150 Cf. 16 August 1599 letter to the elector complaining of the bishop's recent mandate on the marriage jurisdiction of the *Officialatus* and the petition to the *Officialatus* and the petition to the *Reichskammergericht* to uphold, and the town council's request for support from the elector, especially in view of the decision of "Evangelische Stende" not to further tolerate such violations of the Peace of Augsburg. StAS IB/23, Bd. 5, 178ᵛ–180ʳ.

151 Cf. ebb and flow of ongoing marriage jurisdictional disputes of the Prince-Bishopric with the city (StAS IB/8, Bd. 5, 62–63 (1606); GLA 61/11497a, 84 [1618]) and the Elector (GLA 61/11495, 157ʳ⁻ᵛ, 164 [1603]; GLA 61/11497c, 21 [1620]).

deemed necessary. As discussed previously, the break with episcopal marriage jurisdiction on confessional grounds in most cases caught secular authorities unprepared for their newly assumed responsibilities, forcing them to rely on ad hoc mixtures of Scripture, custom, and Canon law, as well as temporary institutional arrangements, sometimes for years before a "new" marriage codification and authority could be agreed upon (see Table 1). Delays in deciding upon new marriage codes might to a certain extent be attributed to the usual inertia of government, but equally significant was the struggle over the substance of such codes between Evangelical theologians and jurists.

Though active in desacramentalizing marriage and promoting secular jurisdiction over it, early Protestant preachers and theologians consistently emphasized the spiritual side of this "worldly thing." Marriage, they argued, must conform to scriptural guidelines first, and worldly law second. All agree, as in the much later (1556) ecclesiastical ordinance of the Palatinate, that "God wills external discipline and has for this purpose given us the law."[152] The question of *which* law however, resulted in a fundamental split between those favoring a marriage law based entirely on Scripture (mainly theologians), and those opposed to too drastic a rupture with existing legal standards (i.e., jurists trained in Canon law).

The sometimes radical and even revolutionary undertone of religious reformers' earliest agendas for marriage and legal reform in general was not lost on the governmental – albeit reform-minded – establishment. As Gerald Strauss points out,

> Persuaded by early Lutheran preaching, people came to believe what they had in the past been taught to accept as given truths were, in fact, only statutes made by men. Rejection of these "human" laws was a way of ridding oneself of unwanted intervention. In its original impulse, therefore, the Reformation was driven by a strong antinomianism. . . . By sounding its call for a return to a primitive condition before written, man-made law, the Reformation at first held out hopes of emancipation from enforced obedience to artificial restraints.[153]

Consequently, only after Protestant reformers had eliminated any such seditionary undertones and began to frame their campaign for marriage reform in a language more amenable to secular authorities – that is,

[152] 1556 *Kirchenordnung; EKO* 187.
[153] Strauss, *Law*, 192.

stricter enforcement of moral standards and prevention of marital disorder and confusion – did they achieve the successes that we have already discussed.

Most notable among these was the extension of dissolution of vows and remarriage (divorce) to cases of proven adultery and malicious desertion, in both instances with scriptural justification. Another was the long-sought invalidation of clandestine marriages of minors without permission of their parents or of any marriage not meeting the requirements for proper publicity. Even in both of these important innovations, though, as with more frequent and stricter sumptuary and other criminal marriage ordinances, the interest of secular authorities in preserving the civil order was clearly served, particularly in view of their new jurisdictional authority. This undeniable preoccupation with regularization, standardization, and rigorous enforcement of marriage law allowed and even forced secular authorities to look past the partisan condemnation of the existing Canon law by many Evangelical theologians and draw heavily from it to meet their immediate needs.

Thus despite the frequent repudiations of papal authority in favor of divine law and Scriptures alone,[154] Protestant civic magistrates and territorial rulers alike clung persistently to what they perceived as tried and proven canonical standards for marriage law, much the same way they persisted in traditional customary trial and punishment of criminal marriage matters. Already blocked in all efforts to gain any independent institutional leverage over marriage,[155] Lutheran and Calvinist religious reformers were forced to accept their chiefly unofficial and nongovernmental roles of advising and admonishing, usually resulting in the previously mentioned reissuances of criminal marriage ordinances with stricter punishments but rarely any changes in substance.

Reformed members of the clergy, for instance, complained constantly of widespread moral dissipation and occasionally succeeded in reissuing or sharpening existing criminal marriage ordinances. Many religious reformers found the fine and imprisonment for adultery in most munici-

---

[154] The preamble to Strasbourg's marriage code of 1534 was typical: "Nun will aber unser fürgenommen reformatio erfordern, das wir nicht nach grobern verstandt der heyden oder Bäpstlichen regeln, sunder nach gottlichen rechten urteilen, dasselbig bestäet in ewigkeit, als ein bestendig gottes wort" (quoted in Wendel, *Le mariage*, 86). Cf. also the language of the marriage ordinances of the Elector of the Palatinate in 1556, 1563, and 1578 (*EKO* 220ff., 264ff., and Press, *Calvinismus und Territorialstaat*, 130).

[155] See my subsequent discussion in this chapter.

pal codes (especially those based on the 1531 municipal diet at Memmingen) much too mild and instead proposed the traditional but rarely enforced death penalty.[156] Although most magistrates resisted such extreme measures, the sheer ferocity of many early Protestant adultery laws and their enforcement remained impressive. One visitor to Constance in 1527 marveled at how fervently "the people of Constance want their city cleansed of all filthy adulterers and fornicators."[157] Sumptuary ordinances, especially those restricting weddings and wedding feasts, were also often issued at the prompting of members of the clergy, though in the instance of these potentially raucous gatherings of two days or more the magisterial concern for order was probably paramount. In Speyer, for example, magistrates issued fourteen such ordinances on wedding feasts alone between 1535 and 1599 (see Figure 3).

Other reformers, such as Calvin and Bucer, spent much of their careers pleading with their respective city councils for comprehensive reformed marriage codes, yet when these finally did appear (in the case of Geneva, twenty years after the establishment of a consistory), the deviation from Canon law remained minimal.[158] Perhaps none of the reformers experienced such frustration at the persistence of canonical influence in marriage as the man whose ceremonious burning of the books of Canon law in 1520 marked the beginning of his own and many others' break with Rome.

In Luther's eyes, the real opponents of a more radically Evangelical as well as customary marriage law were less the order-minded magistrates than the trained jurists who advised them. "There is not a potentate and lord around who doesn't let himself be controlled by a jurist or a theo-

---

[156] Kö II:120, 162ff., 179. Cf. Harvey, "Nürnberg Marriage Laws," 135–41, on Nuremberg.

The 1530s witnessed many failed attempts at marriage codification among Protestant cities, most notably at the diets of Memmingen (1531) and Zurich (1533), the latter resulting in forty-four articles on marriage. Though influential, these agreed standards (e.g., definition of offenses, punishments) were rarely adopted *in toto*, even by those cities participating in the assemblies. Kö I:418ff., II:14–38; and see my comments in Chapter 5.

[157] Quoted in Moeller, "Die Kirche in der evangelischen freien Städten Oberdeutschlands," 157.

[158] The magistrates of Strasbourg and Geneva were both slow to break with episcopal jurisdiction over marriage (cf. Table 1), despite the persistent complaints of their religious reformers of "grosse anstoss und missbruch in den eesachen" (Kö II:387), and likewise resistant of any significant alterations or recodification of the existing civil marriage law once they assumed jurisdiction. Bucer and Calvin, to some extent, also shared in this conservativism regarding the Canon law of marriage (e.g., Calvin's maintenance of affinity prohibitions to the third degree) and instead focused their efforts for marriage reform on urging the magistrates towards stricter criminal marriage laws and enforcement, with varying degrees of success. Cf. Kö II:383ff., 508ff., and especially 627; see my comments in Chapter 2.

Figure 3. Subjects of marital legislation in the Rhineland-Palatinate, 1535–1619.

	Wedding Feast	Clandestine Marriage	Sexual Immorality	Impediments; Divorce
City of Speyer				
Wedding Ordinances:				
1535	*			
1546	*			
1549	*			
1554	*			
1568	*			
1571	*			
1576	*			
1577	*			
1588 (2X)	*			
1597	*			
1598	*			
1599	*			
Moral/Sumptuary Ordinances:				
1540	*		*	
1549	*		*	
Palatine-Electorate				
Police Ordinances:				
1546	*	*	*	
1558	*	*	*	
1561	*	*	*	
1562	*	*	*	
1563	*	*	*	
1565	*	*	*	
1570	*	*	*	
1578	*	*	*	
1583	*	*	*	
1594	*	*	*	
Morals Ordinances:				
1575 (reissued: 1562, 1585, 1606, 1610)			*	
Ecclesiastical Ordinances:				
1556		*	*	*
1563 (reissued: 1565, 1578, 1583, 1610)		*	*	*

continued

Figure 3. *Continued*

	Wedding Feast	Clandestine Marriage	Sexual Immorality	Impediments; Divorce
Marriage Ordinances				
1556	*	*	*	*
1562 (reissued: 1565, 1578, 1583, 1610)	*	*	*	*
Marriage Court Ordinances				
1563		*	*	*
1610		*	*	*
P.-B. Speyer				
Marriage ordinances				
1577 (Wissembourg)		*		
1580 (Joehlingen & Waschbach)			*	
1582 (reissued: 1614)		*		

logian,"[159] he claimed, and in the struggle to reform society and its institutions, it was the lawyers and their Roman or Canon legal concepts that were rapidly winning. In an especially bitter 1536 letter, he lamented that "we theologians can do nothing and count for nothing [in marriage matters] since I have yet to find a jurist who will side with me against the pope in such cases."[160] Luther's tirades against "shameful jurists" and what he considered their amoral machinations were numerous and well known, but nowhere was his wrath more aroused than at any suggestion of subversion of scripturally revealed divine law and truth by papal or other man-made contrivances:

> If all the jurists in the world called a hundred thousand witnesses, but I knew in my conscience that an injustice was being done, I would not let the pope's law stand in the way of doing the right thing. [And if they say] "you are going against the law," [I ask] against what law? Against the imperial law? I shit on the imperial law, and on the pope's law too, and for good measure on the jurists' law as well.[161]

---

[159] *WA* Tischreden 5, no. 5635, in Strauss, *Law*, 98.

[160] Letter of 5 October 1536 to Graf Albrecht von Mansfeld, *WA* Briefwechsel 7:555. Luther attempted to wash his hands of the entire business, twice repeating, "Let the dead bury their dead."

[161] Sermon on 6 January 1544, *WA* 49:294ff., quoted in Strauss, *Law*, 217. See also "Von Ehesachen" (1530), *WA* 30/III:245–46, for complaints about similar infiltration regarding impediments; also Dieterich 44f.; and Strauss's discussion (pp. 214ff.).

It was especially "a thorn in Luther's flesh" that so many Evangelical jurists, such as Melchior Kling, Lazarus Spengler, and even Melanchthon, continued to "hold Canon law in repute and give it authority," and moreover even teach it at reformed universities:

> Jurists have the impudence to give public lectures to our young men on that papal filth, the canon law. So much for our efforts to banish it from our church! . . . We see them bloated with pride as they now reintroduce this stinking filth. . . . But don't provoke me! . . . We theologians are not going to be ruled and dominated by you. Authority and dominion belong to us.

"I could put up with you," he told these jurists, "if you kept to your imperial laws and let go of the papal laws. But all you doctors of both laws are partisans of the pope and his canons."[162] And in this observation, despite the frenzied accusations of betrayal, Luther had captured the essence of Evangelical jurists' and magistrates' persistent refusal to reject Canon law. Unlike him, their almost unqualified acceptance of Roman (imperial) law over most local custom led them to the educated realization that "the two codes had too common a history, and reinforced each other at too many points, to be arbitrarily pried apart."[163]

The "reception of Roman law" in Germany, as we have seen, was already well underway among the jurists of the previous century and earlier, but had only begun to gain the attention of magistrates and territorial rulers in the process of consolidating their power and thus standardizing their laws and courts. By the early sixteenth century, however, the comprehensiveness and flexibility of the *ius commune* (as the early modern version of Roman civil law was often known)[164] found

---

162 *WA* TR 2, no. 2496b; *WA* TR 6, no. 7023; *WA* TR 4, no. 4382b (1543), quoted in Strauss, *Law*, 68, 217–18. Speaking on clandestine marriage, Luther wrote, "Das gehort uns Theologen zu, last sie regieren, wir wollen conscientiam regieren" ("Von Ehesachen" [1530] *WA* 30/III:211).

163 Strauss, *Law*, 68. Luther's most conciliatory statement on the use of the Canon law of marriage was in "Von Eheesachen" (1530) *WA* 30/III:236: "Was mehr felle komen mögen, die befehl ich frumen, gottfurchtigen mennern zu entrichten, das beste sie mögen, es sei nach dem weltlichen odder geistlichen recht, wo es gut ist," but even later in the same treatise (248) he could not refrain from observing "aber is izt so unördig ynn einander geworffen und offt widder einander," that he had neither sufficient time nor space to thoroughly evaluate it.

164 Although it contained some medieval additions (e.g., in marriage, the custom of prenuptial contracts), the *ius commune*, or common law of the empire (not to be confused with English common law), remained overwhelmingly based on the Justinian corpus of the sixth century. Coing, *Europäisches Privatrecht*, 34, 139–40; Strauss, *Law*, 69ff.

appreciative disciples among secular rulers and lawyers alike. Strong and pervasive antipapal sentiment such as that of Luther might have more seriously threatened the adaptation of any "papist"-tainted legal code in newly evangelical principalities had it not been for the already widespread identification of much Roman law as "imperial," and therefore "traditional" in an age where innovation was anathema.[165] Even though this "imperial" law contained increasingly (by the sixteenth century almost exclusively) Roman and canonical principles, the transformation in the name of the German emperor was enough to reduce much of the foreignness in popular perception.

Evangelical jurists, particularly Melanchthon, were no exception to the enthusiasm of most university-educated lawyers for Roman law under any guise, and consequent disparagement for most customary law.[166] Like Luther, who championed the rights of secular authority during the Peasants' War of 1524–25 and thereafter, Melanchthon remained a firm believer in the necessity of written law and authority in the worldly realm, defending it against the "calumnies" of modern "cyclopes and centaurs" who would instead live only by "unwritten principles of right and fairness drawn from Scripture."[167] While Luther, a nonspecialist, preferred Germany's "native, simple, and concise laws" to the "long-winded and far-fetched" imperial laws,[168] Melanchthon turned the ta-

---

[165] Because the designation of "imperial" law (*kaiserliches Recht*) was often extended by jurists to include traditional legal codes such as the *Sachsenspiegel* and *Schwabenspiegel* (usually attributed to earlier emperors such as Charlemagne and Barbarossa), the term itself in fifteenth- and sixteenth-century legal reform literature came to convey two contradictory meanings, referring to Roman law as well as to medieval, customary, anti-Roman "emperors'" law. Consequently, Herman Krause (*Kaiserrecht und Rezeption* [Heidelberg, 1952]) unsympathetically dubbed imperial law the "Trojan horse" by which Roman and Cannon laws finally entered the secular German legal tradition, this time successfully avoiding the fatal characterizations of "foreign" and "innovative," which hampered more open acceptance, even among jurists.

See, Schwab, *Grundlagen*, 228–29, on Protestant use of "imperial" law in marriage laws; and Strauss, *Law*, especially 69ff. and 100ff., on resistance to legal innovation and the importance of the "imperial" designation in the reception of Roman law in Germany.

[166] Strauss notes that throughout this period customary law was almost entirely absent from all German universities' legal curricula, deemed by most jurists as "'unknowable,' a relic of an unenlightened age of chaos and confusion, and a vestigal remnant whose impending eclipse by the orderly, systematic, written imperial law was long overdue." *Law*, 173.

[167] *Oratio de legibus* (1525), quoted in ibid., 227.

[168] "An den christlichen Adel deutscher Nation von des christlichen Stands Besserung" (1520), *WA* 6:459. As was not unusual with the reformer, Luther later reversed his position on imperial law, urging young students to learn, understand, and obey the Roman imperial law, "which is the wisdom and reason inherent in all politics, and a gift of God"; see "Eine predigt, dass man Kinder zur Schulen halten solle" (1530), *WA* 30/II:557, 559, 578.

bles on the appeal to tradition to include and even embody the very same "imperial" law:

> Let it be made clear that we may, indeed, keep the emperors' laws. . . . No existing laws must be nullified, it does not matter how burdensome they are. Our forefathers who made these laws knew that our wild and unruly people must be subjected to harsh commands. Let everyone therefore accept and use the laws of his state . . . [for] Paul himself endorses pagan [i.e., Roman] laws when he says in Romans 13:1 that all authority is of God.[169]

Explicit application of ecclesiastical Roman (i.e., canonical) legal standards in issues such as marriage nevertheless remained a particularly sensitive issue among early Evangelical jurists, especially amid accusations of "popery" and "Romanist invention." In an anonymous tract, Lazarus Spengler, secretary to the Nuremberg city council, published several passages from Canon law, vehemently denying that "like the spider, we suck, draw, and use from these books of church law only matter opposed and repugnant to divine and human truth, Scripture, virtue, and fairness." Rather, he countered, these works contained much "that is godly, Christian, founded in Scripture, and conducive to an upright, honest, and pious life."[170]

A risky public position for an Evangelical leader in 1530, yet it was one that already by the next generation of Protestants had become established, not only in the many secular ordinances on marriage but among almost all Evangelical jurists and theologians as well. Just twenty-six years after the Strasbourg city council had unequivocally rejected all "pagan or papist" rules in its first "reformed" marriage law, a revised ordinance of 1560 spoke only of "divine natural law" and "written imperial law." Within five years the same city council even openly acknowledged the Canon law of marriage as authoritative.[171] The Elector's 1563

---

169 *Unterricht der Visitatorn an die Pfarhern ym Kurfürstentum zu Sachssen* (1528), quoted in Strauss, *Law*, 230.

170 [Lazarus Spengler], *Eyn kurtzer auszug aus dem pebstlichen rechten der Decret und Decretalen* (Wittenberg, 1530), A iii^b–A iv^a, quoted in Strauss, *Law*, 219–20. For the controversy surrounding Spengler's selection, see *WA* 30/II:215–18.

171 The 1565 revision of the 1534 marriage ordinance's section on clandestine marriage, for instance, finds its legal basis in "dem Goettlichen Gesaz, den alten Canonibus, Dazu auch in den keyserlichen Rechten" (Wendel, *Le mariage*, 86–87).

On the significance of Roman law for Protestant reformers, see especially Anneliese Sprengler-Ruppenthal, "Zur Verwendung von Bibelstellen in Kirchengangs des 15. Jahrhunderts," *Zeitschrift der Savigny-Stiftung für Rechtsgeschichte, (Kanonistiche Abteilung)* 98 (1981), 310–38.

marriage court ordinance, composed by a former professor of law, concurred that in

> such cases and matters for which there is no known basis for judgment
> other than the decrees of the popes, if the same are not contrary to divine
> Word or commandment, the marital judges may, after cutting away all that
> is excessive and unnecessary, use such decrees to help them in reaching a
> decision on the matter.[172]

Eventually even Protestant theologians began to acknowledge openly their reliance on the Canon law of marriage and its trained experts,[173] leading Johann Aurifaber, the editor of Luther's *Table Talk*, to confirm the great reformer's worst fears of thirty years earlier, that "politicians, lawyers, and courtiers" run the Church now, "directing religion like worldly affairs."[174]

Aurifaber's estimate of governmental control, though not unfounded, certainly exaggerated the new role of the State in marriage litigation, particularly where the courts themselves were concerned. After breaking with outside episcopal jurisdiction, most Protestant territorial and municipal leaders in fact resisted full and immediate secularization of all marriage authority. Instead they continued, at least ostensibly, a divided secular–ecclesiastical marriage jurisdiction within their own realms, recognizing marriage as a *res mixta*, or "mixed matter." The key change from the pre-Reformation division of authority was that, in both "reformed" and many Catholic polities, all of the ecclesiastical organs involved, with rare exception, stood directly or indirectly accountable to the secular authorities in marriage and other legal or disciplinary matters. Local communal authority – in most cases – remained strong, though increasingly checked in territorial states by a cadre of inspectors, central councils, and, most important, local state officials. More direct

---

[172] *EKO* 293. Written in the margin of one surviving manuscript: "N.B. Jus canonicum no repugnans sacris literis in defectu juris civilis sequendum." The elector's 1556 ecclesiastical ordinance, on the other hand, had spoken of *gottlich*, *naturlich*, and *keyserlich*, but never explicitly *geistlich* (Canon) law (*EKO*, 220ff).

[173] See, for example, Martin Chemnitz, *Examen Concilii Tridentini* (Frankfurt, 1574), part II, 290ff., in which the influential Lutheran theologian consistently rejects any sacramental definition of marriage for Protestants, but openly acknowledges the authority of most Canon law on the subject. See also Coing, *Europäisches Privatrecht* 224–25.

[174] From the preface to Aurifaber's edition of Luther's *Tischreden* (1566), printed in Johann Georg Walch, ed., *Dr. Martin Luthers Sämmtliche Schriften*, vol. 22 (Halle, 1743), 49.

and centralized regulation remained possible only in those relatively few strong and compact city-states. In this way, magistrates and territorial rulers served both of their main concerns in legal reform – namely, taking more direct and complete control of all such issues within their realms while avoiding the disjuncture and confusion of too overt and radical a break with the traditional order.

At the risk of oversimplification, all German marriage jurisdiction after the Peace of Augsburg (1555) may be classified as one of three general types (Figure 4): divided, strongly secular, or mixed. The most common among secular Catholic polities of the period was the first, namely, continuation and even intensification of the traditional divided marriage jurisdiction. Within all Catholic cities and some Catholic territorial states, the bishop's *Officialatus* continued to decide (almost exclusively) marital validity disputes,[175] whereas related criminal and property matters were handled by the usual assortment of local secular and ecclesiastical authorities (Figure 4). Indeed, in many dioceses, the *Officialatus* had already become the Catholic equivalent of a Protestant marriage court. In Constance, the largest German diocese, marital disputes comprised 97.2 percent of all cases between 1551 and 1600.[176] If anything, the resulting jurisdictional divisions between local, secular authorities and regional ecclesiastical ones were more sharply defined than at any time during the Middle Ages.[177]

The second pattern, strong secular jurisdiction, prevailed in Protestant cities where magistrates harbored much more centralizing and exclusive ambitions regarding marriage litigation. The elimination of any independent ecclesiastical authority in this area, though, was far from a foregone conclusion in newly Evangelical cities, at least from the perspective of the earliest reformed clerics or magistrates. Moreover, the relationship between religious reformers and their respective secular authorities remained, in every polity, a complex and unique one.[178] Yet on the question of marriage reform, all reformed clerics played an undeniably common role in secular authorities' establishment of their own

---

[175] The major exceptions to the pattern–Bavaria and all prince-bishoprics–are discussed later in this chapter.

[176] Safley, *Let No Man Put Asunder*, 49.

[177] Cf. the example of the imperial Catholic city of Freiburg; ibid., 91–95.

[178] See, for example, Thomas Brady, *Ruling Class, Regime and Reformation at Strasbourg, 1520–1555* (Leiden, 1978), especially 202ff., on the intricacies of local clergy–magistrate relationships in Strasbourg.

	VALIDITY DISPUTES	CRIMINAL & PROPERTY DISPUTES	EXAMPLES
MIXED/DIVIDED	*Regional Ecclesiastical Court*	*Local Secular Authorities* -village court/elders -town council/city court -territorial court/bailiff OR *Ecclesiastical Authorities* -local lay synod -episcopal or archidiaconal court	All

PRE-1525

1525–1619

	VALIDITY DISPUTES	CRIMINAL & PROPERTY DISPUTES	EXAMPLES
1. DIVIDED	*Regional Ecclesiastical Court*	*Local Secular & Ecclesiastical Authorities*	*All Catholic municipal & some territorial*
2. STRONG SECULAR	*Local Secular Court* (existing or new)	→	Imperial & Swiss cities esp. Zurich, Augsburg, Ulm, Strasbourg, Geneva*, **Speyer**; no known territorial
3. MIXED	*Regional Ecclesiastical OR Secular Court*	*Local Secular & Ecclesiastical Authorities*	Some Protestant cities (e.g., Basel, Bern, Lindau); Catholic ecclesiastical states (including **P.B. Speyer**) & most Protestant & Catholic territorial states (including **Palatine–Electorate**)

*disputes decided *de facto* by consistory, enforced by magistracy marriage jurisdiction.[179] In Zurich, the originator of the strong marital jurisdiction, all marriage cases, including some criminal ones, were initially handled in the first instance by the clergy; even after the establishment of an official marriage court in 1526, the clergy continued to exercise extensive judicial and disciplinary powers.[180] Indeed, in most cities, the very creation of an independent marriage court of general consistory usually came at the prompting of reformed clerics who recognized the need for one uniform, scripturally based standard, with appropriate secular means of enforcement.[181] Not until such institutions actually began operating did those conflicts that in hindsight appear inevitable become likewise apparent to the early partners in reform, on both sides.

It should probably come as no surprise that those cities and territorial states receptive to "a priesthood of all believers" and *sola scriptura* were loathe to recognize any more ecclesiastical or reformed clerical authority than was absolutely necessary. Such sentiments were particularly strong among those rulers who initiated the official break with the Roman hierarchy in favor of their own scripturally inspired enforcement of God's will. Still, one cannot help but be struck by the very ferocity with which almost all of these civic and territorial leaders resisted the creation of any independent ecclesiastical institutions or authority. After all, as reformer Christoph Vischer reminded Protestant rulers and magistrates, they "[could] never be grateful enough to our beloved gospel for having raised [their] estate from the mire into which the papacy and its henchmen had plunged it to the honor and dignity it now enjoys."[182]

The same reformed clerics who played such instrumental roles in convincing secular authorities to make the jurisdictional break in the first place were thus alternately shocked and outraged when they found themselves gradually excluded from any genuine institutional power.

---

[179] Cf. examples of Strasbourg (Kö II:377ff.), Geneva (Kö II:503ff.), and Nuremberg (Kö II:387ff.).

[180] The marriage ordinance of 1526 provided for sharing of initiation in all marriage litigation between the pastors and the newly established marriage court, with punishment by the town council (Kö I:110ff.).

[181] Cf. example of Strasbourg where a group of clerics headed by Bucer, Hedio, and Zell repeatedly demanded of the town council "den offentlichen eebruch abzustellen und den zu strafen und ein gottgefällig ordnung in ehesachen fürzunemen wie zu Zurich und Constentz" (Kö II:387ff.).

[182] *Christliche Auslegung und Erklerung der Haustafel* (Leipzig, 1578); translated in Strauss, *Luther's House of Learning*, 240.

Religious reformers had recognized from the outset the conservative and even authoritarian goals of Protestant magistrates in this area. It was also no secret that governmental control of marriage simultaneously offered magistrates an opportunity for expanded sovereignty over their subjects. Still, most clerics assumed that such concerns remained close enough to their own to ensure them key positions of influence.[183] Throughout the 1520s and 1530s most reformed preachers thus accepted and even encouraged a strong secular marriage jurisdiction, albeit reserving a strong, moral advisory role for themselves. Yet even this consultatory function remained extremely restricted by most secular authorities – a heavy blow to many reformers' original aspirations. To maintain any influence in the reform and enforcement of marriage law, most Protestant clerics were thus forced to accept cooperation with the more powerful secular authorities on whatever terms available.

Consequently, only a few Protestant cities of this period maintained an even balance of power in marriage jurisdiction between two relatively independent secular and ecclesiastical authorities. Within one year after its creation, the marriage court of Bern (handling validity disputes only) had successfully eliminated all appeals of its decisions to the town council. After a longer struggle with its council for control, Ulm's marriage court gained a similar, though short-lived, independence from the magistrates.[184] Still, except for the continuing designation of marriage as a *res mixta*, it would be difficult to term even these relatively independent bodies "ecclesiastical," even in those rare instances when members of the clergy were permitted to be among the judges.[185] Rather, they represented more properly institutions of public morality and discipline – "ecclesiastical" in the same sense as the medieval lay synod. In fact, in most of the reformed polities of the sixteenth century, if such a body

---

[183] Cf. articles of *Memminger Tag* (26 February–1 March 1531), especially regarding judgment of all marriage cases by the local town council, supported by *Zuchtherren*, also appointed by the council. Kö II:30–34; also, Dieterich 83–93 on general clerical support for secular jurisdiction over marriage.

Ironically, as Köhler notes of Zurich, the more these government courts emphasized their "Christian" nature, the more they became administrative rather than judicial organs of the magistrates' theocratic apparatus (Kö II;185–88).

[184] Kö I:322, on Bern; II:73ff., on Ulm. Köhler argues that the source of the delay in Ulm was the lengthy and intense struggle over authority between the magistrates and clerics. Cf. also example of Basel's marriage court (Kö I:268ff.).

[185] Cf. examples of Lindau (Kö II:183–87, 196ff.) and Reutlingen (Kö II:274–78).

existed, it was invariably a reconstruction of an already existing court or police organ, such as the lay synod or morals police.[186]

In those few cities where a more independent and clerical body did develop, it was almost always paralleled by another police organ directly under the secular authorities.[187] Even in Geneva, "the most perfect school of Christ," the de facto legal power and influence of the newly established (1541) consistory in all aspects of marriage practice owed much to the personal authority of Calvin, and was never de jure. Contrary to the theocratic stereotype of the city, both Calvin and the city council consistently recognized and emphasized a division of legal power between secular and ecclesiastical authorities. By law, the powers of the ecclesiastical organ (consistory) remained extremely limited (in Calvin's words, to provide the "norm and standard for all governmental acts") and completely reliant on the generally compliant secular authority for enforcement.[188] Memmingen actually came closer in practice to the Calvinist theoretical division of legal power, though once again the town council supplied both personnel and means of enforcement.[189] If such restrictions were not enough to prevent a strong, independent ecclesiastical legal authority, most of these same magistrates finally took away the only real weapon at such a body's disposal – excommunication.[190] Ecclesiastical authority in these marriage jurisdictions was not entirely illusory, but it was certainly far from being the independent check to secular power that most clerical reformers had intended.

Indeed, for almost all Evangelical and Reformed municipal jurisdic-

---

[186] In Zurich, for instance, the town council combined a network of rural marriage wardens (*Ehegäumer*) with municipal police to intensify enforcement of marital law. See Kilchenmann, *Organisation des zürcherischen Ehegerichts*, 48–76, as well as 86ff., on the council domination of jurisdiction and procedure. On the continuity between lay synods and Protestant consistories and presbyteries, see especially Koeniger's argument, *Die Sendgerichte*, I:1ff.; II:158ff.

[187] Cf. examples of Basel (Kö I:284ff.) and Ulm (Kö II:56ff.).

[188] "norme et critère de tous les actes du gouvernement." Calvin's original proposal for an independent marriage court with only an advisory role for pastors was rejected by the Geneva city council in February 1538. Not until his triumphant return and the council's adoption of his proposed ecclesiastical ordinances in 1541 was his demand for a consistory also accepted. Still, the power of excommunication remained a hotly contested one and never undisputedly at the disposal of the consistory before 1561 (Kö II:517, 557ff., 571ff., 604ff., 640). As a result of this concession, the town council could continue its initial resistance to full secular handling of marriage and other "choses qui ne sont civiles" (Kö II:508–41), while at the same time avoiding the establishment of a completely independent and therefore uncontrollable ecclesiastical organ.

[189] In this case, enforcement was provided by the *Rat's* nine *Zuchtherren*; Kö II:162ff.

[190] See n. 205.

tions, the greater secularization and centralization proposed by Safley for Protestant polities in general does indeed appear to have been the rule.[191] Even in Speyer, a precariously situated and cautious community, the town council maintained a firm, direct control over all marital property and criminal litigation after its break with the bishop's lay synod (mainly through its criminal court), deciding marital vow disputes with no reference whatsoever to clerical advisors (except on questions of consanguinity and affinity) until 1598.[192] Even after the establishment of an ecclesiastical consistory around this time,[193] the role of pastors and theologians remained an extremely restricted one. Already by 1610, for instance, in its installment of ten judges to the consistory, the town council spoke against "perpetuating the practice of appointing clerics to such positions,"[194] explicitly confirming what had already been suggested by the council's previous actions.

At the same time, the terms of the Peace of Augsburg on ecclesiastical jurisdiction required most municipal authorities to maintain at least the semblance of religious authority over marriage. Of all the marriage ordinances issued by German cities during the sixteenth century, only those of Strasbourg conspicuously omitted the usual reference to secular au-

---

[191] Curiously, though his own evidence is based on the Reformed city of Basel, Safley argues that the centralization he finds there is actually more typical of Protestant *territorial* states (*Let No Man Put Asunder*, 122).

[192] Cf. cases of clandestine marriage (8 May 1595; StAS IB/8, Bd. 2, 11ᵛ–13ʳ), malicious desertion (3 May 1597; StAS IB/6, Bd. 2, 6ᵛ), and multiple vows disputes (23 February 1598; StAS IB/8, Bd. 2, 204ᵛ–205ᵛ).

On the role of the clergy before this, we have only a marginal note to the vicar-general's five-point defense of episcopal jurisdiction, which apparently, up to this point, was limited to "handl mit den gradibq. consanguin. und gevatterschaft" (22 September 1597; StAS IB/8, Bd. 2, 166ᵛ).

[193] The exact date of the consistory's formation and assumption of marital jurisdiction is unclear. As late as the time of the city advocate's protest to the bishop in 1598, for instance, there are protocols of the city council handling validity disputes with no reference whatsoever to any ecclesiastical body. Cf. cases of clandestine marriage (8 May 1595; StAS IB/8, Bd. 2, 11ᵛ–13ʳ), malicious desertion (3 May 1597; StAS IB/6, 6ᵛ), and multiple vows disputes (23 February 1598; StAS IB/8, Bd. 2, 204ᵛ–205ᵛ). By 1610, however, the consistory had already been established, as the council considered reappointments of its ten judges (11 June 1610; StAS IB/8, Bd. 5, 397).

[194] "Zuvorderst wie daß Consistorium mit personen zubestellen stetts d.J. dahin daß ein Rhat aus ihren mittel personen dazu zu verordnen hett und ob sie einen von ihren Advocaten dazu bestellen wolten. Nach gelegenheit könt man auch einen oder andern auß die Theologis dazu verordnen doch dazu zu perpetuiren ist nicht rhatsam, haben selbst viel mengel die einer co[gn]ition von nöten, die Materia circa iuram oder obinctum" (11 June 1610; StAS IB/8, Bd. 5, 397). Within five years, however (6 November 1615; StAS IB/8, Bd. 5, 196ff.), the *Rat* did consent to appoint one *Theologer* to the consistory (StAS IA/12; StAS IB/8, Bd. 2, 193ᵛ–194ʳ; also Harster, *Strafrecht*, 187).

thorities assuming marital jurisdiction "in the name of the church."[195] Coing justifiably considers such open "secularization" of marriage authority (as in Holland and Zeeland) the exception to the *res mixta* definition proclaimed by all other reformed governments in Europe.[196] Still, as we have seen, the interpretation of this legal definition allowed considerable flexibility in the actual role of secular authorities in marital jurisdiction: from the relatively independent marriage courts of Bern and Ulm, to those more dependent on the existing city and territorial court, as in Zurich, Basel, and Augsburg,[197] to those instances where marriage litigation formed only a general business area within the already existing court, as in Nuremberg and Constance.[198] Whatever the individual arrangement, one characteristic was clearly common to all: consistent and unswerving dedication to magisterial control in all areas.

This degree of centralization and open secularization was virtually unknown, on the other hand, at the territorial level. Rather, here (and thus throughout the Holy Roman Empire in general) the most common jurisdictional arrangement was a combination of the preceding two types into a third pattern, which may be termed "mixed." In this system, the division of marital jurisdiction into local and regional was generally preserved, but both now answered to the same ultimate legal and political authority: the territorial ruler. This arrangement especially typified large territorial states, such as the Calvinist Palatine-Electorate, but

---

[195] Kö II:409; Wendel, *Le mariage*, 92. On the concept of *christliche Oberkeit* among magistrates, Moeller writes, "Alle ähmlichen Bemühungen in vorreformatorischer Zeit wie auch die vergleichbaren Anstrengungen in den lutherischen Städten wurden kraftvoll überboten und man hatte kein Zweifel daran, daß man so in der rechten Weise Gott die Ehre gebe, man wart überzeugt, daß dieser Eifer und sogar der Aufpasserdienst 'ain christlich werck' sei" ("Die Kirche in den evangelischen freien Städten," 157). See also Hans Liermann, "Evangelisches Kirchenrecht und staatliches Eherecht in Deutschland; Rechtsgeschichtliches und Gegenwartsprobleme," in *Existenz und Ordnung: Festschrift für Erik Wolf* (Frankfurt, 1962) ed. Thomas Wurtenberger, 111.

[196] Coing (*Europäisches Privatrecht*, 225, 231). stresses that technically the secular authorities were empowered by the consistories in this area and not the reverse. "Diese konsistorien waren kirchliche Behörden, die mit Theologen und Juristen besetzt waren," – any related activity on the part of the secular ruler was solely in his role as *Summus Episcopus* of the land. See also Dieterich 246–69 on Protestant marriage jurisdictions in Germany; and Heinz Schilling, "Religion and Society in the Northern Netherlands," in *Religion, Political Culture and the Emergence of Early Modern Society: Essays in German and Dutch History* (Leiden, 1992), 381–88, on civil marriage in the Dutch Netherlands.

[197] On Augsburg, see Kö II:292, 658; and Roper, *Holy Household*, 61–82. On Basel: Staehlin, *Ehescheidung in Basel*, 26ff.; Kö I:240ff.; and Safley, *Let No Man Put Asunder, 121–65*. On Zurich: Kilchenmann, *Die Organisation des zürcherischen Ehegerichts*, 86–205.

[198] Kö II:47, 106ff. 120, 658; Harvey, "Nürnberg Marriage Laws," 102.

Reordering marriage and society

could also be found in a few Catholic city-states, such as Lindau (Figure 4). What most distinguished it from the previous two types of jurisdiction was the frequent, and often indiscriminate, mix of secular and ecclesiastical authorities at all levels. All marital property and criminal jurisdiction in this pattern continued to be handled at the lowest judicial level possible, by some combination of the respective ruler's bailiff and local elders. In this respect, the jurisdictional scenario changed much less with the introduction of the Reformation than might be expected. What did change – drastically even – was the indirect authority that both Protestant and Catholic territorial princes exercised through secular and ecclesiastical officials, now all answerable to the same legal as well as administrative authority.

All German Protestant territorial states, whether based more on the Evangelical episcopal model of Saxony or the Reformed presbyterian structure of Emden, followed the same pattern in marital jurisdiction.[199] In the Calvinist Palatine-Electorate, marriage jurisdiction was centralized in order of legal priority. The most important cases (i.e., divorces and other validity disputes) went to a special regional court, often a consistory but in this instance the Elector's secular marriage court, composed of seven jurists drawn from his supreme court.[200] All lesser criminal and property marital matters were left to the usual network of local

[199] Cf. examples of Württemberg: Günther Erbe, "Das Ehescheidungsrecht im Herzogtum Württemberg seit der Reformation," *Zeitschrift für württembergische Landesgeschichte* 14 (1955), 108ff.; Bernhardt, *Die Zentralbehörden des Herzogtums Württemberg*, 21–22; Kö II:263ff.; Saxony: Karlheinz Blaschke, *Sachsen im Zeitalter der Reformation* (Gütersloh, 1970), 17ff. and 120ff.; Braunschweig: Müller-Volbehr, *Die geistliche Gerichte*, 252ff.

On Protestant consistorial organization, see L. A. Richter, *Geschichte der evangelischen kirchenverfassung in Deutschland* (Leipzig, 1851); Karl Rieker, *Die rechtliche Stellung der evangelischen Kirche Deutschlands ihrer geschichtlichen Entwicklung bis zur Gegenwart*, (Leipzig, 1893); Karl Müller, "Die Anfänge der Konsistorialverfassung im lutherischen Deutschland," *Historische Zeitschrift* 102/93, Bd. 6 (1909), 1–30; Emil Sehling, *Geschichte der protestantischen Kirchenverfassung. Grundriß der Geschichtswissenschaft zur Einführung in das Studium der deutschen Geschichte des Mittelalters und der Neuzeit* 2nd ed. (Leipzig, 1914).

[200] Press maintains, with good indirect documentation, that the Elector's marriage court, operating from about 1558 on, was never anything but a weekly subdivision of his already existing *Hofgericht*: "Nicht einmal die Fiktion eines Ehegericht ist erhalten geblieben; die Säkularisierung der Ehesachen hatte ihre letzte Stufe erreicht, vor der man in Heidelberg noch zurückschreckte" (*Calvinismus und Territorialstaat*, 304; also 133ff.). Cf. *Ehegerichtsordnung* of 1563 (*EKO* 289ff.), reissued in 1582 as part of the general *Landrecht*. Unfortunately, no protocols of the *Ehegericht* have survived from this period.

Württemberg followed a similar practice but in the duchy of Braunschweig, however, a later 1595 edict required strict separation of the chancellory, supreme court, and consistory so that "der allerlei Mißverständnisse unter euch eingerissen" (Müller-Volbehr, *Die geistliche Gerichte*, 270–71).

secular and ecclesiastical authorities.[201] As in Geneva, the boundaries between the secular and the ecclesiastical often blurred so as to become indiscernible. In addition to their usual police duties, for instance, local State officials were also responsible for enforcing Church ordinances, religious instruction, investigating cases of concubinage and desertion, punishing adultery and fornication, and occasionally even deciding marriage contract disputes (though the latter properly belonged to the marriage court).[202] At the same time, ecclesiastical Inspectors and special Superintendents instituted a modified version of pre-Reformation synodal practices under the direction of the newly established central Ecclesiastical Council. In cooperation with local pastors and elders, these Church officials were to visit all parishes and report to these secular authorities any suspected cases of marriage within forbidden degrees, concubinage, illegitimate births, prostitution, adultery, and malicious desertion.[203] Meanwhile, the more numerous cases of lower judicial priority – domestic violence and prenuptial pregnancies – were left entirely to local church presbyteries or consistories.[204] Here traditional lay elders continued to dominate much as they had in medieval lay

---

[201] Cf. my discussion of the Bacharach consistory in Chapter 5; here criminal marriage cases comprised 10–25 percent of the total case load from 1585–1619.

[202] As before the introduction of the Reformation in the Palatinate, criminal marriage matters were all handled by local courts and authorities, usually at the direction of the local *Amtman*. Cf. protocols of the *Rat der vier Täler* of the *Amt* Bacharach (4 July 1570): "Befhalen die amptleute dem gantzen rhat zun vier thalen, das se uber der policeyordnung, sonderlich des hochzeitscostens halber, vleißig halten sollten, sonst wurde er ihren, der burgermeister, nit vergessessen . . ." (LAK 613/502, 60ʳ).

See also examples of bailiff decisions on disputed vows in *Oberamt* protocols of Bacharach, 1609–13 (LAK 4/1631, 17ʳ, 211ʳ⁻ᵛ); 1614–21 (LAK 4/1632, 96, 104–6); also Johannes Casimir's instructions to the *Rat* of Neustadt, 1586 (LAS A1/1753, esp. articles 5 and 6, 110ff.).

[203] *EKO* 231. The *Kirchenrat* was composed of three laymen and three clerics. Cf. instructions to special superintendents and inspectors (*EKO* 231, 249 [1556]; 259 [1558], 538 [1587], etc.), sextons (*EKO* 246 [1556]), *Kirchenrat* (*EKO* 418ff. [1564]). The *Classicalkonvente* (established in 1587, as a result of the excommunication controversy; see n. 205) performed similar police and surveillance functions (*EKO* 527ff.; Press, *Calvinismus und Territorialstaat*, 114ff., 125ff., 575); and Münch, *Zucht und Ordnung*, especially 99–109, on the Palatinate, and 119–51, on presbyterial and clerical organization.

[204] Although electoral ordinances consistently defined both *hurerei* and *völlerie* as serious offenses to be passed on to secular authorities, only adultery cases were clearly recognized as such in practice. Cf. the caseload of the Bacharach consistory from 1585–1619, discussed in Chapter 5. See also E. W. Zeeden, "Calvinistische Elemente in der Kurpfalzischen Kirchenordnung von 1563," in *Existenz und Ordnung: Festschrift für Erik Wolf*, ed. Thomas Wurtenberger (Frankfurt, 1962), 206ff.; J. Estèbe and B. Volger, "La Genèse d'une société protestant: Étude comparée de quelques registres consistoriaux languedociens et palatins vers 1600," *Annales* 31 (1976), 363ff.

synods. Significantly, though, the ultimate ecclesiastical punishment of excommunication remained reserved to the Elector himself (through the Ecclesiastical Council).[205] Thus despite occasional internal political and administrative divisions[206] this system of shared yet hierarchical authority finally secured the Elector's position as *Summus Episcopus* in his own realm, especially in all marital matters.

Catholic territorial states offer perhaps the most surprising example of mixed marital jurisdiction. Indeed, if any territorial states qualify for extensive secularization of marital jurisdiction, they ironically would come from the ranks of such strong Catholic states as Bavaria, Upper Austria, and especially France.[207] In exchange for continuing recognition of clerical privilege, for instance, the archbishop of Salzburg and the bishops of Freising, Passau, Regensburg, and Chimsee granted the duke of Bavaria full sovereignty in almost all other areas of ecclesiastical jurisdiction, including marriage.[208] As in Protestant areas, the 1583 Concordance represented more of an acceptance of the status quo than a sudden expansion. Like their Rhenish cousins, the Bavarian Wit-

---

[205] Controversy over the power to excommunicate was a prominent feature of almost every territorial and municipal Reformation. In the Palatinate the debate was particularly fierce as it involved a fundamental difference in interpretation of Reformed practice, namely between those who favored the Genevan presbyterian model of Church discipline (led by Calvin's disciple Olevian) and those who preferred the strong secular example of Zurich (led by Ursinus). Though Olevian's group did achieve some notable successes toward a strong ecclesiastical discipline – including establishment of the *officium presbyterorum* in 1571 (*EKO* 448ff.), which apparently extended power of excommunication to the elders – the powers of the Elector and his secular administrators remained supreme in this area and the disciplinary system that emerged after the Lutheran interim of 1576–83 bore much more resemblance to that of Zurich than Geneva. While the ecclesiastical branch – *Kirchenrat*, presbyters, and *Classicalkonvente* – maintained some control through inspection and warning, the power of excommunication – as in the original ecclesiastical ordinance of Ottheinrich in 1556 – was reserved to the Elector alone. See Press, *Calvinismus und Territorialstaat*, especially 114–27, and 243ff.; also Ruth Wesel-Roth, *Thomas Erastus: Ein Beitrag zur Geschichte der reformierten Kirche und zur Lehre von der Staatssouveränität* (Lahr, 1954), especially 43–81.
[206] When Johannes Casimir, for instance, inherited the territory of Pfalz-Lautern upon Friedrich III's death in 1576, he argued that marital jurisdiction was an indispensable part of his own *Landeshoheit*, and thus refused to send such matters to the Heidelberg *Ehegericht*. His heir, Ludwig-Philipp made the same claim in 1612, and not until 1620, according to an agreement with Friedrich V, was he to decide whether to recognize the Heidelberg court and pay one-fifth of its budget. Press, *Calvinismus und Territorialstaat*, 304, 502–4.
[207] See Jürgen Bücking, *Frühabsolitismus und Kirchenreform in Tirol (1566–1655): Ein Beitrag zum Ringen zwischen "Staat" und "Kirche" in der frühen Neuzeit* (Wiesbaden, 1972); also Karlheinz Blaschke, "The Reformation and the Rise of the Territorial State," in Tracy, *Luther and the Modern State*, 73ff.; and on France, my comments in Chapter 4.
[208] 1583 concordance; D. Albrecht, "Die kirchlich-religiöse Entwicklung, 1500-1745," in *Handbuch der Bayerischen Geschichte*, ed. Max Spindler, (Munich, 1966), II:629-30. See also E. Mayer, *Die Kirchenhoheitsrechte des König von Bayern* (Munich, 1884), 52ff.

telsbachs had made great inroads into ecclesiastical jurisdiction during the previous century, already by this time effectively controlling most criminal and marital property matters through their own ecclesiastical council and secular officials.[209]

In the much smaller Prince-Bishopric of Speyer, on the other hand, the bishop continued to rely on his traditional *Officialatus* for civil marital cases, while using his privy council (*Hofrat*), local secular officials (*Amtleute, Schultheiße*), and chapters interchangeably in enforcing his criminal marital jurisdiction. In a not untypical adultery case in 1582, for example, Martin Harten of Jöhlingen was arrested by the local village official, tried before the bailiff of Obergrombach, and ultimately judged on appeal by the cathedral chapter.[210] Although some internal jurisdictional rivalries apparently persisted among the archdeacons,[211] the dramatic reduction in the bishop's ecclesiastical jurisdiction actually permitted a much closer identification of his temporal and spiritual realms than at any time since the early Middle Ages. Like the Protestant princes surrounding him, he was *Summus Episcopus* of a united secular and ecclesiastical domain, reigning as ultimate (rather than absolute) lawgiver and judge.

In the conclusion of his monumental overview of sixteenth-century marriage courts and consistories, Walther Köhler proposes that "Zwingli belongs at the head of the development of reformed marriage law and consistories, and the famous Geneva consistory of Calvin is the end, not starting point within this process."[212] Only in Geneva, he argues, did Zwingli's idea and model for ecclesiastical control of marriage reach full fruition, yet even here the blurring of State–Church judicial boundaries ultimately resulted in "the bankruptcy of Church discipline."[213] Thus,

---

[209] Cf. Strauss, *Law*, 155f., on use of the *Rentmeister*; and Hsia, *Social Discipline*, 41, on establishment of a *Geistliche Rat* in 1570; also P. Klein, *Historische Entwicklung der Beamtenbesoldung in Altbayern, 1180–1850* (Innsbruck, 1966).

[210] 26 September 1582; GLA 61/10945, 901. See also other such cases in protocols of 1530–1622 (GLA 61/10933–56), data on adultery prosecutions of the *Hofrat* presented in Table 4, and similar practice in Udenheim, seat of the bishop's government from the mid-sixteenth century on (Nopp, *Geschichte der Stadt Philippsburg*, 79ff.).

[211] There is evidence of continuing operation of the archidiaconal *Officialatus* at least until the end of the Council of Trent and possibly until the council's official adoption by the diocese of Speyer in the 1570s. Cf. court ordinances of ca. 1540 and 1560 with references to "consistorum ecclesiasticorum spirensium." See GLA 67/486, 2–21 (Riedner II, no. 34, 143ff.); GLA 67/277, 8ᵛ–9ʳ (Riedner II, no. 40, 156ff.).

[212] Kö II:653-54. This thesis is also stated in Kö I:231, 448.

[213] Kö II:662.

not only does Köhler dispute Esmein's claim that the trend in marriage jurisdiction was always toward full secular control, but contends that the actual process was – at least initially – in the other direction, toward stronger ecclesiastical involvement.

The evolution of marital jurisdictions as presented here obviously suggests otherwise. While Esmein's model probably exaggerates the movement toward secularization as inevitable or universally forthcoming (though not prevailing in Protestant England, for instance, until 1857), it is unlikely that judicial expansion of all early modern states could have been suppressed, especially considering the inherently dependent nature of ecclesiastical judicial power. Even when, as in the case of the Lutheran interim in the Palatinate under Ludwig VI, the Elector himself attempted to return all marital validity to the ecclesiastical sphere, the secular bureaucratic hold on the matter proved too strong and well established.[214]

At the same time, followers of Esmein misrepresent sixteenth-century Protestant marital reforms when they speak in terms of either "secularization" or "centralization." If secularization means the uniting of all marital litigation under exclusively secular institutions, only a few city-states would qualify, and even then with some reservations. If secularization means granting authority over all secular and ecclesiastical institutions handling marriage to one temporal ruler, then this must also include several Catholic prince-bishops, such as Speyer, thereby refuting the close identification with Protestantism.

The term "centralization," as we have seen, remains even more problematic in defining sixteenth-century changes in marital jurisdiction. Safley's findings for Basel, for instance, are indeed significant, but not in

---

[214] Cf. Elector Ludwig VI's attempts at a Lutheran restoration in the Palatinate during his short reign (1576–83). One of his chief concerns was a return to the traditional Church–State judicial boundaries, which the Reformed government of Friedrich III had, for the most part, eliminated. Still, an early mandate of the new Elector (ca. 1578) on ecclesiastical restitution in all areas was notably reserved on the issue of legal jurisdiction. Whether this reflected his own genuine commitment to a strong secular role in the area of marriage litigation or was more a realistic assessment of probable resistance is open to speculation. Article 8 on hearing witnesses in civil marriage cases is especially revealing: "Ad 8m dörft Eß hart halten, die zeugen in vim iurisdictionis Ecclesiasticae, ohner Sucht der churpfaltz weltlichen herrshafft ad ferendum testimonium zu citiren: doch aber auch ex causis certis nit gerathen sein selbig bey Churpfaltz aber ad Ambtern, sine adiunctione viri Ecclesiastici (:dargleichen sie zu vermeyten preiuditz Ihrer iruisdiction, und wegen eine in ihre sincerität gesagt apprehendirenden mißtrawen schwerlich admittiren werden:) Verhoren zu laßen; cum totalitis decisio in probationibq. iudici factis consistat; alßo dörffte mann sich wohl cum requisitione transmittendorum testium, doch daßsclbige ohn fehlbahelich erfolge, Vergnügen laßen" (GLA 77/4195, 4ᵛ).

terms of the broad confessional pattern he has proposed.[215] Instead he has provided us with opposite ends of the spectrum of sixteenth-century marriage jurisdiction: Catholic city-states such as Freiburg on one end and strong Protestant city-states such as Basel on the other. The majority of German states, however, fell somewhere in between. Not only were most territorial states' legal apparatuses not developed enough to assume the expanded judicial role, but many of their leaders had yet to accomplish the necessary legal standardization throughout their respective realms. Whatever bureaucratic expansion territorial rulers did achieve was gradual – almost glacial in political terms – and started well before the Reformation. Even at the beginning of the seventeenth century, the key local authority figures of bailiff and pastor continued to operate in what one historian has called a "Janus-faced existence" – caught between their loyalties to the commune and those to the lord. As long as both types of leaders continued to be drawn from the local patriciate rather than a pool of professionally trained jurists and functionaries, State authority at the local level must be considered as "officialdom" rather than any effective bureaucratic centralization.[216]

The popular concept of law based on local custom represented an even deeper obstacle to bureaucratic expansion. Early modern statebuilders obviously anticipated Weber's dictum, "no bureaucratization before codification," but just as obviously required much time to allow the popular transition from local notables "finding" law to kings and princes "making" it.[217] Combined with the indispensable professionalization of law and litigation, their early attempts at legal codification, especially regarding marital property, met fierce resistance throughout Germany. Most important, as Robisheaux reminds us, we must be careful not to misrepresent the very nature of early modern bureaucratic growth:

> Power never flowed simply from the top down; and it did not rest solely on violence or coercion. . . . State power did not simply expand in the six-

---

[215] Although his distinctive characterization of Catholics' "persistent inability to establish a formal, institutional connection between the spiritual, religious treatment of [marital] cases and the criminal, civil treatment" (*Let No Man Put Asunder*, 98) might carry some validity at the municipal level, I know of no such Protestant advantage at the larger, territorial level.

[216] On the continuation of local power through elders, churchwardens, and pastors, see Raeff, *The Well-Ordered Police State*, 63ff., 155ff.; Bader, *Rechtsgeschichte*, II:98–99, 299ff; and Carlson, "Marriage and the English Reformation," 510–15.

[217] On the gradual erosion of the medieval concept of *Landesherr* as leader of the *Landesgemeinde* and protector, rather than source, of its laws, see Strauss, *Law*, 48–49, 80–81, 145ff.; and Brunner, *Landschaft und Herrschaft*, 359–67, 387, 423–24.

teenth and seventeenth centuries; it was very often drawn into the village by the villagers themselves. State power was also checked, frustrated, often turned to purposes no ruler completely controlled.[218]

The true basis, then, for differences in marital jurisdictions at this time was only partly confessional in nature. Rather, in the larger context of early modern statebuilding, assumption of full marital jurisdiction had much more to do with the bureaucratic development and even physical size of a polity. Admittedly, Protestant religious reformers were especially influential in spurring their governments to break with episcopal jurisdictions, but even these changes represented cautious and considered political decisions more than spontaneous expressions of religious conviction. Indeed, the striking continuity we have already seen in both Protestant and Catholic marital doctrines appears even more pronounced in marriage law and jurisdiction.[219] We may agree with Köhler that such fidelities to medieval traditions "take nothing away from the significance and originality [of Protestant contributions]."[220] Yet we cannot deny that such extreme legal conservativeness demands at least some modification of the popular association of the Reformation with secularization of marriage. If, then, we revise Esmein's model to describe a much more gradual process of "secularization," from at least the early fifteenth century into the nineteenth century, we at least have a more accurate perspective of the Reformation's contributions. Protestant and Catholic polities did face different legal obstacles in expanding their control over marriage, but the real question that distinguished them was not "Which direction?" but "How soon?" For most absolutist-oriented statebuilders of either confession, the answer was "Not soon enough."

---

[218] Robisheaux, *Rural Society*, 258.

[219] Again, I am not the first to note the great similarity between the confessions, even on the apparently distinctive question of marital jurisdiction. Both Dieterich (150–51, 257) and Coing (*Europäisches Privatrecht*, 48–50) have noted the immaturity of most sixteenth-century territorial bureaucracies, and the consequential preference of many Protestant rulers for maintaining traditional divisions in marriage matters. Hartung (*Deutsche Verfassungsgeschichte*, 80) is even more direct, conceding "Aber in Praxis war der Unterschied zwischen dem protestantischen Landeskirchentum und dem Kirchenregiment der katholischen weltlichen Fürsten nicht allzu groß." Finally, Schwab also considers the *Verweltlichung* of German marital law a long process only reaching fruition in the late eighteenth or nineteenth century (*Grundlagen*, 53–59).

[220] Stated at the outset (I:2) and conclusion (II:624) of the work.

Part II

The social impact of sixteenth-century marriage reform

~~~~~~

4

In loco parentis: Public approval of private consent

> "Wherever God builds a church, Satan also puts a chapel and a tavern next door" . . . under such incitement from the marriage-devil, young people willingly and with their eyes open decide to take and embrace whatever moves them – one out of indecent passion, another out of drunkenness or for other lustful and frivolous reasons – without God's invocation or the divinely ordained mediation of parents and relatives.
>
> Andreas Musculus, the fourth attack of the marriage-devil,
> in *Against the Marriage-Devil* (1556)[1]

The primary target of all sixteenth-century marriage reforms was "proper" formation of the conjugal bond itself. Although the marital union had always involved a precarious balance between private and public concerns, by the sixteenth century many leaders of Church and State believed, as we have seen, that selfish and disrespectful individuals threatened the latter with complete obliteration. Their unanimous response was a vigorous reassertion of the public nature of marriage through a combination of familial, ecclesiastical, and governmental controls – in short, a seemingly total repudiation of the current "individualist" threat embodied by the consensual ideal.

In theory, the goal of this reformation was simple: ensuring the reestablishment of patriarchal authority and thus the orderly joining of persons and property. In practice, though, the legal reforms that ensued involved a much more complicated subtle and complex integration of the private marriage act into the changing social fabric of early modern Europe. Lawrence Stone has called this process "the great transforma-

---

[1] *Wider den Eheteuffel*, in Stambaugh, *Teufelbücher*, IV:109–10.

tion" of European marital and familial authority, producing a gradual schism of marriage's private and public natures. As traditional authority among the family and community declined, he argues, the ideological link between public approval and private consent was shattered, yielding "romantic love" and idealization of the married couple on the one hand and new ecclesiastical and governmental authority over marriage on the other.[2] Thus, although parental and familial authority apparently benefited the most from sixteenth-century reforms, an even greater power over laws and enforcement of the same was reserved to the two new paternalistic rivals of the institutional Church and State.

Our study of the long-term origins of secular and ecclesiastical marriage reforms provides mixed support for this theory. Church involvement in the marriage procedure by this time, as we have seen, had grown so extensive as to be assured unquestioned acceptance among reforming Protestants and Catholics alike. State controls in the marriage process, on the other hand, were slow to displace those of the family and local community, even after the significant growth of legal and bureaucratic apparatuses in the late fifteenth and early sixteenth centuries. Most important, the canonical model of consensual marriage, though attacked, was never fully rejected by secular or ecclesiastical reformers of any denomination. Sixteenth-century reforms, in other words, neither invented the companiate marriage nor rejected it in favor of new paternal, governmental, or ecclesiastical controls.

Rather than one "great transformation" during the sixteenth century, then, we must speak of the intersection of the two great long-term transformations of marriage we have just discussed. The product of the first, the religious reform, was a new conceptualization of marriage that by the time of the Reformation had achieved universal recognition among both Protestants and Catholics: the replacement of Germanic bride-price with Christian consent, or as Michael Schroeter calls it, of *zussamengebens* ("putting together") by *zusammenkommen* ("coming together").[3] At the same time, Church courts and local pastors gradually expanded the role of ecclesiastical approval of all marriages, most visibly in the rising importance of priestly blessing from the thirteenth to sixteenth centuries.

As Schroeter has also pointed out, the combination of consensual

---

[2] See my earlier discussion in the Introduction.   [3] *Wo zwei zusammenkommen*, 266ff.

marriage and declining familial control during this period simultaneously provided an opening for an alternate third party in the wedding, namely, the State or its local representative.[4] As we have seen in the preceding chapter, though, this governmental involvement remained relatively limited throughout our period. The ultimate product of the second transformation was not yet visible during the sixteenth century, only the State's early supplementing of familial and ecclesiastical authority. The wedding procedure itself, consequently, continued to be defined throughout most of German-speaking Europe by the same local ritualistic cycles of generations past.

Consensualist threats to traditional authority

Tensions between the private and public nature of marriage developed relatively late in medieval Europe. Among the Germanic peoples of the early Middle Ages, it had been the father's transferal of legal authority (*Munt; mundium*) over his daughter to the groom that composed the essential "marriage act."[5] As such, the exchange of promises and property was accomplished entirely within familial circles, with very little outside intervention by authorities of Church or State. The ceremonial handing over of the bride to her new husband according to local customs was immediately followed by consummation of the marriage, usually including a procession to the groom's house and ceremonial bedding of the couple in the presence of their families and friends.[6] Customary versions of the procedure varied widely, but for the most part parental approval and consummation[7] remained the standard criteria for public recognition of the marriage as valid.

By the late Middle Ages, the ecclesiastical reforms of the twelfth

---

[4] Ibid., 245–60.

[5] The *Frauenkauf,* or bride purchase, of Germanic peoples consisted of a contract (*desponsatio*) between families or clans passing the family's *Munt* over the bride to the new husband, upon receipt of a gift (*Brautschatz, Munt-Schatz*) from the groom to the bride's family (Mikat, "Ehe," *HRG* 1:810ff). On the origin of Germanic *Munt* in marriage, see Schroeder, *Das eheliche Güterrecht,* I:1–19.

[6] Cf. R. Schmidt-Wiegand, "Hochzeitsgebräuche," in *HRG* 2:188ff. on the many local variations of *Brautlauf* and *Beilage* in Germany.

[7] Cf. numerous customaries equating consummation with validity (for inheritance purposes): Pfaffikon (1427; Grimm IV:345); Binzheim, Atorf, and Neerach in Zurich (1435, 1437, ca. 1500; Grimm I:14; IV:274, 318–19); Gotlieben in Thurgau (1521; Grimm IV:419); Embrach (Grimm IV:342).

century had altered the equation in three significant ways. First, the engagement (*Verlobung; Sponsalia*) resulting from the private negotiation and agreement between the groom and bride's father or guardian was now clearly distinguished from a later public exchange of vows (*Trauung*) between the man and woman themselves.[8] Second, and even more important, this public exchange, or "wedding," had begun to eclipse consummation as the complementary "completion" of a valid marriage. Although still required for validity in most fifteenth- and sixteenth-century customaries, consummation was now pushed to the very end of the cycle, after both the engagement and its public celebration.[9] Still, confusion and disagreement over the validating role of all elements would probably have never been so great had it not been for a third innovation, namely the canonical recognition of *de presenti* vows of the couple alone as sufficient for validity.

The most obvious effect of the Church's new definition of validity was the apparently novel possibility – at least in theory – of a radically different kind of private union, based solely on the authority and consent of the conjugal couple. By dispensing with both the need for parental approval and the various local, ritualistic requirements for valid unions, twelfth-century canonists had introduced both a potentially revolutionary social concept, and – with the enforcement of ecclesiastical courts – the means to implement it.

In practice, however, a variety of outside authorities continued to

---

[8] Schmidt-Wiegand, "Hochzeitsgebräuche," in *HRG* 2:189–90; Harvey, "Nürnberg Marriage Laws," 21ff. The relationship between *Verlobung* and *Trauung* was the subject of an especially heated debate between two late nineteenth-century legal historians, Emil Friedberg and Rudolph Sohm. While both agreed that the familial *Verlobung* formed the basis of the Germanic definition of validity, they differed sharply on the definition and significance of *Trauung* during the following centuries. Friedberg identified the public *Trauung* as a later ecclesiastical innovation, gradually "received" during the fourteenth and fifteenth centuries (*Das Recht der Eheschliessung*, 78ff.). Sohm, on the other hand, argued that the *Trauung* was actually the *Vertrauung*, or traditional handing over of the bride (*traditio puellae*), a thoroughly Germanic and well-imbedded custom long before the legal reforms of the twelfth-century Church (*Das Recht der Eheschliessung*, 59ff.). Also, whereas Friedberg maintained that *Verlobung* and *Trauung* "zeitlich gewöhnlich und später fast immer zusammengefallen in einen Act zusammen eheschliessende Wirkung geübt haben" (21), Sohm countered that the two acts were always separate, especially after the church's gradual assumption of authority in the *Trauung* (89–90; 152ff.). The two also differ on the role of Protestant reformers in the evolution toward a completely civil *Trauung* in the late eighteenth and nineteenth centuries.

[9] Helmholz, on the other hand, finds that in medieval England "the contract which created the marriage bond remained, as it had been in the early Middle Ages, a private act," outside the glare of village publicity, and indifferent to the direction of the Church (*Marriage Litigation*, 30).

provide their own standards of "public approval" to prevent the ill-advised misalliances (*Mißheirathen*) that they feared might otherwise result. Foremost, of course, were the concerns of the parents and families of each potential spouse in securing a socially and financially sound match.[10] Local secular (especially seigneurial) authorities in turn maintained a similar interest in ensuring the successful preservation of persons and property within their respective realms. Finally, ecclesiastical authorities attempted both to protect these interests while at the same time (for mixed reasons) maintaining counterbalances against their more excessive endogamous and authoritarian tendencies. The result was a network of "public" authorities to be consulted in the "free and individual" act of marriage, each threatening a different punishment for noncompliance.

Most local customaries and statutes, for instance, considered marriages of minors without their parents' permission a kind of rape (*raptus in parentes*), comparable with the *Frauenraub* of Germanic times. Since the introduction of ecclesiastical jurisdiction, however, such unions could not be invalidated, only punished. By far the most frequent target of sanctions was the dowry or other property that presumably inspired secret marriages, thus providing a powerful disincentive for unscrupulous fortune hunters (see Table 2). Other reinforcements of paternal authority simultaneously restricted a child's options for legal recourse.[11] Only the true love match, oblivious to disinheritance or other negative consequences, could ignore the necessity of parental approval for a secure marriage.

State regulation of marriage, though concerned primarily with the transferal of property, went well beyond the countless local requirements of parental consent for minors. Seigneurial control of tenant marriages was especially strict, attempting to preserve and expand the local labor

---

10 See the methodological overview of Pierre Bordieu, "Marriage Strategies as Strategies of Social Reproduction," in *Family and Society: Essays from the Annales Economies, Sociétés, et Civilisations*, ed. Robert Forster and Orest Ranum (Baltimore, 1976), 117–44; also Sabean, *Property, Production, and Family*, 329–34, on parents and marriage strategies in eighteenth-century Württemberg.

11 A married daughter, for instance, was not necessarily emancipated from her father. See especially Stobbe, *Handbuch des deutschen Privatrechts*, 4:365–72, 381–83, and 402–6, on legal emancipation of children in late medieval Germany, particularly concerning limitations of parental and other familial *Gewalt*. Cf. Schroeter, *Wo zwei zusammenkommen*, 146–58, on such controls by familial groups in medieval epics.

Table 2. *Punishments for marriages of minors without parental permission*

	Jurisdiction	Punishment[a]
ca. 1250	Imperial prohibition	D
1284; 1308	Eßlingen	D
1297	Frankfurt	D
1310; 1341; 1354	Strasbourg	D
1325	Freising	D (daughter only)
1339	Ravensburg	D (restricted)
1344	Weitnau	D (restricted)
1347; 1379	Zurich	10 lb. Heller F or 10 yrs. B; 20 Marks silver F or prison
1361	Bern	D
1383	Constance	?
1396; 1429; 1457	Memmingen	10 lb Heller for 15 yrs B
1397	Isny	D
1450	Basel	D
1459; 1466	Saint Gallen	10 lb. Heller F
1465	Chur	Magistrates' discretion

[a]D = disinheritance; F = fine; B = banishment.
Sources: Kö I & II; Grimm I, V; *Freisinger Rechtsbuch;* Burghartz, *Leib, Ehre, Gut;* Mone, "Beiträge zur Geschichte des Eherechts."

force by encouraging both early and endogamous unions through the issuance of stiff fines.[12] Some rulers maintained reciprocal agreements on their subjects, culminating in parts of southwest Germany and the Swiss cantons with the equivalent of free trade zones for serf marriages.[13] Most, however, remained jealously protective of all their sub-

[12] Cf. typical German customaries requiring the lord's permission for all marriages: Kircheim in Unter-Alsace, 1329 (Grimm V:434); Tessenberg in Bern, 1352 (Grimm V:38); Chimsee, 1393/1462 (Grimm III:676); Hattgau in Unteralsace, 1400 (Grimm V:508); Eschweiler in Obermosel, 1401 (Grimm II:263); Beyenheim in Wetterau, 1455 (Grimm V:265); and Alfen in Untermosel, 1499 (Grimm V:411). Punishments for offenders ranged from a fine of one gold florin (Eschweiler) to a matching dowry to the lord (Chimsee) to loss of all property to unspecified penalties. See also Schwab, "Heiratserlaubnis," in *HRG* 2:60–66; Walter Müller, *Entwicklung und Spätformen der Leibeigenschaft am Beispiel der Heiratsbeschränkungen; Die Ehegenoßame in alemannisch-schweizerischen Raum* (Simaringen, 1974), 9ff., 24–42; and Schroeter, *Wo zwei zusammenkommen,* 195–203, on the evidence of medieval epics.

[13] See Müller, *Entwicklung und Spätformen,* 67–153, on the *Ehegenoßame paritas* (also known as *genoschaft, consortium in contrahendo matrimonio condordia,* and, by the eighteenth century, *Wechselvertrag*), including those of Zurich (70–85), the twelve and a half abbeys of Lake Constance (85–115), and Saint Gallen (115–26). Of the 450 such agreements analyzed by Müller (43–66), more than three-quarters came from the fourteenth and fifteenth centuries.

jects' persons and goods. All "unequal" marriages between free and unfree persons (*imparitas matrimoni*) were especially prohibited and – like clandestine marriages – as severely punished as theft, particularly if couples attempted to leave the territory.[14]

None of these controls, of course, necessarily eliminated free choice of a spouse. Unequal marriages continued to plague municipal and seigneurial authorities into the sixteenth century, while evidence from German territories suggests that as in English manorial courts "most tenants . . . paid fines instead of marrying the spouse selected for them [by local jurors]."[15] Others, like the free peasants of Grosshembs in Alsace, reveled in their self-proclaimed status as the equals of princes (*fursten gross*) since, "unlike serfs, [they] could marry whomever they pleased."[16] As in requirements of parental approval, seigneurial approval could certainly influence but rarely dictate marriage matches.[17]

Many Swiss and imperial cities claimed the same right of contractual approval as seigneurial officials, occasionally in intentional defiance of the latter.[18] Beyond prohibiting marriages between a citizen and noncitizen before the end of the latter's probationary period (usually a year and

---

For examples, see the customary of Peitgau (Bavaria; ca. 1435) between the dukes of Bavaria and abbots of Etal (Grimm III:648); and 1300 customary of Grosz Bockenheim between Ottenberg and Emrich (Grimm V:623).

14 Cf., for instance, explicit prohibition in the *Sachsenspiegel*, as well as customaries from Romanmotier in Bern (1267; Grimm IV:457), Apple in Waat (1327; Grimm V:12), Hedigen in Zurich (ca. 1400; Grimm IV:293), Winkel in Zurich (Grimm I:80), and a 1312 Memmnigen ordinance (Kö II:143). Mone, "Beiträge zur Geschichte des Eherechts," 58; Rudolf Hübner, *A History of Germanic Private Law*, trans. Francis S. Philbrick (London, 1918), 92ff.

15 Cf. increasing mention in German customaries of fines as punishments for unequal marriages (Müller, *Entwicklung und Spätformen*, 29ff.) and documented fines for such in the *Hausbuch* of Constance's cathedral provost from 1486 to 1489 (Mone, "Beiträge zur Geschichte des Eherechts," 70–72). On England: Elaine Clark, "The Decision to Marry in Thirteenth- and Early Fourteenth-Century Norfolk," *Mediaeval Studies* 49 (1987), 499–502; and similar findings of Barbara Hanawalt, *The Ties That Bind: Peasant Families in Medieval England* (Oxford, 1986), 202ff. See also J. M. Bennett, "Medieval Peasant Marriage: An Examination of Marriage License Fines in the Liber Gersumarum," in *Pathways to Medieval Peasants*, ed. J. A. Raftis (Toronto, 1981), 193–245.

16 1383 customary, cited in Hübner, *Germanic Private Law*, 94.

17 Müller (*Entwicklung und Späformen*, 7–8) argues that seigneurially imposed marriages had disappeared from southern Germany by the thirteenth century. On a related note, I have found only one explicit legal reference to the famous *ius primus noctis* of medieval lords, and a relatively late one at that (1543, from Maur in Zurich; Grimm I:93).

18 Schroeter (*Wo zwei zusammenkommen*, 108ff.) claims that municipal authorities purposely undermined seigneurial authority in this manner. See examples, however, of Isny (1430), Ulm (1440), and Constance (1461), where the reluctance to marry foreigners of any origin signals the beginnings of the exclusionary tendency more associated with the sixteenth century (Kö II:3, 93, 207).

a day), some, such as the Palatinate's Landau, also used the opportunity to postpone or prevent those unions they considered financially insecure.[19] The most active municipal authority in this area before the bureaucratic expansion of the early sixteenth century remained the guild. Journeymen in late fifteenth-century Regensburg, for instance, were even required to produce marriage certificates notified by a priest of *Schultheiß* before admission to one of its guilds.[20]

While most local ecclesiastical authorities actively supported such traditional controls,[21] they were at the same time concerned with securing their own authority over marital validity. Since the early Middle Ages, for instance, Church authorities had attempted to restrict the excessively endogamous practices of recently converted Germanic peoples by imposing a system of impediments of consanguinity and affinity. By the twelfth century, the teaching had so successfully permeated popular practice that, according to some historians, many lords and peasants alike found themselves forbidden from marrying "all the marriageable girls they could possibly know and a great many more besides."[22] While this is no doubt an exaggeration – and certainly offset by the frequency of dispensations up to the second degree of consanguinity[23] – the influence of Church doctrine on practice is certainly indisputable.

The other major "public approval" of the Church also had roots in the

---

[19] Ordinances of 1465 and 1487, cited in Lehmann, *Landau in der Pfalz*, 103. Cf. also similar requirements of Niederingelheim (1385) and Ulm (fourteenth century). Kö II:3; Mone, "Beiträge zur Geschichte des Eherechts," 65–66.

  This was also often extended to weddings as in the prince-bishop of Speyer's 1493 ordinance, requiring notification of "Schultheis, gerichtssleute, oder ander amptleute," before any such ceremony could be held (*Sammlung* 12; and see my subsequent discussion in this chapter).

[20] Regensburg guild ordinances of 1476, 1487, and 1509. Lindner, "Courtship and the Courts," 70–71 (sample certificate on p. 169).

[21] Cf. especially Michael Sheehan, "Marriage of the Unfree and the Poor," *Medieval Studies* 50 (1988), 475ff, on canonical support of free and unfree distinctions.

[22] Flandrin, *Families in Former Times*, 24–26; Ozment, *When Fathers Ruled*, 44ff.; Brundage, *Law, Sex, and Christian Society*, 191ff., and the most notable proponent of ecclesiastical social engineering, Goody, *Family and Marriage in Europe*. All assume, on the basis of primarily legislative evidence, that consanguinity and affinity prohibitions were both widely understood and enforced – a fact in direct contradiction to complaints of almost all sixteenth-century Protestant and Catholic reformers.

[23] Although such frequent dispensations inevitably opened up ecclesiastical authorities to accusations of greed and simony, the practice did apparently serve as an effective counterbalance to unrealistic restrictions in some localities. In the diocese of Speyer, such dispensations were regularly granted by the archdeacons and vicar-general for a moderate charge of 1 fl. Haffner, *Die kirchlichen Reformbemühungen des Speyerer Bischofs Matthias von Rammung*, 16–17; Baumgartner, *Geschichte und Rechts des Archidiakonates der oberrheinischen Bistümer*, 210; also Esmein II:355–414, and my discussion in the next section.

early Middle Ages and likewise grew steadily in importance up to the sixteenth century. First recorded in the ninth century, the custom of a priestly blessing at a wedding ceremony was enthusiastically embraced by the twelfth-century reformers of marriage and eventually required by Lateran IV in 1215.[24] In an attempt to institutionalize the Church's role in the public exchange of vows, canon 51 of the council issued its own definition of public propriety: three public announcements of a forthcoming wedding (banns), and official solemnization "before the Church" (*in facie ecclesiae*) in the presence of at least two witnesses and a priest. Subsequent interpretations of *in facie ecclesiae* varied from any priestly blessing of a marriage to a small ceremony literally "in front of the church." Like its familial and governmental counterparts, the ecclesiastical version of "public approval" could serve as an effective deterrent to what its authors considered misalliances, in this case based on canonical definitions of affinity and consanguinity. What none of the three authorities could prevent, however, was the judicial quagmire produced by the consensual definition of marriage.

By the late fifteenth century, Church courts had become flooded with cases of contested marriage vows, accounting for almost half of all marriage cases heard by the Augsburg *Officialatus* and at least two-thirds of the same case load of the Regensburg episcopal court.[25] The dramatic increase in marital litigation put ecclesiastical authorities in a difficult bind. On the one hand, the fact that the great majority of suits sought recognition rather than dissolution of disputed vows suggested some awareness or even acceptance of both the consensual basis of marriage and the Church's validating role.[26] On the other, the apparently growing

---

[24] Gratian based his endorsement of the priestly requirement on two ninth-century letters, one attributed to Saint Evaristus (pope, ca. 100–109) and the other by Nicholas I (858–67), which both mentioned the custom as part of the wedding ceremony (*Decretum*, C. 30, q. 5). The first Church wedding ritual to include priestly blessings (actually a series of seven benedictions) was the 950 ritual of Durham, later repeated in three eleventh-century Anglo-Norman liturgies; see Jean-Baptiste Molin and Protais Mutembe, *Le rituel du mariage en France du XII ème au XVIème siècle* (Paris, 1974), 29–30.

[25] R. Weigand, "Zur mittelalterlichen kirchlichen Ehegerichtsbarkeit," *Zeitschrift der Savigny-Stiftung für Rechtsgeschichte, Kanonistische Abteilung* 98 (1981), 217–20; Weigand, "Die Rechtsprechung," 407ff. In a case breakdown of the 290 marital disputes before the Regensburg *Officialatus* in 1489, Lindner finds that 229 of these (79 percent) involved disputed vows of one kind or another (Lindner, "Courtship and the Courts," 140–42). For an introduction to the extant sources in this area, see Lindner's survey of late medieval German ecclesiastical courts in Charles Donahue, Jr., ed., *The Records of the Medieval Ecclesiastical Courts and Reports of the Working Group on Church Court Records*, Part I: *The Continent* (Berlin, 1989), 117–22.

[26] While the incidence of private and informal marriages was slow to decline in England, for

abuse of the private exchange of vows to evade traditional controls of all kinds could not be tolerated.

Ecclesiastical judges obviously recognized the dangerous consequences of clandestine vows but remained constrained by the legal elasticity of validity based solely on vows of mutual consent. Consistent (though often ambiguous) directives guided Officials in the interpretations of actual words, of conditions, and of possible impediments, but could not avoid frequent reliance on the participants' testimony as the sole evidence.[27] The result was frequent "dispute, uncertainty, wrangling, and fraud," including the greatest of threats possible to the sanctity and indissolubility of marriage: self-divorce and bigamy.[28]

Local responses to the "window of vulnerability" opened by the canonical legal definition of marriage varied greatly. English synodal statutes beginning in the thirteenth century intentionally obscured the distinction between canonical validity and licity, acknowledging the consensual basis of marriage "almost reluctantly." The intentional confusion – evident in the court testimonies of numerous plaintiffs – probably accounts for the success of English courts in minimizing potential disparities between secular and canonical definitions of a valid marriage.[29] Many French royal ordinances deviated even more from Canon

---

instance, Helmholz finds that the number of litigants seeking proof of marriage in ecclesiastical courts increased dramatically during the thirteenth and fourteenth centuries (Helmholz, *Marriage Litigation*, 28–30). Moreover, in none of the court protocols is there even a hint that lack of solemnity or of any consent other than the couple's invalidated a marriage; in fact, the *verba de presenti* was usually the central issue at stake (267ff.). The evidence for Germany, on the other hand, suggests that the success rate for such suits of recognition was low for both women and men, ranging from 12.5–20 percent, Lindner, see "Courtship and the Courts," 10ff., 53–57; R. Weigand, "Ehe- und Familienrecht in der mittelalterlichen Stadt," in *Haus und Familie in der Spätmittelalterlichen Stadt*, ed., Alfred Haverkamp (Cologne, 1984), 173–74; Weigand, "Die Rechtsprechung," 407, 411–12.

[27] Esmein I:195; Donahue, "Alexander III's Consent Theory," 261. The frequency of the especially difficult *verba de futuro* disputes in French courts was further aggravated by the employment of the *promoteur*, who sought out such illicit unions and added them to the court's already heavy docket. See Lefebvre-Teillard, *Les Officialités*, 108. 164, 170–79; Helmholz, *Marriage Litigation*, 25ff, 31ff.

[28] Helmholz, *Marriage Litigation*, 31, 189ff. While such cases of legal manipulation are naturally difficult to prove, Lefebvre-Teillard (*Les Officialités*, 175–76) finds many cases of French defendants in their third and fourth marriages, displaying surprisingly little fear of excommunication (for perjury) in their denial of vows. See also Sheehan, "Ely Register," 242–47.

[29] Sheehan insists that in vocabulary and intent, "the theories expressed in the statutes were not always consistent nor well understood." In addition, the strict enforcement of banns in England reinforced traditional publicity requirements already in practice by the time of Alexander III. Sheehan, "Ely Register," 228ff.; Sheehan, "Theory and Practice in the Conciliar Legislation," 424, 432, 459; Donahue, "Alexander III's Theory of Consent," 262.

law and continued to require parental consent as necessary for validity into the fifteenth century.[30]

Throughout most of Germany, by contrast, the distinction between "licity" and "validity" appears to have been both recognized and enforced. The records of Speyer's diocesan synod from the fourteenth century on, for instance, reveal no grudging acceptance of the consensual definition of marriage or any deliberate attempts to subvert it.[31] Rather, as Klaus Lindner has demonstrated, German ecclesiastical synods and courts focused their efforts on the punishment of illicit marriages, consistently distinguishing between two types of "clandestine" vows in their punishments.[32] Marriages that failed to comply with the Lateran IV requirements of publicity were considered "incomplete," and punished only if the public church ceremony was refused. Marriages of minors against the will of their parents, on the other hand, were always punished by excommunication in addition to the usual secular sanction of disinheritance.[33]

Whatever the definition of publicity, familial, governmental, and ec-

---

[30] The problems and tensions caused by Alexander III's consensual definition were evident in France from the very beginning. The incomplete and uncertain regulations drawn from Lateran IV were badly applied in practice, despite the severe punishments of synodal statutes. From the *Etablissements de Saint-Louis*, reissued in 1325, into the fifteenth century, the result was an increased reliance on royal and local ordinances, which generally disregarded the decrees of Alexander III and invalidated the marriages of minors without the consent of their parents and friends ("amis charnels"). Etienne Diebold, "L'application en France du canon 51 du IVᵉ concile du Latran d'après les anciens statuts synodaux," *L'année canonique* 1 (1953), 187–95. C. Turlan, "Recherche sur le mariage dans la pratique countumière (XII–XVI siècles)," *Revue historique de droit*, 4th ser., 35 (1957), 483–515; Traer, *Marriage and the family*, 32; Lefebvre-Teillard, *Les Officialités*, 165ff.

For a comparison of English and French enforcement in this area during the late Middle Ages, see Charles Donahue, Jr., "The Canon Law of the Formation of Marriage and Social Practices in the Later Middle Ages," *Journal of Family History* 8/2 (1983), 144–58.

[31] Synodal decrees explicitly condemned "Clandestina quoque matrimonia sub pena Excommunicacionis fieri prohibemus et per plebanos inhiberi sub eadem pena mandamus et precipimus ut fiant in facie Ecclesie publice juxta morem . . ." and refused to excuse any disobedience "per ignoraciam sive contumaciam" (*Collectio* J:5, 115). At the same time, however, there is never any hint that such marriages are invalid, only that they should be judged and punished by episcopal authorities, especially the *Officialis*. Cf. variations of the same prohibition in *Collectio* I:9–10 (1397), 17–18 (1400), 26 (1404), 55 (1410), 71 (1464), 115 (1473), II:5 (1478), 15–16 (1482), 152 (1509), 217 (1524), 385–91 (1582 marriage ordinance); prince-bishop's ordinance of 7 March 1472 (GLA 67/298, 96ᵛff.); and Haffner, *Die kirchliche Reformbemühungen*, 125ff.

[32] Much scholarly confusion, Lindner suggests, stems from indiscriminate medieval statutory references to both kinds of vows as *clandestina* and the influence of the predominantly sixteenth-century issue of marriages of minors on historians' interpretations (Lindner, "Courtship and the Courts," 94–95, 125–28).

[33] Cf. synodal decrees of Trier (1227), Cologne (1281), Regensburg (1377), discussed in Lindner, "Courtship and the Courts," 48ff., and especially those of Speyer mentioned previously.

clesiastical approval all remained standard and essential components of marriage throughout the Middle Ages. Their respective influence over the acceptability of a conjugal match did not disappear with the introduction of a new canonical definition of validity. What had changed, rather, was the balance between public and private consent in the legal equation of marriage. During the centuries preceding the Reformation, German secular and ecclesiastical authorities could prevent or punish unapproved marriages but they could not eliminate them. Private vows, in all forms and despite all attempted disincentives, remained legally valid and binding.

Secular and ecclesiastical "restoration" of traditional authority

Ostensibly all sixteenth-century marriage reforms sought to reestablish the proper balance between private consent and public approval. According to critics, minors and others wishing to avoid parental or public resistance continued to find protection under the canonical definition of marriage, while the same law denied parents, relatives, and friends any legal consideration whatsoever. Moreover, they added, not only the canonical language of betrothal but the very concepts it embodied were foreign to most laypeople. No German, wrote Luther, would ever say, "I will take you" (*Ich werde dich nehmen*), the vernacular equivalent of the *de futuro* promise to marry, just as no authority outside of Canon law would deny the necessity of public approval to a truly godly marriage.[34] Tridentine Catholics of course framed their criticisms of Canon law in less hostile terms, but they vehemently agreed that public propriety must be taken into consideration in the definition of validity.

Traditional authority, consequently, served as the byword among all religious denominations. Although Protestants generally defined "clandestine" as lacking in parental consent *and* publicity, and Catholics limited their prohibition to the latter, the intent of both was the same: reassertion of the public nature of marriage. Amid the secular and religious reformations of the sixteenth century, however, traditional au-

---

[34] "Von Ehesachen" (1530), *WA* 30/III:211–12. Roper's contention that "the Protestant view of marriage approximated more closely to German townspeople's traditional notions of how a marriage was made" may hold true for the issue of pure consensualism, but the pre-Reformation Church strongly encouraged as much adherence as possible to local custom in the ritual cycle. See Lyndal Roper, "Going to Church and Street: Weddings in Reformation Augsburg," *Past and Present* 106 (February 1985), 65.

thority in marriage was no longer limited to the patriarchal family. Rather, the legal reaction against "private" marriages represented a program of social reform designed and implemented by the "public" institutions of Church and State. Church involvement focused principally on securing and even extending its own well-established role as the guarantor of public and moral propriety in the exchange of vows. State regulation, on the other hand, was still growing rapidly in this area, occasionally overlapping with ecclesiastical interests, but remained primarily concerned with the ordered transferal of property from parents to children. This section examines the extent of both kinds of control in the Palatinate during this period, before assessing the consequences for "free and consensual" marriage in the final part of the chapter.

Despite their theological differences, both Protestant and Catholic Church leaders stood firm in their insistence on ecclesiastical controls over the exchange of marriage vows. Although the marriage contract, "just as other worldly contracts, may indeed be validated at the town halls or other common, public, honorable, and civil locations . . . it is considered both proper and Christian," according to the Elector's 1556 ecclesiastical ordinance, "that marrying couples be announced and blessed in the churches before the congregation.[35] The Prince-Bishop's 1582 marriage ordinance was equally explicit about the role of "good, salutary Christian ordinances [for] the holy marriage contract."[36] Significantly, the model for such ecclesiastical controls was the same for both: canon 51 of Lateran IV and its formulaic requirements of publicity.

Both reforms required prospective couples to go first to their parish pastor(s) before the wedding ("well before," in the Electorate) and announce their intentions.[37] Many German Protestant authorities (and some Catholic ones) even introduced guidelines for betrothal, such as in the ordinances of Brandenburg–Nuremberg (1533), Hessia (1557), Strasbourg (1598), and the much-imitated 1559 Württemberg Ecclesiastical Ordinance.[38] If, after a private interview with the pastor and the

---

[35] 1556 *Kirchenordnung; EKO* 165–66.   [36] *Collectio* II:386.
[37] "eine gute zeit darvor," *Kirchenordnungen* of 1556 and 1563; *EKO* 166, 398; *Collectio* 387–88.
[38] Harvey, "Nürnberg Marriage Laws," 48; Sohm, *Das Recht der Eheschliessung,* 210ff. Many, such as the 1575 Hessian *Agenda,* used Luther's *Traubüchlein* as a model (Alfred Niebergall, *Die Geschichte der evangelischen Trauung in Hessen* [Göttingen, 1972], 73; also Schwab, *Grundlagen,* 223). Catholic betrothal formulas, on the other hand, as in 70 of 105 contemporary French Catholic ritual books examined by Burgière ("Le rituel de mariage en France, 641–42), were apparently not as common in Germany; I am aware of only one German Catholic betrothal *ordo*

traditional public announcements of the banns at the couple's parish, no impediment surfaced, the couple was permitted to marry.[39] Clerics of both confessions were strictly enjoined from marrying any of their parishioners to a stranger unless the latter brought "good proof, written or oral, of [his] origin, so that one might ascertain what kind of person [he was], single or married, responsible or dissipated . . . and so that no one may claim ignorance as an excuse."[40] As a final precaution, both the Prince-Bishop and the Palatine-Elector required pastors to keep parish registers of all approved marriages, listing not only the names of the couple, but also those of their witnesses as well as place(s) of origin.[41]

Even more remarkable is the similarity in both confessions' enforcement of impediments. Although the Elector's marriage ordinance eliminated only impediments of affinity and of fourth-degree consanguinity, it still allowed a dispensation for those who, "out of ignorance" married within the third degree of consanguinity.[42] Shortly thereafter, Bishop

---

from the period, namely, from Bamberg in 1587 (H. Reifenberg, *Sakramente, Sakramentalien, und Ritualien im Bistum Mainz seit dem Spätmittelalter* [Münster, 1971], 511).

[39] *Kirchenordnungen* of 1556 and 1563, 1563 *EO; EKO* 166–68, 284, 398; *Collectio* 387. See also pre-Reformation references in 1480 Strasbourg Ritual (Wendel, *Le mariage*, 120–21; excerpt on 215), and 1492 Mainz Ritual (Reifenberg, *Sakramente*, I:485ff.), and 1512 Speyer Ritual "aut in talibus publicis locis in quibis verisimiliter possint ad eorum notitiam pervenire qui sunt de impedimentis informati" (Alois Lamott, *Das Speyerer Diözesanrituale von 1512 bis 1932. Seine Geschichte und seine Ordines zur Sakramentenliturgie* [Speyer, 1961], 237).

Trent also emphasized the same three key points in the priest's interrogation: *nomen, tractatus,* and *fama;* see chapter 7 of *Tametsi* (Schroeder, *Council of Trent,* 188); "Marriage en droit occidental," in *DDC* 6:776; and 1590 requirement of the Speyer chapter at Otterstadt of satisfactory completion by both partners of catechismal interrogation (on faith, commandments, sacraments, etc.) before a marriage was blessed (10 February 1590; GLA 11106).

[40] 1563 *EGO; EKO* 284, 301. The prince-bishop's 1582 ordinance likewise required that "sollte aber bißweilen ein ohnzweiffenlicher oder also glaublicher argwohn sich ereugen und zutragen, daß die vorgenommene ehe boßhafftiger weiß wan soviel verkundigungen solten vorher gehen," then the pastor should prevent the marriage (*Collectio* II:387–89, 390).

[41] Variously referred to as a *verzeichnuß* (1556 *Kirchenordnung; EKO* 145a), *ein besonder buch* (1563 *Kirchenordnung; EKO,* 398), and *ein sonderlich buch* (*Collectio* II:390); also Schroeder, *Council of Trent,* 183–85. The city of Speyer did not order this practice until 1593 (Ohler, in *GStSp* I:584).

Once thought to have been entirely an innovation of the Reformation, the attempt to introduce parish registers of baptisms and marriages dates back at least to Contance Bishop Friedrich II's complaint in 1435 of "Mangel an Beglaubingungszeugnissen für die geistliche Verwandtschaft Seelengefahr entsteht" (Kö I:91). Although they were supported by many ecclesiastical judges in marital disputes, there is no evidence of such reforms being successfully instituted before the sixteenth century.

[42] 1556 *Von den Ehesachen, EKO* 223–24; *EGO, EKO* 314. Both ordinances proposed the following guidelines for *Eherichter* in granting dispensations: "In gradibus juris divini prohibetur matrimonium contrahendum et dirimitur contractum. In gradibus vero human juris prohibetur matrimonium contrahendum, sed non dirimitur contractum." Lev. 18:6–18 and its second-degree

Table 3. *Marital dispensations granted in the diocese of Speyer, 1591–1620*

	3rd-degree consanguinity	4th-degree consanguinity	Affinity (total/spiritual)	Total
1591–1600	31	21	15/4	67
1601–10	10	32	5/3	47
1611–20	16	23	5/1	44

Source: GLA 67/426; 67/427.

Eberhard of Speyer received papal permission to begin similarly dispensing consanguinity impediments of the third and fourth degrees, as well as all degrees of affinity (including spiritual).[43] Both rulers clearly viewed such exceptions as unavoidable until the prohibitions were better publicized, yet the practice endured, at least in the diocese of Speyer, well into the next century. Biannual announcements of the forbidden degrees (as in the Electorate and other neighboring Protestant territories) do appear to have produced a decline in the frequency of third-degree unions among Catholics,[44] but the number of fourth-degree dispensations remained roughly constant (see Table 3). Considered in combination with the declining occurrence of all affinity dispensations, the bishop's adaptation of canonical restrictions resulted in an impediment practice virtually indistinguishable from that of the Electorate and other Protestant territories.

By far the most dramatic example of increased ecclesiastical control among all confessions, though, was the new emphasis on the centrality of the Church ceremony and benediction of the priest or minister (*Trauung*). While long required for licity, the absolute necessity of these two elements for validity was an innovation of the sixteenth century. Protestant and Catholic theologians were unanimous in their support for the

---

prohibitions served as the definitive divine standard; electoral concerns to preserve "erbare zucht bey den underthanen . . . und billiche ordnung" extended the restriction to the third degree of consanguinity. See *above* my comments in Chapter 2.

[43] Apostolic briefs of Sixtus V (27 January 1590; GLA 67/426, 106ᵛ–107) and Clement VIII (24 October 1592; GLA 67/426, 118ʳ–119). While expressly endorsing the doctrine and standards defined by Trent, both went on to give long justification for their favorable response to Eberhard's request, mainly based on the tantalizing availability of marriage within the third and fourth degree in the neighboring Reformed Electorate; GLA 67/426, 107ʳ⁻ᵛ. Cf. similar mandate by Bishop Hugo of Constance at the outset of the Reformation (1522); Kö I:78.

[44] *EKO* 283; *Collectio* II:390; Vogler II:973.

new requirement. Though some popular confusion about the proper sequence of church wedding and consummation obviously persisted,[45] most laypeople by this time obviously also recognized the Church's validating role as essential.

The legitimizing function of the *kilchgang* (literally "church going") was certainly already widely accepted by the sixteenth century, yet until this time the entire ritual itself took place at the front doors – literally the periphery – of the church.[46] Many late medieval churches were even adorned with special *Brauttüre* or *Ehetüre* for the occasion, such as the famous wise and foolish bridesmaids' door at Saint Sebald's in Nuremberg. By moving the ceremony inside to the altar, Protestant and Catholic ecclesiastical authorities reified the centrality of these *de presenti* church vows over the traditional betrothal (*de futuro*) vows within the familial circle and home. Private parallel ceremonies continued in many forms,[47] but clearly the church wedding had established precedence as the guarantor of validity. The public exchange of vows "in full daylight" amid the parish's congregation served as still another check against "early morning secret weddings" and other attempts to circumvent impediment restrictions.[48] If either the priest's interrogation or the public banns had failed to detect an obstacle to ecclesiastical approval, this

---

[45] In 1489, cases of consummation before the church wedding comprised more than one-half of the Regensburg *Officialatus's* "clandestine marriage" case load (Lindner, "Courtship and the Courts," 40–42), and as late as 1550, Calvin complained that many couples had exchanged vows but ignored the church ceremony, living together in "mariages imparfaits" (Kö II:627). Roper ("Weddings in Reformation Augsburg," 66–67), Harvey ("Nürnberg Marriage Laws," 28–29, 58–61), and Köhler (Kö I:103–4) find similar popular confusion on the "completion" of marriage in Augsburg, Nuremberg, and Zurich respectively. See also Chapter 5, on premarital fornication and pregnancy.

[46] Cf. the 1512 diocesan ritual of Speyer, where the entire interrogation, exchange of vows, and benediction take place literally *in facie ecclesiae*, followed by the bridal mass inside (Lamott, *Das Speyerer Diözesanrituale*, 237ff.). By 1592, the vicar-general of Speyer decreed that the couple must wait for the priest "ante ianuas seu templi foras" but then inside for the ceremony (*Collectio* II:400). The change is even more explicit in a comparison of the Mainz *Trauungsritus* of 1480 with that of 1551 (Reifenberg, *Sacramente*, 83–84, 487–90).

[47] In some parts of Germany, such as Lübeck, home ceremonies remained the norm, especially among the patriciate; see Alexander Cowan, *The Urban Patriciate: Lübeck and Venice, 1580–1700* (Cologne, 1986), 130ff. Nuremberg's 1533 *Kirchenordnung* considered a home ceremony sufficient, and some sixteenth-century codes retained the even more confusing relic of a private *Trauung*, officiated by a priest, and separate (usually the next day) *Kilchgang*. Cf. ecclesiastical ordinances of Brandenburg (1540), Calenberg and Göttingen (1542), Austria (1571), Hoya (1581), Lauenburg (1585), and Mecklenburg (1602), cited in Sohm, *Das Recht der Eheschliessung*, 172–73.

[48] ". . . bey hellem haiteren tag und ungefarlich umb die spaten predig oder lesy," in Saint Gallen (Kö I:394). Cf. similar admonition in 1563 *EO* (*EKO* 284) and 1526 Hessian ordinance (Niebergall, *Geschichte der evangelischen Trauung*, 22).

parochial gathering provided a final opportunity to prevent an illicit union, namely, through the now famous question to the congregation: "Does anyone of you here gathered know whether these two persons have any relationship by blood, family, godparenthood or otherwise that hinders them from holy matrimony?"[49] This modification of "public approval" – required by both the Electorate and post-Tridentine diocese of Speyer[50] – might seem slight when we consider the corollary expanded role of the clerical officiator.

In the reformed wedding rituals of sixteenth-century Protestants and Catholics, the role of the priest or minister is clearly and unmistakably the same as that of the father of the bride in the traditional engagement ceremony.[51] As the Elector's 1563 marriage rite explains:

> Just as in paradise the Lord God Himself originally presented Adam with his spouse Eve, so is it just that the marrying couple be brought before the Christian congregation in the church . . . [and] reminded of God's word on their vocation and the peacefulness and fruit of their estate *by the minister.*[52]

While few reformers were as explicit as Zwingli about the congregation replacing the family entirely,[53] the general parallel between the two exchanges of vows was obvious. As André Burgière has noted of contemporary France, even the Catholic priest's formulaic recognition of the union had been widely transformed, by the early sixteenth century, from the traditional "I approve" (*ego approbo*) to "I marry you"(*ego coniugo vos*).[54] Official refences to the ceremony in court protocols likewise

---

49 1512 Speyer Ritual, in Lamott, *Das Speyerer Diözesanrituale*, 241. The reference to spiritual affinity was dropped, of course, from later Protestant versions.

50 1563 *Kirchenordnung, EKO* 398; Vogler II:935–36; *Collectio* II:388–89. Lamott also sees a greater significance to the change: "Das beweist schon die schrittweise Vorverlegung des Trauungsritus aus dem Raum bzw. unter dem Kirchenportal hin vor die Stufen de Altares. Es zeigt sich ebenso im Wandel der Trauansprachen vor und nach der Trauung, in der Ausbildung der Konsensgespräches, der Dexterarum iunctio, der Konfirmation, des Ringritus, und nicht zuletzt in der Bewertung und Gestattung des Segengebetes nach der Trauung" (*Das Speyerer Diözesanrituale*, 237).

51 Schroeter (*Wo zwei zusammenkommen*, 42ff., 295, 321ff.) makes a similar point about ecclesiastical control over marriage but, based on the evidence of epics, dates the change from as early as the thirteenth century in Germany.

52 1563 *Kirchenordnung; EKO* 398 (emphasis added).

53 Cf. Kö I:74ff.: ". . . und keiner dem andren [the pastor's] unterthonen zufüren one sinen gunst und offentlichen, kuntlichen willen."

54 Burgière, "Rituel de mariage en France," 639ff. The evidence is more mixed in Germany, varying from the "Ego coniugo vos legitime, et firmo matrimonium vestrum" of the 1512 Speyer ritual (Lamott, *Das Speyerer Diözesanrituale*, 242) to "Matrimonium inter eos contractum Deos confirmet, et ego illud approbo" of the mid-sixteenth-century Salzburg Agenda (BSB Res.

reflected the shift in emphasis, with the newer *solemnacio* ("blessing" of the priest) almost completely replacing the more traditional *intronisacio* ("crowning" of the bride) during the same period.[55] Protestant emphasis on the minister's role in completion of the marriage was so strong that in some areas his blessing was even referred to as *copulatio sacerdotale*.[56]

The rest of the ceremony, on the other hand, remained strikingly unchanged among Protestants and Catholics alike. With the obvious exception of elimination of the bridal mass, ordinances of the Elector and city of Speyer respected the majority of pre-Reformation practices. Lutheran Speyer preserved the *tempus clausum*, or traditional prohibition of marriage during Advent and Lent (enforced with a ten-gulden fine), and even the Reformed Electorate, under the influence of Spangenberg's *Marriage Mirror*, maintained at least modified restrictions.[57] Indeed, the most significant change proposed by either of these was the substitution of three scriptural readings (Matt. 19:3–9; Ps. 128; Gen. 2:24ff.) and an optional sermon in place of the abolished mass.[58] Like

Cathech. 361/1-(3), 31ʳ), to the 1551 Mainz Agenda: "Matrimonium inter vos contractum Ego confirmo, ratifico, et benedico" (Nibergall, *Geschichte der evangelischen Trauung*, 13).

Local Protestant rites also varied considerably, though the most influential was probably the Ritual of Marbach (1549) adopted in Strasbourg and Geneva: "Et ego hec sponsalia, et hanc vestram mutuam promissionem, authoritate qua fungor, confirmo" (Wendel, *Le mariage*, 110, 122). Sohm (*Das Recht der Eheschliessung*, 220ff.) attempts to identify a north–south pattern in Germany (*coniugo* in north and *confirmo* in south), which is rightfully rejected by Wendel (123) in favor of less regional and more arbitrary distinctions. On the other hand, I find Sohm's (168ff.) argument of parallel development among Catholic and Protestant clerics much more convincing than the confessional divergence in the priest's centrality proposed by Wendel (123). See also early medieval German examples in Otto Opet, *Brauttradition und Konsensgespräch in mittelalterlichen Trauungsritualien. Ein Beitrag zur Geschichte des deutschen Eheschließungsrechts* (Berlin, 1910), 16ff., 94ff.

[55] Lindner, "Courtship and the Courts," 43–45.

[56] An electoral document of ca. 1578 refers to mixed marriages "von einem Catholischen Pfarrherrn seint copulirt worden" (GLA 77/4195, 5ʳ, no. 10). Cf. also 1563 *Kirchenordnung, EKO* 400–401; and many references to *copulatio sacerdotalis* in Wendel, *Le mariage*, 29ff., 109–10, 118–24, 215–16.

[57] Reformed ministers differed greatly on this issue (cf. 1591 Bacharach consistorial decision on *Brotwoch*; AEKK 125/2,242), agreeing unanimously only on *Buß- und Bettag* as a prohibited day for weddings. StAS IA/10, 123ᵛ; Vogler II:935, 938; Wendel, *Le mariage*, 144, 213.

Though preserved in Speyer's post-Tridentine rituals (Lamott, *Das Speyerer Diözesanrituuale*, 235–36), enforcement of forbidden liturgical times (also called *tempus feriarum*) in the Prince Bishopric appears to have been sporadic; cf. Stammer III:125.

[58] The Bern Ritual adopted by the Electorate (1563 *Kirchenordnung, EKO* 400–401) was also preferred by many other reformed polities, such as Strasbourg (Kö II:356; Wendel, *Le mariage*, 121) Cf. the many similarities to the traditional, pre-Reformation ceremony described in Speyer's diocesan ritual book (Lamott, *Das Speyerer Diözesanrituale*, 240ff.), as well as later Catholic liturgical incorporation of the same biblical excerpts and sermon suggestions in the 1551 Mainz Ritual (Reifenberg, *Sakramente*, 489–90, 515–16).

the liturgical specifications of Trent, electoral wedding reforms permitted a surprising amount of local variation within these few established standards.[59] Authority, not ceremony, constituted the central target of reform, and among ecclesiastical leaders of all three confessions this meant merely putting into full practice the same authority that centuries of acculturation had gradually secured for them.

Governmental authorities also attempted to redefine "public approval" of marriage in terms of their own institutional authority but with different immediate objectives. The point at which the early modern state "penetrates" the family,[60] David Sabean has remarked, is regulation of family property, and in the case of marriage this penetration focused almost exclusively on two aspects of the betrothal stage: permission to marry and the exchange of property. As we have already noted, all medieval secular authorities – municipal and seigneurial – took active roles in ensuring "suitable" matches within their jurisdictions. In the sixteenth century, though, State regulation of marriage assumed an even more obviously restrictive and paternalistic form. Like their ecclesiastical counterparts, early modern statebuilders portrayed and most likely perceived their activity in these areas as part of their divinely instituted paternal responsibility. Not surprisingly, they too concentrated on a subtle but intentional usurpation of the key authority in that traditional validation of marriage: the *Hausvater*.

Restoration of parental authority in the marriage process in fact constituted the most often articulated goal of secular reformers. At stake, as both secular and ecclesiastical leaders stressed, was not only the issue of filial duty and respect, but familial property and prestige as well. Luther sums up the argument well:

> If I raised a daughter with so much expense and effort, care and trouble, diligence and work and had bet all my life, body and property on her for so many years, should she not be better protected than if she were a cow who had wandered into the forest, which any wolf could devour? Should my child be so available that any boy, perhaps a stranger or an enemy to me, would have power and free access to steal her secretly from me and

---

59 See my comments in the next section.
60 Sabean, *Power in the Blood*, 137–38; also *Property, Production, and Family*, 26ff. Coing concurs that "man kann das Ancien Régime [also broadly defined] als die Zeit der Verstaatlichung des Familienrechts bezeichnen" (*Europäisches Privatrecht*, 195).

take her home without my knowledge and consent? Does anyone want to leave his money and property standing so openly about that the first one who comes by could take it? Every reasonable person must concede, I say, that this is violence and injustice which could be easily avoided if one prohibited secret engagements . . . No boy would be able to win a child from a pious man or presume to become an heir of property that he had not acquired if he knew that it were useless even if he made a thousand secret engagements.[61]

Luther's analogy of clandestine vows to theft (rather than rape) obviously struck home with Protestant secular authorities who frequently repeated the characterization of children as property. In language strikingly similar to Luther's, the elector's 1563 marriage ordinance unabashedly condemned the suitor "who prowls in corners and the darkness or takes in secrecy; he is a marriage-thief [*ehe diep*] and has dishonestly stolen her, contrary to God and His Word."[62] Unlike the emperor's 1548 ban, which occasionally punished but continued to recognize all marriage vows "without differentiation," ordinances of the Electorate and other Protestant states considered the marriages of minors against their parents' wishes as clearly invalid in the eyes of God and all legal tradition.[63] Henceforth, the couple's exchange of vows alone was not enough to make a valid marriage; it was also to be "orderly, legitimate, and completely proper," including, in the case of "minors," parental approval.[64] Sons in the Palatinate with absent fathers were to

---

[61] "Von Ehesachen" (1530), *WA* 30/III:208–9; translated in Robisheaux, "Peasants and Pastors: Rural Youth Control and the Reformation in Hohenlohe, 1540–1680," *Social History* 6 (1981), 283. Luther repeats the characterization later in the same treatise: "Also mußen wir sagen das ein dieb und sein diebstahl ein reuber und sein raub auch nicht solten von einander zu thun sein" (213).

[62] 1563 *EGO, EKO* 300. The equating of children with property (and even livestock; cf., for instance, 1563 *EGO; EKO* 294) has apparently escaped the notice of those historians who argue without qualification that "from prenatal care to their indoctrination in the schools, there is every evidence that [sixteenth-century Protestant] children were considered special and were loved by their parents and teachers, their nurture the highest of human vocations, their proper moral and vocational training humankind's best hope" (Ozment, *When Fathers Ruled*, 177).

[63] Electoral ordinances repeatedly characterized such unions as "göttlichen, naturlichen und burgerlichen rechten, der erbar- und billickhait zuwider und entgegen." 1556 *Von den Esachen, EKO* 221ff.; 1563 *EGO, EKO* 294ff.; and see my comments in Chapter 2.

[64] 1556 *Von den Ehesachen; EKO* 222; Cf. also 1562 *EO, EKO* 281ff.; 1563 *EGO, EKO* 294ff. As in most of its marriage ordinance, the Electorate follows the age limitation set by Strasbourg (later changed to 24 for men and 20 for women) rather than that of Geneva (20 and 18, respectively). Hughes, *Registers*, 70ff.; Wendel, *Le mariage*, 103–4; Kö II:640. Other Protestant age limitations ranged from 18 and 16 in Schaffhausen to 25 and 22 in Nuremberg (Kö I:360; Harvey, "Nürnberg Marriage Laws," 195).

wait three years before marrying without their permission, and orphans were to obtain approval from their guardians or oldest male relatives. All unions concluded otherwise were, in the words of the Elector's 1563 marriage ordinance, "void, invalid, and nonbinding."[65] Moreover, any who aided minors in such illicit acts were considered guilty of kidnapping, to be "immediately imprisoned and, according to the nature of their offense, punished without mercy by imprisonment, fine, or banishment."[66]

At the same time, municipal and siegneurial authorities continued to expand their own traditional roles in approval of betrothals. Swiss and imperial cities were – predictably – the most active proponents of "successful" unions of persons and property. During the Middle Ages, success had meant protecting the interests of parents and families in choosing their heirs' spouses. By the sixteenth century, though, many town councils had taken much of this familial responsibility on themselves, requiring State approval of all marriage contracts before the church ceremony. Most such restrictions, like those of Landau, simply reflected the usual suspicion of strangers and attempts to promote endogamous unions.[67] The new paternalistic tone of the magistracy, however, is unmistakable. By the late fifteenth century, the normal guild practice of screening all members' potential wives had apparently been extended by many magistrates to the city as a whole. In the paternalistic manner of their composite guilds, the town councils of Nuremberg, Augsburg, and Memmingen, for example, discouraged most exogamous and otherwise "ill-considered" unions while at the same time providing dowries for the marriages of poor but respectable local girls.[68] The sixteenth century, on the other hand, witnessed a more restrictive kind of paternalism, more clearly reflecting an exclusionary backlash from what Gillis calls "the nascent capitalist middle class."[69] Many German cities imitated Augs-

---

[65] 1562 *EO; EKO* 280.

[66] 1562 *EO; EKO* 281. The purposeful unspecificity of the punishment, however, is worth noting.

[67] 1465 and 1487 ordinances of the Palatine city required, like many other municipalities, that strangers wishing to marry into the community bring certificates establishing legitimate origins to the town council before exchanging vows (Lehmann, *Landau in der Pfalz*, 103). Cf. similar ordinances of 1565 and 1577 in Strasbourg (Wiesner, *Working Women*, 21; Wendel, *Le mariage*, 193–201).

[68] Gustav K. Schmelzeisen, *Die Rechtstellung der Frau in der deutschen Stadtwirtschaft* (Stuttgart, 1935), 31–32, 45ff.; Wiesner, *Working Women*, 78; Roper *Holy Household*, 38–39, 72, 150. See also Falk, *Die Ehe am Ausgang des Mittelalters*, 52–66, on similar dowry funds in Hamburg, Cologne, Hildesheim, Halle, Frankfurt, Mainz, and other cities.

[69] Gillis, *For Better, for Worse*, 86ff.

burg's prohibition of "the dissolute, ill-considered and forward marriages of foreign servants and incoming folk" unless they held the prerequisite minimum in property (fifty gulden) necessary for guild membership and citizenship.[70] By 1563, the council was interviewing all nonpatrician or merchant couples to ascertain whether they had sufficient means of support, rejecting and banishing one out of ten applicants.[71]

Territorial rulers were also unambiguous in their opposition to all marriages of unequals, and especially to individuals from outside their jurisdictions. Popular appeals for legalization of unequal marriages largely met with the same results as other social interpretations of Lutheran freedom and equality.[72] The Palatine-Electorate's marriage court ordinance of 1563 staunchly defended the traditional ban on unequal marriages with typical reasoning:

> In the instance where vows have been exchanged between two unequal persons – such as a farm laborer or servant of a noble or knight, or conversely a man of such noble descent [with] a serving girl – the marriage (*if it has not yet been consummated according to the circumstances defined below*) is not to be recognized, since the inequality of persons has repeatedly resulted in such great and widespread licentiousness, and since every individual is certainly capable of finding his equal.[73]

Nor were such concerns limited to Protestant states, as evidenced in minimum property requirements and other marriage restrictions in ordinances of the neighboring Prince-Bishopric of Speyer and much larger Duchy of Bavaria.[74] Like the fathers they claimed to represent, rulers of all confessions considered their own economic stake in such mar-

---

[70] Roper, "Weddings in Reformation Augsburg," 86; the 1537 *EGO* of the city also emphasized that the prohibition on unequal marriages "ist in alle weg zu halten, es were dann, das man des Leibaignen befreiung von seimen herren bekomen möchte. Denn wo nicht, so bleibt das Leibeigen allweg in Gewalt seines Herren" (Kö II:283–84). Cf. similar restrictions in Memmingen, Frankfurt, and Strasbourg, as well as an even stricter 1580 Munich prohibition of marriage for all domestics (Wiesner, *Working Women*, 21, 88).

[71] Roper, *Holy Household*, 139.

[72] Cf. the request of Black Forest peasants in 1524 "dieweil die EE nach göttlicher ordnung fri sein soll" (Müller, *Entwicklung und Spätformen*, 40–41).

[73] *1563 EGO, EKO* 303–5 (emphasis added); and see also 318. Canon law, on the other hand, recognized all such *verba de presenti* between unequals as binding except in cases of error. Cf. Coing, *Europäisches Privatrecht*, 198ff. on continuing prohibition of marriages between free and unfree persons, and my comments in the next section on continuing recognition among Protestants of unconsummated *de futuro* vows.

[74] 1533 *Landesordnung* of Bavaria (Beyerle, *Quellen*, II¹:283–85) and contemporary customary from the Prince-Bishop's village of Gleisweiler (Weizsäcker, *Pfälzische Weistümer*, 664–65).

riages as more than ample justification for greater control of "the greatest contractual agreement and [merger in the world]."[75]

At the same time, the decline of serfdom and increasing labor migration prompted a much more expansive attitude toward marital permission among territorial leaders than their municipal counterparts. By the early sixteenth century, the cost of a governmental dispensation to marry an unequal or foreigner had dropped considerably in most areas, in the Electorate to only one gulder for the native and two gulden for the foreigner.[76] A few rulers even encouraged immigration by granting unrestricted marital rights,[77] though most preferred to exercise their discretionary power to grant exceptions depending on circumstances. Generally, preliminary petitions to marry newly arrived strangers or outside the realm were viewed more favorably by seigneurial authorities than those from already betrothed subjects. Widower Anshelm Schmidt's request to leave the territory to marry was immediately granted by the cathedral chapter of Speyer, as were Hans Greisel's petition for citizenship and marriage in Bauerbach, and widow Catharina Weiland's request to marry her longtime and faithful servant (in order to pass on her property to him in her "old age").[78] Georg Menzering, however, who had already defied the bailiff's ordinance against marriage with "foreigners" by exchanging vows with Barbara Bürkin of Underderdringen, was punished accordingly and denied solemnization or recognition of the vows.[79] Philip Metzler's widow was similarly warned by electoral authorities that her marriage with a foreign serf required official approval and that they should both immediately cease cohabitation or face punishment.[80]

---

75 "die höchste contractverprundung und gemeinschaft undter den menschen" (1563 *EGO; EKO* 294).

76 1519 customary from Mannweiler (Grimm V:667). The fee was split between the Elector and the local commune. Cf. similar fines in Eikel (Westphalia) of 2 fl. (1½ fl. for *middelmessige* and 1 fl. for *allerarmste*), and 5 fl. or *fleurschetz* in Herxheim am Berg, both early sixteenth century; also a similar 72-pfenning fine in 1518 and 1553 Bavarian *Landesordnungen* for servants who marry without their masters' permission or providing sufficient notice. Grimm III:64, V:606; Beyerle, *Quellen*, I²:44–45, II:281–82.

77 Cf. an earlier (mid-fifteenth-century) customary of Kyburg in Zurich, as well as the more common sixteenth-century examples of Nalbacher Thal in the Saarland (1532) and Dammerkirch in Alsace (1578). Grimm II:27, IV:29, 338.

78 14 May 1598; GLA 61/10951, 3–4.

79 GLA 61/10951, 388–89. See Chapter 5 for my comments on the perseverance of the petitionary tradition in early modern Germany.

80 8 December 1611; AEKK 125/2, 363. The woman had also been summoned to the consistory twice before for her "godless" behavior (1605 and 1611; AEKK 125/2, 329, 362). See also Chapter 5.

In view of such an expanded role, the apparent reticence of the State in controlling marital property itself calls for some explanation. Certainly sixteenth-century German states (to the delight of historians) produced an unprecedented amount of bureaucratic paperwork on a variety of matters relevant to marriage, ranging from Church wedding registers to property inventories and assessments. Indeed, "it would be hard to specify," in the words of David Sabean, "any aspect of familial relations in Germany in the early modern period that was not shaped in the crucible of state power." Yet, as the same scholar adds, "the entry point for officials changed once the state learned to mobilize its resources and had gained several centuries of administrative experience."[81] Most governments in our study, as we have seen in the preceding chapter, remained in the earliest phases of legal codification and bureaucratic expansion. Rather than vainly attempting to displace centuries of customary particularism with a single legislative stroke, most sixteenth-century secular authorities sought to enhance State authority in such matters as marital property in a subtler and more indirect manner. Their pattern – similar to their ecclesiastical counterparts – was to establish new institutional authority in the marriage process first and only later attempt significant revisions of the process itself.

Regulation of the exchange of marital property, consequently, focused almost exclusively on the role of the State official as public witness, or notary, of property arrangements made in advance of a marriage.[82] By the beginning of the sixteenth century, many Swiss and imperial cities required official approval of all marriage contracts before the wedding could be held.[83] In language strikingly similar to the religious condem-

---

[81] Sabean, *Property, Production, and Family*, 26.

[82] On marital negotiations and contracts in Germany, see Roper, *Holy Household*, 133ff.; T. Mayer-Maly "Morgengabe," in *HRG* 3:681; Cowan, *The Urban Patriciate*, 126ff.; and especially the contemporary account in *Das Buch Weinberg*, ed. Josef Stein, vols. I and II (Bonn, 1926), discussed in detail in Ozment, *When Fathers Ruled*, 72ff.

See also Sabean, *Property, Production, and Family*, 198–201, on the distinctions between a *Pactum* (sort of an early modern prenuptial contract) and an *Abrede* (written or oral agreement on the size and nature of marriage portions). The first kind of contract was almost always typical of a second marriage for one or both of the partners.

[83] The earliest mention I have found is a 1440 Ulm statute (Kö II:3). See also 1498 Worms *Reformatio* V:5, requiring city's notary or at least five witnesses (Beyerle, *Quellen*, I¹:212ff.), similar 1523 customary from Saint Gallen (Grimm VI:370), and 1603 customary from the duchy of Sayn stipulating a fine of "achthalb rader marck" to the *Vogt* and *Schultheiss* for contracts "verdedingt" outside the realm (Grimm II:500).

A March 17, 1589 decree of the Speyer town council similarly required its own approval of all marriages within the city, although enforcement is unknown. StAS IB/6, Bd.1, 131ʳ, 448ʳ.

nations of clandestine marriages, the 1520 *Reformatio* of Freiburg ordained "that dowries and countergifts should not be established with
vague, unclear promises but with specific and appointed goods, clear
words, and a specific amount," and in any event "not in corners without the
presence of honorable persons."[84] Later territorial codes of Württemberg
(1555), Solms (1571), and Saxony (1572) all adopted similar requirements for publicity with the same notarial role for State officials.[85]

The actual contents of such marriage contracts or legal specifics on
marital property, by contrast, were almost completely ignored by
sixteenth-century legislation. Some states, such as Nuremberg and
Worms, attempted to enforce customary limits on payment of dowries,
while others, such as Frankfurt and Württemberg simply stipulated that
agreements should mention gifts of both the bride and the groom.[86]
Most evaded the issue entirely or relegated it to "custom" (*Land-
esgewohnheit*).[87] Common statutory limits of the bilateral *Morgengabe*, or
morning gift from the groom, for instance (in Speyer, a token one gulder),
clearly represented official recognition of customary evolution since
Germanic times rather than any self-conscious statebuilding agenda.[88]
From the fourteenth century on, both the *Morgengabe* and *Ehesteuer* had
already begun to disappear in the wedding contracts of Strasbourg, and
by the sixteenth century the symbolic nature of the groom's gift appeared
well established.[89] Instead, early modern statebuilders chose to continue

---

84 Freiburg *Reformatio* III.2–4; Beyerle, *Quellen*, I:275–76.
85 Beyerle, *Quellen*, I²:123–24, 209, 283.
86 Nuremberg kept the traditional deadline of one and a half years for payment after signing the
   contract, whereas Worms specified one year if in residence, two years if abroad (Beyerle,
   Quellen, I¹:6–7, 125). See also the 1509 Frankfurt *Reformatio* (Beyerle, *Quellen*, I¹:232); 1555
   Wüttemberg *Landrecht* II:10 (Hess, *Familien- und Erbrecht*, 52, 91ff.).
87 See civil codes of Solms (1571) and Saxony (1572); Beyerle, *Quellen* I²:210, 283; also Ernst
   Eberle, *Probleme zur Rechtsstellung der Frau nach den kursächsischen Konstitution von 1572* (Stutt-
   gart, 1964), 81–83 and 108ff.
      Cf. also customary guidelines for contents of marriage contracts for Westhofen (ca. 1570) and
   Koldingen (Grimm III:43, IV:690).
88 StAS IA/10, 43ᵛ (1535). Cf. customaries of Altselten, Marbach, Bernag, Balgach, and Wil-
   denhaus in Saint Gallen (1475 and ca. 1500); Buenzen in Aargau (1568); and Mülhausen in the
   Palatinate, all limiting the *Morgengabe* to ten lb. pfennig. Grimm V:74, 203, 205; and Hermann
   Arnold, "Das eheliche Güterrecht von Mülhausen i. Elsass am Ausgange des Mittelalters," in
   Deutschrechtliche Beiträge; Forschungen und Quellen zur Geschichte des Deutschen Rechts, ed. Konrad
   Beyerle (Heidelberg, 1908), I:21–25.
89 Wendel, *Le mariage*, 167, 175. In Florence during the same period, the groom's symbolic
   countergift usually comprised clothing and jewelry taken back by the groom's family after the
   wedding (Christiane C. Klapisch-Zuber, "The Griselda Complex: Dowry and Marriage Gifts in
   the Quattrocento," *Women, Family, and Ritual*, 213–46). See also Mayer-Maly, "Morgengabe,"
   in *HRG* 3:678–83.

their efforts toward expanding State authority in the transferal of marital or other property without altering the rules of devolution. A few precociously well organized states such as Württemberg and Upper Austria undeniably achieved much early success in "bureaucratizing" marital and familial property through their comprehensive marital and post-mortem inventories. Yet even in these instances, establishing bureaucratic authority in property transferals was one matter; challenging the very fiber of traditional ownership remained quite another.[90]

Thus, whereas Roman law continued to shape almost every other area of sixteenth-century legal standardization, local custom continued to rule in questions of marital property and inheritance. Not only did the great majority of sixteenth-century civil codes explicitly retain such traditional medieval practices as communal conjugal goods (*Gütergemeinschaft*)[91] and the Germanic definition of male guardianship (*Vormundschaft*),[92] but even the most "Romanized" codifications made only superficial use of Roman legal terminology in defining marital property. Württemberg's 1555 civil code, for instance, employed Roman and German terms for wedding gifts interchangeably, but otherwise eschewed the Roman principles behind the words, particularly the concept of separate dotal property of the wife.[93]

---

[90] Both Sabean (*Property, Production, and Family*, 92ff., 187) and Rebel (*Peasant Classes*) discuss State creation of a peasant aristocracy of "good householders," but Rebel takes the social impact considerably further. See my n. 108.

[91] Cf. civil codes of Nuremberg (1479), Bavaria (1518), and Saxony (1572). Beyerle, *Quellen*, I[1]:8–9, I[2]:49–50; Eberle, *Probleme zur Rechtsstellung der Frau*, 42. Although not so labeled until the *Badisches Landrecht* of 1808, the practice of *Gütergemeinschaft* (in various forms) was almost universal throughout late medieval and modern Germany. Contrary to Roman law's preservation of separate marital goods, customary practice of *Gütergemeinschaft* united all property upon marriage under the husband's administration. Generally (though again, there were countless local variations), upon the death of either spouse, the husband inherited two-thirds of the property, the wife one-third, and the remainder was divided equally among the children. Coing, *Europäisches Privatrecht*, 30ff.; Hübner, *Germanic Private Law*, 621–55; W. Ogris, "Gütergemeinschaft," in *HRG* 1:1871ff., and "Errungenschaftsgemeinschaft," in *HRG* 1:1004–6.

[92] Eberle, *Probleme zur Rechtstellung der Frau*, 45–51; Hübner, *Germanic Private Law*, 625–27. Only the 1555 territorial code of Württemberg rejected the husband's *Vormundschaft* outright, yet even it resisted granting the wife full rights over her marital property and, by the revision of the code twelve years later, had reverted to the previous, traditional practice (Hess, *Familien- und Erbrecht*, 87–88). See also Stobbe, *Handbuch*, IV:516–52.

[93] Cf. *Landrecht* II.10 and synonymous reference to "Zugelt oder Heüratgut, dotem vel donationem" but lack of any clear distinction between husband's and wife's property as well as obvious preference for limited communal goods (*Errungenschaftsgemeinschaft*), leading Hess to conclude "Die Grundstruktur des Familienrechts blieb aaber deutschrechtlich" (*Familien- und Erbrecht*, 91–94, 201). Coing and Ogris concur, the latter observing that "mit der Rezeption fand das römische Dotalsysteme in Deutschland Eingang, das aber unter dem Einfluss inheimischer

On the related issue of inheritance law, most rulers also resisted the one innovation that would have clearly benefited large landowners most – primogeniture inheritance. Historians differ on the sources of dynastic conservatism in this area, as well as the actual inheritance practices that prevailed.[94] The inability or unwillingness of these secular rulers, however, to "tamper" in areas of obvious concern to their own political and economic power suggests greater restraint in statebuilding ambitions than might first be supposed. Even in those parts of Germany and Switzerland where impartibility had become customary by the sixteenth century, codification and uniform enforcement were generally successful only in smaller states, such as the monastic territory of Weingarten.[95] At the same time, the continuing popularity of marriage contracts, another medieval tradition, ensured that the property arrangements of both marrying parties could legally circumvent any customary or statutory condition that did not suit their immediate needs.[96]

In short, the vast majority of all German laws regarding marital property remained traditional in substance as well as form well into the nineteenth century. Even the newly introduced instances of divorce among Protestants displayed marked conservatism on questions of property redistribution. Both the 1529 Strasbourg marriage ordinance and

Rechtsvorstellungen starke Modificationen erfuhr"; See Coing, *Europäisches Privatrecht*, 151–52, 195, 238–41; W. Ogris, "Güterrecht, eheliches," in *HRG* 1:1875. Stobbe (*Handbuch*, IV:149ff.) claims that as late as 1900 less than one-twentieth of the German population lived under Roman dotal law.

94 A recent study by Paula Sutter Fichtner (*Protestantism and Primogeniture in Early Modern Germany* [New Haven, 1989]) attributes the widespread resistance to impartible inheritance among German princes to confessional sensibilities, especially Protestant reformers' teachings on the obligation to care for all offspring equally. While not denying the significance of such teachings among Catholic potentates, Fichtner argues (largely from anecdotal evidence) that the maintenance of large ecclesiastical benefices in their territories offset such financial concerns and made these rulers more receptive to primogeniture than Protestant contemporaries. Thomas Robisheaux (*Rural Society*, 81–82, 122ff.) confirms a mid-sixteenth-century reversal of the previous trend toward acceptance of primogeniture among German rulers, but suggests more non-religious factors in a general economic conservative reaction that apparently affected both confessions equally. David Sabean argues that the entire debate on partible versus impartible inheritance practices is actually a false one and that most areas were typified by very complicated and interconnected systems between these two artificial poles (*Property, Production, and Family*, 13ff., 186–87).

95 Sabean, *Property, Production, and Family*, 15; and cf. Robisheaux, *Rural Society*, 81–83, 123–38, on unsuccessful attempts by the dukes of Hohenlohe to enforce strict impartibility in a region where versions of it had already become customary by the fifteenth century. See also H. Weitzel, "Primogenitur," in *HRG* 3:1955–56.

96 Sixteenth-century jurists disagreed on the validity of statutory regulation of marriage contracts for subjects living outside of their territory, but all agreed that such contracts could make stipulations counter to local custom (Coing, *Europäisches Privatrecht*, 151ff.).

later 1563 marriage court ordinance of the Palatine-Electorate stipulated adherence to the "imperial law" as much as possible, and explicitly used the rules of *Gütergemeinschaft* to the disadvantage of the divorced or divorcing woman.[97] The magistrates of Strasbourg, for instance, specified that property divisions in divorce were to grant two-thirds of the communal property to the innocent party, but also that the property of an innocent woman went to her children or – in the case of no offspring – went toward the "common good" of the poor. Other Protestant authorities were less harsh toward a divorcing wife – the Palatine-Electorate granting her one-third of communal goods, Basel two-thirds, and all in Lindau (since an adulterous spouse was considered legally dead) – but all retained male guardianship over all women, especially divorced ones.[98]

The early modern State did not limit its paternal assumption of authority in marriage to the area of betrothal and the exchange of property, however. Rather, as we have seen in the preceding chapter, in most Protestant areas and some Catholic ones, secular and ecclesiastical controls were often intermingled and administered by a variety of authorities. Long before the institution of civil marriage in Germany, for instance, many town halls were already building additions exclusively for wedding banquets (and occasionally ceremonies).[99] The most striking example of State hegemony in traditionally religious functions, however, was not that of any Protestant territory but of Europe's largest Catholic state – France. Already by the publication of *Tametsi*, the French monarchy had claimed the right to keep the local marriage registers ordered by Trent, and in 1586 the French assembly of the clergy made the witnessing priest, as in most Protestant areas, a representative of the State.[100] By 1612, the rupture between theology and enforcement that had led to total marital jurisdictional assumption by Protestant states had

[97] Wendel, *Le mariage*, 170; *EKO* 323–24.
[98] In divorces of the electorate, an innocent woman without children received "ihres ehebruchigen mannes zugebrachte widerlag und morgengab und der dritte thayl seiner andern gueter frey ledig neben ihrem heyrathgut heimfallen" (*EKO* 324). On Basel and Lindau, see Thomas M. Safley, "Civic Morality and the Domestic Economy;" in *The German People and the Reformation*, ed. R. Po-Chia Hsia (Ithaca, N.Y., 1988), 180–81.
[99] Cf. the example of Geislar town hall and the 1607 addition often referred to as the *Hochzeithaus* (Tütken, *Geschichte des Dorfes und Patrimonialgerichtes Geismar*, 207–8); also *Kirchenordnungen* of Württemberg (1553; Friedberg, *Das Recht der Eheschließung*, 200–201) and the Palatine-Electorate (1556; *EKO* 166) on weddings held at the *Rathaus*.
[100] Bels, *Le mariage des protestants franais*, 87, 197; Basdevant, "Des rapports de l'Eglise," 72, 87. With the Edict of Nantes (1598), this designation was extended to Protestant ministers as well.

resulted in a similarly strong secular role in France, despite its Catholic allegiances.[101] Whatever the jurisdictional arrangement, though, secular and ecclesiastical authorities of the sixteenth century were determined to remake marriage along "traditional" lines, securing their own "paternal" authority in the process.

Private consent and public approval in the patriarchal age

Despite their many criticisms of Canon law's consensualist doctrine, sixteenth-century reformers were by no means irreconcilably opposed to it in principle. Protestant and Catholic authorities viewed new legal restraints of parental, ecclesiastical, and governmental approval more as necessary counterbalances rather than nullifications of consensual marriage. The great majority of legal reforms, consequently, aimed at a restoration in balance between public and private concerns in marriage and not an "everyday tyranny" of fathers supported by the Church and State.[102]

Even within such modest goals, however, the limited effect of new or "restored" public controls over marriage must have disappointed ambitious religious leaders and statebuilders. Our examination of the long-term origins of their reforms should leave us less surprised at their successes and failures. For although sixteenth-century secular and religious reformers shared the same high expectations of their involvement in the marriage process, they did not share the same history of accomplishment. For better or worse, the canonical model of marriage had become well entrenched in both legal theory and practice, and could not be dismissed by the most aggressive opponents of consensual validity. Nor for that matter could traditional local rituals of legitimation be easily displaced in attempts by the Church and State to monopolize this function. New legal and bureaucratic expansions of traditional ecclesiastical and secular authority could build on long-established communal practices, but could rarely replace them. In the traditions that ruled popular perception and practice, the State's reform of marriage was too much of the newcomer to hope for more.

Certainly, parental authority in marriage does not seem to have suf-

---

[101] Royal edicts of 1606, 1629, 1639, and 1697 served to reinforce in law what had already become general practice in all aspects of marital control, especially civil litigation. Bels, *Le mariage des protestants français*, 126; Traer, *Marriage and the Family*, 32–35; Esmein I:33–34.

[102] Jean-Louis Flandrin, *Les amours paysannes: Amour et sexualité dans les compagnes de l'ancienne France (XVIe–XIXe siècles)* (Paris, 1975), 55.

fered from the legal reforms of Protestants. On the contrary, new requirements of their consent for validity gave sixteenth-century parents (especially fathers) an apparently unprecedented legal stranglehold on their children's choice of mate. Although more and more municipal and territorial codes restricted the parents' right to disinherit children in unapproved marriages,[103] secular and ecclesiastical courts routinely enforced the same parents' wishes in contested vows, apparently dissolving or recognizing them upon request. In 1598, for instance, the Lutheran magistrates of Speyer unquestioningly supported the demand of Hans Flochen's widow that Hanns Ingstein's clandestine betrothal to her daughter be recognized over his subsequent promise to another.[104] A similar exchange of vows just three years earlier had been summarily dissolved by the same body, despite the presence of one witness, at the request of the woman's guardian.[105] Findings for other contemporary Protestant marriage courts apparently confirm the same strong alliance between parents and the magistracy on this issue. Of 110 disputed engagements before the Hohenlohe-Langenburg marriage court from 1550 to 1679, for instance, 71.2 percent were initiated by parents and pastors and all were invalidated.[106]

---

[103] Though completely prohibited by some medieval German authorities (e.g., 1479 Nuremberg *Reformatio*), disinheritance in such cases was generally limited by most sixteenth-century cities and territories to cases involving a "dishonorable" individual, such as a prostitute or executioner (see Chapter 5). Cf. Municipal Reformations of Worms (1498) and Freiburg (1520), and territorial codifications of Bavaria (1553) and Solms (1553) (Beyerle, *Quellen*, I¹:7, 215, 302; I²:220; II¹:236–37) as well as customaries of Haszloch (1492), Saint Gallen (1523), and Spesbach (1570), all requiring the *Amtman's* permission to disinherit children (Grimm V:579, 672; VI:371).

[104] 12 January 1598; StAS IB/8, Bd.2, 193ᵛ. Apparently, though, the magistrates were particularly swayed by the mother's assertion that Ingstein "Irer dochter nicht allein die Ehe versproch., sund. (auch und ir die unzimliche werck volbracht ab. dess. ungedacht) sich mit einer ander ehlich verlobt." See my subsequent comments on consummated *de futuro* vows.

[105] 8 May 1595; StAS IB/8, Bd.2, 11ᵛ. Cf. similar case in Bacharach: 15 April 1612; LAK 4/1631, 240ʳ.

[106] At least twenty-three youths (28.8 percent) attempted to outmaneuver such parental objections with suits of their own, only to meet with the same disappointing result. Robisheaux, "Peasants and Pastors," 294–96. Cf. similar results in the marriage court of Reutlingen for roughly the same period, where 97 percent of all cases (ninety-five total) involved diputed vows, 79 percent of which were declared nonbinding (Allen, "Crime and Punishment in Reutlingen," 249–50), and invalidation in Augsburg of fourteen of sixteen disputed vows without parental permission (Roper, *Holy Household*, 160).

    Carlson, on the other hand, finds no such pattern in English matrimonial disputes – quite the opposite: "Parents, amazingly, seemed no more inclined to agitate for legal reinforcements for their authority than writers were to recommend them." Only two of over two thousand from the diocese of Ely, for instance, included any provisions restricting the matrimonial choices of legatees, with a similar pattern in York ("Marriage and the English Reformation," 469–74).

Some historians have concluded from such evidence of increased control exercised by parents over their children's marriage and inheritance rights that the sixteenth century marked a turning point toward what Stone calls "the Restricted Patriarchal Nuclear Family."[107] Hermann Rebel even contends that the sixteenth-century State's increasing regulation of property redistribution and inheritance resulted in a complete restructuring of familial relations within the early modern peasant household, creating a "class struggle" between propertied parents and their scrambling heirs.[108] Other scholars, such as Steven Ozment, acknowledge the strong patriarchal character of the change, but emphasize instead a more affectionate and close-knit family as a result of Protestant innovations.[109]

Once again, though, we risk overestimating the goals and capabilities of sixteenth-century secular authorities in this area and underestimating their fundamental social and legal conservativeness. Most rulers, in fact, were apparently just as concerned with parental abuses of the consensual ideal as those by disobedient children. Ordinances of the Elector expressed outrage at such "unfatherly" patriarchs who "hindered [their children] not only in proper Christian discipline, but also in securing timely and suitable marriage."[110] Still worse were those unloving and irresponsible parents who "[paid] less attention to their children than cows, letting them do whatever they want – running off to dances, wedding feasts, and other parties and gatherings,"[111] If parents themselves abused their God-given authority, then it was up to their govern-

---

107 See especially *Family, Sex, and Marriage,* 138ff.
108 "This notion [that relations to the house became more important to one's kin] . . . tears asunder the positivist perceptions of the relations between role and kin relations at least as far as the society in question here is concerned. Relationships that appear to be personal – based on sentiment, shared beliefs, and the affectionate interplay of family members, were in fact something different altogether" (*Peasant Classes,* 178). Unfortunately, Rebel's description of the centralized "invader" State" of Upper Austria (esp. 159ff.) not only appears inapplicable to other German territories but, even more problematic, his characterization of the familial – economic relationship at the heart of the entire social and political struggle – namely, between the pensioning stem elder (*Auszügler*) and dispossessed children – depends on one contemporary example (despite thorough analysis of 867 household inventories) (172).
109 *When Fathers Ruled,* especially 53ff.
110 1556 *Von den Ehesachen; EKO* 222. Cf. many similar municipal and territorial ordinances cited in Dieterich 200–1.
111 1563 *EGO; EKO* 294. Cf. an earlier version of the same in 1556 *Von den Ehesachen* (*EKO* 221) and Vogler II:956ff. on the duties of parents toward their children as defined by the ecclesiastical authorities of the Electorate. See also similar sentiments of Luther ("Von Ehesachen" [1530], *WA* 30/III:215), Calvin (Sermon 123 on Deut. 21:18–21; *Corpus Reformatorum,* 27:676ff.), and the *Hausväterliteratur* in general (Hoffmann, *Hausväterliteratur,* 151ff.).

mental counterparts – princes and magistrates – to provide the proper paternal guidance. Or, in the words of the Elector's coreligionist John Knox, "then the ministry or magistracy may enter into the place of the parent . . . for the work of God ought not to be hindered by the corrupt affections of worldly men."[112]

No parent, according to electoral ordinances, was to force his or her children into marriage, "which is and should remain a free estate."[113] In language identical to the contemporary Catholic pronouncements of Trent and the Prince-Bishop of Speyer, such parental coercion was considered a violation of the sanctity of the institution, in the Electorate punishable by an unspecified fine.[114] Nor should a father unfairly hinder a marriage "without just and legitimate grounds" since

> the written imperial laws sensibly decree and ordain that parents with children still in their charge who unfairly forbid them to take husbands and wives, and stand in their way, or withhold a dowry or trousseau, should be forced . . . by the *Amtleute* and *Landvogt* to give [the couple] permission to marry and their share of the patrimony.[115]

Parental consent, as Protestant authorities repeatedly stressed, was an extension of the consensualist doctrine of marriage, and not a nullification of it. Free and mutual consent continued to be recognized by all sixteenth-century jurists, Protestant as well as Catholic, as the irrefuta-

---

[112] *The Book of Discipline* (1560), in J. Knox, *The History of the Reformation of Religion in Scotland*, ed. Cuthbert Lennux, (London, 1905), 411–12.

[113] 1563 *EGO; EKO* 299. Cf. Luther's tract on the subject: "Das Eltern die Kinder zur Ehe nicht zwingen noch hindern sollen" (1524), *WA* 15:155–69; also "Von Ehesachen" (1530), *WA* 30/III:236–40.

[114] Chapter 9 of *Tametsi* (Schroder, *Council of Trent*, 189) and 1582 marriage ordinance of the Prince–Bishopric of Speyer, where pastors were instructed, "Und wo auff beschehene erkundigung einiger mißverstand, widerwillen, oder nötigung vermerckt unnd gespürt als balt bei gebürlicher straff nach unserer ermeßigung von deren vermelung gentzlich sich enthalten" (*Collectio* 389).

1556 *Von den Ehesachen; EKO* 222. Electoral ordinances, however, left determination of parental *zwang* up to the discretion of the *Eherichter*: "Man khan aber keine gewisse regel oder maß in causa metus ordnen und furschreiben, sondern haben sich verstendige eherichter nach gestalt gelegenheit der personen, des orts, der zeit, des zwangs und sonst aller andern umbstenden des handels zu vorhalten, auch darnach zu sprechen und urthaylen, wie dann alle rechtsgelerten, auch die canones einhelligklich alßo schliessen," which concludes, "und dieweil die civila und canonica iura in diesen fellen nichts unpillichs oder ungöttlichs geordnet, mögen sich die eherichter derselbigen hierin gebrauchen" (1563 *EGO; EKO* 198). Cf. similar treatment of 1565 Strasbourg marriage ordinance (Wendel, *Le mariage*, 197) and Neuchâtel marriage judges (Watt, *Making of Modern Marriage*, 63–4).

[115] 1563 *EGO; EKO* 281, 297–98. Cf. predecessor 1556 *Von den Ehesachen* (*EKO* 223); and 1562 *EO* (*EKO* 281).

ble legal basis of every valid marriage. While reformers differed by confession on the additional public requirements for legitimacy, none disputed the ultimate authority of the marrying individuals to accept or reject a proposed union.[116]

Protestant legal enforcement, consequently, continued to rely much more on the traditional canonical *de futuro* and *de presenti* vows of the couple themselves than the more frequent assertions of parental authority might suggest. Consummated *de futuro* vows, for instance, were routinely recognized by all secular and religious authorities of the Palatinate as binding, regardless of parental knowledge or approval.[117] The continuing significance of consummation in Protestant marriage law in fact provided minors the same opportunity of parental defiance as before the Reformation. The most startling evidence of such continuity ironically comes at the conclusion of a long condemnation of clandestine marriages of minors in the Elector's 1563 marriage ordinance:

> In the event, though, that after the clandestine betrothal has taken place, the aforementioned disobedient child remains intent in his course against the will of his parents, and cannot be swayed or talked out of his existing commitment . . . then the vows should be recognized as binding by our marriage judges, although their parents are not obliged to provide any dowry, trousseau, gift, or anything else.[118]

Truly determined couples, in other words, could successfully circumvent familial opposition in much the same way as before the Reformation. The 1612 decision of the Bacharach bailiff to recognize the marriage of Hermann Lehen and Elisabeth Bidbach – "who, without the knowledge of their parents and guardians, had become engaged to one another" – appears a typical example. In accordance with directions of

116 Dieterich 121–26, 154–55, 200ff.; Coing, *Europäisches Privatrecht*, 230. In the Electorate, see 1563 *EO* (*EKO*, 280–81 and 1563 *EGO* [295ff.]; and cf. examples of Zurich and Ulm (Kö I:93–103, II:49–50), Basel (Staehlin, *Ehescheidung in Basel*, 40ff.), Nuremberg (Harvey, "Nürnberg Marriage Laws," 48–60), and Strasbourg (Wendel, *Le mariage*, 94ff.; Kö II:435ff).

117 Though Luther and other religious reformers resisted this canonical carryover, the only two courts I have found that annulled consummated vows are Augsburg (Roper, *Holy Household*, 160) and Hohenlohe (Robisheaux, *Rural Society*, 108). Some authorities even made marriage mandatory in such cases; cf. consistorial ordinances of Geneva (1541), Brandenburg (1577), and Prussia (1584). Schwab, *Grundlagen*, 232; Friedberg, *Das Recht der Eheschliessung*, 221–222.

118 1562 *EO; EKO* 280. The paragraph concluded "Und gedencken wir vor uns, auch soliche mutwillige verechter göttlicher, natürlicher und unserer ordnung nach gestalt und gelegenheyt der sachen ernstlich strafen zu lassen." Cf. similarity to pre-Reformation codes in n. 11 and Table 2.

the 1562 marriage ordinance and the 1563 marriage court ordinance, the bailiff declared that the couple "be on this account punished, but afterward – since they do not wish to separate – be allowed to complete their vows with the normal church ceremony," simultaneously annulling another betrothal.[119]

Parental coercion, while difficult to prevent or punish, was similarly viewed with disfavor by marital judges and, in one 1601 Bacharach case, even considered a strong mitigating factor in a nineteen-year-old's poisoning of his older, unwanted wife.[120] A young woman from the same district also claimed parental force eight days after her 1599 public engagement to a local youth of whom "she could say nothing dishonorable but simply didn't want him." The case for dissolution was referred to the marriage court in Heidelberg. [121] The practice of a forced, or "shotgun," wedding (*Zwangstrauung*) was officially prohibited by the 1563 marriage court ordinance, which clearly stated that while the impregnator of a young maiden should wish to marry her out of "Christian love and honor," he was not to be compelled by any "worldly or physical force." Upon refusal he was required merely to provide just compensation of mother and child depending on the financial circumstances of each.[122]

Undoubtedly, the actual role of sixteenth-century parents in their children's marriages was more complex and varied than any model drawn from legal evidence alone could suggest. "Reading [only] cause papers," as Carlson writes of contemporary English marital cases, "it is

---

[119] 1562 *EO* and 1563 *EGO* (*EKO* 281, 296); *Amtman* decision of 24 April 1612 (LAK 4/1631). The two had already been jailed the year before for exchanging secret vows (3 July 1611; LAK 4/1631, 237ᵛ). Cf. 1565 Strasbourg marriage ordinance that also automatically annuls clandestine marriages *unless* "es weren dann dermassen vmbstend vnd christliche Ehrliche vn hochbewegende vrsachen vorhanden, Das die Annullation oder vernichtigung der Ehe, den Kindern vnd Eltern mehr zü nachtheil vnd verkleinerung dann zü vortheil vnd wolfart gelanden möcht" (Wendel, *Le mariage*, 197–98).

[120] Vogler II:978. Not only was the youth abused by his wife, but also by his father, who continued to beat him even after the forced marriage. The Bacharach consistory appears to have been particularly sensitive to cases of domestic violence, censoring thirteen parents in thirty years for verbal and physical cruelty to their children. Vogler II:956ff.; and see my discussion in Chapter 5.

[121] The public engagement included the *"Handstreich in Gegenwertigkeit zweyer Tisch vol Leut gehalten, auch die Braut den Treuschatz von Breutigam genommen."* 18 July 1599; Schüler, *Die Konventsprotokolle*, 100–2. In a similar case before the bailiff in 1619, the woman was required to return the dowry as well as pay all court costs (*LAK* 4/1632, 356).

[122] *EKO* 311. Cf. similar instructions in territorial codes of Baden (1495) and Prussia (1577); Beyerle, *Quellen*, II¹:148, 377.

possible to find evidence for any view of the role of parents in actual practice."[123] Even Flandrin admits that "among the individuals constituting the household there were, in former times just as nowadays, extremely varied relationships of affection, fear, condescension, respect, etc., depending both on the character of each individual and on the circumstances" – certainly a proviso against reductionism and formularization.[124] That courtship continued to be monopolized by young people themselves appears fairly certain. That parents continued to apply a combination of moral pressure and threats of disinheritance to prevent unwanted unions is also surely true. But to conclude that sixteenth-century courts and laws, especially Protestant ones, offered one group an insurmountable and inflexible advantage over the other we simply need more evidence.[125]

New Protestant and Catholic requirements of Church or State approval for validity can likewise be misleading. Authorities of all religious confessions, as we have seen, reacted strongly against recognition of the private exchange of *de presenti* vows, "that result in terrible disasters such as perjury, fornication, immorality, and other troublesome annoyances."[126] Most acknowledged that the existing imperial requirement of seven witnesses (for licity) was probably unrealistic for all cases and, instead, like the Elector and Prince-Bishop of Speyer, set the minimum at two or three "close relatives or in-laws. or, if none are at hand, two respectable, pious, and responsible persons."[127] Only those unions that met these and the previously mentioned requirements for publicity (three public banns, interrogation, witnessing of vows by own parish pastor, etc.) were to be recognized as valid, since – in the words of the

---

[123] "Marriage and the English Reformation," 415. Safley agrees that the nature of court evidence "makes it impossible to determine whether parents played a larger role in Protestant litigation than in Catholic" ("Civic Morality and Domestic Economy," 186–87). See also Watt, *Making of Modern Marriage*, 83ff., on this subject.

[124] *Families in Former Times*, 112. Flandrin concludes this sentence, of course, with the qualification "which are not our concern in this study." See also Richard Van Dülmen, "Fest der Liebe. Heirat und Ehe in der frühen Neuzeit," in *Armut, Liebe, Ehre: Studien zur historischen Kulturforschung*, ed. Richard Van Dülmen (Frankfurt, 1988), especially 72ff., on the mixture of individual choice and family concerns in this process.

[125] Gillis argues that only the number of informal marriages in England probably declined (*For Better, for Worse*, 92), whereas Ingram concludes that it is "highly doubtful whether the changes of the period 1570–1640 altered the balance between individual and family interests to any significant extent." Ingram, *Church Courts, Sex, and Marriage*, 137ff., 202–4.

[126] 1563 *EGO; EKO* 299.

[127] 1563 *EO; EKO* 281–82. Cf. identical restrictions of Chapter 1 of *Tametsi* (Schroeder, *Council of Trent*, 104) and bishop of Speyer's marriage ordinance (*Collectio* 387).

Elector's marriage ordinance – "marriage is a public estate ordained by God, and not a matter for corners or the dark."[128]

Forbidding private and informal vows, however, did not necessarily eliminate them altogether or prevent Protestant and Catholic courts from recognizing them as valid, especially when consummated. Customary exchange of drinking toasts, rings, and even property, for example, were expressly declared inadequate for validity by the Elector's marriage ordinance,[129] yet local officials appeared generally willing to formalize and solemnize such bonds rather than dissolve them. The gift of a *thaler* coin, a ring, and a belt clearly lent the 1591 clandestine vows of two Bacharach minors a greater significance in the minds of both the couple and the authorities.[130] Jurists, too, tended to focus their efforts more on the eradication of frivolous and potentially litigious betrothals concluded "in heated and rash desire or with words of jest and cursing"[131] (such as eating a sausage "in the name of love"), rather than the many private, customary practices that continued to be treated as binding.[132]

Consummated informal vows, though punished by secular authorities, continued to be routinely regularized with the public church wedding

---

[128] 1563 *EO; EKO* 300. The ordinance immediately follows this with the legal dictum: ". . . und soll diß die generalregel sein: das allewegen hierin privata publicis weichen caeteris paribus, das ist, heimbliche verlöbdnus soll dem offentlichen weichen, alßo auch heimlich beyschlafen dem offentlichen beyschlaffen."

[129] 1563 *EGO; EKO* 299–300. The Genevan Ecclesiastical Ordinances of 1561 were equally explicit: "All promises of marriage should be made honourably and in the fear of God and in no way dissolutely or frivolously, as when merely touching glasses when drinking together without first having made a sober proposal, and those who do otherwise shall be punished; but at the request of one of the parties, claiming to have been taken by surprise, the marriage shall be rescinded." Hughes, *Register of the Company of Pastors of Geneva*, 73.

[130] In addition to the *Treuschatz* (supposedly unwittingly supplied by the boy's father), the vows were consummated, thus putting the cases within the jurisdiction of the *Amtman*. 26 August 1591; Schüler, *Die Konventsprotokolle*, 61.

[131] 1563 *EGO; EKO* 302. Conditional vows, recognized "biß anhero in babstumb und sunst an mehr orten" as binding were likewise invalidated by the Elector's 1562 *EO* (281) and the *EGO*. Cf. secular punishment of the typical tavern vows by Melchior Hoücher of Bacharach: 3 January 1619; AEKK 125/2, 398.

[132] This excludes, of course, instances involving fraud or previous engagements. See Watt, *Making of Modern Marriage*, 65–70, on the sausage and other customary exchanges; also *Vierrichter* cases StAS IB/8, Bd.2, 204ᵛ–205ʳ and StAS IB/16, Bd.1, 12ʳ⁻ᵛ, both involving informal (with "rorige wort"), customary vows (in the latter, with the gift of a bird) and both resolved with solemnization "inner vierhalb Jahrs." Safley finds the persistence of such traditional beliefs and practices so strong as to conclude that "the legal prerequisite of due publicity and formality, consistently enforced by the *Ehegericht*, found no immediate, universal acceptance in Basel" (*Let No Man Put Asunder*, 154).

(without, however, the bride's wreath and usual wedding feast).[133] Even multiple-vow disputes, the greatest challenge to any marital court, were resolved along traditional canonical standards of the first legitimate *de presenti* vows or the first consummated.[134] Thus Otilia Leinhart was able to have her 1613 engagement to Balthes Mohr annulled by claiming previous vows and sexual intercourse with Arnold Chur, a notorious local rake (the Bacharach bailiff, however, also ordered her to pay Mohr forty gulden in damages).[135] Protestant and Catholic courts also annulled those vows that lacked public proof, but only at the request of one of the participants or, as in the requirement for parental consent, a member of one of their families. Otherwise, private vows were as valid as those before the Reformation, able to be "legitimized" whenever the need arose.

Ironically, secular and ecclesiastical attempts to extend further their own roles in the marital process occasionally provided a means for marrying couples to circumvent the usual public controls. In the confessionally splintered Palatinate, for instance, some couples used the political and religious rivalries to their advantage, offering their service and allegiance (illegally) to whichever authority would approve their marriages. After an Inspector of the Elector had denied a female subject's 1594 request to marry because of her fiancé's illegitimate child and previous vows in Frankfurt, the determined woman simply obtained a certificate of birth from the magistrates and crossed the Rhine to be married by an obliging Catholic priest.[136] Reformed authorities in the Electorate instructed local pastors (particularly those near Catholic areas) to warn parents and couples of the dangers of intermarriage with "idolaters," yet the many mixed marriages in both Bacharach and the prince-bishopric indicate the limited effectiveness of such admonitions.[137] In fact, the

---

133 1563 *EO; EKO* 282; Vogler II:1005–8. In most cases, the offenders were also punished by secular authorities for fornication. (See Chapter 5.)

134 *Eherichter* of the Elector were instructed to apply the traditional canonical standard "Quod semel placuit, amplius displicere non potest," adjusting it to the revised standards for licity (1556 *Von den Ehesachen;* 222). Cf. the proscribed procedure "in strittigem ehelubdnussen," also section 22 "Von dem beschlafenen Mägden," in 1563 *EGO* (*EKO* 330–33).

135 15 June 1613; LAK 4/1631, 211 ʳ⁻ᵛ. See also Chapter 5 on other misadventures of Arnold Chur.

136 AEKK 125/2, 259; cf. a similar 1558 case cited in Vogler (II:1108) of a young Protestant suitor, anxious about his own clergy, who sought out a Catholic priest to marry him and his fiancée.

137 Mixed marriages were discouraged but reluctantly recognized by all confessions if they met the respective requirements for publicity. Cf. GLA 77/4195, 4ᵛ–5ʳ (Documents of the Lutheran

1541 Genevan law against marriage to "those who do not profess the gospel" represents one of the few explicit sixteenth-century prohibitions of intermarriage.[138] Sometimes couples, displaying an astonishing lack of confessional conviction, used the religious division to get around even more minor restrictions, such as Catholic and Lutheran prohibitions on marriages during Lent and Advent. The Reformed pastor of Winningen was hesitant to bless and witness the 1598 marriage of two strangers giving such an excuse, but he eventually agreed with the bailiff that marriage was preferable to "a whore's life" for the young bride.[139] All secular authorities, of course, forbade and condemned such actions by their own subjects[140] – not least because of the damage to their own political and legal sovereignty – yet appeared ready to accept such cross-overs from other states.

Undoubtedly the most outstanding evidence of traditional standards of validation, though, comes from the many popular customs that had become so intertwined with the betrothal and wedding rituals. Some, such as the exchange of rings, were already so completely assimilated as to be considered intrinsically "Christian" by Protestant and Catholic reformers alike.[141] Others, particularly those practices considered "pagan" and "superstitious," were expressly forbidden. Yet while the family and community might accept the authority of Church and State in the

Restoration under Elector Ludwig VI, ca. 1578), articles 9 (*Punctus separationis a thoro et mensa zwishen Eheleuthen differenter religion*) and 10 (*Benedictio differenter religion*) and Vogler II:1109 on the Palatine-Electorate; also Naz, "Mariage en droit occidental," in *DDC* 6:784–86, on Trent's position.

    The number of examples in electoral parish registers (Vogler II:1109–11) and Catholic Prince-Bishopric (Stamer III:215ff.) suggests a lower frequency of mixed marriages than the parishes of nearby Strasbourg, for example, which recorded almost one a year (148 total) from 1529 to 1681 (Hsia, *Social Discipline*, 75).

[138] Article 112, cited in Wendel, *Le mariage*, 129. See also Esmein I:216ff. on interfaith marriages.

[139] AEKK 125/83/3, 621.

[140] The 1614 reissuance of the prince–bishop's marriage ordinance had particularly harsh words for those young couples who left the territory to contract "heimlichen verporgene Ehehafften," without their lord's permission or release from serfdom. 15 July 1614; *Sammlung* 36. Cf. similar complaints concerning evasion of impediment restrictions in n.22.

[141] Cf. W. D. Wechernagel, "Ehering," in *HRG* 1:840–41; Schmidt-Wiegand, "Hochzeitsgebräuche," in *HRG* 2:190–91. While shoes remained the traditional object of exchange for most couples throughout the Middle Ages, rings were also popular, dating back to the early Germanic tribes "als funktionelle Geräte von religiöser, sozialer, magischer, und sakraler Bedeutung."

    For an intriguing study of similar acculturation of wedding customs in contemporary Italy, see Christiane Klapisch-Zuber, "Zacharias, or the Ousting of the Father: The Rites of Marriage in Tuscany from Giotto to the Council of Trent." in *Women, Family, and Ritual*," 178–212, especially 202ff.

enforcement of traditional standards, neither was willing to alter those standards significantly – standards defined, to a large extent, by popular, local custom.[142]

"As many places, so many different customs," Luther wrote on marriage rituals, concluding, "it is not for us clerics or ministers to order or regulate, but should be left to every city and land which customs and traditions to follow."[143] Luther excluded the church ceremony from such regional variation, but overall displayed an openness to diversity that most of his Evangelical and Reformed successors did not share. Traditional rites of passage, such as the kidnapping of the groom by prostitutes or single women, drunken serenading of the bride-to-be by the single men (and other *charivari* variations) as well as the noisy procession from bride's house to church to feast (*"kirche und strasse gehen"*)[144] were thus all attacked by religious reformers as "Jewish and evil customs."[145] Unfortunately, these same clerics also found such rivals to their own validating authority remarkably resistant to change. Even the ceremonial bedding of the newly married couple (see Figure 5b), despite clerical attempts at abolishment, was tenaciously preserved in even the most fervently Evangelical of cities.[146] Catholic reforms, though

---

[142] As André Burgière notes of France, "le rituel religieux et le rituel populaire ne sont radicalement distincts ni dans leur histoire ni dans leur fonctions," and "tout se passe comme si la pratique populaire assumait désormais un rôle d'intégration sociale (d'ou, peut-être, en developpement des rites qui affirment les droit territoriaux de la communauté locale, comme le 'vin de mariage' de la barrière) [in Germany, the "love drink" of St. John] abandonnant à l'Église le le magistère moral et le controle juridico-administratif des mariages" (Rituel de mariage en France," 638, 648). See also Roper, *Holy Household,* 145–46, on related *Ansingwein* customs.

[143] Introduction to "Traubüchelin" (1529), *WA* 30/3:79.

[144] On late medieval and early modern German marriage customs, see J. Bolts, "Hochzeitsbräuche," *Alemannia* (1886), 14:188ff.; Schmidt-Wiegand, "Hochzeitsgebräuche," in *HRG* 2:192ff.; Roper, "Weddings in Reformation Augsburg," 84ff.; Jacques LeGoff and Jean-Claude Schmitt, *Le charivari* (Paris, 1981); David Fabre, "Families: Privacy versus Custom," in *A History of Private Life,* ed. Philip Ariès and Georges Duby (Cambridge, Mass., 1989) III:533ff.; Van Dülmen, "Fest der Liebe," 94ff.; and cf. Christiane Klapisch-Zuber, "The 'Mattinata' in Medieval Italy," in *Women, Family, and Ritual,* 261–82. See also Iwan Bloch, *Die Prostitution* (Berlin, 1912), I:709ff., 763, on the role of prostitutes in wedding rituals.

[145] Vogler II:942. Cf. similar complaints by the Strasbourg clergy in Kö II:399.

[146] Cf. Roper, "Weddings in Reformation Augsburg," 92ff., on attempts of the Augsburg magistracy to abolish the *Ansingwein* and ceremonial *Beilage;* Werner Danckert, *Unehrliche Leute: Die verfemten Berufe* (Bern, 1963), 79–80, on similar complaints about the customary *Hochzeitsbade* of the entire wedding party (a.k.a. *Wenzeltag,* or *Walgernacht*); also Burgière, "Rituel de mariage en France," 645ff., and Molin and Mutembe, *Le rituel du mariage,* 255–70, on corollary attempts by Catholic Counter-Reformers to emphasize conjugal chastity over fecundity in their rituals.

Figure 5. Three popular targets of Protestant and Catholic marriage reform: (a) prenuptial sexual relations, as in the popular *Fensterlehen*, or nocturnal visits by the prospective groom.

generally more tolerant of local diversity,[147] met with similar resistance in any attempted "tampering" with popular customary concepts of propriety.

The one aspect of the entire marriage ritual to receive the most

---

[147] Cf. *Tametsi* on weddings: "If any provinces have in this matter laudable customs and ceremonies in addition to the aforesaid, the holy Council wishes earnestly that they be by all means retained" (Schroeder, *Council of Trent*, 185). The council only objected to anything that inordinately delayed consummation (Naz, "Mariage en droit occidental," in *DDC* 6:767).

Figure 5. (b) traditional and allegedly pagan rituals such as the blessing of the marital bed and singing of obscene songs.

legislative attention among Protestant and Catholic reformers alike was the symbol of communal "public approval" itself: the wedding feast. More than any other element of the betrothal and wedding process, this culmination of all local standards of propriety would clearly mark the limitation of expanded Church and State influence. In sheer number and frequency alone (see Figure 3), the restrictive ordinances of all Palatine states on this issue indicate both the frustration and gradual acceptance by authorities of this fact.

Figure 5. (c) riotous and gluttonous wedding feasts, as in Brueghel's famous portrayal (Vienna Kunsthistorisches Museum).

Official concern over wedding feasts was twofold in nature. First and most obvious, almost all sixteenth-century secular authorities shared the same reservations about the excessive spending involved in such celebrations. The size of the feast, like the amount of the dowry, indicated social prestige and status, prompting many proud fathers to exceed their means in order to enhance their reputations.[148] In the tradition of many late medieval sumptuary ordinances,[149] secular authorities throughout Germany attempted to limit both the size and duration of the celebration. In the Palatinate, both the Electorate and the city of Speyer issued slightly altered versions of the Prince-Bishop's 1472 limitations. Whereas Bishop Mathias had set the limit on guests at thirty (twenty in the

[148] Cf. Roper ("Weddings in Reformation Augsburg," 74ff.) and August Jegel ("Altnürnberger Hochzeitsbrauch und Eherecht," *Mitteilungen des Vereins für Geschichte der Stadt Nürnberg* 44 [1953], 238–74), on the enormous amounts spent by members of all social classes to impress friends and neighbors. See also Gillis, *For Better, for Worse*, 55–83, on "The Politics of Big Weddings."

[149] See my Chapter 3; also Jegel, "Altnürnberger Hochzeitsbrauch," especially 244–48.

Figure 5. (d) "The Wedding Feast" of Brueghal (ca. 1567). In the foreground, the groom pours wine for his guests while the bride sits contentedly at the center of the table (Vienna Kunsthistorisches Museum).

country), ordinances of the Elector raised the limit to thirty-two and later forty guests, while decrees of Speyer's town council fluctuated wildly over a seventy-year period between twenty and sixty.[150] Ordinances of all three polities similarly regulated the number and content of meal courses (four, including baked cheese and fruit), total meals (three to five), and

[150] *Ordnung, wie es hinfür mit den Brautläuffen, Kintbetterinnen, Eschermittwoch, uneelichen Leuten und anderem gehalten werden soll* (7 March 1472; GLA 67/298, 96ᵛff.); also in the bishop's 1479 *Landgebot* (GLA 67/298, 36ᵛff.) and 1493 *Hochzeit* ordinance (*Sammlung* 11–12).

In the Electorate: 1546 *Polizeiordnung* (*EKO* 105–6); 1558 *Polizeimandat* (*EKO* 262–63); and frequent reissuances of the same (see my Figure 3). Sponheim also set a limit of forty guests (Vogler II:940). Members of the ruling class, of course, were exempt from such restrictions, as the Elector's police mandate makes clear the exception of "unserer hohen rethe und des adels."

The city of Speyer issued thirteen wedding ordinances during 1535–99 (see Figure 3), first setting a limit at sixty guests in 1539, in 1571 reducing it to twenty, before restoring it to sixty again just six years later. StAS IA/10, 43ʳ–44 (1535); 75ᵛ–76ᵛ (1546); 93ᵛ–95ᵛ (1549); 110ʳ–11ᵛ (1568); 111ʳ–112ᵛ (1571); 113ʳ–114ʳ (1577); 114ᵛ–118ʳ (1577); 119ʳ–120ᵛ (1589); 122ʳ–124ᵛ (1589); IB/6,9ᵛ Bd.2, (1597); 28ᵛ (1598); 43ʳ⁻ᵛ (1599).

On similar wedding ordinances in France and the Lowlands, see Muchembled, *Popular Culture and Elite Culture*, 133ff.

duration of the entire feast (usually no more than two days)[151] (see Figure 5d). In addition, each restricted the celebration to invited guests and close relatives, also limiting the value of presents to the married couple.[152] In a final tribute to medieval sumptuary tradition, the Elector's alms ordinances of 1570 and 1574 suggested that "when the meal begins, a small locked box or sack should circulate and the people be admonished to give alms [for the poor]."[153]

The second concern of sixteenth-century reformers was much more characteristic of their times, namely, the "unchristian" character of such feasts. Electoral ordinances repeatedly complained of "much immorality and frivolity at dances, during the day as well as night," and "grave sins that stopped with the pagans and should be found much less among Christians[154] (see Figure 5c). The enduring combination of drinking and dancing not only led to much sexual immorality, but also frequent fighting and violence.[155] Moreover, in the general atmosphere of worldly, sensual pleasure that prevailed, many religious leaders feared that the spiritual nature of marriage was ignored, if not completely forgotten. Spangenberg compared the guests at most weddings to "crude, rancid, monstrous swine," and Electoral Superintendant Johann Telones complained similarly: "From feast to dance, from dance to feast, God is least."[156] Guests should not come to a wedding for good food and drink, implored the preachers of Speyer in 1569, "but rather much more for the glory of God and the well-being and salvation of the married couple."[157]

---

[151] While all agreed on a two-day limit, the city of Speyer was by far the most precise in its regulation, specifying no more than four courses per meal, including baked cheese and fruit (apparently an oft-attempted loophole), and no more than three meals total, two on the first day. StAS IA/10, 43ᵛ, 94ᵛ, 110ᵛ, 111ᵛ, 113ᵛ, 115ᵛ; *Sammlung* 11–12; *EKO* 105, 263.

[152] The 1493 ordinance of the Prince-Bishopric limited gifts from strangers to 3 shillings. The 1558 *Polizeimandat* of Electorate limits gifts from any nonrelatives to 1 rhenish florin (with a 10 fl. fine for offenders), while municipal ordinances of Speyer varied from a limit of 1/3 to 1 fl. on "outsider" wedding gifts. *Sammlung* 12; *EKO* 104, 262–63; StAS IA/10 94ᵛ, 116ʳ.

[153] *Allmusenordnung der statt Haydelberg* (ca. 1570; *EKO* 443); also *Almosenordnung* (1574; *EKO*, 470).

[154] 1546 *Polizeiordnung; EKO* 105.

[155] Next to complaints of *unuberschwenglicher kosten*, the *unordnunge und unbescheidenheiten* typical of such feasts were the principal target of all secular legislation on weddings. Cf. 1558 *Polizeimandat* that complains of guests "beyeinander im Sauß und unordenlichem vihischem leben verharrt" (*EKO* 263); also StAs IA/10, 43ʳff,; Vogler II:941–42; and see my comments in Chapter 5.

[156] "grobe, garstige, unflätige Sewe" (Spangenberg *Ehespiegel*, 288); "vom essen zum tantzen, vom tantzen zum essen, gottes vergessen" (HStAMü Kasten blau 389/9b, 311ᵛ).

[157] 1569 *Gutachten*, cited in Ohler, in *GStSp* I:633.

The impact of attempts at "Christianization" on such firmly entrenched practices, however, was apparently minimal. Authorities of Church and State could succeed in enforcing those concepts and practices that had already gained popular acceptance, but eliminating rather than simply adding on to custom proved more difficult than they had anticipated. Thus when the elders of Bacharach repeatedly fretted about "all sorts of frivolity" at wedding celebrations, they also apparently expected an unsympathetic reticence on the part of secular authorities.[158] Even the universally accepted church wedding was caught between two much older rituals – the wedding breakfast (*Morgensuppe*) and wedding feast – suffering greatly, according to its defenders, as a result. All three polities of our study complained of wedding parties arriving late from the breakfast, and many guests who skipped the church ceremony altogether to get ready for the subsequent feast.[159] All three decreed that those individuals not in church by ten o'clock should be turned away, and if this included the wedding party, the ceremony canceled.

Despite the frequent issuance of fines,[160] though, most people apparently considered the ordinances at worst intrusive and at best just another expense to be carried by the bride's father. The Reformed pastor of Weisel reported that at a recent wedding "the people disliked and cursed [such regulations], to which he retorted that they should not blame him but the groom, who brought more guests (as a promise to the cook) than he had originally indicated."[161] The increasingly frequent reissuances of the same ordinances, moreover, suggests both the limitations of secular officials' authority in such matters and their own recognition of the same fact. Even if the rules were widely understood and the fines consistently

---

158 Cf. 7 May 1602 and 25 July 1619; AEKK 125/2: 301, 401. See also Chapter 5.
159 1589 wedding ordinance of city of Speyer (StAS IA 10, 119ʳ⁻ᵛ); 1592 instruction from vicar-general (*Collectio* 400–401); and Elector's 1558 *Polizeimandat; EKO* 263; Vogler II:937ff.

On the old and widespread custom of the *Morgensuppe*, see Schmidt-Wiegand, "Hochzeitsgebräuche," in *HRG* 2:192ff.; and Roper, "Weddings in Reformation Augsburg," 70–71.
160 The records of the Kaub *Amtman* from 1583ff. include a number of fines for wedding violations, usually ranging from 1 to 8 fl., but, in the case of a *Zollbeamter*, 100 fl. to the poor for an extra table. Schüler, *Die Konventsprotokolle*, 165–66. See also a 1615 fine of 50 fl. for a Kaiserslautern wedding (1/2 fl. per extra person); Vogler II:941.
161 23 February 1609; Schüler, *Die Konventsprotokolle*, 165.

administered,[162] popular and customary definitions of propriety were not likely to change overnight.

Thus, though consistently resisted by most local and secular authorities since its twelfth-century introduction, the consensualist ideal of validity did succeed in eventually penetrating not only judicial perceptions but popular practice as well. Sixteenth-century legal reactions among members of the Protestant and Catholic "establishment," while successfully extending the consensual definition to include parents and relatives, had otherwise limited effects on actual practice. For all their claims of paternal reinforcement, Protestant secular authorities never considered rejecting the consensual basis of marriage and, by implication, the primacy of the marrying couple over their families. Attempts by clerical reformers of both confessions to "Christianize" many customary rituals, such as the marriage feast, were especially frustrated, often meeting with indifference and even defiance on the part of the laity.[163] As we will see in the enforcement of marital morality, local and traditional "public" controls continued to exercise much more influence in questions of propriety than any similar controls of the institutional Church or State.

The most significant accomplishment of sixteenth-century secular and ecclesiastical reformers was their successful identification with the traditional paternal role in the entire betrothal and wedding process. By bringing the central validating ritual into the church and eventually the town hall, both of these public authorities in turn validated their own essential roles in the wedding cycle. Certainly ecclesiastical regulation had a more entrenched tradition than its governmental counterpart, but in the sixteenth century authorities of both spheres continually expanded their own controls over marriage exercised in *loco parentis*. Parental and communal authority was not – nor was it soon to be – replaced by either of them, but the necessary ideological and institutional transformation had at least already begun.

---

[162] Cf. obvious confusion among Catholic pastors regarding the new marriage ordinance (from Visitation, Stamer III:401); instructions of prince-bishop (*Sammlung* 12), Elector (*EKO* 106, 263); and especially increasingly desperate complaints of popular indifference in the municipal wedding ordinances from 1535 to 1599 (StAS IA/10, 43ʳff.). James M. Kittelson ("Successes and Failures in the German Reformation: The Report from Strasbourg," *Archiv für Reformationsgeschichte* 73 (1982), 170–71) reluctantly comes to a similar conclusion about the effectiveness of Strasbourg wedding ordinances.

[163] See my Conclusion.

5

〜〜〜〜〜〜〜〜〜〜〜〜〜〜〜〜〜〜〜〜〜〜〜〜〜〜〜〜〜〜〜〜

"Against the marriage-devil": Sexual discipline and domestic stability

Q. What does the seventh commandment require?
A. That all unchasteness is abominable to God and we should thus banish it from our hearts and live chastely and virtuously, whether in the holy estate of marriage or outside it.
Q. Is God forbidding only adultery and similar violations in this commandment?
A. Since both our body and soul are temples of the Holy Spirit, He wants us to keep both of them clean and holy. He therefore forbids all unchaste acts, gestures, words, thoughts, desires and whatever might lead people to such.
Questions 108 and 109, *Heidelberg Catechism* (1563)[1]

In the introduction to one of the most popular works on marriage of the sixteenth century, Andreas Musculus prepared his readers for the relentless adversary they faced in the "Marriage-Devil": "No work, ordinance, or institution of God is so disagreeable, grievous, and hateful to the Devil as the estate of matrimony."[2] Musculus's subsequent detailed description of the marriage-devil's strategies in fact closely corresponded to the foremost concern of all secular and religious reformers of marriage after formation of the marital bond, namely, protection of the resulting conjugal unit. In practice, just as in the pamphlet discourse, this "protection" almost invariably carried the connotation of "discipline," more specifically, restriction of all sexual relations to within properly formed marriages. Illicit sexual relations, reformers reasoned,

---

[1] *108. Frag* (41st Sunday), *EKO*, 364. Cf. *Institutes* II.viii.41.
[2] *Wider den Eheteufell*, in Stambaugh, *Teufelbücher*, IV:85.

harmed not only a specific union, but the institution of matrimony as a whole. The often indiscriminate legal application of terms such as *Ehebruch* (adultery; literally, "marriage breaking") and *Unzucht* (fornication; literally "undiscipline" or "immorality") to all sexual offenses[3] suggests an even more fundamental contrast among reforming authorities: the "virtuous, lawful ordinance of God and Nature" (marriage) on the one hand; sexual anarchy on the other.[4] Moreover, as in the debate over clandestine marriage, the goals of religious reformers again configured nicely with those of secular authorities: better enforcement of moral standards with as little disruption of the social order as possible.

Unfortunately for religious reformers' high aspirations, the nature and goals of secular enforcement – as in the formation of the marriage bond – remained too traditional for new biblically inspired standards to make much impact. Secular authorities usually embraced the stricter standards of local preachers but remained constrained by primitive procedural methods and traditional definitions of culpability and punishment based more on personal honor than the nature of the offense itself. Under the prevailing double standards of social status and gender, for instance, single women faced the strictest sanctions for sexual (and thus marital) transgressions and married men the mildest. Moreover, greater pressure for moral reform usually only intensified traditional tensions, yielding – as in the contemporary witch craze – more accusations and punishments involving the socially marginal. Reformed officials undoubtedly made the most extensive attempt to transform popular values and perceptions of marriage, but the results were disappointingly similar to those of their Lutheran and Catholic neighbors.

To understand fully the impact of sixteenth-century "protection" of the conjugal unit, we must examine moral and legal reforms in terms of their three principal objectives: prevention, prosecution, and preserva-

---

[3] Other scholars have also noted the broad use of *Ehebruch* and *Unzucht* among sixteenth-century secular and religious authorities alike. Sabean, *Power in the Blood*, 136ff.; Roper, *Holy Household*, 123–24; Safley, *Let No Man Put Asunder*, 109; and Ingram, *Church Courts, Sex, and Marriage*, 239, 282ff., on the English equivalent of "bawdy."

On definitions of "normalcy" and the relationship of sexual deviance to the moral standards of a society, see Safley, *Let No Man Put Assunder*, 5ff., and Guido Ruggiero, *The Boundaries of Eros: Sex, Crime, and Sexuality in Renaissance Venice* (New York, 1985), 9ff., and 146–68.

[4] From the Zweibrücken *Eheordnung* of 1605, quoted in Vogler II:973. On the apparent increase in sexual anxiety during the sixteenth and seventeenth centuries, see William J. Bouwsma, "Anxiety and the Formation of Early Modern Culture," in *After the Reformation: Essays in Honor of J. H. Hexter*, ed. Barbara C. Malament (Philadelphia, 1980), 215–46; also Muchembled, *Popular Culture and Elite Culture*, 189ff.

tion of the conjugal unit. First, many marriage reformers, especially among the Protestants, believed that many of the sexual offenses threatening marriage could be prevented by abolishing all officially or unofficially sanctioned opportunities for them to occur in the first place, particularly brothels and popular dances. Second, all agreed that effective prosecution and punishment of all remaining *Unzucht* could significantly reverse the perceived spread of such immorality. Third, and most important, both Protestant and Catholic reformers concurred that, whatever the means involved, the primary goal of all their actions remained the preservation of already existing unions – not their dissolution. After comparing Protestant and Catholic programs in all three areas of reform, we will then again consider the relative conservatism of all sixteenth-century criminal prosecution, especially in the preservation of most traditional, pre-Reformation practice.

Prevention

During the late Middle Ages, prostitution was widely tolerated throughout Europe, especially in urban areas.[5] The common justification among magistrates and even religious authorities was an old one: Like sewers, brothels drained off excessive lust and thus prevented worse offenses and sexual anarchy in general.[6] Many cities, consequently, even maintained official civic brothels, regulating all aspects of the trade, from fees and work hours to the food and drink served.[7] Public baths, which also

[5] According to Brundage (*Law, Sex and Christian Society*, 521ff.), widespread toleration in European cities did not actually begin until the late fourteenth century. The most thorough introduction to late medieval and early modern prostitution is still Bloch, *Die Prostitution*. See also Richard Trexler, "La prostitution florentine au XVe siècle: Patronages et clienteles," *Annales* 36/6 (1981), 983–1015; Leah L. Otis, *Prostitution in Medieval Society: The History of an Urban Institution in Languedoc* (Chicago, 1985); and most recently, Jacques Rossiaud, *Medieval Prostitution*, trans. Lydia Cochrane (New York, 1988).

[6] In the words of the annual oath taken by the brothel keeper of Ulm, such houses existed "to further the interest and piety of the city and its folk, and to warn and keep it from harm" (Lyndal Roper, "Discipline and Respectability: Prostitution and the Reformation in Augsburg," *History Workshop* 19 (Spring 1985), 5ff., 9. Ruggiero agrees that in a merchant city like Venice civic brothels did indeed serve the public interest, "(providing) a sexual environment for many transients that did not seem to directly threaten the wives and daughters of residents" (*The Boundaries of Eros*, 170, n. 4).

[7] In Ulm and Augsburg, the brothel keepers even took annual oaths and played a great role in civic rituals (Roper, "Prostitution," 4ff.). Cf. also Bloch, *Die Prostitution*, I:766ff., and prostitution regulations of Strasbourg in Johann Karl Brucker, ed., *Strassburger Zunft- und Polizei-Verordnungen des 14. und 15. Jahrhunderts* (Strasbourg, 1889), 456–60, 468–69; and Wiesner, *Working Women*, 97ff.

enjoyed reputations as "refuges of frivolity," were similarly numerous throughout Germany, even in small and medium-sized cities.[8] Although there is no record of such statutory approval of prostitution by the magistrates of Speyer during the same period, unofficial complicity was apparently not uncommon. In 1486 the municipal court settled a dispute between the madame of an unspecified brothel and a young cooper's apprentice acting as interim procurer during the regular pimp's absence; no punishment of either the acknowledged prostitution or procurement is mentioned.[9] Frequent references to known brothels and relatively mild punishments by the city's lay synod for procurement also suggest a kind of official tolerance unknown during the Reformation era.[10]

Sixteenth-century reform of prostitution in Germany, Lyndal Roper has pointed out, passed through at least two phases.[11] The first aimed only at preventing and punishing illegal visits to brothels, especially by married men and clerics. Theoretically, sex with a prostitute had always been considered adulterous for married men in Germany, but not until this morally charged time was the prohibition consistently enforced. Many of the cities operating their own brothels were thus forced to choose between enforcing the prohibition on married clients by close police surveillance as in Zurich, or complete closure as in Ulm.[12] Because the practice was never officially sanctioned in Speyer, there is no recorded change of policy in this area.

By the second half of the sixteenth century, reform of prostitution in the Palatinate and throughout Germany had entered the much more ambitious phase of complete prohibition and intolerance. Many religious reformers now reversed the traditional image of prostitution and pollution, arguing as Johannes Brenz, "Some say one must have public brothels to prevent greater evil – but what if these brothels are schools in which one learns more wickedness than before?"[13] (see Figure 6b).

[8] Large cities generally maintained several at a time; late medieval Ulm, for instance, had eleven, Nuremberg had twelve, and Vienna twenty-nine. Danckert, *Unehrliche Leute*, 64–68.
[9] StAS IA [A.B. II, 1486], cited in Harster, *Strafrecht*, 192.
[10] A fourteenth-century Speyer municipal ordinance stipulated four-week imprisonment and banishment for convicted pimps (*riffan*), but the one-pound wax fine of Wendel Wafenschmidt, "der hellt bubery mit namen eyn geistlich fraw und ein pfaffen," was probably more representative of the city and synod's prosecution of the offense. See also references of magistrates to *Hurenstuben* in the city's *Spital* (Hospital) and "*Betzenloch des Altpörtels*" (Harster, *Strafrecht*, 190ff.).
[11] Roper, "Prostitution," 1off.
[12] Bloch, *Die Prostitution*, I:767; 811ff.; Kö I:144–45 (Zurich); Roper, "Prostitution," 3ff. (Ulm).
[13] *Vom Ehbruch und Hürerey* (Frankfurt, 1543), H 4ᵇ, quoted in Roper, "Prostitution," 12.
  Cf. similar arguments about *Gunckelhäuser* in Hans Medick, "Village Spinning Bees: Sexual

Figure 6. Three common manisfestations of the "Marriage-Devil": (a) clerical concubinage and the resulting resentment among laypeople.

Some historians have also emphasized the significance of a concurrent outbreak of syphillis and the genuine public health concerns of civic officials. In any case, secular and religious authorities were in agreement, closing down all brothels and public baths within their jurisdictions and prosecuting all forms of prostitution vigorously.[14]

Culture and Free Time among Rural Youth in Early Modern Germany," in *Interest and Emotion: Essays on the Study of Family and Kinship*, ed. H. Medick and David W. Sabean (Cambridge, 1984), 317–39.

[14] As usual, imperial legislation on the matter was extremely influential and widely imitated throughout Germany. See, for instance, article 123 of the *Carolina* on pandering, as well as the

Figure 6. (b) brothels and the lechery, frivolity, and theft associated with them.

Whether, on the other hand, the increased prosecution and suspicion of prostitution eliminated or even significantly reduced the practice is doubtful.[15] If anything, legal prohibition of the world's oldest profession appears to have succeeded only in driving the practice underground or at least into territories with less stringent enforcement. In 1560, four men of Zweibrücken were forced to travel to the neighboring Duchy of Bitsch to find an operating brothel; all were nonetheless discovered and pun-

general prostitution prohibitions of the *Reichspolizeiordnungen* of 1548 (25:3) and 1577 (26:3). Augsburg was one of the first German cities officially to close its civic brothel in 1532, followed by Basel in 1534, Nördlingen and Geneva in 1536, Ulm in 1537, Regensburg in 1553, and Frankfurt in 1560. Cf. Dr. Von Posern-Klett, "Frauenhäuser and freie Frauen in Sachsen," *Archiv für die sächsische Geschichte 12 (1874), 63–89;* also Ludwig von Maurer, *Geschichte der Städteverfassung in Deutschland* (1870; reprint: Aalen, 1962), III:103ff.; Biéler, *L'homme et la femme;* and Wiesner, *Working Women,* 104ff.

15 Vogler (II:999) makes the largely unsubstantiated claim that this was the one area in which reforms of extramarital relations appear to have had an effect in Zweibrücken, Sponheim, and the Electorate.

Figure 6. (c) adulterous relations at home (when the spouse is gone) or in forests and other hidden places.

ished by their own consistory.[16] More frequently, as in Speyer, traveling prostitutes would merely work in an area as long as possible before being banished. Even then they occasionally returned.[17] Other governments made only token gestures of enforcement, such as Evangelical Augsburg, which, during the height of Reformation fervor, averaged 3.2 convictions a year (in a city of 30,000!).[18] Sanctions against such women remained – as we will see – invariably harsh, yet for a variety of reasons too complex to discuss here,[19] neither the supply of prostitutes nor the

16 All four were sentenced by the consistory to carry the *Lasterstein* ("stone of shame"). Vogler II:998. On use of the *Lasterstein* as punishment, see subsequent discussion in this chapter and Figure 7e.
17 Harster reports that some lingering or returning prostitutes were "mit Kot beworfen und neuerding ausgetrieben" by the magistrates (*Strafrecht*, 190ff.). Cf. StAS IA/705, 15ʳ (27 May 1578) and subsequent discussion of the expulsion of nine prostitutes by the magistrates of Speyer from 1576 to 1581.
18 Figures from 1528 to 1548 in Roper, *Holy Household*, 113–14, 124ff. Cf. similar statistics provided by Van Dülmen (*Theater des Schreckens*, table 4) for Nuremberg, with an annual average of 1.9 convictions for 1578–1615 (at least one-third of those including charges of theft).
19 Carlo Cipolla (*Before the Industrial Revolution* [New York, 1976], 84ff.) and Roper ("Prostitution," 19ff.), for instance, both credit demographic pressures, capitalism, and the subsequent declining job market for women with the continuing supply of willing prostitutes despite increased prosecution. Rossiaud (*Medieval Prostitution*, 33ff.) also views late medieval prostitution as one of the few options left rape victims and other already "dishonored" women.

demand of their willing clientele was adversely affected by the climate of moral and legal reform – only the openness of the practice.

After civic brothels and public baths, the most frequently cited occasions of sexual misconduct were popular festivals and dances. From the perspective of most religious reformers, such popular gatherings served no other purpose than to promote ungodly frivolity.[20] Particularly aggravating were the many informal balls for young people held on traditional feast days such as Carnival, Pentecost, and Saint John's. At the slightest rumor of such gatherings, observed the author of the *Dance-Devil*, youths rushed off regardless of the weather, yet nobody ran so eagerly to church when they heard the bells of Sunday service ringing.[21] Of the four categories of dance identified by Spangenberg in the *Marriage-Mirror*, such "knaves' dances" (*Bubentänze*) were undoubtedly the worst, breeding "luxury, arrogance, cockiness, contempt for others, indecency, discord, quareling, murder, adultery, whoring, secret engagements, and other scandals and disgraces."[22] A 1590 ordinance of the Electorate concurred, calling such balls both "Epicurean" and "pagan,"[23] and a contemporary observer in Voralberg went into even more lurid detail:

> At parties and gatherings, in inns or other enclosed places . . . single boys and girls prance about indecently. . . . The scandalous and depraved practice of walking the streets and (climbing through lovers' bedroom windows) [in German, all one verb: *fensterlen* – see Figure 5a] is common, as well as nightime dancing in houses or corner of courtyards . . . and single boys singing indecent knaves' songs and carrying on other foolishness and misdeeds on the streets at night, all with screaming and cheering.[24]

---

[20] "leichtfertigkeiten," "saltationes impudicas"; cited in Vogler II:989.

[21] Daul, *Tanzteufel*, in Stambaugh, *Teufelbücher*, II:89–93.

[22] With undisguised glee, Spangenberg proceeds to recite numerous historical instances of the divine wrath incurred by such gatherings, including heart attacks, bolts of lightening, and collapsing bridges (the last killing over two hundred revelers in 1277 Utrecht). Spangenberg, *Vom Tanz* (45th sermon from *Ehespiegel*) in Daul, *Tanzteufel*, in Stambaugh, *Teufelbücher*, II: 155–626.

[23] Vogler II:989.

[24] Undated manuscript (ca. 1600) of Zams deaconry, quoted in Hermann Heidrich, "Grenzübergänge: Das Haus und die Volkskultur in der frühen Neuzeit," in *Kultur der einfachen Leute: Bayerisches Volksleben vom 16. bis zum 19. Jahrhundert*, ed. Richard Van Dülmen and H. Heidrich (Munich, 1983), 22.

On the youth culture in Germany, see Medick, "Village Spinning Bees," 317–39. *Spinnstuben* and *Gunckelhäuser* were notorious for the same drinking, dancing, and physical contact between the sexes that characterized popular festivals and wedding feasts.

After much petitioning by the Protestant clergy, the Elector and city of Speyer each agreed to prohibit or at least closely supervise such gatherings. Both would have no doubt shared the belief expressed by the pastors of Hohenlohe that restriction of at least the opportunities for "unseemly love and licentious behavior" at the same time contributed to the "preservation of marital piety."[25] Henceforth, the only dances permitted were those held "in a decent, honorable manner, without excessive immodesty, spinning, jumping, or other frivolities."[26] Local requests for official permission to hold dances were quick to adopt the appropriately solemn tone. A 1592 petition by the youth of Traben was the model of efficacy, asking the bailiff for "an honorable dance, since we must otherwise busy ourselves the entire year long . . . with chopping, digging and other hard work." Approval of a "modest little dance" was immediate.[27]

Still, it is doubtful that the small fine imposed by the Elector for participation in unsupervised dances had more of an effect than earlier punishments threatened by the city and Prince-Bishopric of Speyer.[28] For many youths, such gatherings provided the only opportunity to meet eligible members of the opposite sex (an argument anticipated and vehemently denied by Daul in his *Dance-Devil*).[29] Whether due to the economic pressures to marry or the more immediate urges that reformers sought to restrain, official restrictions only succeeded in transferring dances to more isolated spots, rather than eliminating them. Pastors, of course, were aware of this circumvention of the law but could do little more than complain to secular authorities – as they did at least ten times

[25] More specifically, the pastors requested that the court appoint official supervisors of the dances and end the gatherings before dark "so that girls and boys end at the right time of day and go home to their masters, lords, and mistresses." Ordinances of 1586, 1588, 1592, and 1654 subsequently banned *all* dances in Hohenlohe. Robisheaux, "Peasants and Pastors," 289.

[26] 1558 *Polizei Mandat; EKO* 263. Cf. later 1618 *Polizeiordnung* totally forbidding "Fastnacht, Mummerei, Johanissfeuer, sonderlich aber do Lehenausrufen, verbotene Winkel- und Feiertagstänze, heimlicher zusammenkünfte in spinnstuben, schändliche Lieder, und was dergleichen heidnische, unflätige, und unchristliche Dinge mehr sind . . ." (Schüler, *Die Konventsprotokolle,* 147–48).

[27] LAK 33/4947, 16–17.

[28] Cf. pre-Reformation predecessor (ca. 1460) permitting parish priests to forbid dances, exacting a fine of 3 pfennig for any violation (Grimm I:353). The 1604 ordinance of the Elector specified a 14-fl. fine, but the only two references to enforcement I have found fined two youths of Bacharach 21 Albus and 14 pfennig in 1609 (LAK 4/1631, 232) and eleven youths 13 Albus each in 1619 (LAK 4/1632, 357–59). The punishment for the same offenses in Calvin's Geneva was considerably harsher, including three days' imprisonment on bread and water and a minimal 60-sols fine (Biéle, *L'homme et la femme,* 123).

[29] Daul, *Tanzteufel,* in Stambaugh, *Teufelbücher,* II:101.

in Bacharach between 1592 and 1606.[30] Local governmental officials in turn intervened when possible – as in the 1596 case of a Bacharach widow sponsoring dances at her house[31] – but surely recognized the futility of their task. As in the Palatinate's Keffenbach and Alberweiler, the local youth would merely "scurry elsewhere to other villages where they knew of dances."[32]

Almost all legal authorities were aware, of course, that brothels and dances were not the only locations where sexual misconduct could occur. Still it was a distinctive mark of sixteenth-century Protestant – and to a lesser degree Catholic – secular and religious reform that the two spheres should be as one where public discipline and welfare were concerned; what was moral should be legal and vice versa. Thus as religious intolerance of many traditional and "pagan" sexual practices increased during the late fifteenth century, the corollary cry for legal prohibition never lagged far behind. The prevalent modern criterion for new laws – namely, their practicality – was not irrelevant to these social reformers, but neither was it of primary importance. When judged by this same modern standard, the reform of prostitution and popular dances was indeed not practical and, in that sense, not successful. If evaluated, however, by the characteristic sixteenth-century goal of effectively uniting moral and legal standards, the reforms were not necessarily as ill-conceived or naive as we might wish to label them.

Prosecution

In both goals and implementation, Protestant and Catholic prosecution of marital offenses was almost identical. Despite the extreme severity suggested by most Evangelical and Reformed rhetoric, the men who enforced the laws and moral standards of their communities displayed remarkable fidelity to traditional definitions of culpability and exoneration. Even those offenses that clearly were punished more severely by sixteenth-century Protestants than previously – specifically prostitution and concubinage – were likewise more harshly disciplined among Cath-

---

[30] Complaints were registered in the records of the Bacharach *Konvent* on 17 May 1592, 28 June 1592, 21 June 1593, 27 April 1598, 18 July 1599, 1 August 1605, and 12 June 1606 (Schüler, *Die Konventsprotokolle*, 67, 69, 77, 96, 105, 147, 151); and in the records of the Bacharach consistory on 7 May 1602, 9 July 1602, and 13 July 1606 (AEKK 125/2, 301, 334).

[31] 24 July 1597; AEKK 125/2, 274.

[32] Quoted in Vogler II:992. Cf. similar enforcement problems described in Wright, *Capitalism, the State, and the Lutheran Reformation*, 170–71.

olic contemporaries. Most important, traditional double standards based on social status and gender continued to exercise much more influence in actual punishment than any universal religious standard. In short, regardless of confession, all sixteenth-century authorities shared not only the same moral standards and hierarchy of offenses, but the same traditional vision of crime and punishment as well.

The source of their common vision was something that anthropologists and cultural historians refer to as the *Gemeinschaft* mentality. This conceptualization of society and criminal deviance recognizes two generally distinct groups within each community: the members on the "inside," namely married couples and especially burghers; and those marginal, suspicious individuals on the "outside": domestic servants, shepherds, vagabonds, widows, and particularly those readily identified as "dishonorable" (*unehrliche*) – Jews, prostitutes, executioners, and many others.[33] Among magistrates, the distinction between "scoundrel" (*bösewicht*) and "goodman" (*biedermann*) was invariably the first and most important determination of the court in sentencing of a convicted offender.[34] According to Bruce Lenman and Geoffrey Parker, this distinctly early modern double standard in fact represented the product of two completely separate medieval systems of law, one based on community law and restitution, the other founded on State law and punitive measures: "The justification for this division lies in the fact that compensation originated in feuds which only flourished between those social equals capable of sustaining a private conflict."[35] This basic mental division of society continued to exercise more influence in individual

---

[33] This sociological distinction was first proposed by Ferdinand Tönnies, *Gemeinschaft und Gesellschaft* (Leipzig, 1887), and was further refined by Max Weber in *Wirtschaft und Gesellschaft*, 5th ed. (Tübingen, 1976). The prototypical *Gesellschaft* – as opposed to the small, face-to-face *Gemeinschaft* – is a much larger and more modern association of diverse individuals, such as a business partnership or other formal organization, artificially created, with limited and specific interests. See Danckert, *Unehrliche Leute*, especially 9–12, on the legal distinctions between *unehrlichkeit*, *echtlosigkeit*, and *rechtlosigkeit*, as well as a list of "dishonorable professions" on p. 12; O. Benecke, *Von unehrlichen Leuten, Culturhistorische Studien und Geschichten aus vergangenen Tagen deutscher Gewerbe und Dienste* (Berlin, 1889): also K.-S. Kramer, "Ehrliche/ unehrliche Gewerbe," HRG 1:855–58; and Van Dülmen, *Theater des Schreckens*, 66ff.

[34] Allen, "Crime and Punishment," 143–165a, especially 155ff. Cf. corollary French distinctions between people of "condition honneste" and "personnes viles et abjectes" (Muchembled, *Popular Culture and Elite Culture*, 193); and English reliance on "common fame" (Ingram, *Church Courts*, 326–37).

[35] Bruce Lenman and Geoffrey Parker, "The State, the Community, and Criminal Law in Early Modern Europe," in *Crime and the Law: The Social History of Crime in Western Europe since 1500*, ed. V. A. C. Gantrell et al. (Oxford, 1980), 27.

punishment for all marital offenses throughout the sixteenth century than any confessionally or legally inspired innovation, again reflecting the overwhelming preference for continuity in legal enforcement.

The severity of an offense (and thus also of official sanction) in turn depended on the particular confluence of two related factors: honor and wealth. Consequently, adultery – involving both – was generally considered a much more socially disruptive and serious problem than fornication between two unmarried and legally unconnected persons. Only when the latter offense also involved questions of honor and property – as in illegitimate births and undesirable heirs – was it treated by secular authorities with the same dispatch and gravity. It was no coincidence, then, that in both Protestant and Catholic states adultery was prosecuted and punished by secular authorities, whereas fornication and concubinage were usually left to weaker ecclesiastical bodies. Like prostitution, sexual relations between unmarried individuals also threatened the marital estate but, in the instance of fornication, only indirectly. We will thus first examine prosecution of marital offenses within these two levels before turning to the question of confessional distinctions in enforcement and punishment.

Until the late Middle Ages, adultery was defined exclusively as a crime committed by a married woman with an outsider (the *Ehebrecher*) and whose punishment in theory belonged to the cuckolded husband alone. Only as the involvement of secular and especially ecclesiastical authorities grew in this area was the offense gradually extended to include married men who had relations outside of marriage.[36] Even then, except in cases of open or *in flagrante delicto* adultery (*handhafter Ehebruch*), only the husband could petition a court for action.[37] More-

---

[36] The Church first attempted to introduce the concept of male adultery with the Franks, arguing that since both adulterous husbands and wives harmed the institution of marriage equally, they should be punished equally. The practice was already widespread in Italy by the eighth century, but faced a much longer struggle for acceptance in Germany. As late as the thirteenth century, both the *Sachsenspiegel* and *Schwabenspiegel* mentioned only the wife's adultery, in Speyer (according to the 1246 *Zollweistum*) still adjudicated by the hot-iron ordeal. Not until the *Bambergesnsis* and *Carolina* were both kinds of adultery officially recognized as at least theoretically equal. Lieberwirth, "Ehebruch," in *HRG*, 1:836–38; Harvey, "Nürnberg Marriage Laws," 113ff.; Harster, *Strafrecht*, 187; and see my discussion in Chapter 3.

[37] Though the cuckolded husband's right to petition, however, was eventually extended to wives by the *Carolina*, enforcement of this right varied. The Elector's *Ehegerichtsordnung* of 1563, for instance, clearly stipulates that "die weiber aber ihre menner nit dieses lasters [adultery] furzufordern mocht, fug und recht haben soll," providing the traditional scriptural and Roman legal justification of the man alone as head of the household. *EKO* 310, 320; Lieberwirth, "Ehebruch," in *HRG* 1:838; Mikat, "Ehe," in *HRG* 1:828–29.

over, as late as the sixteenth century, criminal codes such as the *Bambergensis* (1507) and *Carolina* (1532) continued to recognize the husband's traditional right to kill his wife and her lover if caught in the act.[38] In 1555, for instance, a baker from Lußheim in the Prince-Bishopric of Speyer was arrested for the stabbing death of his wife's lover and then released from custody on just such grounds while his adulterous wife was sentenced by the same authorities to death by drowning.[39]

Still, by the same time, at least one major deviation from tradition had become evident and that was the increasingly frequent prosecution of married men for adultery. In some areas of the Palatinate, in fact, men were apparently prosecuted far more often than women for adultery, accounting for at least 75.8 percent of total adultery convictions by the Catholic prince-bishop's Privy Council (*Hofrat*) and 90.9 percent of the same total in the Lutheran city of Speyer's criminal court (*Vierrichter*).[40] Do such statistics actually signal a significant change in criminal prosecution and the role of gender, or is there another explanation? A breakdown of adultery case types provides the best starting point.

Most married men convicted of adultery in the Palatinate during the second half of the sixteenth century had at least one characteristic in common: Their paramours were of servile or marginal social status. In the rural areas, this role was often filled by the family maid, as in at least half of

[38] *Tötungsrecht*, or *Rachbefugnis*, was considered by all secular authorities throughout Germany an inalienable right of all males for restoring their honor and thus fiercely preserved (Harvey, "Nürnberg Marriage Laws," 115; Lieberwirth, "Ehebruch," in *HRG* 1:839.

  In other parts of Europe, however, the act was by no means considered automatically justified by the emotional circumstances. Gratian, for instance, had expressly rejected such an act of private retribution, citing several of the Church Fathers (including Augustine) in support (Brundage, *Law, Sex and Christian Society*, 248). Most states influenced early by "the written law" appear to have likewise supported the canonical position. Cf. prosecution of such causes in fifteenth-century Venice (Ruggiero, *The Boundaries of Eros*, 67ff.).

[39] GLA 61/11491, 70ᵛ (25 May 1555). Cf. a similar 1528 incident in Ulm, cited by Harvey ("Nürnberg Marriage Laws," 119–20), of a barber who killed both his wife and her lover and was released by authorities on the same grounds.

[40] Including cases of double adultery (5), 47 of 62 cases of the *Hofrat*, 1585–1620; at least 10 of 11 cases of *Vierrichter*, 1576–81 (the marital status of Agatha von Fenberg, executed for incest in 1577, is not clear). If all males of unknown marital status among the *Hofrat's* married-women convictions are considered (8), this percentage could rise slightly to 78.6 percent. The same tendency is evident in the marriage prosecutions of the contemporary Reformed courts of Neuchâtel (63.6 percent males, 1547–1618) and the Palatinate's Bacharach (88.8 percent of those recorded for 1590–1615) Watt, *Making of Modern Marriage*, 89; LAK 4/1631–32.

  Cf., on the other hand, adultery divorces of Basel's Reformed *Ehegericht* from 1529 to 1554, where women are cited as the guilty party 65.2 percent of time. Staehlin, *Ehescheidung in Basel*, 181–98.

the married male convictions in the Prince-Bishopric of Speyer.[41] After servants, most women convicted of adultery with married men were of broadly defined marginal social status: "common vagabond," "day laborer," and more generally "common women" or "whores."[42] Often, these women were the same domestic servants already mentioned, in this instance promised money or, in some desperate cases, even marriage in return for sexual favors. Coercion and rape were apparently also not uncommon, though occasionally we come across individuals such as the unnamed maid of Heinrich von Finkenbach who preferred to quit her position than to give in to her employer's advances.[43]

Usually, such indiscretions occurred, as in the case of Hans Schweinvater, "one day when his wife was away"[44] (see Figure 6c) but, as we shall see, concubinage among separated or widowed men, especially older ones, was also not infrequent.[45] Almost invariably, though, not until the maid was visibly pregnant or had already delivered a child was the matter brought before authorities.[46] At that point, both were arrested, imprisoned, tried, and punished individually.

Many sixteenth-century legal codes, from the *Carolina* to the Elector's 1575 morals ordinance, defined adultery in theory as a capital offense.[47] In practice, the offense was only rarely punished by death, and then

---

[41] 53.2–76.6 percent of 47 convictions, 25 are explicitly "mit seiner magd"; in 11 cases the social position of the woman is not mentioned. See typical Bacharach case of Friederich Becker and his maid (18 October 1590; AEKK 125/5, 241). Vogler has found a comparable frequency of maid adulteries during the same period in the records of neighboring Sponheim and Zweibrücken (Vogler II:979, 994), as does Watt in Neuchâtel (*Making of Modern Marriage*, 93–96). Ingram estimates that maids accounted for at least 70 percent of unwed mothers in late sixteenth-century England (*Church Courts, Sex and Marriage*, 264).

[42] The references include *gemeine landstreicherin, taglohnerin, gemeine weiber, dürn, metz;* see Bloch, *Die Prostitution*, I:732–35, for list of late medieval and early modern German terms for prostitutes.

[43] HStAMü II/K.b. 390/1c, 625ᵛ. On the question of maid–employer sexual relations, see Wiesner, *Working Women*, 86–90, and Ingram, *Church Courts, Sex, and Marriage*, 265–67.

[44] GLA 61/11497, 23ᵛ. In this case, the wife was out of town ("nit in heimish gewesen").

[45] *Ehebruch* was also occasionally applied to widows and widowers, as in the 1606 case of Hans Schreiber and two widows in the Lautterberg district (GLA 61/11496, 111ʳ), and Jacob Rupsch of Scheithal, fined "dieshalb in wehrenden witwastand deflorirt" in 1620 (GLA 61/11497c, 31). A 1580 Vierrichter adultery conviction of Bertrundt Mayer "so ein nonne im kloster zu S. Claren gewesen" is ambiguous as to whether Mayer had married or her religious vows were still considered binding (StAS IA/705, 25ᵛ). Cf. subsequent discussion in this chapter on concubinage.

[46] At least 20 of 22 cases (90.9 percent) in the Bishopric of Speyer where "maid" was specified; 30–36 of 42 total convictions (71.4–85.7 percent) when women of unspecified status are included.

[47] Lev. 20:10ff.; article 120 of *Carolina*, cited in Lieberwirth, "Ehebruch," in *HRG* 1:838ff.; 1575 *Sittenmandat* (*EKO* 487); Harvey, "Nürnberg Marriage Laws," 116–19.

almost always in connection with some more serious crime, such as incest.[48] Rather, punishment for adultery could range from public church penance to banishment, depending on the offender and, occasionally, the scandalousness of the offense. Yet, as Tables 4 and 5 illustrate, the severity of the sentence was hardly a random affair. Usually the married man was fined according to his personal worth and given a church penance: among Protestants a public confession of guilt and carrying the "stone of shame" (*Lasterstein;* see Figure 7e); among Catholics carrying a candle around the altar of his parish church at the beginning of three consecutive Sunday masses.[49] The single woman, on the other hand, was usually given "until she was able to stand from the birth bed" to get out of the territory.[50] Only occasionally did the court also direct the man to make some kind of financial provision for the child's support before it and the mother were banished.[51]

More than religious doctrine, institutional limitations, or even the

---

[48] A 1508 Nuremberg case, for instance, of a married woman burned alive for "grosser hurery" was very unusual (Harvey, "Nürnberg Marriage Laws," 130–31), as was the 1527 Zittau drowning of a woman for adultery with sixty-three men (Allen, "Crime and Punishment," 254). Generally, German municipal courts relied exclusively on fines, corporal punishment, and/or banishment (cf. Allen, 275, n. 53; Van Dülmen, *Theater des Schreckens,* tables 4 and 5). On the great discrepancy between the severity of sixteenth-century German legal codes and practice, see Allen, 32–56, 105–23, 321ff.

[49] In Bacharach, public humiliation was accompanied in at least two cases by fines (1 May 1612; 18 February 1613) and in three instances (1 May 1612; 28 January 1613; 24 May 1615) by brief imprisonment (LAK 4/1631, 240ᵛ-242ᵛ). For the Palatine-Electorate's penance formula for adultery, see Vogler II:973. I have found no evidence that this was accompanied by excommunication as was frequently the case in Geneva (E. William Monter, "Crime and Punishment in Calvin's Geneva, 1562," *Archiv für Reformationsgeschichte* 64 [*1973*], (*283*). On use of the *Lasterstein* as punishment, see Eberhard von Künssberg, *Über die Strafe des Steintragens* (Breslau, 1907).
 Among Catholics, the sentence was the same as that of the pre-Reformation lay synod: ". . . ascensis candelis demum extinctis et in terram projectis ac pulsatis campanis infra missarum et aliarum divinarum horarum solemni" (GLA 67/417, 172ʳ; 14 November 1506). Of 47 convictions of married men by the *Hofrat,* 40 (85.1 percent) carried penalties of fine and/or the public penance, alternately referred to as the *gewohnliche kirchuß* or *kertzentrag.* Occasionally brief imprisonments were also tacked on to the sentences (GLA 61/11496, 184ᵛ, 224ʳ, 253ᵛ, 263ʳ), and banishment for more serious offenses, such as multiple vows (GLA 61/11497, 306ᵛ). See Table 4. At least seven of these *Hofrat* punishments were accompanied, however, by court-ordered separations ("alle offne eheliche zeich. und gesellschafft vermeiden soll") until otherwise notified (GLA 61/11495a, 15ᵛ, 36ʳ⁻ᵛ, 38ʳ, 105ᵛ· 108ʳ, 110ᵛ; GLA 61/11496, 184ᵛ, 306ᵛ).

[50] GLA 61/11496, 181ᵛ. See my subsequent comments on frequency of banishment for maids.

[51] Courts did not directly decide or negotiate such settlements, but rather directed the accused "das kindt zuenderhalten oder sich mit der Mutter suvergleichen" (StAS IA/705, 25ᵛ). In only one instance of our sample (StAS IA/705, 306ᵛ) is the amount (in this case fifty thaler) set by the *fauth* himself; otherwise his role is that of the traditional medieval arbitrator of last resort. Cf. StAS IA/705, 25ᵛ; GLA 61/11496, 73ᵛ, 110ʳ, 177ʳ.

Table 4. *Adultery punishments of P.-B. Speyer* Hofrat *(Catholic), 1585–1619*

	Married		Single[a]	
	Male	Female	Male	Female
Fine and/or penance	40[b]	15	2	2[e]
Prison sentence & fine/penance	4	—	1	—
Corporal and banishment	2[cd]	1	10	12
Death	1[d]	—	—	1[d]
Unknown	—	4	2	27
Total	47	20	15	42

[a]Includes 8 males and 11 females of unspecified marital status; omission reduces the sample size but does not significantly alter distribution.
[b]7 accompanied by court-ordered separations.
[c]Multiple vows.
[d]Incest or bestiality.
[e]Widow.
Source: GLA 61/11495–97.

Table 5. *Adultery punishments of the city of Speyer's* Vierrichter *(Lutheran), 1576–81*

	Married		Single	
	Male	Female	Male	Female
Oath	4[a]	—	—	1
Fine	3	—	—	—
Loss of *Burgrecht*	1	—	—	—
Banishment	2[bc]	—	—	6[e]
Death	1[d]	—	—	1[d]
Unknown	—	—	—	2
Total	11	0	0	10

[a]Including 2 cases of settlement with mother when child involved.
[b]Leper.
[c]From Strasbourg.
[d]Incest.
[e]Includes 4 prostitutes, 1 maid, and 1 ex-nun.
Source: StAS IA/705, 1r–26r.

Figure 7. The tools of marital discipline (significantly concentrating on public humiliation of women): (a) an "iron maiden" for unruly single or married women (Mittelalterliches Kriminalmuseum Rothenburg ob der Tauber).

nature of the offense itself, the primary basis for gradation of punishment among all secular authorities of the Palatinate remained the social position of the offender.[52] As throughout the Middle Ages, the central issue for offending members inside the *Gemeinschaft* was public honor

---

[52] Cf. Keith Thomas, "The Double Standard," *Journal of the History of Ideas* 20 (1959), 195–216; Roper, *Holy Household*, 82–88; and the similar findings of Ruggiero for Venice (*The Boundaries of Eros*, 152ff.).

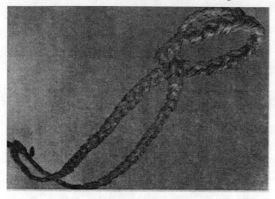

Figure 7. (b) the straw wreath of shame for fornicating unmarried women (Mittelalterliches Kriminalmuseum Rothenburg ob der Tauber).

and restitution, hence continuation of the Germanic *wergeld* tradition and the ecclesiastical counterpart of public penance to ensure reconciliation with the community.[53] In our sample of the Prince-Bishop's Privy Council, this was the sentence for 93.6 percent of known married male offenders and 75 to 95 percent of married female offenders; the much smaller sample from the city of Speyer reflects the same pattern of social distinction.[54]

As in the sentences of the lay synod, the amount of the fine varied with the nature of the adultery and wealth of the offender. Open or multiple adultery, for example, were considered more serious than an

---

[53] On punishments of "honor," see Rudold Quanter, *Die Schand- und Ehrenstragen in der deutschen Rechtspflege. Eine kriminalistische Studie* (1901); (Reprint: Aalen, 1970); Hans von Hentig, *Die Strafe*, vol. I: *Frühformen und kulturgeschichtlicke Zusammenhänge* (Berlin, 1954).

Van Dülmen's claim (*Theater des Schreckens*, 76ff.) that public church penance was more prevalent among Protestants than Catholics is not borne out in the records of the *Hofrat* and *Vierrichter*, where the opposite was true.

[54] *Hofrat* figures include four cases of brief imprisonment. If offenders of unspecified marital status are included, 44–49 of 55 male convictions (80–89 percent), 15–19 of 31 female convictions (48.4–61.3 percent). The same tendency is clear in adultery punishments of the *Vierrichter*, with 8 of 11 married men receiving similar sentences, and no recorded prosecution or punishment of married women.

Cf. Ruggiero, *The Boundaries of Eros*, table 2, 52, on the same pattern of comparative leniency.

Figure 7. (c) the "house dragon" mask for bad wives (Mittelalterliches Kriminalmuseum Rothenburg ob der Tauber).

employer sleeping with his maid and fined accordingly.[55] Similarly, men of wealth, such as Martin Fimpelt of Bruchsal and Georg Schmidt of Neipsheim, could each be fined "by his estimated property" as much as 800 and 200 gulden annually (compared to the usual 10 to 100 gulden

[55] Harster (*Strafrecht*, 187) also remarks on the similarity in gradation of adultery offenses by the reformed *Vierrichter* to pre-Reformation standards. A sentencing guide of the lay synod in 1492, for instance, prescribes fine of 1 fl. for concubinage and adultery of an employer with his maid, 2 fl. for "usual" adultery, and 2 fl., 20 schilling *Heller* and unspecified corporal punishment for adultery between a Christian woman and a Jew (Walther Kohl, "Das Laiensengericht in Speyer," 67). The city of Speyer's 1616 *Vierrichterordnung* sets the fine for adultery at 5 pound *Heller* or the equivalent prison sentence (StAS IA/12, 284).

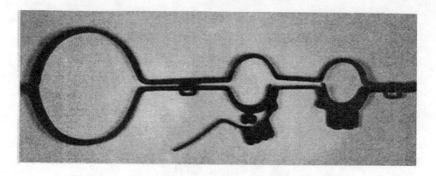

Figure 7. (d) hand-irons for public display of male or female offenders (Mittelalterliches Kriminalmuseum Rothenburg ob der Tauber).

Figure 7. (e) the stone of shame, to be borne in procession by convicted adulterers or fornicators (Mittelalterliches Kriminalmuseum Rothenburg ob der Tauber).

fine).[56] In 1580, two men of the city of Speyer were even fined differently (30 gulden and 100 gulden) for relations with the same prostitute on the same day.[57] Only rarely was the privileged legal status of enfranchised and otherwise accepted members of the community even threatened by authorities.[58]

Those offenders considered marginal to the *Gemeinschaft*, on the other hand, received quite different treatment. Here, corporal punishment and banishment were the norm, comprising 66.7 to 80 percent of single male sentences for adultery, 85.7 percent of known single females' sentences of the Prince-Bishop's Privy Council, and 70 to 90 percent of all single women's punishment by the city's criminal court (see Tables 4 and 5).[59] As Guido Ruggiero has noted of fifteenth-century Venice, sexual relations *within* this group appear to have been little regulated, if at all, by secular authorities, even after religious reforms of the sixteenth century.[60] Only when a marginal individual was publicly known to have "carnally mixed" with a member inside the community did authorities take action, though by quite different standards than those already discussed.

Because secular authorities were generally less concerned with "eradicating a moral vice (than) reconstituting the family unit and protecting property,"[61] their attitude toward individuals outside that sphere was significantly different. Whereas the goal of punishment of those within the *Gemeinschaft* was to restore, by fine or penance, lost status in the community, marginal offenders had no such status to regain. Instead, the

---

56 GLA 61/11495, 39ᵛ, 41ʳ, 136ᵛ. Cf. similarly high fines by Bacharach *Amtman* of 150 fl. in 1613 and 100 fl. in 1619 (LAK 4/1631, 243ʳ; LAK 4/1632, 357).

57 20 April 1580; StAS IA/705, 24ᵛ–25ʳ.

58 Mason Hans Becker was warned by the magistrates that if he ever repeated his adultery, "woll ein Rath Ihnen zum burger nit gedulden" (10 January 1581; StAS IA/705, 27ᵛ) and Jeremias Neumeyer actually has his *burgerrecht* "ufgezogt" (18 February, 1577; StAS IA/705, 6ᵛ) but these are the only such mentions of the privilege in connection with punishment of adultery.

59 If female offenders of unknown marital status are also included, 13–40 of 42 *Hofrat* convictions (28.6–92.9 percent), 7 of 9 *Vierrichter* convictions of single women. While certainly not all single persons were necessarily considered marginal, based on the punishment in those cases where social status is identified (all 12 women and 7 of 10 men in *Hofrat* adultery convictions), the correlation remains generally valid.

Cf. sentences of prostitutes in Speyer (StAS, IA/705, 6ᵛ, 8ʳ, 15ʳ, 24ᵛ–25ʳ, 27ᵛ), and findings of Roper, "Prostitution," 19; Harster, *Strafrecht*, 190.

60 Ruggiero, *The Boundaries of Eros*, 39ff., 61ff. Cf., however, two cases of fornication between servants before the Bacharach consistory in 1585 (13 June 1585; AEKK 125/2, 211).

61 Ruggiero, *The Boundaries of Eros*, 69. See also Brundage, *Law, Sex, and Christian Society*, 542, on the connection between adultery and property.

focus here was on public humiliation of the offender and purification of the community from the same undesirables, usually by physical banishment. Speyer's 1576 banishment of Einhardt Krantz, "an impure (leper) who carnally mixed [*fleischlich vermischt*] with a pure person in the lepertorium" provides an appropriate metaphor for punishment of all marginal offenders for adultery.[62] Often the "infection" identified with such marginal groups went beyond the symbolic, as with prostitutes and the sixteenth-century epidemic of venereal disease.[63] Unlike married and propertied individuals, marginal persons – at least according to the magistrates – had little or no stake in the community and therefore few means or reasons to promise restitution. The community, in turn, had even fewer reasons for providing such an opportunity, permitting a severity in punishment much closer to the letter of the law.

Prosecution of married women for adultery displayed at least two similarities to that of men. In the Prince-Bishopric of Speyer, at least one-third and perhaps as much as 75 percent of adultery charges against married women involved single men of servile status.[64] In addition, almost all were caught in the act while still married or were charged after physically deserting their spouses for a prolonged period of time; according to extant petitions the wronged husband is explicitly cited as the initiator only once.[65] As in the prosecution of male adultery, it was generally only the same open impropriety with an individual of low social status that prompted authorities to take action. When the wife of Jacob Zihn took up with another man in the local inn and on the streets of Niderfeldt, it was the public "stain [*schandfleck*] on all honor-loving matrons" that prompted the elders of Bacharach to have her imprisoned by the bailiff.[66] Usually, the outcome for the guilty parties was also similar: fine and public penance for the adulterous wife, banishment (and some-

---

[62] 6 June 1576; StAS IA/705, 1ᵛ. Cf. similar case of leper Anna Magdt in Bacharach (5 October 1604; AEKK 125/2, 316); and Van Dülmen, *Theater des Schreckens*, 176ff., on "Selbstreinigung der Gesellschaft." Rossiaud (*Medieval Prostitution*, 57–58) also remarks on the many similarities in official pronouncements against the "pollution" of Jews, lepers, and prostitutes.

[63] Roper ("Prostitution," 4ff.) argues that prostitutes were by far more closely identified with the disease in popular literature than mercenary soldiers or other groups who participated in its spread.

[64] A total of twenty adultery convictions includes seven known servants, five married men (double adultery), and eight of unspecified social or marital status. Cf. similar Bacharach case of Katherina Winter and the *Wirth* at Engel (17 November 1609; AEKK 125/2, 351).

[65] 1579 *Vierrichter* case of Anna Steinberger, arrested on order of her husband, Hans Harder of Würzburg (Harster, *Strafrecht*, 190).

[66] 21 April 1605; AEKK 125/2, 321.

times also a fine) for her male partner.[67] In cases of adultery involving Catholic clerics, disciplining of the male offenders varied more but the punishment, if any, of married women was invariably mild.[68]

Adultery between two married parties (double adultery) was certainly not unheard of during this period, but apparently less commonly prosecuted. Such offenses probably made up less than 10 percent of total adultery cases of the Prince-Bishop's Privy Council and at most two of eleven such cases recorded by the city of Speyer between 1576 and 1581.[69] Here insufficient documentation makes generalization difficult, especially considering the range of circumstances and punishments. The case of four married people (none to each other) apprehended in group debauchery in 1616 appears an extraordinary one, yet the Privy Council's sentence – the usual public penance "to provide an example for others" – seems peculiarly routine.[70] Georg Schwarz and Otilia Adam, on the other hand, were sentenced for their 1598 adultery to imprisonment for several days on bread and water, fines, public penance, and legal separation from their respective spouses until further notice.[71]

---

67 Banishment was the most frequently mentioned sentence for single young men, as in the typical case of Hans Wagener of Niedt aus der Wederaw, a *bender* apprentice arrested "deswegen, das er mit Seyfridt Geyeissbergers eheweib, welllliche ausgerissen, fleischliche unzucht getriben, uff gewohnlichen urpheden erlassen unnd ime dabey asugesagt worden, der statt Speir hinfuro müessig zu gehen" (10 January 1579, cited in Harster, *Strafrecht*, 188). See Tables 4 and 5.

68 Ingram (*Church Court, Sex, and Marriage*, 249–59) finds remarkably similar patterns in the prosecutions of adulterous wives, constituting at most 10–20 percent of all adultery cases. Brundage (*Law, Sex, and Christian Society*, 539ff.) claims that by the fifteenth century, most jurists and ecclesiastical authorities had given up altogether trying to punish women involved with clerics. Ruggiero, however suggests more serious treatment by Venetian authorities of such offenses, considered "crimes against God" (*The Boundaries of Eros*, 71ff.). See my subsequent comments on the prosecution of sexual offenses among clerics.

69 The *Hofrat* percentage ranges from 5 explicit cases of double adultery (8.1 percent) to a possible total of 26 (41.9 percent) out of all 62 adultery convictions. Since married women were invariably identified in relationship to their husband (e.g. "Appolonia Nicolas Lamben zu Schifferstadts hausfraw"), the higher figure, based on cases of unspecified marital status, appears highly improbable.

The *Vierrichter* case of Bertrundt Mayer, "so ein nonne im kloster zu S. Claren gewesen," is ambiguous as to whether Mayer's vows were considered still binding, she had remarried, or only the adultery of her partner, Niclaus Wöberin, was in question (30 May and 8 June, 1580; StAS IA/705, 25ᵛ). The marital status of Agatha von Fenberg, executed in 1577 for incestuous relations with her daughter's husband, is likewise ambiguous (21–22 June, 1577; StAS IA/705, 10v).

I have found no mention of this kind of adultery among the ten recorded prosecutions of the Bacharach consistory from 1590 to 1615.

70 4 November 1616; GLA 61/11497, 18ᵛ.   71 16 March 1598; GLA 61/11495, 44ʳ.

Apparently the only kind of double adultery eliciting the same reaction from all secular authorities of the Palatinate was the intentional procurement by some husbands of their own wives to other men. When the bishop's bailiff of Rottenburg arrested Lanng Lawer and Bader Hennsling for adultery in 1560, the charge that Lawer's husband "had sought in a suspicious and disreputable manner to bring them together" was enough for all three to end up in the tower.[72] The court's justification for the subsequent flogging and imprisonment of "not only the adulteress but her husband as well" is especially interesting. According to the judges, not only was such an offense forbidden by "the Almighty and [Emperor Charles V]," but it was becoming so common "at this time" that such suspicion alone constituted grounds enough to initiate *ex officio* action and punishment.[73] Functionaries of the Elector and city of Speyer apparently reacted with similar dispatch and severity in such cases.[74]

The other target of the sixteenth-century marital discipline was sexual incontinence among unmarried persons. Such activities had always been considered sinful by ecclesiastical authorities, of course, but again, the harshness and urgency of sixteenth-century condemnations is particularly striking. Nor was the ubiquitous Protestant literary topos of the "whoring devil"[75] limited to clerical elites. When the Reformed elders of Germersheim complained in 1598 that "[the practice of] fornication is out of hand and nearly without shame,"[76] their frenzied fear of sexual anarchy was easily a match for that of any popular preacher or polemicist. According to the Elector's 1546 police ordinance, these "undisciplined and harmful frivolities against God's commandment" were – together with adultery – "currently widespread" and "shamelessly practiced by clerics and laity [alike]."[77] In the legal and moral offensive that ensued, though, authorities consistently distinguished between two kinds of sexual activity outside of marriage: isolated or short-term liaisons (fornication); long-term cohabitation without official betrothal or

---

[72] 5 November 1560; GLA 11492a, 32ʳ. Cf. Kö II:394.
[73] Articles 122 and 123 of *Carolina;* GLA 11492a, 31ʳ–32ʳ. Almost as an afterthought: "dergleich den Bub anh gefenglichen Inzieg. Im Thurm nach gepur. straffs mit Ruthenn zuchtig: und daruff bessern zucht zusagen solle . . ."
[74] Cf. the 1625 *Vierrichter* case of a husband procuring his wife to a Carmelite monk (Harster, *Strafrecht,* 192) and similar punishment by authorities of Electorate, Zweibrücken, and Sponheim (Vogler II:97ff.).
[75] See my discussion in Chapter 2.   [76] LAS D2 363b/I, 74.   [77] 1546 *Policey ordnung; EKO,* 104.

Church blessing (concubinage). As we shall see, it was – as in adulterous relationships – the long-term repudiation of marriage that secular authorities perceived as most injurious to the dignity of the estate and consequently the focus of the most ambitious reforms.

In prosecuting and punishing fornication, both Protestant and Catholic authorities made the same distinction between completely frivolous relations and those where marriage was suggested or at least possible. Cases of the first type, usually involving marginal individuals, present another clear example of the gender-based double standard. Presumably since the institution of marriage was never directly threatened, men convicted of fornication only were generally released on oath without punishment.[78] Unmarried women, however, were punished for the same crime with imprisonment, rods, irons, and usually banishment.[79] Overall, prosecution of this largely unprovable offense appears to have been infrequent, even in Reformed areas.[80]

Fornication resulting in pregnancy was an entirely different matter. Here it appears that secular authorities considered the sexual offense secondary in importance to the abuse of betrothal and consequent dangers to the institution of marriage (as well as the patrimony). If preceded by a public and indisputed betrothal, premarital sexual relations were generally punished as they had been before the Reformation, with a fine or public penance, or both, before solemnization of the vows.[81] Only

---

[78] StAS IA/705, 8ʳ⁻ᵛ, 10ʳ, 24ʳ, 24ᵛ⁻25ʳ, 26ᵛ; GLA 61/11496, 316ʳ; GLA 61/11497, 170ʳ, AEKK 125/2, 211, 282, 351. Occasionally (StAS IA/705, 24ᵛ⁻25ʳ; LAK 4/1631, 237ᵛ), small fines were also levied.

[79] StAS IA/705, 6ʳ, 6ᵛ, 24ᵛ⁻25ʳ, 25ᵛ⁻26ʳ, 27ᵛ; AEKK 125/2, 211, 282, 312, 351; LAK 4/1631, 235ʳ, 242ʳ⁻ᵛ. The similarity to treatment of prostitutes was not coincidental, as will be discussed.

[80] I have found only nine cases of fornication without pregnancy or marital vows in the records of the Bacharach consistory (AEKK 125/2, 211), thus constituting about one-quarter of all fornication cases from 1585 to 1619. Vogler has found thirty-two cases for the neighboring Reformed Zweibrücken consistory for 1558–89, but punishment also appears light and the prosecution rate of about one case per year is not significantly higher than those of contemporary Nuremberg (.74) or Frankfurt (.42) (figures based on Van Dülmen, *Theater des Schreckens*, tables 4 and 5).

[81] Usually, as before the Reformation, the couple was told to formalize its union if both were eligible (including "equal" in social status) and pay a small fine (4–7 fl. in Reformed Bacharach compared with a 2-pound wax and 1 fl. fine of the pre-Reformation lay synod). The 1556 synod of Kassel added that the *kirchgang* should take place "ohne alles gebrenge, pfeifens, danzens, schenkens" (Niebergall, *Die Geschichte der evangelischen Trauung*, 49). See also E. William Monter, "The Consistory of Geneva, 1559–1569," *Bibliothèque d'humanisme et renaissance* 38 (1976), 476–84.; Lehmann, *Landau in der Pfalz*, 103–4; Harster, *Strafrecht*, 189ff; *EKO* 287; and Friedberg, *Das Recht der Eheschiliessung*, 278. Cf. similar tolerance in England (Gillis, *For Better, for Worse*, 52ff.; Carlson, "Marriage and the English Reformation," 449; and Ingram, *Church Courts, Sex, and Marriage*, 225–27).

the Reformed states of Zweibrücken and Geneva appear to have had stiffer penalties of imprisonment and public penance with the "stone of shame."[82] In the Palatine-Electorate, prenuptial pregnancy and its punishment delayed official solemnization until six weeks after the birth but did not preclude lawful marriage.[83] If, though, the vows had been secret, "frivolous," or were otherwise contested, both parties faced severe sanctions. When the Prince-Bishop's Privy Council, for instance, learned that shepherd Hans Schreiber had not only committed fornication with two widows in Lauttenburg but also given one of them the Elector's penny as a token of betrothal, the "frivolous fellow's" sentence was immediately changed from the usual public penance to banishment.[84]

By far the most widely decried threat to marriage among unmarried persons, however, was the continuing repudiation of the sacred bond and legal contract represented by concubinage. During the Middle Ages, such informal and unsolemnized union had been both widespread and generally tolerated, even among clerics.[85] Beginning in the late fifteenth and early sixteenth centuries, though, religious and secular authorities launched a combined legal and moral offensive against all irregular unions, lay as well as clerical. Countless local ordinances (including two from the magistrates of Speyer in 1540 and 1549) echoed the condemnation and punishment of concubinage proclaimed by both Lateran V

---

82 Zweibrücken specified three weeks in prison, a 20-fl. fine, and three weekly processions with the *Lasterstein;* Geneva, six days' imprisonment and a 60-sols fine, although excommunication was clearly more frequent in practice (160 from 1564 to 1569). Vogler II:1007; Bièler, *L'homme et la femme,* 124; Monter, "The Consistory of Geneva," 479–81. Some of the fifty-six cases of premarital fornication in Hohenlohe-Langenberg (1550–88) were also punished with short prison sentences (Robisheaux, *Rural Society,* 108).

The magistrates of fourteenth- and fifteenth-century Venice also displayed an increasing strictness in their punishment of fornication, often including long jail sentences. Cf. Ruggiero, *The Boundaries of Eros,* 16–42.

83 Cf. Bacharach consistory's censoring of six prenuptial fornication cases, including two for babies born too soon after the wedding: 8 September 1587, 1 August 1599, 17 May 1601, 31 January 1608, 4 May 1617, 15 March 1620; AEKK 125/2, 226, 282, 295, 342, 388, 404; LAK 4/1631, 239ᵛ, 243ʳ. See also the Elector's 1579 "Forma wie personen, so wider göttlich und weltlicher obrigkeit verlobt in unzucht betreten, der kirchen abbitung thun und derenselben wider eigesönet werden sollen" (*EKO,* 601).

84 31 January, 1606; GLA 61/11496, 111ʳ. Cf. similar reactions to frivolous vows in the Elector's 1563 *EGO* (*EKO* 311) and similar cases before Bacharach consistory (3 January 1619; AEKK 125/2, 398); and my comments in Chapter 4.

85 Cf. H.-W. Strätz, "Kebsehe, -kind," in *HRG* 2:695–96; D. Giesen, "Konkubinat," in *HRG* 2:1074–75; Brundage, *Law, Sex, and Christian Society,* 98–103, 297–300, 369, 444–47. A 1459 Genevan ordinance provides an early exception (Bièler, *L'homme et la femme,* 186).

(1514) and the emperor's police ordinances of 1530 and 1548,[86] all of them consistently singling out the same two groups as worst offenders: widows and widowers, and clerics.

Widows and widowers comprised a significant portion of the population in all early modern European societies.[87] Due to the occasionally ambiguous use of the term *Ehebruch* and *Hurerei*, however, it is difficult to know how many of those men prosecuted for adultery with their maids were actually widowers. According to most religious reformers, such concubinage of "unequals" remained all too frequent and only occasionally punished. Lorenz Frenel and Adam Metzler were each called before the Bacharach consistory for their cohabitation with "suspicious females," but without admissions of guilt, neither could be punished.[88] Another Bacharach man accused of impregnating his maid was still permitted to cohabitate with her for the final two months of the pregnancy and required only to make public penance at the child's baptism.[89] Most widowers, moreover, defended these informal arrangements as preferable to living alone or, worse yet, redividing the inheritance with a formal union. Indeed, in two cases of the Prince-Bishop's Privy Council, it was only when children of widowers feared their patrimony was in jeopardy that they denounced their respective fathers' concubinage to authorities.[90]

---

[86] *Gepot das Gots leütern / schweren /Eebrechen / unelich beywonen / egrerlich halten / auch zudrinken belagend* (1540); *Verbot stuchen zudrucken ebruch und lastermessigen beywonen belang* (1549). StAS IA/631, 1ᵛ–2ʳ, 6ʳ–ᵛ; Giesen, "Konkubinat," in *HRG* 2:1075. See also Brundage, *Law, Sex, and Christian Society*, 514, 557–58, 569–70.

[87] Some historians have estimated that as many as 20 percent of all women at any given time were widows, with a similar or even higher percentage among the male population, for example, Stone, *The Family, Sex, and Marriage*, 42ff. Peter Zchuncke (*Konfession und Alltag in Oppenheim* [Wiesbaden, 1984], finds that 41.8 percent of all marriages from 1568 to 1798 in Oppenheim involved at least one widow(er).

[88] 28 March 1613, 19 January 1617; AEKK 125/2, 374, 388. Cf. similar results among widows and male cohabitants (3 October 1585, 30 April 1587, 6 July 1604, 3 April 1614, 8 February 1613; AEKK 125/2, 213, 313, 371, 377).

[89] Michael Schwindt denied the charge but received the same sanction of public penance as the woman "nach vollendung Ihres Kindbett" (3 August 1600; AEKK 125/2, 291).

[90] Georg Ehem of Arzheim was turned in by his two sons-in-law, Peter Hora and Hanns Zorn, merely on suspicion of concubinage (26 September 1597; GLA 61/11495a, 32ʳ), as was Anthonius Natz of Allerweyler by his son and son-in-law (29 December 1610; GLA 61/11496, 224ʳ). In both cases, the fathers were accused of *Ehebruch* and plans to appropriate their dead wives' property for themselves. Cf. Vogler II:995ff.; and my comments in Chapter 4.

I have found no sixteenth-century mention of *Morgantische Ehe*, or *Ehe zur linken Hand*, the practice of maintaining completely separate property and inheritance rights, with no legal union between the couple. W. Leiser ("Morgantische Ehe," in *HRG* 3:676–77) maintains that until

Less serious, but equally prevalent, many remarrying widows and widowers began cohabitation almost immediately after their spouses' deaths and long before official solemnization. In 1561, the consistory of Zweibrücken complained that the majority of widows within its jurisdiction continued to live with their fiancés during engagement, although expressly forbidden by several ordinances since the fifteenth century.[91] The Elector's 1582 territorial code also explicitly condemned this "completely frivolous practice . . . giving rise to all kinds of trouble and injustice . . . against the written law and all civil respectability."[92]

Yet beyond reiterating the set waiting period for remarrying widows and widowers (usually nine months – for obvious reasons of propriety) and raising the fine from lay synod standards (in Bacharach to ten gulden in 1600), legal reforms of lay concubinage rarely differed from their pre-Reformation predecessors.[93] The better enforcement sought by religious reformers could only have been achieved by a more radical transformation of governmental involvement than most would have considered practical or even desirable. Moreover, most secular authorities apparently shared lay people's reprehension only in openly scandalous situations, such as the 1602 cases of two Bacharach widows who became engaged and began cohabitation within three to four weeks of their spouses' deaths.[94] Simple cohabitation among widows and widowers, such as the 1598 case of Matthes Larner and Elisabeth Larner, was rarely an issue. When the couple approached the consistory's secretary after the prescribed waiting period and asked for permission to proclaim their engagement, he merely asked them "with great seriousness" whether they had slept with one another during their long cohabitation, to which they "very modestly" answered in the negative.[95]

the twentieth century, such unions were considered both valid and sacramental in Germany and most European countries.

[91] Vogler II:998. The consistory subsequently decreed a 10-fl. fine for all such illegitimate cohabitation. See Vogler II:995ff. on general difficulties encountered by Protestant reformers of the Palatinate in the area of illicit sexual relations.

[92] 1582 *Landrecht,* XIIII titul; *EKO,* 287.

[93] Again, the severity of the Zweibrücken consistory (a prison sentence of eight to fifteen days or banishment) appears to have been the exception more than the rule in the Palatinate (Vogler II:996). Roman law required a delay of ten months for remarrying widows (Max Kaser, *Roman Private Law,* trans. Rolf Dannenbring, 4th ed. [Pretoria, 1984], 289).

[94] 22 March 1602; AEKK 125/2, 299–300. Cf. similar scandal caused by Hans Greuß, drunkenly roaming the area for two years with a "frivolous old female" (14 May 1608: AEKK 125/2, 343).

[95] 25 June 1598; AEKK 125/2, 278. Though still suspicious, the secretary was instructed in the absence of any proof to allow them to proclaim their banns. Cf. similar warning to Claus Schapp

Indifference to clerical concubinage was evidently an even more pervasive problem in the Palatinate. Since the earliest records of Speyer's diocesan synod in the fourteenth century, rarely a meeting of the biannual assembly passed in which the practice was not addressed and condemned. Usually the bishops issued threats of excommunication "against nefarious concubine holders" to the clergy at large, but occasionally individual offenders were summoned to appear and ordered to separate from their mistresses within eight days or suffer suspension.[96]

Actual implementation of this long-standing policy, however, appears to have been highly sporadic and often nonexistent. In the fall synod of 1493, the synod's secretary complained that many clerics used special ecclesiastical occasions, such as the celebration of a neighboring parish's dedication or patron's feast day, as a pretext for "openly and shamelessly" cavorting with their concubines "or other foolish females . . . finally returning glutted and bragging about their carrying on."[97] Indeed, in the wake of Bishop Matthias's largely failed clerical reforms of the 1460's, most episcopal officials appeared to suffer from declining expectations on the subject. Another synodal meeting of the same period, for instance, addressed not the abolition of such unions but merely the issue of propriety, forbidding priests' children from living with them or serving at mass.[98]

By the beginning of the sixteenth century, open criticism of clerical concubinage was again frequent, but this time among the laity. Of all clerical abuses decried in polemical pamphlets, the issue of sexual hypocrisy was undoubtedly the most recurrent, particularly in cities such as Speyer where clerics made up a larger percentage of the population[99] (see Figure 6b). Evangelicals, of course, were especially eager to point out

and Margaretha Mollens to regularize their long-standing engagement with a church wedding (3 October 1585; AEKK 125/2, 213) as well as a couple's scandalous cohabitation during the winter of 1592–93 (AEKK 125/2, 253).

96 Cf. *Collectio* I:3ff. (1390–1610). Occasionally, an exorbitant and rarely enforced fine was also threatened (e.g., 100 fl. in 1405; *Collectio* I:31).

97 Martini synod, 1493. *Collectio* II:58, 71.

98 Martini synod, 1487. *Collectio* II29. Preaching against corruption, on the other hand, never went out of vogue, as in Bishop Ludwig's first address to the synod (Martini 1478) on the subject: ". . . maxime autem concubinatus detestabile vitium quo altissimus ejusque intemerata et castimissa virgo et mater Maria patrona nostra graviter haud dubium offenduntur ac sacrosancte ecclesie auctoritas . . ." (*Collectio* II:3). Cf. Brundage, *Law, Sex, and Christian Society*, 537–39, on European-wide attempts by fifteenth-century ecclesiastical authorities to curb clerical concubinage and fornication.

99 In 1500, 7–8 percent, or about 469 clerics; Alter in I:475–76.

what they considered a quintessential abuse of the Roman church.[100] Even the leaders of the Peasants' Revolt and Speyer considered the practice significant enough to be included in their eight mainly political articles:

> Fifth, they do not want the clergy or anyone else to live in sin [*zu Unehr sitzen*], which we consider when a person lives suspiciously with another, without just cause or reason.[101]

The responses of the various confessions to clerical concubinage, as we have seen, differed markedly. In newly Protestant cities and territorial states throughout Germany (including Speyer and the Electorate), abolition of clerical celibacy was almost always the first officially sanctioned reform, thus ostensibly eliminating the very occasion for clerical concubinage altogether.[102] The effects were immediately obvious: While complaints of clerical ignorance (especially concerning the Eucharist) and drunkenness continued to plague the ecclessiastical leadership and laity of the Reformed Palatinate, the once paramount issues of sexual immorality among clerics was rarely mentioned.[103]

Some reform-minded Catholics also questioned the enforceability and necessity of clerical celibacy. The Bavarian representative to the Council of Trent put the case succinctly:

> Many other men who are aware of the current state of affairs in Germany ... believe that chaste marriage would be preferable to sullied celibacy. They further warn that the most able and knowledgeable men in the population would rather have wives without ecclesiastical benefices than benefices without wives.[104]

---

[100] See Chapter 1, on theme of clerical "whoring" in early Protestant polemic.

[101] Quoted in Alter, in *GStSp* I:492. Cf. similar tone of grievance no. 67 at the 1521 Diet of Worms (Gerald Strauss, *Manifestations of Discontent on the Eve of the Reformation* (Bloomington, 1971), 61).

[102] In the Palatine-Electorate: *Bedencken des durchleuchstigen pfaltzgraven Friedrichs* . . . (13 April 1546; *EKO* 93–94).

[103] Vogler (*Le clergé protestant rhènan*, 295–303) finds only six cases of dismissal for sexual immorality among Protestant clerics in Zweibrücken during the entire period of 1555–1619. Still, complaints of *epikuräisch* and *ergerlich* life-styles among Protestant clerics did not disappear entirely. Cf. 1580 electoral instruction for offices of *kirchendiener* and *schulmeister*, as well as 1584 mandate to the entire clergy (*EKO* 510–15). See also Vogler, ibid., 344–56, on general attempts to improve reputation and status of pastors by regulating dress and behavior.

[104] Quoted and translated in Brundage, *Law, Sex, and Christian Society*, 568. Cf. similar proposals in correspondence between the bishop of Worms and the cathedral chapter of Speyer in 1564 (Forster, *Counter-Reformation*, 23).

Since the 1520's, many provincial synods explored the possibility of marriage for priests[105] but in the end all Catholic authorities held firm to the traditional marriage prohibition. From the 1549 *Reformatio* of Charles V to *Tametsi* (1563) of Trent to the 1588 ordinance of reform bishop Eberhard of Speyer, enforcement rather than doctrine would be the focus of clerical reform.[106]

Most Catholic authorities recognized, as had their Protestant counterparts, that clerical *concubinatos* threatened not just "their own souls [with] damnation" but brought "trouble to other [lay] people," as well.[107] At the same time, reform-minded ecclesiastical officials faced widespread apathy among both clergy and laity. Archbishop Albrecht of Mainz, rarely noted for his reformist tendencies, complained to Nuncio Morone in 1542 that all of his priests were *concubinatos*.[108] Jesuit Peter Faber was equally dismal in his assessment of Worms: "Grant God, that in this city of Worms there are only two or three priests who aren't living in forbidden relationships or other public depravity."[109]

The diocese of Speyer was no exception. In his 1583 visitation of the rural chapters of Hambach and Deidesheim, Vicar-General Beatus Moses found that at least twelve of the twenty-two clerics he interviewed lived openly with their concubines and children in their rectories.[110]

---

[105] Discussion of the issue at the 1522 meeting of the bishops of Chimsee, Freising, and Passau (with representatives of Brixen and other secular authorities) was followed by similar debates at the provincial synods of Cologne (1536) and Salzburg (1537), as well as the 1537 papal commission on general ecclesiastical reform (Franzen, *Zölibat und Priesterehe*, 64–77).

[106] Charles V's 1549 *Reformatio* on clerical reform is typically traditional: "Si fornicaretum autem, vel adulterium committeret, etiam extra Ecclesiam abijeiendum ed ad poenitentiam inter Laicos agendam redigi debere. Ut autem non ferant haec secula tantem seuritatem, et sit mitius agendum, Sacerdos, Diaconus, et Subdiaconus fornicationis, Adulterij, aut suspectae familiaritatis convictus, remota protinus concubina, prima non poena peccuniaria, sed suspensione ab officio, et beneficio secundum scandali gravitatem plectendus est . . ."; see *Collectio* II:309; Schroeder, *Council of Trent*, 188–89; F. X. Remling, *Urkundenbuch zur Geschichte der Bischofe zu Speyer* (Mainz, 1854), II:578–79.

[107] 1546 *Policey Ordnung; EKO* 93.

[108] Stamer II:315.

[109] Quoted in B. Duhr, *Geschichte der Jesuiten in den Ländern deutscher Zunge im 16. Jahrhundert* (Freiburg, 1907), 5ff. The complaint is echoed in practically every diocese of Germany, such as the representative of the duke of Bavaria to the Council of Trent's assertion that 96 or 97 of the 100 priests in his realm maintained concubines. Even by the most conservative estimate, at least one-third to one-half of all sixteenth-century German priests lived with concubines and/or children. August Franze, *Die Visitationsprotokolle der ersten nachtridentischen Visitation im Erzstift Köln unter Salentin von Isenberg im Jahre 1569* (Münster, 1960), 123ff.; Franzen, *Zölibat und Priesterehe* 84, 88–91; Forster, *Counter-Reformation*, 22–23.

[110] Stamer III:91–92. The pastor of Niederlauterbach even admitted to fathering eleven children, four of whom had already died.

Indeed, according to witnesses, his very first subject, the pastor of Hambach, had already had at least two concubines before his current partner, a runaway wife and recently mother of a child by him.[111] Moreover, despite the Church hierarchy's equation of such concubinage with "licentious heresy,"[112] many laypersons apparently accepted the practice as unexceptional. When questioned by the vicar-general, the bellringer of Hainfeld, for instance, readily admitted that his pastor lived with his cook and their four children, "as is customary with pastors."[113]

In view of such widespread abuse, the means of correction appear curiously restrained. In the diocese of Speyer, for instance, the traditional procedure (also endorsed by Trent)[114] of three successive warnings and automatic excommunication was only occasionally supplemented by more active prosecution of offenders. Following the Visitation of 1583–88, for instance, all clerics with concubines were ordered to pay ten Marks silver and separate within six weeks or face suspension, banishment, and possible secular punishment.[115] Yet while at least thirty-two clerics were punished for sexual misconduct during this period of Counter-Reform (1583–1610), the annual rate of prosecution (1.13) was only slightly higher than that of the preceding thirty-four years (.73).[116]

Apparently, as in cases of lay adultery, it was generally only in very public and prolonged relationships that secular or ecclesiastical authorities took any notice whatsoever.[117] Open concubinage, consequently,

---

[111] Vischer was also accused of impregnating his maid and paying her off for silence, as well as an openly immoderate life-style where food, drink, and dancing was concerned. Moses suspended him from his position immediately, and within a few days the local chapter had elected a replacement (Stamer III:92–93).

[112] 18 May 1585 letter from newly crowned Sixtus V to Bishop Eberhard of Speyer, quoted in *Nuntiarberichte von der Görresgesellschaft*, ed. Gerhard Müler, part I (1533–59) (Gotha, 1892–) Vol. I:81ff.

[113] Stamer III:92. See also Forster, *Counter-Reformation*, 24ff.

[114] Chapter 8 of *Tametsi;* Schroeder, *Council of Trent*, 188–89.

[115] Martini synod 1588; Ammerich, "Formen und Wege der katholischen Reform," 300ff.; Stamer III:112ff.

[116] The statistics are based on *Urpheden* of imprisoned clerics from the episcopacies of Philip (1529–60), Marquad (1560–83), and Eberhard (1583–1610). GLA 67/318, 423, 424. From 1549 to 1583, twenty-four such oaths are recorded for clerics, with twenty-eight during the years 1583–1610. See also Forster, *Counter-Reformation*, 42–49, 77ff., and cf. similarly higher pre-Reformation average of 5 per year out of 450–600 clerics in the lower Rhine. See Josef Lohr, *Methodische kritische Beiträge zur Geschichte der Sittlichkeit der Klerus besonders der Erzdiözese Köln am Ausgang des Mittelalters* (Münster, 1910), 59ff.

[117] As in the continuing open concubinage of Johann Hurnlinger (11 November 1585; GLA 67/424, 20ʳ) and Pelagius Birchoff (29 May 1589; GLA 67/424, 31ᵛ) with their housekeepers. Both were arrested, temporarily suspended, and fined.

received the most consistent scrutiny and by the 1620s, according to Marc Forster, was completely eliminated in the diocese of Speyer.[118] In one extraordinary case, Frederick Cunzman, vicar of Saint Germain and Mauritius, was frequently warned but only ultimately arrested and punished after compiling an impressive list of offenses, including adultery and concubinage with the bellringer's wife, fathering two illegitimate children by the same, seducing another married woman after a clandestine feast during Lent, exchanging marriage vows with (and subsequently impregnating) a country maiden, frequent late-night parties with bad company, and – according to letters found in his room – still more instances of adultery and fornication. Cunzman's subsequent financial punishment[119] was admittedly harsh – particularly when compared with pre-Tridentine punishments – but how representative was it of Catholic enforcement overall? To answer that question, we must return to a broader scope of comparison.

Were Protestant secular authorities more active or successful than their Catholic counterparts in prosecuting marital offenses? Based on his comparative study of Reformed Basel and Catholic Freiburg, Thomas Safley argues that they were. Protestant and Catholic magistrates, according to Safley, "brought varying concerns and attitudes" to this area of social control and thus "took different actions in accordance with their religious convictions and the needs of their communities."[120] Not only did Protestant secular authorities expand the traditional scope of their prosecuting authority, but they acted quickly, decisively, and, concludes Safley, more effectively than their Catholic counterparts in all areas of marital regulation:

> Protestants could sweep aside the legal and institutional obstacles confronting Catholics. The reformers consolidated the regulation of mar-

---

[118] Forster, *Counter-Reformation*, 82, 89–93.

[119] After his arrest, Cunzman was held (perhaps ironically) in the nuns' cloister at Saint Martin's in Altspeyer before being tried by his own chapter (rather than the vicar-general). Based on his 1589 assessed value of 2,600 fl. and "etliche guld an vermöge," he was then ordered to pay the newly established fine of 10 marks silver for concubinage, settle with the bell ringer of Saint Martin and his wife as well as his two illegitimate children, write and compensate his country "wife" and her child, avoid all other women with whom he had had relations, "Unnd hab darauff desen alles zu noch mehrer sicherheit" to pay the sizable sum of 1,000 fl. as compensation to his fellow burghers, at a rate of 15 or 60 bazern (approximately 1–4 fl.) each, according to his property (28 August 1592; GLA 67/424, 47ʳ–52ᵛ).

[120] Safley, *Let No Man Put Asunder*, 1. While Protestants emphasized "communal peace and stability," the "limits in canon law and the concerns of the court . . . prevented any broader response to the marital problems of the faithful [by Catholic authorities]" (90).

riage, redefined the role of marriage within a Christian community, and established laws to transform reform into reality. The Catholic Church could not offer reforms commensurate with those of the Protestants. As a result, Protestants achieved a more comprehensive and effective regulation of marriage in early modern Europe.[121]

At the same time, however, Safley's own findings provide a less conclusive basis for his generalization than he suggests. The common presumption of an increase in litigation and prosecution only after the Reformation, for instance, is never substantiated by court protocols or police records. Nor is the much discussed decline in case volume of the Constance *Officialatus* after 1550 really as significant as the relatively long delay before any corresponding increase in the same volume of Basel's marriage court (1606) – a lacuna of more than eighty years after the introduction of the Reformation in the city. Moreover, because the vast majority of marital offenses had always been handled by local secular authorities, the enhancing effects of Basel's jurisdictional centralization remain far from obvious. In fact, when prosecution of marital offenses alone is considered, the Catholic city actually had a much higher annual rate (12.02) than its larger Protestant neighbor (5.43).[122]

What are we to make of such conflicting data? Unfortunately, the sparse records of Palatinate authorities before and after the Reformation provide little basis for a thorough quantitative comparison. Local consistories of the Elector and Zweibrücken, for instance, appear to have taken an active role in disciplining marital behavior but whether this was significantly different from their Catholic predecessors or contemporaries is unclear. The same holds true for the very incomplete records of Speyer's criminal court, which are equally inconclusive on the question of increased prosecution with the onset of reformed teachings. Only the Prince-Bishop's Privy Council shows clear signs of increased persecution from the 1580s on, but even this probably represents a decline in local authorities' autonomy rather than a new intensity of prosecution.[123] An increase in both Protestant and Catholic prosecution in this

---

[121] Ibid., 195.

[122] Safley ingeniously turns the higher prosecution rate of Freiburg into a point in Basel's favor: "That extramarital relations were prosecuted more frequently in Freiburg than in Basel may reflect the dissatisfaction of the Catholic laity with the legal means at their disposal to rectify marital dysfunction"–in effect, the magistrates of Basel were that much more successful in *preventing* instances of adultery than those of Freiburg. Ibid., 185.

[123] Until the episcopacy of reform bishop Eberhard (1581–1610), the *Hofrat* served almost exclu-

area does seem likely, especially in view of Van Dülmen's dramatic findings for all criminal prosecution of the period,[124] yet the precise degree of such an increase in the Palatinate is impossible to establish.

On way to circumvent the dearth of relevant statistics is by examining the one aspect of prosecution that is well documented enough to permit comparison, namely the means of legal initiation. Despite the undeniable influence of Canon and Roman law by this time, prosecution of marital offenses at the local level remained largely unchanged from medieval times. In other words, the only offenses even considered by most secular authorities were those brought before them by a direct accuser or general "hue and cry" (*Notruf*). Except for the morals police of a few Swiss and imperial cities, German states possessed no equivalent of the French courts' *promoteur* to detect crimes.[125] Contrary to the common stereotype of official surveillance, all German authorities of the late sixteenth century (including Calvinists) displayed the same hesitance to transgress the traditional boundary between house and community both figuratively and literally represented by the front door's threshold. In the Electorate, for instance, only the husband of an adulterous wife could bring suit against her.[126] Unless an offense could be consid-

---

sively as a court of appeals. Its assumption of adultery and other previously local litigation was part of an overall administrative centralization initiated by Eberhard and his vicar-general, Beatus Moses. See Chapter 3.

[124] The findings of Van Dülmen's *Theater des Schreckens* on general criminal prosecution in several German cities (Frankfurt, Nuremberg, Breslau, Augsburg, Mecheln, and Zurich) suggest a peak both in rate and severity of prosecution during the second half of the sixteenth century, with a notable decline in the same two areas during the next hundred years. Cf. 47, 62ff., 113ff., especially tables 4–8.

Michael Weisser (*Crime and Punishment in Early Modern Europe* [Sussex, 1979], 77ff.) notes a similar increase in both reported crimes and executions throughout sixteenth-century Europe, particularly England.

[125] Cf. Lefebvre-Teillard, *Les Officialités*, 34, 179ff., and Fournier, *Les Officialités*, 29ff., on the role of the French *promoteur* in marital and adultery litigation. Even in the eighteenth century, though, France maintained only 3,882 members of the rural police force (*maré chausée*) to perform such a function for all of the kingdom, and 468 of these were senior administrators (Lenman and Parker, "The State, the Community, and the Criminal in Early Modern Europe," 19). See also the dramatic expansion of the role of the English J.P. in cases before common pleas courts from 1490 (2,100) to 1606 (23,453) (Lenman and Parker, 16).

Even the *Ehegaumer* of Zurich's *Ehegericht* functioned more like traditional jurors or church wardens in bringing cases to the court's attention (Kilchenmann, *Die Organisation des Zürcherischen Ehegerichts*, 48–76). On the relatively active role of some German and Swiss municipal morals police in this respect, especially in Basel, Ulm, and Strasbourg, see H. Planitz, *Grundlagen des deutschen Arrestprozesses* (Leipzig, 1922); Kö II:3–6, 146–47, 236–37, 360.

[126] 1563 *EGO*; *EKO* 310. This right, however, did not extend equally to the wife of an adulterous man.

ered "open, undoubted and scandalous," as in concubinage and out-of-wedlock pregnancies, public officials preferred to leave it within the "realm of honor" (i.e., the patriarchal household) or the local community at large and its own coercive techniques of shame and violence, such as charivari.[127] In a typical case, Stephan Müller of Bacharach was brought by public outcry before the consistory for adultery with his maid, but in the absence of any proof, he received merely a stern admonishment to dismiss the accused woman and was sent home.[128]

The primary and often exclusive prompters to official action remained suspicious pregnancies and illegitimate births, all closely monitored by local authorities in the Palatinate.[129] Bailiffs investigated every rumor of out-of-wedlock pregnancy and some pastors even refused to marry visibly pregnant women without government approval.[130] Some German towns such as Strasbourg and Nuremberg provided housing for unwed mothers and their children while the town council attempted to track down fathers and secure financial support.[131] In the Rhineland-Palatinate, the consistory of Zweibrücken prosecuted 106 cases of fornication and illegitimate births from 1558 to 1589, including 13 denials of paternity.[132] If the birth was the result of an "unequal" union (e.g., employer and maid) or – as was especially common among itinerant shepherds and soldiers – a pregnant woman could not produce a father to regularize the union, she and her baby then risked all the legal and moral vilification reserved for prostitutes and bastards.

---

[127] Quoted from the *Bambergensis* (1507) in Harvey, "Nürnberg Marriage Laws," 117. Imperial police ordinances of 1530, 1548 (tit. 25 § 2) and 1577 (tit. 26 § 2) all recommend the same restraint by authorities in adultery cases except in cases of open and continuous concubinage. Cf. Segall, *Geschichte und Strafrecht der Reichspolizeiordnungen von 1530, 1548, und 1577;* and Lieberwirth, "Ehebruch," in *HRG* 1:839.

On authorities' continuing preference for out-of-court settlements and deals ("composition"), see Roper, *Holy Household,* 198ff.; and Weisser, *Crime and Punishment* 20ff.

On the *Bereich des Ehres* in early modern German society, see Heidrich, "Grenzübergänge," 17–41; and Van Dülmen, *Theater des Schreckens,* 8, 13ff.; and Amussen, *An Ordered Society,* 96ff. On communal coercion and disciplining, see K.-S. Kramer, "Rügerbräuche," in *HRG* 4:1198–99.

[128] 7 May 1605; AEKK 125/2, 325. Cf. similar findings of Bernhard Müller-Würthmann, "Raufhändel: Gewalt und Ehre im Dorf" in *Die Kultur der einfachen Leute,* ed., Richard Van Dülmen (Munich, 1983), 79–111, where all but one of twenty-six cases before the Starnberger *Landgericht* during 1593–94 were initiated by complaint rather than *ex officio* action.

[129] The figures are 32–49 percent of 62 total *Hofrat* adultery convictions (51.6–79 percent).

[130] Cf. Reformed pastors of Rehborn and Germersheim (Vogler II:1007).

[131] Wiesner, *Working Women,* 43; most, though, were still imprisoned or expelled soon after the birth.

[132] Vogler II:994, 1006, 1009ff.

Illegitimate children had always faced legal discrimination, but the late fifteenth and early sixteenth centuries were particularly harsh.[133] During this time, many secular authorities not only refused to recognize the legitimization procedure offered by the Church, but extended the social stigma of bastards as well. An unpublished ordinance of the Elector in 1587, for instance, affirmed that even if baptized, illegitimate babies were condemned to Hell.[134] Mindful of the desperate quandary often connected to such pregnancies, many secular authorities therefore also treated all reports of stillborn births and secret burials as potential infanticide cases. In France, Henri II ordered all infant deaths following clandestine pregnancies and burials to be presumed homicides and punished accordingly.[135] The same presumption of guilt until proof of innocence appears to have prevailed in Germany as well, where infanticide prosecution also increased dramatically in the sixteenth and seventeenth centuries.[136] In two unrelated Privy Council cases of suspected infanticide in 1618 and 1620, both Catherine Drerlich and Appolonia Dietz, after extensive interrogation and witness testimony, were cleared of any wrongdoing yet still exiled from the bishopric.[137]

As a whole, though, the nature of official inquiry remained over-

---

[133] Cf. case of Katharina Franz Zimmermans tochter, imprisoned twice within five years for fornication and having illegitimate children (22 April 1604; AEKK 125/2, 312). Illegitimacy was punished through the Rhineland by fines and/or imprisonment: usually fewer than 10 fl (5 pound *Heller* in the city of Speyer) and immediate solemnization of the union (if possible) constituted the official remedy. StAS IA/12, 284ʳ.

[134] Cited in Vogler II:1009. The consistorial records of Bacharach include only four such baptisms from 1585 to 1623 (AEKK 125/2, 415). See also Brundage, *Law, Sex, and Christian Society*, 543ff.

[135] Natalie Zemon Davis, *Fiction in the Archives: Pardon Tales and Their Tellers in Sixteenth-Century France* (Stanford, 1987), 86, 193–95. Enforcement of the 1556–57 edict was apparently much more rigid than that of other capital offenses. In a study of over 200 appeals of infanticide verdicts to the Parlement of Paris, Alfred Soman ("Les procès de sorcellerie au Parlment de Paris [1565–1640]," *Annales* 32 [1977], 797) finds that two-thirds of the women were still condemned to death. William Monter's comparison of female executions for infanticide (25 of 31 convictions) to those for witchcraft (19 of 122) in Geneva, 1592–1712, reflects a similar rigidification of punishment in this area; see "Women in Calvinist Geneva," *Signs* 6/2 (1980), 189–209. See also Richard Van Dülmen, *Frauen vor Gericht. Kindsmord in der Frühen Neuzeit* (Frankfurt, 1991).

[136] Convictions in Nuremberg, for example, increased from a total of four in 1500–50, to twenty in 1550–1600, twenty-one in 1600–50, before again shrinking to six in 1650–1700 (Hsia, *Social Discipline*, 144–45). Cf. also Wiesner, *Working Women*, 70–72, on the role of midwives in this respect.

[137] Catharina Salamon Drerlich zu Landthausens tochter: 2 April 1618; GLA 61/11497, 39ᵛ–40ʳ. Appolonia Dietz von Schleittal: 21 and 28 February, 19 March 1620; GLA 11497c, 23, 25, 31. Both sentences, however, were reduced upon appeal: Dietz's to two years' banishment (still more than the fine issued the father of the child) and Drerlich's to an oath.

whelmingly reactive. Even in the less frequent petitions for action from angered spouses or children, suspected adulterers could only be convicted by public proof (i.e., pregnancy or several witnesses) or their own admission of guilt,[138] thus reinforcing traditional reliance on private retribution. Philip Düttelsheimer's suspicion of his wife's adultery, for instance, came to the attention of the bailiff of Bacharach only after the accused lover, Johann Schmidt the elder, filed assault charges against the outraged husband. Düttelsheimer denied the charge and produced two witnesses in his defense, but the bailiff decided for the visibly beaten plaintiff and, at the same time, ordered the husband to prove his allegation of adultery within one month or drop the matter.[139]

Most of the continued resistance to more active prosecution of marital and other offenses also stemmed, of course, from structural limitations of the legal institutions themselves. In most polities of early modern Germany, as we have seen in Chapter 3, "prison sentences were unknown and police supervision or control unworkable."[140] Larger principalities faced even greater obstacles, with moral and legal enforcement dispersed among a variety of local and regional authorities, most operating independently and occasionally even in competition with one another. Visitations by ecclesiastical inspectors of all three confessions provided some semblance of legal uniformity throughout their respective realms, but occurred too sporadically to alter dramatically much customary practice, especially in such thoroughly traditional issues as the prosecution of adultery.

As we have also seen in Chapter 3, only city-states and small territorial states were capable at this time of even conceiving of the kind of comprehensive legal reform and increased bureaucratic centralization required to ensure greater control, and even this was slow to develop. With

---

[138] From the Elector's 1563 *EGO:* "Der ehebruch wirt nit allein beweisen, wann zway mit der that beyeinander in unzucht ergriffen, gefunden oder gesehen werden, sondern auch aus stadtlichen und unzweifelhaften vermutungen, als nemblich, wann zwey oft an heimlichen, verporgenen und zu sochen verpotenen lastern bequemen orten, auch zu sondern stunden, bevorab wann einem ein, zwey, oder drey solchs undersagt oder zu entpoten worder, sich einer sollichen argwöhnischen zusammenkhunft zu mussigen, durch welche presumptiones, die man violentas nennet, vermug der kayserlichen rechten, darbey wir es auch in diesem fall bleiben lassen, der ehebruch ganugsam bewiessen werdern khann." *EKO,* 321–322.

See Weisser, *Crime and Punishment,* 72ff., on the difficulty of securing criminal proof in early modern Europe.

[139] 30 June 1613; LAK 4/1631, 215ʳ.   [140] Van Dülmen, *Theater des Schreckens,* 8.

the exception of extraordinary cases of incest and bestiality,[141] for example, the records of our sample rarely even suggest the use of inquisitorial methods to obtain confessions of guilt. Even in those few cases where the town council of Speyer felt compelled "by office and magistracy" to initiate an investigation of accused adultery, it was with much apparent reluctance and repeated written justification of the action. In the 1597 adultery case of Wolff Rosenfeld and Wolf Schwarz's wife, only after a detailed and unsolicited statement by Rosenfeld's servant did municipal authorities feel justified to initiate interrogation and, even then, a unanimous verdict from the entire town council was required for conviction.[142]

Beyond simple procedural limitations, though, sixteenth-century prosecution of marital offenses remained fundamentally hampered by a more profound inability or unwillingness to move beyond traditional communal concepts of justice and punishment. Contrary to the state-building standard of a uniform code classified by crime, local secular authorities continued to fit punishments to the criminal, thus perpetuating subjective judgments based on social status and gender. Moreover, in keeping with their extremely conservative agenda, Protestant and Catholic legal reforms not only supported traditional *Gemeinschaft* double standards but made the dividing lines even more rigid. Already in the late fifteenth and early sixteenth centuries, many German cities, including Speyer, had begun stricter enforcement of the traditional dress codes of clearly defined social status. Similar to a contemporary yellow star requirement for Jews, for instance,[143] secular authorities ordered all prostitutes to wear broad green stripes or red berets at all times for ready identification as "dishonorable" individuals.[144] "Common women" such as Elisabeth Reudel of Speyer who brazenly defied the visible boundary

---

[141] See my subsequent discussion.

[142] 3 January 1597; StAS IB/8, Bd.2, 128ʳ–130ʳ. "Hatt ein Rhat von ampts weg. Eod. (Rosenfeld) laßen darin zu Inquiciscion." Rosenfeld was ultimately tried and found guilty before a meeting of the entire *Rat*.

[143] The requirement of distinctive dress for Jews actually dates back at least to canon 68 of Lateran IV (1215); Paul Guèrin, *Les conciles gènèraux et particuliers*, vol. II (681–1326), 3rd ed. (Paris, 1897), 424.

[144] Other "marks of infamy" for prostitutes included yellow trim (Frankfurt), bonnets (Hamburg), black and white hats (Strasbourg), and in Vienna a yellow patch "a hand wide and a span long." See Block, *Die Prostitution*, I:814ff.; Brundage, *Law, Sex, and Christian Society*, 524ff.; and Wiesner, *Working Women*, 103–04.

of honor by copulating in the bride's wreath (symbolizing virginity and respectability) were imprisoned, flogged, and banished wearing the equally symbolic straw wreath of shame[145] (see Figure 7b).

In such a morally charged atmosphere, the social and legal status of all women remained especially precarious. Similar to contemporary accusations of witchcraft, sexual "ill-fame" of any kind could destroy even the purest of reputations.[146] Married women, as suggested by the relatively low rate of adultery prosecutions, appear to have fared better but were by no means above constant surveillance and suspicion. In 1575, a Diffenbach woman was summoned before the local consistory because of her "shameful whorish" vocabulary and "sodomist, whorish disposition" but dismissed because of lack of solid evidence.[147] Widows, as women living "under their own smoke," were apparently particularly susceptible to rumors and accusations of impropriety, with almost every suspicious house visit reported to local authorities.[148] A widow of Bacharach was questioned and imprisoned in 1613 on the basis of her comportment "as a common whore": going out late at night on back roads with frivolous company and – more suspiciously – turning away a suitor whom she considered "too pious."[149]

[145] 30 January 1577; StAS IA/705, 6ʳ. Cf. 1514 ordinance of Nuremberg to same effect (Harvey, "Nürnberg Marriage Laws," 125); and see H. Moser, "Jungfernkranz und Strohkranz," in *Das Recht der kleinen Leute. Festschrift für Sigismund Kramer*, ed. Konrad Köstlin and Kai Detlev Sievers (Berlin, 1976), 140–61; and Roper, *Holy Household*, 143–44.

[146] See 1563 *EGO* (*EKO* 308) on inquiries about female reputations; also Roper, "Prostitution," 94–95, on the gender double standard in this respect. Weisser, ("Crime and Punishment in Early Modern Spain," in *Crime and Punishment*, 94) notes that in the villages of Castille, accusations of prostitution were much more common among unpopular women than charges of witchcraft.

[147] HStAMü II/K.b. 390/1c, 607ᵛ, 614ʳ. Cf. similar concerns of contemporary Calvinists of the French Midi, where 21 percent of all synodal regulations concerned feminine "frivolity" in appearance. J. Garrison-Estèbe, *Protestants du Midi, 1559–1598* (Toulouse, 1980), 306.

[148] Cf. case of Christoff Berkin's widow (5 March 1577; StAS IA/705, 8ʳ), summoned before the *Vierrichter* of Speyer "weg. verdechtigen zugangs in Georg Glorkens haus und ueberstendig und komen herren Burgermeister fernutz Permienteren gewachen," though subsequently released on her oath. The widow of the Bacharach schoolmaster, Phillip Wagner, faced similar rumors in 1598 (Schüler, *Die Konventsprotokolle*, 96). See Wiesner, *Working Women*, 6ff., 190ff.; and Roper, *Holy Household*, 49–54, on "masterless" women in sixteenth-century Germany; also Roper, "'Willie' und 'Ehre': Sexualität, Sprache, und Macht in Augsburger Kriminalprozessen," in Wunder and Vanja, *Wandel der Geschlechterbeziehungen*, 191–93, on the question of female honor.

[149] 8 February 1613, 21 February 1613; AEKK 125/2, 371–72; also LAK 4/1631, 211ʳ⁻ᵛ, 242ᵛ. Otilia Lindaman, it should be noted, was later convicted of fornication with the notorious Arnoldt Chur (5 October 1613; AEKK 125/2, 375); see also Chapter 4 for my comments on a broken engagement with *Schulteiß*'s son. Cf. a similar case before the *Vierrichter* of Hans von der Strassen's widow, accused of "ubel haushaltens mit Jungen leuthen" and given eight days to

Women outside of marriage faced an even stricter double standard. Whereas fornication by single men was generally dismissed by secular authorities with an oath, the same act by single women put them in the legal as well as moral category of "whores," subject to the usual flogging and banishment.[150] According to a contemporary Neuchâtel legal formula:

> A girl will be considered a virgin if she has good morals and a good reputation without any suspicion, and if she does not give in to the will of a young man unless he had first promised her faith of marriage in the presence of at least two honorable witnesses.[151]

Any accusation of multiple partners made maids and other marginal women particularly vulnerable to the prostitute classification. Once Hans Schorr had convinced authorities that the maid he had impregnated was "a common whore who had also carried on with others," his fine was reduced and "this strumpet" banished.[152] Anna Hempl accused with another woman in 1577 of sleeping with three men in the city of Speyer's Predigerkloster, was similarly classified by the court as a "whore" despite her long-standing employment as a maid at the cloister.[153] Moreover, since such "common women" could not "legally" be raped in many German cities, Hempl's counteraccusation of rape and defloration by the cloister's married organist was summarily dismissed by the magistrates as irrelevant; she (though curiously not her companion) was subsequently flogged and banished while all men connected to the incident were released on oath.[154] Another man tried the same year

---

get rid of them (24 July 1577; StAS IA/705, 11v); also Steffan Müller's widow, accused of behaving "wie ein gemein dirn" (3 April 1614; AEKK 125/2, 377).

[150] German authorities show no evidence of recognizing a sexual "gray area" between prostitution and marriage for women as Ruggiero finds among Venetian magistrates (*The Boundaries of Eros*, 153ff.). Cf. Roper, "Prostitution," 10ff., and my subsequent comments on general classification of *unzuchtige* women as *dirne*.

[151] Watt, *Making of Modern Marriage*, 90–91. Cf. the related custom of the bridal examination administered by the Zurich *Ehegericht* fourteen days before a wedding (Kö I:103–4; also 1439 customary in Grimm I:14).

[152] 22 September 1608; GLA 61/11496, 177r.

[153] 8 March 1577; StAS IA/705, 8r. The full charge against Hemplin included much guilt by association – "das sie ein zeitlang mit gemein Metzen umbgezogen, In Unzucht gelebt, nochmals Im Prediger Kloster kamen, Bei dem Jungen und zweien Conventualn auch geschlaffen . . ." – despite the court's own acknowledgment of her virginity before this incident!

[154] Wiland Jung, the organist, had already (2 March) been summoned on such charges and released upon oath, but was again briefly imprisoned after Hemplin's charge on her 8 March arrest that "doch anderlich vorgeb. mehrgemellter Organist hab Ihr [Hemplin] die Jungfrawschafft genommen und genotzuchtigt, do er doch vorhin ein ehefraw hatt" – presumably more for the adultery than the rape. There is no further mention of Jung in the protocols. StAS IA/705, 7v–8r.

for attempted rape of "a maid" was released on oath by Speyer's magistrates merely on the condition that he ask her pardon for the offense.[155] The crime of rape itself, while defined by the *Carolina* (article 119) as capital offense, was in practice much less severely punished, if it was even prosecuted, by secular authorities in Germany.[156] A 1537 Augsburg ordinance officially sanctioned such laxity, simultaneously demoting rape from a violent to a sexual offense and invalidating all cases where the judges considered the plaintiff to have provided any encouragement "by word or deed."[157] As Lyndal Roper concludes, it is difficult to argue that the theoretical equality of genders espoused by Protestant reformers had any more of a social impact than similar egalitarian implications of a "priesthood of all believers."

> The Reformation, which seemed at first to offer a sexual ethic identical for men and women, and appeared to bestow a new dignity on the married wife, suspected all women, single or married, of being ever ready to surrender themselves to their lust for debauchery.[158]

Only one category of sexual offense appears to have been consistently punished the same by secular authorities regardless of social status or gender, namely, those "crimes against the order of Nature" traditionally considered the most abhorrent: incest, homosexuality, and bestiality. All three, in keeping with Mosaic, Germanic, and imperial law were considered capital offenses.[159] Usually, as in the incest case of Matthias Seitz and his mother-in-law Agatha von Fenberg, the man was hanged "from the gallows at daybreak" and the woman condemned "from life to death

---

On the legal status of prostitutes in late medieval Europe, see Brundage, *Law, Sex, and Christian Society*, 529ff.

155 18 August 1576; StAS IA/705, 2ᵛ.

156 Cf. Allen, "Crime and Punishment," 258, 277 n. 79; Strasbourg ordinance in Kö II:363; and Brundage, *Law, Sex, and Christian Society*, 530ff. In fact, Rossiaud (*Medieval Prostitution*, 11–30) sees the rape act (particularly gang rape) as an integral part of male sexual initiation, and Ruggiero even argues that "from rape to fornication to marriage appears to have been a relatively common progression" (*The Boundaries of Eros*, 31). Cf. German literary treatment of rape and its relation to social status in Wiltenburg, *Disorderly Women*, 223ff.

157 Roper, *Holy Household*, 83–84. The only exception I have yet found in Germany is Nuremberg, which executed six rapists between 1600 and 1692 (also encompassing the Thirty Years' War, it should be noted). (Van Dülmen, *Theater des Schreckens*, 94, table 5.)

158 Roper, "Prostitution," 21.

159 Articles 116 and 117 of *Carolina*, Lev. 20:11–21; and on Germanic customary law, see Harster, *Strafrecht*, 185, and Brundage, *Law, Sex, and Christian Society*, 533ff. In some cities, however, such as Reutlingen, incest was often punished only with fines and banishment (Allen, "Crime and Punishment," 256–57). Cf. similar lenient punishment described by Ingram in England (*Church Courts, Sex, and Marriage*, 245–49).

by [drowning]."[160] In cases of bestiality and sodomy (both considered crimes against God as well as nature), authorities also followed the traditional gender distinction, burning male offenders and drowning their female counterparts.[161] Yet even here, the system was not without its checks for protecting the community's interests. In 1608, for instance, the Prince-Bishop's Privy Council only banished Stoffel Hertzog for his incestuous and adulterous relations with his wife's sister while simultaneously executing the sister-in-law. Two years later he was even readmitted to the Prince-Bishopric after persistent petitioning "by the entire community, including the dean and chapter of Bruchsal" (and spending eight days in the tower on bread and water).[162] The apparent significance of Hertzog's social status in both acts of clemency leads us to the one area of judicial discretion in punishment not yet discussed – appeal.

As in Hertzog's case, the court's decision to judge by the letter of the law (*nach strengem Recht*) or with mercy (*nach Gnade*) represented the final appraisal of the offender's value to the community and could literally make the difference between life and death. Many offenders, consequently, made the most of their marital and familial ties and obligations in order to mitigate their sentences. Sara Mayer, the wife of Adam Echenlaub, and Georg Bracken, the hangman of Ubstatt, each made enough of an issue of their "small children" to obtain significantly reduced sentences from the Privy Council.[163] Spouses, parents, and assorted relatives also interceded frequently, usually with good results.[164] The same was true of influential friends, government employees, and

---

[160] 21–22 June 1577; StAS IA/705, 10ᵛ. Incestuous relations between relatives by marriage, especially stepfathers and their wives' daughters, was apparently the most frequent kind of incestuous adultery in the Palatinate. Unlike Italy and France, though, where fines, corporal punishment, and banishment were the usual punishments (Ruggiero, *The Boundaries of Eros*, 42ff.; Brundage, *Law, Sex, and Christian Society*, 534–35), such offenses in Germany almost always resulted in execution. Cf. cases cited by Vogler II:1011; Nopp, *Philippsburg*, 85ff.; and Van Dülmen, *Theater des Schreckens*, 190–93, tables 4 and 5.

[161] Cf. cases of the *Vierrichter* (Harster 66ff., 184–85); *Landgericht* of Udenheim (Nopp, *Philippsburg*, 103); and *Hofrat* (GLA 61/11497, 147ʳ⁻ᵛ, 157ᵛ–158ʳ); Roper, *Holy Household*, 255–58; also Ruggiero, *The Boundaries of Eros*, 109–45.

[162] 3 October 1608 and 3 February 1610; GLA 61/11496, 177ᵛ, 212ʳ. Cf. similar leniency in the 1579 incestuous adultery case of a woman of Knaudenheim and her husband's brother, sentenced by Udenheim authorities to flogging and banishment only (Nopp, *Philippsburg*, 86).

[163] GLA 61/11495a, 14ᵛ–15ʳ; GLA 61/11496, 73ᵛ, 85ᵛ–86ʳ; GLA 61/11497, 113ᵛ–114ʳ, 116ʳ, 117ʳ).

[164] Usually the relative was specified (e.g. "in ansehung seines alt vatter"), but occasionally an appeal was granted simply "in ansehung der eheliche freundschaft." GLA 61/11495, 83ʳ, 87ᵛ–88ʳ, 94ʳ⁻ᵛ; GLA 61/11496, 110ʳ, 322ʳ; GLA 61/11497, 46ᵛ.

almost anyone else willing to act as a character witness, including in one case "an old, decrepit maid . . . long in [the guilty party's] employ."[165] As long as the reputation and social value of the offender could be affirmed, some degree of clemency was almost certain.

Among members of the community, age and financial resources could also provide grounds for leniency by the court. Adulterers Georg Ehem and Georg Franck, for instance, were both immediately released from custody and the usual public penance on account of their "advanced age" (in Franck's case seventy years old).[166] Authorities also generally showed clemency to offenders who claimed insufficient means of support, though only after some rudimentary investigation and financial assessment.[167] Steffan Bugler, the miller of Waldhambach, attained a reduction of his adultery fine and penance "on the grounds that he was loaded with debts" and because the Privy Council did not with to punish his innocent wife and children. When, however, authorities subsequently learned that Bugler's assets were much greater than he pretended, the original fine of 300 gulden was restored and the miller imprisoned until his debt was paid.[168] Other abuses of the clemency procedure, if discovered by authorities, were punished with similar dispatch and severity.[169]

---

165 17 February 1609; GLA 61/11496, 184ᵛ–185ʳ. See also instances of intercession by a well-placed friend (23 February 1598; GLA 61/11495, 127ʳ) and even by the *fauth* himself (22 January 1606; GLA 61/11496, 110ʳ), probably a much more common occurrence than the records reflect.

166 26 September 1597; GLA 61/11495a, 32ʳ (Georg Ehem of Arzheim); and 10 July 1604; GLA 61/11496, 39ʳ (Georg Franck of Neigsheim). Both were released from the usual *kertzentrag* but not from their respective fines of 200 fl.

167 In the cases of Hans Helferich of Roth and shepherd Hartmann Becker of Dortheim, the *Hofrat* first ascertained that their respective assets were indeed "gering" before reducing their fines, twice in the latter's case (who repeatedly claimed to be "an gelt entpfrembt"). GLA 61/11495a, 105ᵛ; GLA 61/11496, 181ᵛ, 183ʳ.

168 3 July 1592; GLA 61/11495, 110ʳ. The original reduction from 300 to 200 fl. and the release from the *kertzentrag* came "uß ursach er mit schulden besterkt" and "dieweil des supplicant weib und kinder durch diß kertzentrag unschuldiger weiß auch gesherckt worden möcht." The court's subsequent discovery of Bugler's wealth is written in the margin and undated: ". . . hat es hernacher facta relatione gleichwol bey erlaßung des kertzentragens verplieben lasses aber soviel die geltstraff belangt db. der supplican in der fengnuß understenden außshublech und sich seines vielen gelt so sich berichnen die bestengte geltpon, der 300 fl. annachleslich zu bezahlen behanet darauff auch dem Amptman uff Magenburg der gestalt shriftlicher bevelch zufertigt . . ."

169 Occasionally, of course, authorities did err on the side of mercy. Cf. the case of the already banished Sebastian Silber of Joehlingen, granted temporary readmittance by the *Schultheiß-gericht* on 7 September 1574, permanent residence on 19 March 1575, and then expelled for new adulterous relations with Apollonia Größ on 28 May 1575 (also "ist bedeckt zu Abschlägy antworth zu geben"). GLA 61/10944, 142–43, 233, 259.

Overall, though, the use of appeal and clemency appears to have been both common and successful among the convicted adulterers and adulteresses of our study. Only four such appeals were refused outright by the Prince-Bishop's Privy Council, resulting in an 86.7 percent success rate in attaining some degree of sentence reduction.[170] The power to pardon, as many historians have pointed out, constituted an essential component of legal sovereignty and consequently was often exercised by political rulers of all kinds during the early modern period.[171] Yet, as in the original sentencing, the basis for judgment remained unshakably traditional – reputation and status in the *Gemeinschaft*. Significantly, almost all appeals in adultery cases came from within the "honorable" group, and exclusively from men. Whether marginal offenders saw no point in appealing or such requests were simply not recorded is open to speculation.[172]

In short, although Protestant and Catholic secular authorities may have supported reformers' calls for improved legal enforcement and prosecution of marital offenses, most were still unwilling or unable to make the basic institutional changes needed. Instead, they continued to rely on such traditional medieval practices as initiation by public outcry and even oath helping, investigating *ex officio* hesitantly if at all. While some quantitative increase in prosecution – among Catholics as well as Protestants – does appear likely during the sixteenth century, it is difficult to characterize this alone as "better" or "more effective" or even significantly different without some clearer evidence of deviation from previous practice.[173]

---

170 Of thirty appeals of *Hofrat* adultery convictions, twenty-six resulted in reduction or elimination of fines and/or other punishments. Reasons for refusal, as in Wolff Bertsel's appeal of a remarkable twelve-year *kertzentrag* sentence (31 October 1573; GLA 61/11494a, 50ʳ), are difficult to infer beyond the court's standard justification "damit ander darab ein exempel und beyspiel nehm. mog."

171 Cf. Davis, *Fiction in the Archives*, 52ff., 61ff., on use of clemency by political rulers of the period, and Van Dülmen, *Theater des Schreckens*, 46–48, on the power represented by reduction and pardoning of criminal sentences: ". . . so unterlag die konkrete Gerichtspraxis aufgrund des ausgebildeten Fürbittensystems doch wieder den sozial starken, lokalen Gruppen, die durch ehrbare Bürger, hochgestellte Geistliche und Adelige auf das Urteil einwirken konnten. . . . Wie mächtig ein Grundherr oder eine Zunft waren, zeigte sich nicht selten in ihrer Einfluß-möglichkeit auf Gerichtsurteil."

172 Paul Frauenstädt ("Drei Malefizbücher," *Zeitschrift für die gesamte Strafrechtswissenschaft* 23 [1903], 269–88) actually finds a hardening of summary judgment by social status and related decline of judicial mercy during the seventeenth century in Germany.

173 Cf. similar conclusions of Vogler II:1012ff.

Preservation

The third and ultimate goal in the sixteenth-century defense of marriage was preservation of existing unions. Prevention and prosecution of marital offenses remained crucial, but only inasmuch as they led to the reconciliation of estranged spouses and the restoration of marital stability. All official intervention was directed to this end, as was punishment of all disruptions of established marriages.

Of all the practices considered threatening to this marital stability, the one most feared by secular and religious authorities alike was that of private separation, usually in the form of malicious desertion, and often leading to concubinage or even bigamy. The Elector's marriage ordinance of 1563 typically lamented the multiple moral and legal woes produced by such "irresponsibility":

> Meanwhile, some men are so crazy and robbed of all human and fatherly sense that they take wives and stay with them for a while, seizing and enjoying all their worldly goods, even having children with them, before secretly deserting them or going off to war – out of sheer caprice and frivolity, without [the wives'] knowledge or approval, and often despite prohibition by the civil authority to whom they owe obedience and service. Thus the wives, with or without children, remain for many years without help or consolation, provided with nothing – against all that is just – pitifully left to ruin. Not only does this then lead to fornication among such wives, but sometimes even engagement and marriage, along with the great disputes, troubles, and terrible disturbances that necessarily follow.[174]

As in the instance of clandestine vows between minors, it was mainly the threat of social and legal anarchy represented by such "frivolous" individuals that both Protestant and Catholic marriage ordinances emphasized. And, once again, the significant distinction in denominational responses to the threat remained one of degree.

Most sixteenth-century authorities realized that the real enforcement problems posed by malicious desertion had less to do with punishing the guilty party than with preventing moral and legal anarchy in marriage. Often abandonment represented a kind of self-divorce for those unwilling or unable to continue cohabitation with their spouses. The reasons

[174] *EO* 1563; *EKO* 286. Cf. more indulgent description of deserting wives in the same ordinance (*EKO* 326).

given ranged from drunkenness and infidelity of a spouse to the simple exasperation of a deserting miller from Wolfenstein who in 1575 told his wife, "go find another knave to support you; I've done the best I can by you long enough."[175] Some were consensual separations, some temporary, but all were illegal. Unfortunately, since such separations almost invariably took the deserter out of the proper authorities' jurisdiction, the largely unpreventable offense was likewise unpunishable.[176]

Even more distressing and potentially explosive was the legal and moral quandary of the remaining spouse. All abandoned spouses were required by Canon law to wait at least seven years before their deserting husband or wife could be considered legally dead. Any sexual relations before the expired waiting period could be prosecuted as adultery and punished accordingly.[177] On the other hand, any attempt to legitimize such relations by a church ceremony or otherwise might be considered bigamy, a "much worse crime" than adultery according to the *Carolina*. Some received lenient treatment: The abandoned wife of mercenary Arnolt Stier received only a consistorial reprimand for her premature engagement and cohabitation, and Caspar Weber of Speyer was apprehended by the magistrates and similarly released on oath in 1577 before he could make good his bigamous vows.[178] Most others, however, were not as fortunate, consequently suffering flogging and banishment or, in at least one case, even death.[179] Still, just as for their deserting counter-

---

175 Vogler II:979. In his examination of divorce petitions to the consistory of Zweibrücken, Vogler finds grounds given for abandonment generally the same among both genders (physical or "spiritual" incompatibility) with the occasional exceptions among women of love for another man or merely a desire to wander (Vogler II:981–82).

176 Only if the spouse returned to the territory could he or she be prosecuted, and even then, as in two *Hofrat* cases (GLA 61/11495a, 14ᵛ–15ʳ; GLA 61/11496, 183ᵛ) authorities made no distinction from common adultery either in prosecution or punishment.

177 Cf. GLA 61/11496, 261ʳ, 306ᵛ; GLA 61/11497, 18ᵛ–19ʳ; and see my comments in Chapter 2.

178 2 January 1606; AEKK 125/2, 328. 19 November 1577; StAS IA/705, 13ʳ. Since she had waited only eight months after his departure and remarried "ohn gewissen grund seines todts," Stier's wife was ordered by the Bacharach consistory to separate from her new husband until she heard of Stier's fate. Cf. more serious cases of Niclaus Mangerin (22 March 1607) and Elisabeth Leyeindenkerin (31 August 1594) who each married knowing that their respective first spouses were still alive. AEKK 125/2, 259, 338.

  More often, bigamy cases involved the abandoning spouse remarrying in his or her new location, as in the cases of Lorenz Hopf from Newedorf in 1597, and Georg Geyer from Magdenburg in 1611 (GLA 61/11495a, 15ʳ; GLA 61/11496, 232ʳ).

179 While harsh, the usual punishment of flogging and banishment was still not as severe as the death penalty demanded by Lev. 20:10ff. and some Protestant pastors. The 1512 execution of a bigamous mason in Zweibrücken, for instance, and a similar execution in seventeenth-century Nuremberg appear to provide merely the exceptions that prove the rule (Vogler II:1011; Van Dülmen, *Theater des Schreckens*, table 5). Cf. Brundage, *Law, Sex, and Christian Society*, 539–42,

parts, the number of legally adulterous or bigamous spouses who were actually prosecuted probably represents but a small fraction of the real number of such self-divorces and remarriages occurring. Two married couples in Bacharach who privately agreed to separate were only summoned to the consistory and chastised when each of the remaining wives attempted to conduct business in her husband's absence.[180] When we consider, moreover, Hans Helferich's misguided appeal of his 1600 adultery conviction on the grounds that his wife had given him permission both to sleep with and to exchange vows with their maid,[181] it is obvious that canonical definitions of marital indissolubility had not yet permeated every level of society. Such at least was the conviction of reformers who remained convinced that desertion and self-divorce were clearly problems that would only grow worse unless authorities acted.

The response of the various secular authorities of the Palatinate was – as in control of the marriage procedure itself – a uniform one: intensification of bureaucratic enforcement. First and foremost, many local consistories and municipal authorities took the unprecedented step of more active intervention in cases of marital strife and potential desertion. While Safley's assertion that "Protestants took a much broader view of marital responsibilities than did Catholics"[182] remains questionable, there does appear to be some basis for differentiation in this area of enforcement. The elector's local presbytery in Bacharach, for instance, intervened at least 108 times (see Figure 8) in 64 cases of domestic discord from 1585 to 1619 (an annual average of 3.0), whereas the only record of official Catholic intervention in the bishopric consists of seven cases by the secular authority of Jöhlingen from 1563 to 1623 (.11 annually).[183] Confessional differences among municipal authorities, on

and Allen, "Crime and Punishment," 275–76 (esp. n. 61), on the variety of civil and ecclesiastical penalties for bigamy during this period.

[180] The *Zollschreiber* refused to let Rörich von Kaub's wife buy a horse without her husband present (20 November 1597; AEKK 125/2, 275), and Maria Maden informed the *Zollschreiber* that her husband had refused to pay a 500-fl. debt (9 October 1600; AEKK 125/2, 291). Both were referred to the consistory and ordered to reunite. Cf. similar illegal separation in Neuchâtel (Watt, *Making of Modern Marriage*, 152–54).

[181] 4 September 1600; GLA 61/11495a, 110v. Helferich's fine was reduced from 100 to 60 fl. in view of his "gering" assets, but his request to remarry was denied "als contra canonicum."

[182] Safley, *Let No Man Put Asunder*, 158, also 163ff.

[183] AEKK 125/2, 202–402. Indirect references to other interventions by the consistory (e.g., AEKK 125/2, 285) suggest that not all cases were recorded. For similar cases of the Jöhlingen *Vogtgericht* (a secular court, and therefore unequal comparison), see GLA 61/6981, 432–33, 440–41 and GLA 61/15536. I am indebted to Marc Forster for this last citation.

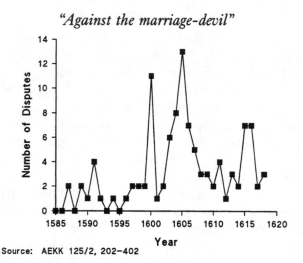

Source: AEKK 125/2, 202–402

Figure 8. Domestic disputes before the Bacharach consistory (Palatine-Electorate), 1585–1619

the other hand, were apparently much less pronounced in this respect, with the annual prosecution rate of Catholic Freiburg (1.7) comparable with that of Lutheran Speyer (1.5).[184]

More significant, the Reformed consistory of Bacharach displayed a striking sophistication in its approach to marital strife. Beyond simple warning or punishment of offenders, the ecclesiastical leaders of this community consistently sought the root of discord as well, attempting such remedy as was within their powers. Among more than half of the 64 couples summoned (37), the husband's behavior was singled out as the source of trouble, including overlapping references to excessive violence (29), drunkenness (12), physical absence (4), and general godless behavior (17). Wives fared somewhat better, designated the chief disruptors in only 8 cases, but they frequently shared the blame with their husbands

Cf. the average intervention rates of German Reformed consistories and those of their French and Swiss counterparts: .66 annually in Valangin (Neuchâtel), 23.2 in Cardaillac, 26.5 in Montauban, 50.33 in Geneva, and 55.9 in Meyrueis (Bernard Vogler and J. Estèbe, "La genèse d'une société protestante: Étude comparée de quelques registres consistoriaux langue-dociens et palatins vers 1600," *Annales* 31 (1976), 326ff.; Watt, *Making of Modern Marriage*, 149; Monter, "Women in Calvin's Geneva," 194).

[184] Figures are based on eighty-five cases of abuse prosecuted by the Freiburg magistracy from 1550 to 1600 (Safley, *Let No Man Put Asunder*, 117–18) and nine similar cases (five for wife beating, four for *Ubelhaushaltung*) of the *Vierrichter*, 1576–81 (StAS IA/705, 1ʳff.). See also Roper, *Holy Household*, 165–205, 256ff., on Augsburg.

on account of their nagging (12), swearing (9), drunkenness (2), or laziness (1). Indeed, the popular literary stereotypes of the hard-drinking, short-tempered husband and shrewish *böse Weib* found many real-life corollaries among the sparring couples of Bacharach. Usually men were cited more for physical abuse and women for verbal abuse, though one 1614 Bacharach case involved a woman who struck her smaller and weaker husband, ultimately "beating him with a pot at the market and throwing an iron at his head."[185] Several husbands received solemn lectures and even threats from consistory members on the virtue of restraint in drink and violence.[186] "Bitter" or "godless" wives, on the other hand, were more frequently admonished to curb their tongues and avoid provoking their husbands.[187]

Often the consistory's investigation moved beyond the couple's own disruptive behavior to a deeper conflict rooted in the extended family and its dynamics. In at least nine instances, ecclesiastical authorities traced marital discord back to ongoing and violent arguments with an in-law or blood relative.[188] Usually, as in the 1600 case of Anthes Podtz and his wife, the relative (in this case, the wife's father) was also summoned and asked to testify, before all three took traditional oaths to uphold their respective familial stations and keep the peace.[189] On other occasions, family members petitioned the consistory to effect reconciliation, as in the case of Philip and Anna Rommel, who had separated shortly after

---

[185] 16 January 1614; AEKK 125/2, 377. Cf. domestic violence cases of Zweibrücken, Bacharach, and Obermoschel in Vogler II:975ff.

[186] See Vogler and Estèbe, "La genèse d'une société protestante," 379ff., on the Reformed campaign against drunkenness in the Palatinate; and Roper, *Holy Household*, 182–85, on similar reform efforts in Augsburg. See also Hoffmann, *Hausväterliteratur*, 102ff. and 209ff., on polemical campaigns against the *Sauffteuffel*.

[187] See cases of Paul Thurm's wife (4 May and 15 June 1600), Suzanna Heitzent (24 May 1591), Margaretha Trier (19 August 1604), Katherina Kauber (20 June 1612); AEKK 125/2, 246, 288–89, 315, 366–67; also Hoffmann, *Hausväterliteratur*, 129–30, on bitter wives.

[188] Cf. problems with the wife's brother (17 October 1592), wife's mother (18 April 1602, 20 November 1608, 26 February 1615), wife's father (13 January 1600), husband's mother (17 June 1599, 4 March 1603, 14 July 1605), and both sets of parents (25 August 1594). AEKK 125/2, 249, 259, 281, 285, 300, 306, 324, 345, 380. Watt (*Making of Modern Marriage*, 151ff.) finds a similar concern with familial dynamics among the marriage judges of Neuchâtel.

[189] 13 January and 3 February 1600; AEKK 125/2, 285–86. Hans Krämer testified that his concern about mistreatment of his daughter had been answered by Podtz calling him "einen alten Lander, Böswicht, und Morder." Since previous imprisonment had made no difference, however, Krämer was satisfied with a promise of better treatment of his daughter; the consistory likewise forgave Podtz "in ansehung seines Jugent," and dismissed him after his oath.

their wedding and returned to their respective parents' homes.[190] Finally, in at least five instances, Church officials scolded quarreling couples for parental neglect and the other harmful effects of their squabbles on their children.[191] In short, the Reformed consistory of Bacharach clearly considered the connection between marital discord and larger disruptions as much a social reality as a polemical theme.

At the same time, such increased intervention remained necessarily limited in scope and effect. More than one out of three couples summoned by the Bacharach consistory appeared more than once, some more than five times.[192] Most cases were brought to the attention of authorities only after fights between married couples had become too loud and frequent for neighbors, as in the regular two-hour plus rows between Matthes Käßler and his wife.[193] In 1590, Michael Gross and his wife were summoned before the Zweibrücken consistory for such brutal and constant fighting that "even God in Heaven would weep . . . chasing one another out of the house and yard, cursing one another as 'thief' and 'murderer,' 'whore' and 'sorceress.'"[194] Sometimes official intervention resulted in successful reconciliation between spouses, as in as least eleven cases of the Bacharach consistory.[195] More often, though, mediation and sanctions simply proved too little too late. Like their pre-Reformation predecessors, local authorities had but two choices in cases of incompatibility: forced cohabitation or forced separation. With verdicts of the first kind – officially discouraged by the Elector's marriage ordinance[196] – desertion was clearly nourished rather than impeded by official efforts at reconciliation, as in the case of a Bacharach woman

---

190 6 April 1604; AEKK 125/2, 332. Anna accepted full responsibility on account of her "sehr stringen mutwilligen kopf," but also agreed to the consistory's suggestion of a six-month trial reconciliation. Cf. similar case of Jacob and Johanna Hutt (4 May 1617; AEKK 125/2, 388).

191 29 September 1589, 28 March 1591, 17 October 1592, 18 May 1600, 22 July 1609, 30 June 1615 (AEKK 125/2, 237, 244, 289, 349, 383).

192 Eleven couples were summoned twice, nine three times, one four times, and two more than five times.

193 3 August 1600; AEKK 125/2, 291.

194 Vogler II:977. Cf. similar cases of Paul Thurm and his wife who "roppfeln und schlagen tag und nacht" and "uff den gassen fluchen sehr" (5 July 1605; AEKK 125/2, 324). See also Sabean, *Production, Property, and Family,* 239–45 and 334–39, on the symbolism of abusive language in early modern Germany.

195 It is probably also significant that forty-two of the sixty-four couples (65.6 percent) were summoned only once.

196 1563 *EGO; EKO* 327.

who claimed to prefer eternal damnation to forced cohabitation with her husband.[197] The second kind of solution (forced separation) though officially sanctioned and more frequently applied,[198] was equally unsatisfactory in promoting marital stability and preventing adultery.

Significantly, few authorities, Protestant or Catholic, ever considered physical abuse in itself – except in life-threatening situations – as worthy of serious punishment. Seven of the nine cases of domestic violence in Speyer from 1579 to 1583, for instance, were dismissed by the magistrates with promises of improvement alone.[199] The more interventionist Reformed officials of Bacharach likewise usually threatened imprisonment only after a third summons, and even then appeared reluctant or unable to carry such threats out.[200] Relying almost exclusively on warnings and threats of excommunication to achieve their end,[201] ecclesiastical officials surely found the possibilities for significant behavior modification extremely limited, to say the least. Three ecclesiastical censures within four years, for instance, appear to have little deterred a brewer of Bacharach who continually beat his wife "not only with his fists but with large sticks, like a wild animal."[202] In one particularly infamous case, the oft-censured wife beater Bonificius Metzler eventually beat his wife to

---

[197] 24 May 1591; AEKK 125/2, 246. The woman was also found by the consistory, however, to be a "sehr gotloses weib." Cf. similar case of a Bacharach man imprisoned in 1611 for wife beating who, upon release, preferred jail to cohabitation with his wife (LAK 4/1631, 117).

[198] Cf. 1563 *EGO* (*EKO* 329), one-year separation "zu dische und Beth" by Speyer *Rat* for a case of wife beating (6 May 1598; StAS IB/6, Bd.1, 21ʳ), and other Protestant uses of canonical separation (formerly reserved for apostasy and malicious desertion). See E. Hubrich, *Das Recht der Ehescheidung in Deutschland* (Berlin, 1891), 36ff.; Günther Erbe, "Das Ehescheidungsrecht im Herzogtum Württemberg seit der Reformation," *Zeitschrift für Wüttembergische Landesgeschichte*, 14 (1955) 97–100; Watt, *Making of Modern Marriage*, 146ff.; and my discussion in Chapter 3.

[199] Georg Kirmer (19 June 1580; StAS IA/705, 26ʳ) was imprisoned briefly before being released on oath, and Martin Bronnern Plattnern (13 March 1581; STAS IA/705, 28ʳ⁻ᵛ) had "sein burgerrecht ufgesagt, mitt anzeig, das er sein nahrung anders wo suchen mögen." Cf. Roper, *Holy Household*, 171ff., 185–94, on similar lenient punishment of wife beating by the Augusburg magistracy.

[200] While at least nineteen cases were referred to the bailiff or *Zollschreiber*, the incomplete records of Bacharach provide only three mentions of imprisonment for wife beating in consistory protocols (AEKK 125/2, 286, 314, 371) and three references in the bailiff's records (LAK 4/1631, 235ᵛ, 236ᵛ, 237ᵛ).

[201] Although the Bacharach consistory began a more frequent application of excommunication from 1604 on, it never approached the level of the Geneva consistory and its 302 excommunications for domestic disputes during 1564–69 (Monter, "The Consistory of Geneva," 479–81).

[202] 7 May 1615, 16 June 1616, 22 February 1618 (AEKK 125/2, 382, 386, 392). An unrepentent Johann Scharlier, however, blamed his wife Eva entirely and said contemptuously of the magistrates "[weiss] ich nicht wz recht od. wz ich thun soll, so hat man doch gut recht alhie."

death in 1616.[203] Sometimes the perceived futility of the consistory's efforts even entered the official protocols, as in the secretary's weary assessment after one oath of improvement that such a change "was not even to be hoped for [in this case]."[204] A Bacharach woman, though, who returned on her own to the consistory to demand stricter punishment of her abusive husband was judged a "thoroughly bitter wife, without the slightest grounds," and "warned of her office and how she should behave."[205] A Nuremberg woman who similarly sued her husband for being "too rough" in bed was immediately imprisoned by the local town council as an example to all wives who questioned their husbands' authority within the household.[206] As much of the *Hausväterliteratur* taught, a "certain amount" of force and discipline was always within the husband's prerogative; total denial of such would risk emasculating the man and undermining the proper marital relationship.[207]

If for whatever reason desertion did occur, the remaining spouse was strictly enjoined from marrying, "much less sleeping with" a new partner, without consulting the secular authorities.[208] In the Electorate, both the abandoned party and the authorities were first to establish through a series of public inquiries and announcements that the missing spouse left "out of his own malicious caprice" and that his or her whereabouts was truly unknown. If, in the meantime, the guilty party returned, he or she was required to show "genuine and legitimate grounds" for the absence, or otherwise (if a man) forced to pay restitution and then banished.[209] If, as in at least five such cases in the Prince-Bishopric of Speyer, the deserting partner had also been guilty of adultery during the separation, he or she was punished in the usual manner.[210]

---

203 Metzler was summoned at least four times for wife beating (3 June 1603, 25 January 1605, 30 November 1606, 22 February 1607; AEKK 125/2, 306, 329, 334, 337) and subsequently tried and executed for the murder in 1616 (Schüler, *Die Konventsprotokolle*, 114).
204 5 May 1611; AEKK 125/2, 360. Peter Letar had been summoned for wife beating, drunkenness, swearing, and telling Jewish children that they could go to church.
205 4 May and 15 June 1600; AEKK 125/2, 288–89. Cf. LAK 4/1630, 74ʳ.
206 The same day, the Nuremberg town council passed a decree threatening the same to all other married couples who did not first attempt private reconciliation. Harvey, "Nürnberg Marriage Laws," 162. See a similar moral lesson in Hans Sachs, *Die Sieben Clagenden Weiber* (1531), in Edmund Goetze, ed., *Sämtliche Fabeln und Schwänke von Hans Sachs* (Halle, 1893), I:34–39.
207 See Chapter 2.
208 1563 *EO*; *EKO* 286. See also 1556 *Visitationsinstruktion* (*EKO*, 249); 1558 *Spezialsuperintendent instruktion* (*EKO* 259–60); and 1563 *EGO* (*EKO* 320ff.).
209 *EKO* 245, 259, 286; enforcement of this ordinance is unknown. Cf. general description of procedure in establishing abandonment in Hecker, "Ehescheidungsprozeß," in *HRG* 1:843.
210 GLA 67/11495a, 14ᵛ–15ʳ; GLA 61/11496, 261ʳ, 304ᵛ; GLA 61/11497, 18ᵛ–19ʳ, 23ᵛ.

In the event that secular and ecclesiastical authorities were unable to prevent or remedy a case of malicious desertion, Protestants introduced the measure of last resort (*ultima ratio*) to restore marital stability: remarriage of the remaining spouse. All agreed that the innocent spouse should not be "burdened by the guilty [person's] wickedness and forced to remain without marriage,"[211] but differed on the prerequisites for legal remarriage. In many Protestant territories, the canonical presumption of death after a waiting period of seven years was modified to allow relatively quicker remarriage of abandoned spouses, sometimes within one year of desertion.[212] In this sense, Protestant divorce represented what Roderick Phillips has characterized as a substitute death certificate.[213]

At the same time, all Protestant authorities displayed obvious apprehension about making divorce and remarriage too accessible. As in the only other generally accepted ground for official repudiation of vows, adultery, magistrates attempted to dissuade potential divorce plaintiffs as much as possible. Basel's marriage court judges, for instance, were explicitly directed to "allow divorce [only] with great difficulty and necessity, to prevent and hold it up as long as possible . . . and take all possible pains to prevent granting the divorce" – all through a combination of officially mediated attempts at reconciliation and intentional prolonging of the trial and expenses.[214] Judges in the Palatine-Electorate received similar instructions to exercise "great caution" and warn "both parties to consider their honor, children, and family" and the "shame and scandal" that a divorce might inflict upon all.[215]

Moreover, almost all sixteenth-century Protestant secular authorities

---

[211] 1556 *Kirchenordnung*; *EKO* 224.

[212] The main innovation was to distinguish between those often absent and others who probably were dead. (See Chapter 2.) In the Electorate, the waiting period was at least one year, with further extension left entirely to the discretion of the judges (and actual practice unknown). 1563 *EGO*; *EKO* 324–26. The Duchy of Württemberg adopted the same policy (Erbe, *Familen- und Erbrecht*, 106).

Cf. the waiting periods of three years in Zurich and Basel (one year for men), six or seven years in neighboring Zweibrücken, Württemberg, and Neuchâtel, and ten years[!] in Geneva, although after one year a wife could swear that she had absolutely no knowledge of her husband's whereabouts. Kö I:112–13, II:638; Staehlin, *Ehescheidung in Basel*, 29, 104–5, 111; Watt, *Making of Modern Marriage*, 145; Erbe, *Familen- und Erbrecht*, 107; Vogler II:970, 985.

[213] Phillips, *Putting Asunder*, 91.

[214] Staehlin, *Ehescheidung in Basel*, 64, 82. Cf., on the other hand, attempts at judicial expediency in the Electors' 1563 *EGO* (*EKO* 330–31).

[215] 1563 *EGO*; *EKO* 321.

(including the Electorate) rejected outright all other grounds for divorce and remarriage – including excessive abuse, insanity, and disease – as unbiblical and otherwise insufficient justification. The Elector's 1563 marriage ordinance also refused all divorce petitions where it was discovered that a spouse had given the other "advice, aid, or assistance" in adultery, and in cases of adultery by force (rape) or without the knowledge of the woman (confusion of identity).[216] Only the Reformed marriage courts of Basel and Neuchâtel, apparently, consistently granted divorces on grounds other than adultery or desertion, and all Protestant courts continued to issue trial separations and annulments.[217] Marriage, stated the Electoral marriage ordinance, had been ordained by God as an "indissoluble bond of souls, bodies, and goods," and those "wicked, discontented married couples [who] out of urging by Satan and evil meddling people . . . [bore] great jealousy, anger, hatred, and other ill will toward one another" should be legally separated, punished if applicable, and banished if necessary, but not divorced.[218]

Divorce, consequently, remained a relatively little exercised option among early modern Protestant authorities. Records of the Electorate and city of Speyer are unfortunately sparse in this area,[219] but other Reformed and Evangelical courts show a clear trend of considerable restraint (see Table 6). Reformed Zweibrücken and Neuchâtel, for instance, both only had annual divorce rates of .02 per 1,000 of general population, and even the most active sixteenth-century court – Basel – averaged only .57 (cf. the 1980 U.S. rate of 5.2).[220] On an individual basis, of course, there was at least the possibility of legal remarriage where there had not been before – a confessional distinction painfully apparent to Veronica Sulz after the Catholic Privy Council's rejection of

---

216 1563 *EGO* (*EKO* 322). The same reasoning held for insanity (since experts could not agree on a definition) and disease ("da alle zeit gute besserung zu hoffen und ein ehegemahl des andern creutz zu tragen, auch alle lieb, treu, und hulf zu beweisen schuldig ist."). *EKO* 223–25; 285ff; 320ff., and see my comments in Chapter 2.

217 Almost one-fifth of the divorces granted by the Reformed *Ehericter* of Basel (1529–1600) and Neuchâtel (1547–1706) were on grounds other than adultery. Based on slightly overlapping statistics of Staehlin, *Ehescheidung in Basel*, 181–98; Safley, *Let No Man Put Asunder*, 142, table 2; and Watt, *Making of Modern Marriage*, 121–24. See also Dieterich 69ff.

218 1563 *EO; EKO*, 284–85.

219 Except for an occasional excerpt from the city's *Ratsprotokolle* (e.g., StAS IB/6, Bd. II, 6ᵛ: 1597 appeal for divorce on grounds of desertion), we must rely on statuatory evidence alone for both principalities.

220 *World Almanac and Book of Facts 1989* (New York, 1989), 807.

Table 6. *Divorce rates in sixteenth-century Protestant courts*

Location (years)	Divorces granted	Annual % per 1,000 population
Zurich (1525–31)	28	.74
Basel (1525–92)	374	.57
Augsburg (1537–46)	86	.29
Württemberg (1544–47; 1567–90)	221	.02
Neuchâtel (1547–1706)	93	.02
Zweibrüken (1557–96)	57	.02
Geneva (1559–69)	3	.01

Sources: Kö I:413; Staehlin, *Ehescheidung,* 181–98; Safley, *Let No Man Put Assunder,* 167; Roper, *Holy Household,* 158; Erbe, "Das Ehescheidungsrecht," 115; Watt, *Making of Modern Marriage,* 123; Vogler II:986; Monter, "Consistory of Geneva," 476.

her husband's thirteen-year absence as sufficient basis for her new marriage to Georg Degen.[221] But among the general population, the threat of free and collusive self-divorce continued to be considered so great by Protestant authorities that they would not even consider allowing remarriage unless the innocent spouse was free of any suspicion and willing to endure a series of legal and financial obstacles intended to dissuade him or her from such a course.[222] Catholic or Protestant, reconciliation remained the foremost goal. Where respective authorities differed was only on those few cases that all confessions were willing to recognize as hopelessly irreconcilable.

What conclusions can we draw about marital discipline? First, the fiery rhetoric of moral reform preached by sixteenth-century leaders does indeed appear to have coincided with a universal increase in all criminal

---

[221] 2 January 1601; GLA 61/11495a, 108ʳ. Even though she claimed her husband had for thirteen years "in Niderland gewesen," Veronica Sulz's request for permission to exchange "die eheliche verspruchnuß mit dem kirchgang bestetig" with Georg Degen zu Odenheim was denied "wo aber die supplic. glaubliche urkind und kundschafft ferpring, daß ermelter Peter Sulz von todt abgang od. in krieg gliben stell iren als dem gebettener maß willfahret werden . . ."

[222] As Köhler reluctantly concludes, "Damit kehrte man zu dem ursprünglichen Gedanken zurück, der Glaubensdifferenz keinen Enfluß auf die Ehescheidung einzuräumen, vielmehr nach sonstigen Rechtsgründen (desertio vorab) zu strafen" (Kö I:138). Staehlin (*Ehescheidung in Basel,* 94) also points out that forbidding self-divorce did not always prevent the court from making it stand in cases where both had committed adultery, where the "guilty" party was defined as the first to do so.

prosecution. Whether both were merely symptomatic of larger demographic and economic pressures during the period is an issue less easily resolved. That prosecution rates of adultery and other marital crimes also increased appears likely but remains similarly difficult to prove in the case of the Palatinate and its legal authorities.

What is clear, however, is that differences between Protestant and Catholic legal treatment of marital offenses during this time were minimal, if any. Rather than applying a stricter absolute standard to all cases before them, the Lutheran magistrates of Speyer and Calvinist authorities of the Electorate, like their Catholic counterparts, continued to try and to punish adultery by the same traditional values of the *Gemeinschaft:* rarely initiating investigation or proceedings and sentencing by the same double standards of social utility. Moreover, in the heightened atmosphere of moral intolerance and suspicion that characterized all confessions at the time, the character of all women, particularly unmarried ones, was continually suspect, rendering them ever vulnerable to the same severe treatment usually reserved for "dishonorable" marginal individuals. Although the continued protective treatment of adulterous married women is difficult to establish on the basis of our small samples alone, obvious social discrimination in other areas of "public morality," such as prostitution and concubinage, suggests the same adherence to traditional standards among Protestants and Catholics. In other words, however sixteenth-century Protestants and Catholics chose to characterize the "Marriage-Devil," their moral and legal remedies were virtually identical: Prosecute when possible, punish and purge by social status, and, above all, restore the stability of existing marriages and the community as a whole.

Conclusions

Marriage represents one of the most fundamental links between the public and the private, between society and the individual. It is hardly a coincidence that sixteenth-century critics and twentieth-century historians alike have found it a useful and generally reliable gauge of early modern social tensions and changes. Unlike sixteenth-century observers, though, we often remain constrained by our teleological perspective – we know what happens next. Obviously modern Western marriage is quite a different customer from its medieval ancestor. Yet with our long-term hindsight, it is difficult to avoid casting such fundamental ideological and practical changes of marriage in terms of more general transformations of the same period. The changing concept of "society" itself, for instance, from the medieval village *Gemeinschaft* to the modern *Gesellschaft* with its nuclear family and State (later nation)[1] cannot help but color our interpretation of marriage reforms. How do we escape the teleological traps laid for us in such knowledge?

The best alternative, I hope the reader by now agrees, lies in adopting the perspective of sixteenth-century reformers themselves as much as possible. Like all reformers, they sought to reconcile an ideal with reality, in this case an essentially medieval and scholastic definition of marriage with an increasingly sophisticated and interconnected society. Like all human beings, they were largely the products of their environment, in this instance the university and public office, but also traditional and conservative cultures. Their goals were thus ostensibly conservative; their methods, on the other hand, somewhat innovative; their success

---

[1] See especially *A History of Private Life*, particularly vol. 3: *The Renaissance*.

273

mixed. Again, the key to this paradox lies in the long-term origins of the reforms themselves.

As we have seen, all sixteenth-century marriage reformers, regardless of confession, professed the same goal: better and increased legal enforcement of traditional Church teachings, with as few ideological and legal changes as possible. Their universally conservative agendas might be attributed to the very nature of all institutional power, but such a facile explanation does not address the apparently genuine aspirations of all marriage reformers for actual social transformation. Rather, we must look instead to the long-term religious "Reformation" described in Chapter 2, involving the twelfth-century introduction and gradual popular acceptance by the sixteenth century of the Church's definition of marriage as holy, consensual, and indissoluble. Protestant and Catholic marriage reformers differed on specific legal interpretations of this ideal – particularly the crucial definitions of "clandestinity" and "consent" – but unanimously accepted the essence of the canonical definition as well as the Church's role in protecting it. In view of the diversity and often irreconcilability of marital customs in late medieval Europe, the long process of acculturation to the new ecclesiastical definition of the most basic of social institutions was indeed a remarkably successful "Reformation."[2]

The immediate social significance of this ideological Reformation in terms of "confessional formation," however remains ambiguous. Certainly, legal reforms of all confessions on questions of clandestinity, impediments, sacramentality, and especially – among Protestants – divorce had an important impact in the area of marital litigation. But all of these had much less immediate effect on the institution of marriage in sixteenth-century Germany than the Protestant abolition of the celibate religious ideal, especially as it affected moral reform and pastoral care.[3] This reversal of the centuries-old preference for chastity pervaded all

---

[2] In this respect I agree with the perspective adopted by Jean Delumeau, *Catholicism between Luther and Voltaire* (London, 1978), and Bossy, *Christianity in the West, 1400–1700*, both of whom stress the strong similarities between sixteenth-century Protestant and Catholic religious reforms, in intent as well as in content. I also share Bossy's reservation (viii), that in emphasizing the resemblances between the forms of sixteenth-century Christianity, there is a danger of exaggerating the unity of pre-Reformation Christianity.

[3] Cf. similar conclusion of Steven Ozment: "No institutional change brought about by the Reformation was more visible, responsive to late medieval pleas for reform, and conducive to new social attitudes than the marriage of Protestant clergy"; see *The Age of Reform, 1250–1550: An Intellectual and Religious History of Late Medieval and Reformation Europe* (New Haven, 1980), 383.

Conclusions

Protestant writings and sermons on marriage, popular or learned, throughout the century, culminating in the Lutheran *Hausväterliteratur* and its imitators. Catholic reforms, while maintaining a sacramental definition of marriage, focused on curbing the abuses of celibacy (concubinage, adultery, etc.) rather than the ideal itself. Thus a clear contrast emerged, in examples if not in practice, between a married Protestant ministry, preaching to and counseling married parishioners, armed with an arsenal of popular works with practical advice, and a celibate Catholic clergy, attempting to maintain a comparable influence with a divided literary and exemplary set of ideals.

At the same time, legal documents and even literary ones remain notoriously precarious means of measuring marital affection and prevailing social attitudes. The moral influence of books, sermons, and pamphlets is not quantifiable;[4] we can never know the number of acts of adultery not committed, clandestine marriages prevented, or general improvement of relations between spouses that might have resulted from such preaching. Thus, while there *was* an obvious distinction both in the quantity and content of Protestant writings on marriage and the family, it is far from obvious that "despite the conservatism *to which it often succumbed*, the Reformation still dramatically changed traditional attitudes toward the institutions of celibacy and marriage during the course of the sixteenth century."[5]

Nor does it appear that Protestant or Catholic marriage reforms of the sixteenth century were closely tied to any immediate demographic changes in familial and household structures. Certainly the ideal of the companionate marriage by no means remained restricted to sixteenth-century Protestants, nor, for that matter, did the transition from extended to nuclear family necessarily even take place in the century of the Reformation.[6] Rather, the occasional coincidence of the two and the teleologi-

---

[4] Cf. Vogler's attempts to gauge familial affection by terms of endearment in Protestant testaments; Vogler II:974.

[5] Ozment, *When Fathers Ruled*, 49 (emphasis added); but see also this scholar's own admission of the difficulty of assessing such impact on attitudes in *Protestants: The Birth of a Revolution* (New York, 1992), 169ff. The same argument applies to negative and restrictive characterizations of early modern marriage and the family, such as those of Muchembled and Flandrin; cf. my comments in Chapter 4.

[6] Both Goody and MacFarlane, for instance, argue that the transformation occurred in England during the thirteenth century (see my Introduction). Since such structures also obviously differed considerably regionally, we need much more work done on the medieval and early modern German family before such theorizing is even conceivable.

cal temptation seem too much for some scholars to resist, encouraged of course, by a perilous overreliance of learned literature. For as our examination of clandestine marriage has shown, the canonically inspired model of the couple and traditional familial controls both predated and survived the Reformation.

"Confessionalization" arguments positing Protestantism as a willing ally or tool of early modern statebuilding face even more obvious obstacles in the instance of marriage reform. Increasing codification of marital laws along canonical and Roman standards did indeed aid most early modern secular authorities in expanding their sovereignty, but this could hardly be considered either "secularization" or "centralization." For although many secular authorities were clearly expanding their marital jurisdictions by the time of the Reformation, very few of them used the occasion of religious rupture to attempt full secularization or centralization of marriage jurisdictions within their respective realms. Only those states with already well codified laws and sufficiently developed judicial and police organs – generally Swiss and imperial cities – could provide the kind of rigorous enforcement demanded by religious reformers of marriage.[7] In larger territorial states, most rulers were still at the step of legal standardization within their respective jurisdictions, relying on traditional local networks and procedures for enforcement with a minimum of centralized supervision. Moreover, there is no evidence that any territorial ruler of sixteenth-century Germany, Protestant or Catholic, ever desired more than the pre-Reformation Prince-Bishop's role of *Summus Episcopus* – ultimate legal authority and instance of appeal in ecclesiastical matters. Legal codification in all areas, including marriage, certainly constituted a prerequisite to the absolutist state, but should not be confused for the same.

Perhaps the most important evidence against sixteenth-century confessionalization, though, comes from the demonstrated continuity of local and customary dominance of almost all aspects of marriage. Certainly the role of the Church (especially in the church wedding) was by now secure and that of the State increasingly acknowledged, but from

---

[7] Such isolated examples provide a shaky foundation indeed for Safley's confessional generalization that "the Reformation not only centralized institutional control of marriage but inspired greater sensitivity, as revealed in its court verdicts, to the needs of petitioners . . . [improving] the control of marriage, protecting marital harmony and stability and providing a legal refuge of sorts for women" (*Let No Man Put Asunder*, 180).

marriage contract negotiations to prenuptial rituals to wedding feast, the entire marriage cycle continued to be dominated by local custom and traditional patriarchal authority. Criminal prosecution of adultery, prostitution, fornication, and other sexual offenses proved especially resistant to change, relying on both traditional means of enforcement (public accusation) and traditional values of honor and reputation within the *Gemeinschaft* to determine punishment. Admittedly, Protestant religious and secular authorities were probably more vocal than their Catholic counterparts in their condemnations of "frivolous" customs and sexual immorality. But whether due more to very immature State bureaucracies, tenacious local and familial power, or the fundamentally conservative nature of sixteenth-century German society as a whole, the results were disappointingly similar.[8]

In general, then, sixteenth-century marriage reform was typified by commonly high religious standards, with commonly inadequate means of implementation. Protestant reformers by the second half of the century might have increasingly blamed governmental indifference or even corruption,[9] but clearly most of their expectations for morals enforcement exceeded the capabilities of any state, much less an early modern one.[10] Many sixteenth-century laypeople apparently also considered the new sexual standards of reformers humanly impossible, protesting as a delegation of Genevan citizens did to Calvin that, at the current rate of

---

[8] Cf. Vogler's conclusion on the effectiveness of Protestant social reform in the Palatinate: "Les Eglises territoriales résulterent au contraire [to the hopes of earlier religious refomers] d'efforts lents et obstinés, patients et méthodiques, souvent tâtillons et sans gloire, que compromettaient parfois les résistances sourdes des populations ou tout simplement leur inertie. Vues avec le recul de l'histoire, ces efforts apparaissent beaucoup plus comme l'oeuvre de bureaucrates que de missionnaires . . ." (Vogler II:1276). See also Vogler II:762–69) on the weakness of Reformed consistories and II:872 on popular indifference.

Cf. similar conclusions of Roper ("Weddings in Reformation Augsburg," 100–1) and Robisheaux (*Rural Society*, 123, 272ff.) on the continuing popular definition of marriage, as well as Kingdon ("The Control of Morals in Calvin's Geneva," in *The Social History of the Reformation*, ed. Lawrence P. Buck and Jonathon W. Zophy [Columbus, 1972], esp. 11–12) on the disciplining of morals, particularly sexual offenses.

[9] Cf. complaints by Hoppenrod of "die grosse nachlessigkeit aller Obrigkeit" in sexual discipline (*Hurenteufel*, in Stambaugh, *Teufelbücher*, II:192ff.); and similar protests by Daul in his *Tanzteuffel* that secular authorities "durch die finger sehen" when it comes to matters of public drunkenness and immorality (Stambaugh, Teufelbücher, II:68ff.). Not surprisingly, both authors decry their own period as "the worst and last" of times.

[10] Cf. the well-known conclusion of Strauss on the Lutheran reform of education and its "apparent failure to transmit a clear religious message that could be consciously received and adopted" (*Luther's House of Learning*, 223ff.). See also 305ff. on the weakness of State bureaucracies vis-à-vis local communal authorities.

consistorial intervention, all their wives "might end up sewed up in sacks and drowned in the river for adultery."[11] The greatest success of Protestant reformers, rather, came at the level of ideology, and here it was ironically in conveying (with slight modification) the same sacral and consensual ideal of marriage that their pre-Reformation predecessors had struggled to promulgate.

What are the implications for the historical viability and significance of "Reformation"? Clearly the new social influence of theologians and jurists from the fifteenth century on cannot be discounted as irrelevant to larger long-term transformations. That their ideas or attempted reforms qualify as socially "revolutionary," however, also appears dubious, particularly from what we have just seen of marriage reform. In the ever precarious balancing of long- and short-term historical change, the definition of "Reformation" most consistent with our findings might be that of Euan Cameron in his recent survey of the subject.[12] The "series of parallel movements" that he proposes certainly permits us to recognize both the medieval roots of marriage reform as well as the important distinctions in language and form peculiar to the sixteenth century. Nor does recognizing the fundamental basis for confessional similarities diminish their differences, particularly in view of the growing divergence of confessional cultures in the centuries to follow. Whether these emerging confessional formulations of "modern" marriage also necessarily paralleled larger, long-term transformations of the family and "society" itself remains debatable. That most of their immediate reform goals necessarily yielded to the evolutionary pace of such social transformations, however, appears uncontestable.

[11] Kingdon, "The Control of Morals in Calvin's Geneva," 12. The delegation was scolded as frivolous and had its leader imprisoned. Shortly thereafter, however, the consistory's moral campaign slackened.
[12] *The European Reformation* (Oxford, 1991), 1–2.

Appendix on sources

The majority of archival sources employed in this study are located in the Badisches Generallandesarchiv (GLA) in Karlsruhe and the Stadtarchiv Speyer (StAS), with the remainder coming from the Landesarchiv Speyer (LAS), Landeshauptarchiv Koblenz (LAK), Archiv der Evangelischen Kirche in Rheinland, Archivstelle Koblenz (AEKK), and Bayerisches Haupstaatsarchiv München (HStAMÜ). Among the three Palatine states in question, the records of the Prince-Bishopric of Speyer are undoubtedly the most intact for the period, with those of the city of Speyer less continuous, and those of the Palatine-Electorate (due to the combined destructive effects of the Thirty Years' War and French invasion of 1689) the most damaged and – to a great degree – lost.

Legal primary sources, composing the bulk of my archival evidence, may be divided into three types. For the first – ordinances, statutes, and various codifications – I have relied on manuscript registers of the city council of Speyer (mainly StAS IA/8, IA/10, IA/12, IA/631) as well as the published collections of the Prince-Bishopric of Speyer (*Collectio; Sammlung*) and the Palatine-Electorate (volume 14 of the Sehling series *Die Evangelischen Kirchenordnungen des XVI. Jahrhunderts [EKO]*). All of these represent unilateral governmental decrees on all aspects of marriage litigation and prosecution and, while valuable in determining official intent, they have little to say about actual reception and implementation. The six-volume collection of customaries by Jacob Grimm, as well as the Palatine collection of Weizsäcker, have proved invaluable sources for pre-Reformation legal customs, although, here, too – as Bader warns

279

us – we must remember the significance of seigneurial hegemony and clerical redaction in their composition.[1]

Specific jurisdictional and procedural issues involving marriage were drawn from a second kind of legal source, namely the letters, treaties, and court formulas contained in registers (*Kopialbücher*) of all three. These include those of the Prince-Bishopric from 1478–1615 (GLA 67/277, 304, 316, 318–20, 322–23, 341, 409, 414, 417, 425–27, 486 [excerpts published in Riedner II]; LAS F1/71), city of Speyer from 1568–1699 (StAS IB/1, Bd. 7; IB/6, Bde. 1, 2; IB/8, Bde. 2, 5; IB/22; IB/23, Bde. 4, 5; IB/29, Bd. 9; IB/30), and the Palatine-Electorate from 1559–1620 (GLA 67/860, 928–30, 986, 4195,; HStAMÜ II/K.b. 273/7, 8, II/K.b. 339/20, II/K.b. 398/1 I/4; LAS A1/1753, A1/2366, B24/9). These records, especially official letters of protest and agreement between governmental leaders, provide more of an insight into the daily machinery of marital litigation (especially on disputed legal jurisdiction) as well as overall political relations between the three polities during the period of our study.

Undoubtedly the most important – though often also the most frustrating – sources on both marriage law and practice are the records of the courts themselves: acts and protocols. For historians of early modern Europe, the forensic interplay between popular practice and legal principle provides one of the few firsthand experiences we can have of marriage in the larger society. Yet as every scholar who has worked with these documents can testify, the protocols themselves – whether highly detailed or, as in most cases, laconic to a fault – at most provide glimpses of the many social interactions and issues involved. Lawsuits and criminal prosecutions remain precarious indicators of general attitudes and practices within a society and must therefore be approached by the historian with circumspect caution as a basis for broader theorizing and generalization.[2]

Historical generalization is particularly difficult in the case of the Palatinate for another reason all too familiar to historians of this period, namely, the paucity and irregularity of the sources themselves. The only

---

[1] Bader, *Studien zur Rechtsgeschichte*, 3:211. See also K. Kollnig, "Probleme der Weistumsforschung," in *Deutsches Bauerntum im Mittelalter*, ed. Günther Franz (Darmstadt, 1976), 394–423.

[2] See Burke, *Popular Culture in Early Modern Europe*, 65–87; and Carlo Ginzburg, *The Cheese and the Worms* (New York, 1982), xiv–xxii. Cf., however, Safley's application of Durkheim's theory of criminal deviance to the sixteenth-century prosecution of marital crime and dysfunction (*Let No Man Put Asunder*, 5–8).

extant pre-Reformation marriage protocols of the diocese of Speyer's episcopal court (*Officialatus*), for instance, are those few scattered summaries copied into two early sixteenth-century registers of miscellaneous ecclesiastical matters (GLA 67/417 and 67/487).[3] Records of the city of Speyer's criminal court (*Vierrichter*) are even more disappointing for the same period, as are those of the Elector's supreme court (*Hofgericht*) on the subject of marriage. Although two *Achtbücher* of the *Vierrichter* have survived from this period (StAS IA/694 [1396–97]; StAS IA/704 [1415–1510]), as well as three registers of the Elector's *Hofgericht* decisions from 1468–80 (GLA 67/951–53), I have found no reference to any marriage or adultery cases, and only one dowry dispute before the *Hofgericht*.

Protocols and acts from the main period of our study, 1555–1619, are somewhat better, if unevenly so. Once again, the Prince-Bishopric of Speyer is the best documented, with protocols of the cathedral chapters' meetings and jurisdictional disputes (GLA 61/10943–56; the records of 1500–17 have been transcribed by M. Krebs), clerical synodal summaries until 1600 (GLA 67/411–13, 419; also published in *Collectio*), oaths of purgation (*Urpheden*) from 1529–1616 (GLA 67/318, 423–24), and although no records of the *Officialatus*, the mostly complete records of the Prince-Bishopric's Privy Council (*Hofrat*) from 1547–1620 (GLA 61/11488–98). Judicial records of the city of Speyer are considerably fewer, composed mainly of *Vierrichter* criminal sentences from 1576–81 and 1605 (StAS IA/705; IB/16, Bd. 1) and indirect discussions of marriage cases in registers of clerical and juridical consultations (StAS IB/8, Bde. 2, 5; IB/20; IB/22). No records of either the Elector's marriage court (*Ehegericht*) or supreme court have survived for the period and the one extant volume of the central ecclesiastical council (*Kirchenrat*; GLA 61/9532) covers only the years 1569–71, with extremely little material touching on marriage. Consequently, I have focused instead on the one administrative district with the fullest documentation available – Bacharach – and made use of the range of marital offenses and disputes recorded by the bailiff (*Amtman*) from 1600–21 (with lacunae; LAK 4/1630–32), consistorial protocols from 1585–1620 (AEKK 125/2, 202–402), and the local clerical council (*conventus*) protocols of 1587–

---

[3] For records of other German episcopal courts, see the report of Klaus Lindner in Charles Donahue, Jr., ed., *The Records of the Medieval Ecclesiastical Courts and Reports of the Working Group on Church Court Records*, part I: *The Continent* (Berlin, 1989), 117–22.

1620 (Archiv der Evangelischen Kirche in Rheinland, Düsseldorf A IX/B 1; also published by Schüler, *Die Konvents protokolle*).

The records of the Prince-Bishop's *Hofrat* and of the Bacharach (Electoral) consistory are undoubtedly the most integrally intact of the group, well preserved and covering a generally uninterrupted period, yet even these bear witness to the inherent taciturnity of the sources. In the instance of the *Hofrat*, the acts touch on only one aspect of marriage (adultery), and then provide only very brief case summaries, listing the names and places of origin of the offender(s) and sometimes the plaintiff, nature of complaint, and nature and date of the decision and punishment. The consistorial protocols yield slightly more information, occasionally even direct quotations from the summoned offenders, but often return to formulaic recitations of the offense and its punishment. Records of the *Vierichter* and of the bailiff of Bacharach, while fewer, remain similarly limited in content and form.

In addition to all of these, I have made use of two kinds of nonlegal primary sources: pamphlets and ecclesiastical visitations. For the first I have relied primarily on the excellent *Flugschriften* collection compiled by Dr. Hans-Joachim Köhler and his Special Research Group in Tübingen,[4] as well as various other pamphlets and reformers' writings that I have located in the Bayerische Staatsbibliothek in Munich and the Newberry Library of Chicago or in published collections (see published primary bibliography). While these polemical and theological sources convey the self-described intent of early marriage reformers, visitation records offer some measure of their effect on practice. Unfortunately, the visitation records of our three states provide only indirect evidence of such social impact on marriage at best. There are no such records for the city of Speyer, and the Palatine-Electorate's extant visitation records of 1556, 1582, and 1609 say very little about the issues of marriage and celibacy per se.[5] Two volumes from the diocese of Speyer's 1582–87 visitation have survived (GLA 61/11262; LAS D2/306/10) and these,

---

[4] For a description of the project and its methodology, see Hans-Joachim Köhler, "Fragestellungen und Methoden zur Interpretation frühneuzeitlicher Flugschriften," in Köhler, *Flugschriften*, 1–27. Indexes have currently been published from A–L: *Bibliographie der Flugschriften des 16. Jahrhunderts. Teil I. Der frühe 16. Jahrhundert, 1501–30* (Tübingen, 1991–).

[5] Cf. G. Biundo, "Bericht und Bedenken über die kurpfälzische Kirchenvisitation im Jahre 1556," *Jahrbuch der Kirchengeschichtlichen Vereinigung in Hessen und Nassau* 10 (1959), 1–41; K. Hardtfelder, "Kirchenvisitation der Stadt Heidelberg, 1582," *Zeitschrift für Geschichte des Oberrheins* 34 (1882), 239–56; H. F. Macco, *The Church Visitations of the Deanery of Küsel in the Palatinate 1609* (Philadelphia, 1930); and Forster, *The Counter-Reformation*, especially 19–143.

in combination with the previously mentioned *Urpheden* of the clergy, provide some evidence on the enforcement of clerical celibacy. Other than two questions on the sacramentality and nature of marriage, however, the records say nothing about this aspect of the religious reform and thus have limited value for our purposes.

Bibliography

I. PRIMARY SOURCES CITED

A. Manuscript Sources

Archiv der Evangelischen Kirche in Rheinland, Archivstelle Koblenz (AEKK)

125/2	Misc. Eccles. Bacharach (including presbytery protocols, 1584–1633)

Generallandesarchiv Karlsruhe (GLA)
Hochstift Speyer

42/306	Ehevertrag zw. Bernhart Wüt von Grumbach u. Agata Zofstein (16.2.1525)
61/6981	Jöhlingen Vogtsgerichtprotokolle (1573–90)
61/10933–56	Protokolle des Domkapitels Speyer (1574–1622)
61/11104–09	Kapitelsprotokolle des Stifts St. Guido (1573–1629)
61/11262	Visitatio Capituli sedes Ruralis Lautterbach modo Steinfelsen alios Weysenberg (1584)
61/11488–98	Protokolle des Hofrats Speyer, (1528, 1529, 1537–66, 1573–1624)
61/15536	Jöhlingen Vogtsgerichtprotokolle (1594–1623)
67/277	Eid und Gerichtsbuch (ca. 15th Century)
67/298	Liber officiorum Matthiae (1464–78)
67/303	Rechtsspruche d. Bischofs Ludwig (1479–1504)
67/304	Liber contractuum Ludovici (1478–1504)
67/316	Liber contractuum Rudolphi (1552–60)
67/318–19	Verträge, Urteile, Urpheden, etc. Episc. Spir. (1529–60, 1560–74)
67/320	Liber officiorum Marquadi (1560–81)
67/322	Liber contractuum Eberhardi (1581–1610)
67/323	Liber officiorum Eberhardi (1581–1610)

Bibliography

67/341	Bruchsal Verhandlungen u. Verträge mit der Pfalz (1454–1615)
67/409	Misc. Bistum Speyer (1521–1600)
67/411	Synodalprocesse, Incorporationen, Reformationen, Wahlen (1495–1593)
67/412	Synodalbrieffe d. Dompropsts Georg v. Gemmingen u. d. Bish. Ludwig Pfründurkunden, mit älteren Beilagen (1488–96)
67/413	Bruchsal Processus synodales (1478–1516)
67/414	Liber spiritualium (1355–1478)
67/417	Super Materiis in libris spiritualium Ludovici, Philippi, et Georgii Episc. Spir. (1491–1528)
67/419	Copiarum Procces. synod. (1513–76)
67/423	Urfehden protokolle sub Marquadi epis. (1560–81)
67/424	Urfehden prot. sub Eberhardi (& Christoph) (1581–1610, 1610–16)
67/425–27	Libri spiritualium (1561–81, 1581–1610, 1610–51)
67/486	Liber variorum iuramentorum, ordnungen, u. Eide des geistl. Gerichts (ca. 1550)
67/487	Urkunden meist. geistl. betr. (1399–1634)
67/489	Bruchsal Stadtbuch über Privatsachen (1567–1620)
78/2406	Polizeiordnung Philipp II von Speier (28.11.1548)

Kurpfalz

61/9532	Protokolle des Kirchenrats (1569–71)
65/245	Gerichtsordnung für Großeicholzheim u. Hardersbach (1578)
65/1160	Polizei-Ordnungen, Mandate, Trakate, Flugblätter (ca. 17th century)
67/860	Liber officiorum Fried. IV (1592–1610)
67/928	Liber officiorum J. Casimirs Admin. (1583–91)
67/929–30	Libri officiorum (1592–1620)
67/951	Hofgerichtsurteile (1468–80)
67/974	Kirchenraths Dokumentenbuch, Bd. II (1562–1703)
67/978	Kirchenraths Dokumentenbuch, Bd. VI (1564–1790)
67/980	Kirchenraths Dokumentenbuch, Bd. VIII (1035–1700)
67/986	Liber officiorum Fried. III (1559–75)
77/4195	Ecclesiastica (ca. 1578)
77/4277	Evang. Reformation in der kufürstl. Oberpfalz (1542–58)
77/9674	Relig. misc. (1565)

Hauptstaatsarchiv München (HStAMÜ)

II/K.b. 273/7, 8	Acta comitalia versch. Anhalt./Spirens (1570)
II/K.b. 339/20	Summarische Verzeichnis der Pfalz-Neuberg Kammergerichts (1599–1601)

II/K.b. 390/1c	Meisenheim Visitationen
II/K.b. 398/1,	Gerichts u. Urteilsbuch über
Fasc. I/4	die kurpfälzisch-speyerischen Hoheitsirrungen (1503)

Landesarchiv Speyer (LAS)

A1/1753	Vertrag zw. Joh. Casimir und Rat zu Neustadt (1586)
A1/1938	Ottenberg Statuten von J. Casimir (1581)
A1/2366	Vertrag zw. Kurpfalz und Stadt Worms (19.9.1611)
A2/1178.9, II	Gemeinen Amttage u. Einführung eines Gerichtsbuch zu HochSpeyer (1489–1702)
B24/9	Landauer Vertrag (zw. Kurpfalz u. Zweibrücken) (1612)
D2/306/10	Liber visitationis sämtlichen Pfarreiren in den Ämter Kirrweiler, Edesheim u. Marientraut (1583)
D2/363b/I	Prot. Presbyterii Germersheim (1591–1600)
E2/19	Reichskammergericht Akten betr. Ehevertrag zw. Conrad v. Tübingen u. Johanna v. Zweibrücken-Bitsch (9.7.1532)
F1/71	Verträge des Hochstifts Speyer mit der Reichstadt Speyer (1422–1518)
F5/47	Schifferstadt Gerichtsbuch (1542–1622)
F5/132	Impflingen Gerichtsbuch (1607–83)
F5/286	Heiratskontraktenprotokolle Ilbesheim bei Landau (1593–1629)

Landeshauptarchiv Koblenz (LAK)

4/1630–32	Protok. des Oberamtes Bacharach (Kurpfalz) (1600–4, 1609–13, 1614–21)
4/4064	Gerichtsbuch von Eckenroth (1566–1619)
33/4947	Sponheim Visitationen
613/501–4	Stadt Bacharach Ratsprotokolle (1559–74, 1606–23)

Stadtarchiv Speyer (StAS)

IA/8	Versammelten Statuten, Ordnungen (16th–18th century)
IA/10	Statuten, Ordnungen u. Herrengebote (1535–93)
IA/12	Gerichtsordnungen (16th–17th century)
IA/20	Bürgerliche Beschwerden und Aufstand gegen den Magistrat, (1512–13)
IA/85	Formularanweise der Kanzlei, 2 Bde. (15th–16th century)
IA/631	Aufsicht auf die Sitten (1523–1764)
IA/694	Achtbuch (1396–97)
IA/704	Criminalia Rechtspflege: Frevelgericht (Vierrichter) Misc. (15th–16th century)

Bibliography

IA/705	Vierrichter Amts-Protokolle über Frevel u. Urphehden (1576–1610)
IB/1, Bd. 7	Ratsprotokolle Speyer (1599–1600)
IB/6, Bde. 1, 2	Protocullum decretorum et secretorum senatis (1568–1623)
IB/8, Bde. 2, 5	Protocolla consultationem (1574–1637)
IB/16, Bd. 1	Vierrichter Amtsprotokolle (1605–99)
IB/20	Protokolle richtlicher Bedenken u. Urtheile (1562, 1573–79, 1582, 1587, 1589–96)
IB/22	Protocullum clericale (1575–1621)
IB/23, Bde. 4, 5	Protokolle missivalia (1586–1604)
IB/29, Bd. 9	Misc. Kopialbuch des 18. Jh. (ca. 16th century)
IB/30	Kopialbuch etlichen Privilegien, vertrag. u. anders (1516–45)

B. Printed Sources

Agricola, Franz. *Diatriba evangelien de coniugio et coelibatu sacerdotum.* Cologne: M. Cholinum, 1581.

Biblischer Ehe-Spiegel/ Jn Siben Catholischen Ehe- oder Braut Predigen verfasset. Cologne: Bernhard Wolther, 1599.

Alberus, Erasmus. *Das Ehebüchlein/ Ein Gesprech zweyer weiber/ mit namen Agatha und Barbara* . . . Strasbourg, 1539.

Althamer, Andreas. *Ain Sermō von dem eelichen stand/ dz er auch den priestern frey sey/ gethon zu Schwebischen Gemuünd* . . . Augsburg: Philip Ulhart d. Ä., 1525.

Arnoldi, Bartholomäus [de Usingen]. *Sermo de matrimonio sacerdotum et monachorum.* Erfurt: Hans Knappe d. Ä., 1523.

Barbali, Barbali, *Ein Gespräch. Kurtzwylig wie ein müter wolt Dz jr tochter in ein kloster solt* . . . Zurich: C. Froschauer, 1526.

Barbaro, Francesco. *Eyn gut Buch von der Ehe, was die Ehe sei, was sie guts mit sich bringe* . . . Trans. Erasmus Alberus. Hagnaw: V. Kobian, 1536.

Benrath, Gustav Adolf. "Die kurpfälzischen Kirchenvisitationen im 16. Jahrhundert." *Blätter für Pfalzische Kirchengeschichte* 42 (1975), 17–24.

Berger, Arnold E. *Die Sturmtruppen der Reformation; Flugschriften der Jahren 1520–25.* Leipzig, 1931; reprint: Darmstadt, 1964.

Beyerle, Franz, gen. ed. *Quellen zur neueren Privatrechtsgeschichte Deutschlands.* 2 vols. Weimar, 1936–.

Beza, Théodor de. *Tractatio de repudiis et divortiis.* Geneva, 1573.

Bezold, Friedrich von, ed. *Briefe des Pfalzgrafen Johann Casimir.* 3 vols. Munich, 1882–1903.

Biundo, G. "Bericht und Bedenken über die kurpfälzische Kirchenvisitation im Jahre 1556." *Jahrbuch der kirchengeschichtlichen Vereinigung in Hessen und Nassau* 10 (1959), 1–41.

Böcking, E., ed. *Ulrichs von Hutten Schriften.* 4 vols. and 2 suppls. Leipzig, 1859–70; reprint: Aalen, 1963.

Bibliography

Der bösen weiber Zuchtschůl. Eyn Schöner Dialogus odder gesprech/ von Zweyen Schwestern . . . Frankfurt a.M.: Christian Egenolff, ca. 1535.

Brenz, Johannes. *Wie yn Ehesachen/ und inn den fellen/ so sich derhalben/ zutragen/ nach Götlichen billichen Rechten/ Christenlich zu handeln sey. Mit einer Vorrhede Mart. Luthers.* Wittenberg, 1531.

Catechismus Deutsch. Nuremberg: Valentine Newber, 1550.

Frühschriften. Ed. Martin Brecht, Gerhard Schäfer, and Frieda Wolf. 2 vols. Tübingen, 1974.

Brucker, Johann Karl, ed. *Strassburger Zunft- und Polizei-Verordnungen des 14. und 15. Jahrhunderts, aus den Originalen des Stadtarchivs.* Strasbourg, 1889.

Bucer, Martin. *De Regno Christi ad Eduordum Sextum Angliae Regem libri duo (1550)*, in *Opera Latina*, vol XV. Ed. François Wendel. Paris, 1955.

Bugenhagen, Johannes. *Wye man die/ so zu der Ehe greyffent/ Eynleitet zu Wittenberg.* Magdeburg: Hans Knappe d. J., 1525.

Von dem ehelichen stande der Bischoffe und Diaken. Wittemberg: Josef Klug, 1525.

Vom Ehebruch und Heimlichen Weglauffen. Wittenberg, 1541.

Bullinger, Heinrich d. Ä. *Der Christlich Eestand.* Zurich, 1540.

Calvin, John. *New Testament Commentaries.* Ed. David W. Torrance and Thomas F. Torrance. Grand Rapids, Mich., 1959–74.

Institutes of the Christian Religion. Ed. J. T. McNeil. Trans. Ford Lewis Battles. 2 vols. Philadelphia, 1960.

Canisius, Peter. *Catholischer Catechismus.* Cologne, 1563.

Clausen, Hans-Kurt, ed. *Das Freisinger Rechtsbuch.* Weimar, 1941.

Clemen, Otto, ed. *Flugschriften aus den ersten Jahren der Reformation.* 4 vols. Halle, 1906–11.

Flugschriften aus der Reformationzeit in Faksimiledrucken. 2 vols. Neue Folge der Flugschriften aus den ersten Jahren der Reformationzeit. Leipzig, 1921–22; reprint: Nieuwkoop, 1967.

Collectio processum synodalium et constitutionem ecclesticarum Diocesis Spirensis ab anno 1247 usque ad annum 1720. Ed. Speyer Bishop August von Lindburg-Stirum. Bruchsal, 1786.

Coras, Jean de. *Des Mariages clandestinement et irreverement contractés par les enfans de famille, au decceu, ou contre le gré, vouloir, et consentement de leurs pères et mères, petit discours, et brieve resolucion.* Toulouse: Pierre du Puis, 1557.

Corpus Reformatorum. Berlin, Leipzig, Zurich, 1834–.

Corpus scriptorum ecclesiasticorum latinorum. Vienna, 1866–.

Culmann, Leonard. *Jungen gesellen, Jungfrauwen und Witwen/ so Ehelich wöllen werden/ zu nutz ein unterrichtung/ wie sie sich in ehelichen stand richten sollen.* Magdeburg: H. Waltherther, 1534.

Eberlin, Johann. *Wie gar gfarlich sey / So Ain Priester kain Eeweyb hat / Wye Unchristlich / und schedlich aim gmainen Nutz Die menschen seynd / Welche hindern die pfaffen Ain Eelichen stand.* Augsburg: Melchior Rammingel, 1522.

Egli, E., and C. Finsler, eds. *Huldrich Zwingli, Sämtliche Werke.* Berlin, 1906.

Enders, Ludwig, ed. *Johann Eberlin von Günzberg, Sämtliche Schriften.* 2 vols. Halle, 1896–1900.

288

Bibliography

Erasmus, Desiderius. *Complete Works.* Toronto, 1969–.

Eyb, Albrecht von. *Das Ehebüchlein.* Nuremberg: Anton Koberger, 1472; facsimile: Wiesbaden: G. Pressler, 1966.

Ob einem mannen gezimen zunemmen ein Eeweib oder nit, sampt der Antwort darauff. S.l., 1540.

Flad, Philipp W. L. *Specimen anecdoten iuris Palatini de successione ab intestato ante statutum Palatinum.* Heidelberg, 1743.

Franck, Sebastian. *Weltbüch, Spiegel und bildtnisz des gantzen erdtbodens.* Tübingen, 1534.

Friedberg, Emil, ed. *Corpus Iuris Canonici.* Vol. I: *Decretum Gratiani* (ca. 1140). Vol. 2: *Decretalium collectiones.* Leipzig, 1879–81; reprint: Graz, 1955.

Glasschröder, Franz X. *Urkunden zur Pfälzischen Kirchengeschichte im Mittelalter.* Munich and Freising, 1903.

Neue Urkunden zür pfälzischen Kirchengeschichte im Mittelalter. Speyer, 1930.

Grimm, Jacob, ed. *Weisthümer.* 6 vols. 2nd ed. Göttingen, 1840–78. Reprint: Berlin, 1957.

Güttel, Kaspar. *Ueber den Evangelion Johannis/ da Christus seyne Mutter such seine Junger/ waren auff die Hochzeyt geladen . . . Eyn Sermon dem Ehlichen standt fast freudesam und nützlich.* Zwickau: Jörg Gastlel, 1524.

Hardtfelder, K. "Kirchenvisitation der Stadt Heidelberg, 1582." *Zeitschrift für Geschichte des Oberrheins* 34 (1882), 239–56.

Hilgard, A. *Urkunden zur Geschichte der Stadt Speier.* Strasbourg, 1886.

Hughes, Philip Edgcumbe, trans. and ed. *The Register of the Company of Pastors of Geneva in the Time of Calvin.* Grand Rapids, Mich., 1966.

Kluckhohn, August. *Briefe Friedrich des Frommen.* 2 vols. Braunschweig, 1868–72.

Koeniger, Albert M. *Quellen zur Geschichte der Sendgerichte in Deutschland.* Munich, 1910.

Krebs, Manfred, ed. "Die kurpfälzischen Dienerbücher, 1476–1685." *Mitteilungen der Oberrheimischen Historischen Kommission* 1. Supplement to *Zeitschrift für die Geschichte des Oberrheins,* 92 (1942).

——— ed. *Die Protokolle des Speyer Domkapitels, 1500–1517.* Stuttgart, 1968–69.

Lansberger, Johannes. *Eyn schöne Vnderrichtung was die recht Ewangelisch geystlicheit sy/ vnd was man von den Clösteren halten soll.* Cologne: Eucharius Cervicornus, 1528.

Laube, Adolf, Annerose Schneider, and Sigrid Loos, eds. *Flugschriften der frühen Reformationsbewegung, 1518–24.* 2 vols. Vaduz, 1983.

Luther, Martin. *D. Martin Luthers Werke: Kritische Gesamtausgabe.* Weimar, 1883–. Reprint, 1964–68.

Macco, Hermann Friedrich. *The Church Visitations of the Deanery of Kusel in the Palatinate 1609.* Philadelphia, 1930.

Menius, Justus. *Erynnerung was denen so sich ynn Ehestand begeben zu bedencken sey.* Wittemberg: N. Schirlentz, 1528.

Menzel, Karl. "Regesten zur Geschichte Friedrich I." In *Quellen zur Geschichte Friedrich I. des Siegreichen Kurfürsten von der Pfalz,* part III, ed. Konrad Hoffmann. Munich, 1862; reprint: Munich: Scientia Verlag Aalen, 1969.

Meuche, Hermann. *Flugblätter der Reformation und des Bauernkrieg.* Leipzig, 1976.

Moeckard, Johannes. *Ain Christliche ainfältige/ und zu dieser zeit seer notwendige er-*

manung/ an die jugent darinnen angezaigt wirdt was kinder iren Eltern zuthun schuldig seind. Augsburg, 1550.

Monumenta Germaniae Historica, Fontes Iuris Germanici Antiqui, Nova Series. Ed. Karl August Eckhardt. Nos. 1, 4–6. Munich, 1933, 1960–64.

Mutis, Joannes. *Tractatuli duo metrici, quorum/ primus continent reccomendationem mulierum contra viros (p. I. Motis)/ Secundus remedium virorum contra concubinas atosque coniuges* (a P. de Corbolio). Reutlingen: M. Greff, 1490.

Remling, Franz X., ed. *Urkundenbuch zur Geschichte der Bischöfe zu Speyer.* 2 vols. Mainz, 1852–53; reprint: Aalen, 1970.

Riedner, Otto. *Die geistlichen Gerichtshöfe zu Speyer im Mittelalter.* Vol. II. Paderborn, 1915.

Sammlung der Hochfürstlich-Speierischen Gesetze und Landesverordnungen. Part I (1470–1720). Bruchsal, 1788.

Schatzgeyer, Kaspar. *Vnivs articvli dissolvbilitatem matrimonij contingentis vera dec/ contra Lvtheranv dogma in cadem materia declaratio, & per sacra scriptvram svfficienter roborata* . . . Tübingen: Ulrich Morhart d.Ä., 1525.

Schroeder, H. J., ed. *Canons and Decrees of the Council of Trent.* St. Lovis, 1941.

Schüler, Heinz. *Die Konventsprotokolle der reformierten Klasse Bacharach, 1587–1620.* Schriftenreihe des Vereins für Rheinische Kirchengeschichte, 51. Cologne, 1977.

Schwerin, Claudius, Freiherr von. *Quellen zur Geschichte der Eheschliessung.* 2 vols. Bonn, Berlin, Leipzig, 1920–33.

Schwitalla, Johannes, ed. *Deutsche Flugschriften, 1460–1525.* Tübingen, 1983.

Sehling, Emil, gen. ed. *Die Evangelischen Kirchenordnungen des XVI. Jahrhunderts.* Vol. XIV (Kurpfalz), ed. J. F. G. Goeters. Tübingen, 1969.

[Sitzinger, Ulrich]. *Ein getrewe vermanung eins liebhabers des Euangelischen warheyt an gemeyne Pfaffheyt nit zu widderfechten den Ehelichen standt/ so ein Ersamer Priester zu Wormbs (im von Got im neüwen vnnd Alten Testament zu gelassen) an sich genomen hat.* Speyer: Jacob Schmidt, 1523.

Spalatin, Georg. *Vierzehen ursachen/ die billich yederman bewegen sollen/ den Ehestand lieb und hoch zuhaben und achten/ sich gerne darein zubegeben/ und denselbigen ehrlich und wol/ trewlich unnd freundlich zu halten durch Georgum Spalatinum/ aus der heiligen Götlichen Schrifft gezogen.* Erfurt: Andreas Rauscher, 1531.

Spangenberg, Cyriakus. *Ehespiegel/ Das ist/ Alles was von dem heyligen Ehestande/ nutzliches/ noetiges/ unnd troestliches mag gesagt werden/ In LXX Brautpredigen/ zusammen verfasset.* Strasbourg: Theodor Rilel, 1570.

Stambaugh, Ria, ed. *Teufelbücher in Auswahl.* Vols. 2–5. Berlin, 1970–80.

Stör, Thomas. *Der Ehelich standt von Gott mit gebenedeyung auffgesetzt / soll umb schwärhait wegen der seltzsamen gaben der Junckfrawschafft yederman frey sein / und niemant verboten werden.* Nuremberg: Hans Hergot, 1524.

Vives, Joannes Ludovicus. *De officio mariti.* Basel: R. Winter, 1538.

Weech, F. von. "Pfälzische Regesten und Urkunden," *Zeitschrift für die Geschichte des Oberrheins* 22 (1869), 177–216, 361–79, 401–17; 23 (1871), 155–79; 24 (1872), 56–103, 269–326; 32 (1880), 190–233.

Weizsäcker, Wilhelm. *Pfälzische Weistümer.* Speyer, 1957–68.

Bibliography

Zoepfl, H., ed. *Die Peinliche Gerichtsordnung Kaiser Karls V nebst der Bamberger und der Brandenburger Halsgerichtsordnung.* 2nd ed. Leipzig and Heidelberg, 1876.

SELECT SECONDARY LITERATURE

A. Marriage and Theology

Baranowski, Siegmund. *Luthers Lehre von der Ehe.* Poznan, 1906.

Basdevant, Jules. "Des rapports de l'Eglise et de l'Etat dans la legislation du mariage du Concile de Trente." Ph.D. dissertation, Paris, 1900.

Biéler, André. *L'homme et la femme dans la morale calviniste: La doctrine réformée sur l'amour, le mariage, le célibat, le divorce, l'adultère et la prostitution, considérée dans son cadre historique.* Geneva, 1963.

Bossy, John. "The Counter-Reformation and the People of Catholic Europe." *Past and Present* 47 (1970), 51–70.

Christianity in the West, 1400–1700. Oxford, 1985.

Bouwsma, William. *John Calvin: A Sixteenth-Century Portrait.* Oxford, 1988.

Boswell, John. *Christianity, Social Tolerance, and Homosexuality.* Chicago, 1980.

Delumeau, Jean. *Catholicism between Luther and Voltaire.* London, 1978.

Doherty, Dennis. *The Sexual Doctrine of Cardinal Cajetan.* Regensburg, 1966.

Douglass, Jane Dempsey. *Women, Freedom, and Calvin.* Philadelphia, 1985.

Dugan, Eileen Theresa. "Images of Marriage and Family Life in Nördlingen: Moral Preaching and Devotional Literature, 1589–1712." Ph.D. dissertation, Ohio State University, 1987.

Falk, F. *Die Ehe am Ausgang des Mittelalters.* Freibourg, 1908.

Franzen, August. *Zölibat und Priesterehe in der Auseinandersetzung der Reformationszeit und der katholischen Reform des 16. Jahrhunderts.* Vereinschriften der Gesellschaft zur Herausgabe des Corpus Catholicorum, 29. Münster, 1969.

Gaudemet, Jean. *Le mariage en Occident. Les moeurs et le droit.* Paris, 1987.

Godefroy, L. "Le mariage au temps des Pères." In *DTC* 9: 2077–2123.

"Le mariage dans l'Ecriture Sainte." In *DTC* 9: 2044–77.

Hendrix, Scott. "Christianizing Domestic Relations: Women and Marriage in Johann Freder's *Dialogus dem Ehestand zu Ehren.*" *Sixteenth Century Journal* 23/2 (1992), 251–66.

Hoffman, Julius. *Die 'Hausväterliteratur' und die 'Predigten über den christlichen Hausstand': Lehre vom Hause und Bildung für das häusliche Leben in 16., 17., und 18. Jahrhundert.* Göttinger Studien zur Paedagogik, 37. Weinheim, 1959.

Jedin, Hubert. *A History of the Council of Trent.* Trans. Dom Ernst Graf. London, 1957.

Crisis and Closure of the Council of Trent. Trans. N. D. Smith. London, 1967.

Karant–Nunn, Susan C. "The Transmission of Luther's Teachings on Women and Matrimony: The Case of Zwickau." *Archiv für Reformationsgeschichte* 77 (1986), 31–46.

"Kinder, Küche, Kirche: Social Ideology in the Sermons of Johannes Mathesius." In *Germania Illustrata: Essays on Early Modern Germany Presented to Gerald Strauss,* ed.

Bibliography

Susan C. Karant-Nunn and Andrew L. Fix, 121–40. Sixteenth Century Essays and Studies, 18. Kirksville, Mo., 1992.

Kawerau, Waldemar. *Die Reformation und die Ehe. Ein Beitrag zur Kulturgeschichte des 16. Jahrhunderts.* Coll. Schriften des Vereins für Reformationsgeschichte, 39. Halle, 1892.

Köhler, H. J., ed. *Flugschriften als Massenmedium der Reformationszeit; Beiträge zum Tübinger Symposion 1980.* Stuttgart, 1981.

Lähteenmäki, O. *Sexus und Ehe bei Luther.* Schriften der Luther-Agricola-Gesellschaft, 10. Turku, 1955.

Lamott, Alois. *Das Speyerer Diözesanrituale von 1512 bis 1932; seine Geschichte und seine Ordines zur Sakramentenliturgie.* Quellen und Abhandlungen zur mittelrheinischen Kirchengeschichte, 5. Speyer, 1961.

LeBras, Gabriel. "La doctrine du mariage chez les théologiens et les canonistes dupuis l'An Mille." In *DTC* 9:2123–2220.

Leclercq, Jean. *Monks on Marriage: A Twelfth-Century View.* New York, 1982.

Lettmann, R. *Die Diskussion über die klandestinen Ehen und die Einführung einer zur Gültigkeit verpflichtenden Eheschliessungsform auf dem Konzil von Trent.* Münsterische Beiträge zur Theologie, 31. Münster, 1967.

Miller, Thomas F. "Mirror for Marriage: Lutheran Views of Marriage and the Family, 1520–1600." Ph.D. dissertation, University of Virginia, 1981.

Moeller, Bernd. "Die Kirche in den evangelischen freien Städten Oberdeutschlands in Zeitalter der Reformation." *Zeitschrift für die Geschichte des Oberrheins,* n.s., 73 (1964), 147–62.

Molin, Jean-Baptiste, and Protais Mutembe. *Le rituel du mariage en France du XIIème au XVIème siècle.* Thélogie Historique, 26. Paris, 1974.

Niebergall, Alfred. *Die Geschichte der evangelischen Trauung in Hessen.* Veröffentlichungen der Evangelischen Gesellschaft für Liturgieforschung, 18. Göttingen, 1972.

Noonan, John T. *Contraception: A History of Its Treatment by the Catholic Theologians and Canonists.* Cambridge, Mass., 1965.

Oberman, Heiko. *Luther: Man between God and the Devil.* Trans. Eileen Walliser-Schwarzbart. New York, 1989.

Pfeiffer, Charles W. "Heinrich Bullinger and Marriage." Ph.D. dissertation, St. Louis University, 1981.

Rehermann, Ernst. *Das Predigtexempel bei protestantischen Theologen des 16. und 17. Jahrhunderts.* Schriften zur niederdeutschen Volkskunde, 8. Göttingen, 1977.

Reifenberg, H. *Sakramente, Sakrametalien, und Ritualien im Bistum Mainz seit dem Spätmittelalter.* Vol. I: *Bis 1671.* Liturgiewissenschaftliche Quellen und Forschungen, 53. Münster, 1971.

Selderhuis, Herman. "Martin Bucer und die Ehe." In *Martin Bucer* and *Sixteenth-Century Europe,* ed. Christian Kriege and Marc Lienhard, 173–84. Leiden, 1993.

Tentler, Thomas. *Sin and Confession on the Eve of the Reformation.* Princeton, 1977.

Vancandard, E. "Célibat ecclésiastique." In *DTC* 2:2068–87.

Villien, A. "Divorce." In *DTC* 4:1455–78.

Bibliography

Wahl, Johannes. *Die Stellung der Spanier zu dem Problem der klandestinen Ehen in den Verhandlungen auf dem Konzil von Trient.* Bonn, 1958.

Yost, John. "Changing Attitudes toward Married Life in Civic and Christian Humanism." *Occasional Papers of the American Society for Reformation Research* 1 (1977), 151–66.

Zeeden, Ernst W. "Calvinistische Elemente in der Kurpfalzischen Kirchenordnung von 1563." In *Festschrift für Erik Wolf,* ed. Alexander Hollerbach et al., 183–214. Frankfurt, 1962.

B. Marriage and Law

Allen, Richard Martin. "Crime and Punishment in Sixteenth-Century Reutlingen." Ph.D. dissertation, University of Virginia, 1980.

Arnold, Hermann. "Das eheliche Güterrecht von Mülhausen i. Elsass am Ausgange des Mittelalters." In *Deutschrechtliche Beiträge; Forschungen und Quellen Zur Geschichte des Deutschen Rechts,* ed. Konrad Beyerle, I:1–72. Heidelberg, 1908.

Bader, Karl Siegfried. *Studien zur Rechtsgeschichte des mittelalterlichen Dorfes.* 3 vols. Weimar, 1957–73.

Bader, Karl Siegfried, and Grete Bader-Weiß. *Der Pranger: Ein Strafwerkzeug und Rechtswahrzeichen des Mittelalters.* Freiburg im Br., 1935.

Below, Georg von. *Die Ursachen der Rezeption des römischen Rechts in Deutschland.* Munich, 1905; reprint: Aalen, 1964.

Bennecke, Hans. *Die strafrechtliche Lehre vom Ehebruch.* Marbourg, 1884.

Bernhardt, Walter. *Die Zentralbehörden des Herzogtums Württemberg und ihre Beamten, 1520–1629.* Veröffentlichungen der Kommission für geschichtliche Landeskunde in Baden-Württemberg, 70–71. Stuttgart, 1972–73.

Brundage, James A. *Law, Sex, and Christian Society in Medieval Europe.* Chicago, 1987.

Brunner, Otto. *Land und Herrschaft.* Darmstadt, 1965.

Coing, Helmut. *Römisches Recht in Deutschland.* Milan, 1964.
Europäisches Privatrecht. Vol. I: *Älteres Gemeines Recht (1500-1800).* Munich, 1985.
ed. *Handbuch der Quellen und Literatur der neureren europäischen Privatrechtsgeschichte.* 2 vols. Munich, 1976–77.

Dauvillier, Jean. *Le mariage dans le droit classique de l'eglise, depuis le Décret de Gratian (1140) jusqu'à mort de Clement V (1314).* Paris, 1933.

Demelius, Heinrich. *Eheliches Güterrecht im spätmittelalterlichen Wien.* Osterreichische Akademie der Wissenschaften Philosophische-Historische Klasse, 265/4. Vienna, 1970.

Diebold, Etienne. "L'application en France du canon 51 du IVe concile du Latran d'après les anciens statuts synodaux." *L'année canonique* 2 (1953), 187–95.

Dieterich, Hartweg. *Das protestantische Eherecht in Deutschland bis zur Mitte des 17. Jahrhunderts.* Munich, 1970.

Donahue, Charles, Jr. "The Policy of Alexander III's Consent Theory of Marriage." In *Proceedings of the Fourth International Congress of Medieval Canon Law,* ed. S. Kuttner, 252–81. Vatican City, 1975.

Bibliography

"The Canon Law on the Formation of Marriage and Social Practice in the Later Middle Ages." *Journal of Family History* 8/2 (1983), 144–58.

Eberle, Ernst. *Probleme zur Rechtsstellung der Frau nach den kursächsischen Konstitution von 1572.* Stuttgart, 1964.

Erbe, Günther. "Das Ehescheidungsrecht im Herzogtum Württemberg seit der Reformation." *Zeitschrift für württembergische Landesgeschichte* 14 (1955), 95–144.

Erler, Adalbert. *Kirchenrecht.* 5th ed. Munich, 1983.

Esmein, Adhémar. *Le mariage en droit canonique.* 2 vols. Paris, 1891.

Faurey, Joseph. "Le droit écclésiastique matrimonial des calvinistes français." Ph.D. dissertation, Paris, 1910.

Feine, Hans E. A. *Kirchliche Rechtsgeschichte.* 5th ed. Cologne, 1972.

Fichtner, Paula Sutter. *Protestantism and Primogeniture in Early Modern Europe.* New Haven, 1989.

Fournier, P. *Les Officialités au Moyen Age.* Paris, 1880.

Freisen, Joseph. *Geschichte des kanonischen Eherechtes bis zum Verfall der Glossenliteratur.* Tübingen, 1888; reprint: Paderborn, 1963.

Frensdorf, F. "Ein Urteilsbuch des geistlichen Gerichts zu Augsburg zus dem 14. Jahrhundert." *Zeitschrift für Kirchenrecht* 10 (1871), 1–37.

Friedberg, Emil. *Das Recht der Eheschliessung in seiner geschichtlichen Entwicklung.* Leipzig, 1865; reprint: Aalen, 1965.

Verlobung und Trauung. Leipzig, 1876.

Gantrell, V. A. C. et al., eds. *Crime and the Law: The Social History of Crime in Western Europe since 1500.* London, 1980.

Gottlieb, Beatrice. "Getting Married in Pre-Reformation Europe: The Doctrine of Clandestine Marriage and Court Cases in Fifteenth-Century Champagne." Ph.D. dissertation, Columbia University, 1974.

"The Meaning of Clandestine Marriage." In *Family and Sexuality in French History,* ed. Robert Wheaton and Tamara K. Hasrevcn, 49–83. Philadelphia, 1980.

Harrington, Joel F. "Reformation, Statebuilding, and the 'Secularization' of Marriage: Jurisdiction in the Palatinate, 1450–1619." *Fides et Historia* 23/3 (Fall 1990), 53–63.

"The Impact of Protestantism and Roman Law on the Marital Property Rights of Women in Sixteenth-century Germany." In *Marriage and the Family in History,* ed. Roderick Phillips. Toronto, 1994.

Harster, Theodor. *Das Strafrecht der freien Reichstadt Speier in Theorie und Praxis.* Untersuchungen zur deutschen Staats- und Rechtsgeschichte, 61. Breslau, 1900.

Hartung, Fritz. *Deutsche Verfassungsgeschichte vom 15. Jahrhundert bis zur Gegenwart.* 7th ed. Stuttgart, 1959.

Harvey, Judith Walters. "The Influence of the Reformation on Nürnberg Marriage Laws, 1520–1535." Ph.D. dissertation, Ohio State University, 1972.

Hashagen, Justus. "Zur Characteristik der geistlichen Gerichtsbarkeit vornehmlich im späteren Mittelalter." *Zeitschrift der Savigny-Stiftung für Rechtsgeschichte, Kanonistische Abteilung* 6 (1916), 205–92.

Hattenhauer, Hans. *Geschichte des Beamtentums.* Handbuch des öffentlichen Dienstes, 1. Cologne, 1980.

Bibliography

Hecker, A.-P. "Ehescheidungsprozeß." In *HRG* 1:843–46.

Helmholz, Richard. *Marriage Litigation in Medieval England*. London, 1974.

Hess, Hans. "Gerichtswesen und Gerichtsordnungen der Stadt im Spätmittelalter und in der frühen Neuzeit." In *Landau in der Pfalz*, ed. H. Hess, 151–62. Landau, 1974.

Hess, Rolf-Dieter. *Familien- und Erbrecht im württembergischen Landrecht von 1555*. Veröffentlichungen der Kommission für geschichtliche Landeskunde in Baden-Württemberg, Series B: Forschungen, 44. Stuttgart, 1968.

Hilling, Nikolaus. *Die Offiziale der Bischöfe von Halberstadt im Mittelalter*. Kirchenrechtliche Abhandlungen, 72. Stuttgart, 1911.

"Die Bedeutung der iurisdictio voluntaria und involuntaria im römischen Recht und im kanonischen Recht des Mittelalters und der Neuzeit." *Archiv für katholisches Kirchenrecht* 105 (1925), 449–73.

"Kirchliche Gerichtsordnungen des 14. bis 16. Jahrhunderts aus deutschen Bistümern." *Archiv für katholisches Kirchenrecht* 109 (1929), 577–83.

Hinschius, Paul. *Das Kirchenrecht der Katholiken und Protestanten in Deutschland*. 6 vols. Berlin, 1869–95.

His, Rudolf. *Das Strafrecht des deutschen Mittelalters*. 2 vols. Weimar, 1920; reprint: Darmstadt, 1969.

Houlbrooke, Ralph A. *Church Courts and the People during the English Reformation, 1520–1570*. Oxford, 1979.

Hradil, Paul. *Untersuchungen zur spätmittelalterlichen Ehegüterrechtsbildung nach bayrisch-österreichischen Rechtsquellen*. Teil I: *Das Heiratsgut*. Vienna, 1908.

Hübner, Rudolf. *A History of Germanic Private Law*. Trans. Francis S. Philbrick. London, 1918.

Ingram, Martin. *Church Courts, Sex, and Marriage in England, 1570–1640*. Cambridge, 1987.

Johanek, Ingeborg. "Geistlicher Richter und geistlicher Gericht im spätmittelalterlichen Bistum Eichstätt." Ph.D. dissertation, Universität Würzburg, 1981.

Karlowa, O. *Über die Reception des römischen Rechts in Deutschland, mit besondern Rücksicht auf der Churpfalz*. Heidelberg, 1878.

Kaser, Max. *Roman Private Law*. Trans. Rolf Dannenbring. 4th ed. Pretoria, 1984.

Kilchenmann, Küngolt. *Die Organisation des zücherischen Ehegerichts zur Zeit Zwinglis*. Quellen und Abhandlungen zur Geschichte des schweizerischen Protestantismus, 1. Zurich, 1946.

Kimminich, Otto. *Deutsche Verfassungsgeschichte*. Frankfurt, 1970.

Köhler, Walther. *Zürcher Ehegericht und Genfer Konsistorium*. 2 vols. Leipzig, 1932–42.

Koeniger, Albert M. *Die Sendgerichte in Deutschland*. Vol. I. Munich, 1907.

Kohl, Walther. "Das Laiensendgericht in der mittelalterlichen Stadt Speyer." J.D. dissertation (masch.), Mainz, 1951.

Langbein, John H. *Prosecuting Crime in the Renaissance: England, Germany, France*. Cambridge, Mass., 1974.

Lefebvre-Teillard, Anne. *Les Officialités à la Veille du Concile de Trente*. Paris, 1973.

Leiser, W. "Morgantische Ehe." In *HRG* 3:676–78.

Bibliography

Lieberwirth, R. "Ehebruch." In *HRG* 1:836–39.

Liermann, Hans. "Evangelisches Kirchenrecht und staatliches Eherecht in Deutschland; Rechtsgeschichtliches und Gegenwartsprobleme." In *Existenz und Ordnung: Festschrift für Erik Wolf*, ed. Thomas Wurtenberger, 109–21. Frankfurt, 1962.

Lindner, Klaus M. "Courtship and the Courts: Marriage and Law in Southern Germany, 1350–1550." Th.D. dissertation, Harvard, 1988.

Maschke, R. "Aus dem Urteilsbuch des geistlichen Gerichts Augsburg." In *Festgabe der Kieler Juristen Fakultät*, 215–53. Kiel, 1907.

Maurer, W. "Reste des kanonischen Rechts im Frühprotestantismus," *Zeitschrift der Savigny-Stiftung für Rechtsgeschichte, Kanonistische Abteilung* 82 (1965), 190–253.

May, Georg. *Die geistliche Gerichtsbarkeit des Erzbischofs von Mainz in Thüringen des späten Mittelalters*. Erfurter Theologische Studien, 2. Leipzig, 1956.

Mayer-Maly, T. "Morgengabe." In *HRG* 3:678–83.

Merzbacher, F. "Ehe, kirchenrechtlich." In *HRG* 1:833–36.

Mikat, P. "Ehe." In *HRG* 1:809–33.

Mitteis, Heinrich, and Heinz Lieberich, eds. *Deutsche Rechtsgeschichte*. 18th ed. Munich, 1988.

Mone, Franze Joseph. "Wirksamkeit der westfälischen Gerichte am Obberrhein." *Zeitschrift für die Geschichte des oberrheins* 7 (1856), 385–446.

"Beiträge zur Geschichte des Eherechts vom 13.–15. Jahrhundert (in Bayern, Hessen, Badden, Elsass, und der Schweiz)." *Zeitschrift für die Geschichte des Oberrheins* 19 (1866), 58–73.

Müller, Walter. *Entwicklung und Spätformen der Leibeigenschaft am Beispiel der Heiratsbeschränkungen; Dei Ehegenoßame im alemannisch-schweizerischen Raum*. Vorträge und Forschungen des Konstanzer Arbeitskreises für mittelalterliche Geschichte, 14. Simaringen, 1974.

Müller-Volbehr, Jörg. *Die geistliche Gerichte in den Braunschweig-Wolfenbüttelschen Landen*. Göttinger Studien zur Rechtsgeschichte, 3. Göttingen, 1973.

Naz, R. "Mariage en droit occidental." In *DDC* 6:740–87.

"Divorce." In *DDC* 4:1315–25.

Ogris, W. "Errungenschaftsgemeinschaft." In *HRG* 1:1004–6.

"Gütergemeinschaft." In *HRG* 1:1871–74.

"Güterrecht, eheliches." In *HRG* 1:1874–76.

Phillips, Roderick. *Putting Asunder: A History of Divorce in Western Society*. Cambridge, 1988.

Raeff, Marc. *The Well-Ordered Police State: Social and Institutional Change through Law in the Germanies and Russia, 1600–1800*. New Haven, 1983.

Riedner, Otto. "Das Speierer Offizialsgericht im 13. Jahrhundert." *Mitteilungen des Historischen Vereins der Pfalz* 29–30 (1907), 1–107.

Rodeck, Franz. *Beiträge zur Geschichte des Eherechts deutscher Fürsten bis zur Durchführung des Tridentinums*. Münster, 1910.

Safley, Thomas M. *Let No Man Put Asunder: The Control of Marriage in the German Southwest: A Comparative Study, 1550–1600*. Kirksville, Mo., 1984.

Schmelzeisen, Gustav K. *Die Rechtstellung der Frau in der deutschen Stadtwirtschaft*.

Bibliography

Arbeiten zur deutschen Rechts- und Verfassungsgeschichte, 10. Stuttgart, 1935.

Schrader, Gerhard. "Die bischöflichen Offiziale Hildesheims und ihre Urkunden im späten Mittelalter (1300–1600)." *Archiv für Urkundenforschung* 13 (1935), 91–176.

Schroeder, Richard. *Geschichte des ehelichen Güterrechts in Deutschland.* 4 vols. Stettin, 1863–74.

Lehrbuch der deutschen Rechtsgeschichte. Leipzig, 1889.

Schwab, Dieter. *Grundlagen und Gestalt der staatlichen Ehegesetzgebung in der Neuzeit bis zum Beginn des 19. Jahrhunderts.* Bielefeld, 1967.

"Heiratserlaubnis." In *HRG* 2:60–66.

"Heiratszwang." In *HRG* 2:66–69.

Segall, Josef. *Geschichte und Strafrecht der Reichspolizeiordnungen von 1530, 1548, und 1577.* Strafrechtliche Abhandlungen, 183. Breslau, 1914.

Sohm, Rudolf. *Das Recht der Eheschliessung aus dem deutschen und canonischen Recht geschichtlich entwickelt.* Weimar, 1875.

Trauung und Verlobung: Eine Entgegnung auf Friedberg: Verlobung und Trauung. Weimar, 1876.

Kirchenrecht und Eherecht. Strasbourg, 1882.

Staehlin, Adrian. *Die Einführung der Ehescheidung in Basel zur Zeit der Reformation.* Basel, 1957.

Stobbe, Otto, gen. ed. *Handbuch des deutschen Privatrechts.* Vol. 4: *Familienrecht,* ed. H. D. Lehrmann. 3rd edition. Berlin, 1900.

Straub, Heinrich. *Die geistliche Gerichtsbarkeit des Domdekans im Alten Bistum Bamberg von den Anfängen bis zum Ende des 16. Jahrhunderts.* Münchner Theologische Studien, Kan. Abt., 9. Munich, 1957.

Strauss, Gerald. *Law, Resistance, and the State: The Opposition to Roman Law in Reformation Germany.* Princeton, 1986.

Traer, James. *Marriage and the Family in Eighteenth-century France.* Ithaca, N.Y., 1980.

Trusen, W. "Offizialat." In *HRG* 3:1214-18.

Tütken, Hans. *Geschichte des Dorfes und Patrimonialgerichtes Geismar bis zur Gerichtsauflösung im Jahre 1839.* Studien zur Geschichte der Stadt Göttingen, 7. Göttingen, 1967.

Van Dülmen, Richard. *Theater des Schreckens: Gerichtspraxis und Strafrituale in der frühen Neuzeit.* Munich, 1985.

Villien, A. "Divorce." In *DTC* 4:1455-78.

Weigand, R. "Die Rechtsprechung der Regensburger Gerichts in Ehesachen unter besonderer Berücksichtigung der bedringten Eheschliessung nach Gerichtsbüchern aus dem Ende des 15. Jahrhunderts." *Archiv für katholisches Kirchenrecht* 137 (1968), 403–63.

"Ehe- und Familienrecht in der mittelalterlichen Stadt." In *Haus und Familie in der Spätmittelalterlichen Stadt,* ed. Alfred Haverkamp. Cologne, 1984.

"Kirchenrechtliche Bestimmungen mit möglicher Bedeutung für die Bevölkerungsentwicklung." *Saeculum* 39/2 (1988), 173–83.

Weisser, Michael. *Crime and Punishment in Early Modern Europe.* Sussex, 1979.

Bibliography

Wendel, François. *Le mariage à Strasbourg à l'Epoque de la Réforme, 1520–1692.* Collections d'études sur l'histoire du droit et des institutions de l'Alsace, 4. Strasbourg, 1928.

Wilhelm, Rudolf. "Rechtspflege und Dorfverfassung nach nieder-bayerischen Ehehaftsordnungen vom 15. bis zum 18. Jahrhundert." Ph.D. dissertation, Universität Munich, 1953.

Wunderli, Richard. *London Church Courts on the Eve of the Reformation.* Speculum Anniversary Monographs, 7. Cambridge, Mass., 1981.

C. Marriage and Society

Amussen, Susan Dwyer. *An Ordered Society: Gender and Class in Early Modern England.* Oxford, 1988.

Anderson, Michael. *Approaches to the History of the Western Family, 1500–1914.* London, 1980.

Ariès, Philippe. *Centuries of Childhood: A Social History of Family Life.* Trans. Robert Baldwick. New York, 1962.

Ariès, Philippe, and Georges Duby, eds. *Histoire de la vie privée.* Vol. II: *Le Moyen Age,* ed. G. Duby. Paris, 1986.

Bels, Pierre. *Le mariage des protestants français jusqu'en 1685.* Paris, 1968.

Berkner, Lutz. "The Stem Family and the Developmental Cycle of the Peasant Household." *American Historical Review* 77 (1972), 398–418.

Bloch, Iwan. *Die Prostitution.* 2 vols. Berlin, 1912–25.

Bossy, John. "The Counter-Reformation and the People of Catholic Europe." *Past and Present* 47 (1970), 51–70.

Christianity in the West, 1400–1700. Oxford, 1985.

Boswell, John. *Christianity, Social Tolerance, and Homosexuality.* Chicaago, 1980.

Brady, Thomas. *Ruling Class, Regime, and Reformation at Strasbourg, 1520–55.* Leiden, 1978.

Burgière, André. "Le rituel du mariage en France: Pratiques ecclésiastiques et pratiques populaires (XVIe–XVIIIe s.)." *Annales* 33 (1978), 637–49.

Burke, Pete. *Popular Culture in Early Modern Europe.* New York, 1978.

Burghartz, Susanna. *Leib, Ehre und Gut: Delinquenz in Zürich Ende des 14. Jahrhunderts.* Zurich, 1990.

Carlson, Eric Josef. "Marriage and the English Reformation." Ph.D. dissertation, Harvard University, 1987.

Chojnacki, Stanley. "Dowries and Kinsmen in Early Renaissance Venice." *Journal of Interdisciplinary History* 4 (1975), 571–600.

Clark, Elaine. "The Decision to Marry in Thirteenth- and Early Fourteenth-Century Norfolk." *Mediaeval Studies* 49 (1987), 496–516.

Cowan, Alexander F. *The Urban Patriciate: Lübeck and Venice, 1580–1700.* Quellen und Darstellungen zur Hansischen Geschichte, N.S. 30. Cologne, 1986.

Danckert, Werner. *Unehrliche Leute: Die verfemten Berufe.* Bern, 1963.

Davis, Natalie Zemon. "Ghosts, Kin, and Progeny: Some Features of Family Life in Early Modern France." *Daedalus* 106/2 (1977), 87-114.

Bibliography

Delumeau, Jean. *Catholicism between Luther and Voltaire.* London, 1978.

Diefendorf, Barbara. "Widowhood and Remarriage in Sixteenth-Century Paris." *Journal of Family History* 7/4 (1982), 379–95.

Duby, Georges. *Medieval Marriage: Two Models from Twelfth Century France.* Trans. Elborg Forster. Baltimore, 1978.

The Knight, the Lady, and the Priest: The Making of Modern Marriage in Medieval France. Trans. Barbara Bray. New York, 1983.

Flandrin, Jean-Louis. *Families in Former Times: Kinship, Household, and Sexuality.* Trans. Richard Southern. Cambridge, 1979.

Foucault, Michel. *Discipline and Punish: The Birth of Prison.* Trans. Alan Sheridan. New York, 1977.

Gaudemet, Jean. *Le Mariage en Occident. Les Moeurs et le droit.* Paris, 1987.

Gillis, John R. *For Better, for Worse: British Marriages, 1600 to the Present.* New York, 1985.

Goody, Jack. *The Development of Family and Marriage in Europe.* Cambridge, 1983.

Goody, Jack, et al., eds. *Family and Inheritance: Rural Society in Western Europe, 1200–1800.* Cambridge, 1976.

Hanawalt, Barbara. *The Ties That Bind: Peasant Families in Medieval England.* Oxford, 1986.

Harrington, Joel F. "*Hausvater* and *Landesvater:* Paternalism and Marriage Reform in Sixteenth-Century Germany." *Central European History* 25/1 (1992), 52–75.

Heidrich, Hermann. "Grenzübergänge: Das Haus und die Volkskultur in der frühen Neuzeit." In *Kultur der einfachen Leute: Bayerisches Volksleben vom 16. bis zum 19. Jahrhundert,* ed. Richard Van Dülmen and H. Heidrich, 17–41. Munich, 1983.

Herlihy, David. *Medieval Households.* Cambridge, Mass., 1985.

Herlihy, David, and Christiane Klapisch-Zuber. *Les toscans et leur familles: Une étude du catasto florentin de 1427.* Paris, 1978.

Houlbrooke, Ralph A. *The English Family, 1450–1700.* London, 1984.

Howell, Martha. *Women, Production, and Patriarchy in Late Medieval Cities.* Chicago, 1986.

Hsia, R. Po-Chia. *Social Discipline in the Reformation: Central Europe, 1550–1750.* London, 1989.

ed. *The German People and the Reformation.* Ithaca, N.Y., 1988.

Hughes, Diane Owen. "From Brideprice to Dowry in Mediterranean Europe." *Journal of Family History* 3 (1978), 262–96.

Jegel, August. "Altnürnberger Hochzeitsbrauch und Eherecht." *Mitteilungen des Vereins für Geschichte der Stadt Nürnberg* 44 (1953), 238–74.

Kawerau, Waldemar. *Die Reformation und die Ehe. Ein Beitrag zur Kulturgeschichte des 16. Jahrhunderts.* Coll. Schriften des Vereins für Reformationsgeschichte, 39. Halle, 1892.

Klapisch-Zuber, Christiane. *Women, Family and Ritual in Renaissance Italy.* Trans. Lydia Cochrane. Chicago, 1985.

Lafon, Jacques. *Les epoux bordelais (1450–1550): Régimes matrimoniaux et mutations sociales.* Paris, 1972.

Bibliography

Laslett, Peter. *Household and Family in Past Time.* Cambridge, 1972.

Family Life and Illicit Love in Earlier Generations. Cambridge, 1977.

Lebrun, François. *La vie conjugale sous l'Ancien Régime.* Paris, 1975.

Macfarlane, Alan. *Marriage and Love in England: Modes of Reproduction, 1300–1840.* New York, 1986.

Maschke, Erich. *Die Familie in der deutschen Stadt des späten Mittelalters.* Sitzungsberichte der Heidelberger Akadamie der Wissenschaften, phil.-hist. Kl., 4. Heidelberg, 1980.

Medick, Hans. "Village Spinning Bees: Sexual Culture and Free Time Among Rural Youth in Early Modern Germany." In *Interest and Emotion: Essays on the Study of Family and Kinship,* ed. H. Medick and David W. Sabean, 317–39. Cambridge, 1984.

Mitterauer, Michael, and Reinhard Sieder, eds. *From Patriarchy to Partnership: The European Family from the Middle Ages to the Present.* Trans. Karla Oosterveen and Manfred Horzinger. Chicago, 1982.

Monter, E. William. *Enforcing Morality in Early Modern Europe.* London, 1987.

Mount, Ferdinand. *The Subversive Family: An Alternative History of Love and Marriage.* London, 1982.

Muchembled, Robert. *Popular Culture and Elite Culture in France, 1400–1750.* Baton Rouge, 1985.

Müller-Wörthmann, Bernhard. "Raufhändel: Gewalt und Ehre im Dorf." In *Die Kultur der einfachen Leute,* ed. Richard Van Dülmen, 79–111. Munich, 1983.

Otis, Leah L. *Prostitution in Medieval Society: The History of an Urban Institution in Languedoc.* Chicago, 1985.

Ozment, Steven. *When Fathers Ruled: Family Life in Reformation Europe.* Cambridge, Mass., 1983.

Pavan, Elisabeth. "Police des moeurs, société et politique à Venise à la fin du moyen age." *Revue historique* 536 (1980), 241–88.

Plattard, J. "L'invective de Gargantua contre les mariages contractées sans le sceu et adveu des parents." *Revue du XVIe siècle* 15 (1927), 381–88.

Rebel, Hermann. *Peasant Classes: The Bureaucratization of Property and Family Relations under Early Habsburg Absolutism, 1511–1636.* Princeton, 1983.

Robisheaux, Thomas. *Rural Society and the Search for Order in Early Modern Germany.* Cambridge, 1989.

Roper, Lyndal. "Discipline and Respectability: Prostitution and the Reformation in Augsburg." *History Workshop* 19 (1985), 3–28.

"Going to Church and Street: Weddings in Reformation Augsburg." *Past and Present* 106 (1985), 62–101.

The Holy Household: Women and Morals in Reformation Augsburg. Oxford, 1989.

Rossiaud, Jacques. *Medieval Prostitution.* Trans. Lydia Cochrane. New York, 1988.

Roth, Klaus. *Ehebruchschwänke in Liedform: Eine Untersuchung zur deutsch- und englischsprachigen Schwankballade.* Munich, 1977.

Ruggiero, Guido. *The Boundaries of Eros: Sex, Crime, and Sexuality in Renaissance Venice.* New York, 1985.

Bibliography

Sabean, David W. *Power in the Blood: Popular Culture and Village Discourse in Early Modern Germany.* Cambridge, 1984.

Property, Production, and Family in Necharhausen, 1700–1870. Cambridge, 1990.

Safley, Thomas Max. "Civic Morality and the Domestic Economy." In *The German People and the Reformation,* ed. R. Po-chia Hsia, 173–90. Ithaca, N.Y., 1988.

Schilling, Heinz. *Religion, Political Culture and the Emergence of Early Modern Society: Essays in German and Dutch History.* Studies in Medieval and Reformation Thought, 50. Leiden, 1992.

Schmidt-Wiegand, R. "Hochzeitsgebräuche." In *HRG* 2:186–197.

Schochet, Gordon J. *The Authoritarian Family and Political Attitudes in Seventeenth-Century England.* 2nd rev. ed. Oxford, 1988.

Schroeter, Michael. *"Wo zwei zusammenkommen in rechter Ehe . . ."; Sozio- und psychogenetische Studien über Eheschließungsvorgänge vom 12. bis 15. Jahrhunderts.* Frankfurt, 1985.

Schwarz, Ingeborg. *Die Bedeutung der Sippe für die Öffentlichkeit der Eheschliessung im 15. und 16. Jahrhundert.* Schriften zur Kirchen- und Rechtsgeschichte, 12. Tübingen, 1959.

Screech, M. A. *The Rabelaisian Marriage.* London, 1958.

Sheehan, Michael. "The Formation and Stability of Marriage in the Fourteenth Century: Evidence of an Ely Register." *Medieval Studies* 33 (1971), 228–63.

"Theory and Practice in the Conciliar Legislation and Diocesan Statutes of Medieval England." *Medieval Studies* 40 (1978), 408–60.

"Choice of Marriage Partner in the Middle Ages: The Development and Mode of Application of a Theory of Marriage." *Studies in Medieval and Renaissance History* 4 (1978), 3–33.

"Theory and Practice: Marriage of the Unfree and the Poor." *Medieval Studies* 50 (1988), 457–87.

Shorter, Edward. *The Making of the Modern Family.* New York, 1975.

Stauffenegger, R. "Le mariage à Genéve vers 1600." *Mémoires de la société pour l'histoire du droit et des institutions des anciens pays bourguignons* 27 (1966), 319–29.

Stone, Lawrence. *The Family, Sex and Marriage in England, 1500–1800.* New York, 1977.

Strauss, Gerald. *Luther's House of Learning: Indoctrination of the Young in the German Reformation.* Baltimore, 1978.

Taillandier, Pierre. "Le mariage des protestants français sous l'Ancien Régime." J. D. dissertation, Poitiers, 1919.

Trexler, Richard. "La prostitution florentine au XVe siècle: Patronages et clienteles." *Annales* 36/6 (1981), 983–1015.

Turlan, C. "Recherche sur le mariage dans la pratique coutumière (XIIe–XVIe siècles)." *Revue historique de droit,* 4th ser., 35 (1957), 477ff.

Van Dülmen, Richard. "Fest der Liebe. Heirat und Ehe in der frühen Neuzeit." In *Armut, Liebe, Ehre: Studien zur historischen Kulturforschung,* ed. Richard Van Dülmen, 67–106. Frankfurt, 1988.

Vogler, Bernard, and J. Estèbe. "La genèse d'une société protestante: Étude comparée de quelques registres consistoriaux languedociens et palatins vers 1600." *Annales* 31 (1976), 362–78.

Wackernagel. W. D. "Ehering." In *HRG* 1:840–43.

Walker, Mack. *German Home Towns: Community, State, and General Estate, 1648–1971.* Ithaca, N.Y., 1971.

Wall, Richard, et al. eds. *Family Forms in Historic Europe.* Cambridge, 1982.

Watt, Jeffrey. *The Making of Modern Marriage: Matrimonial Control and the Rise of Sentiment in Neuchâtel, 1550–1800.* Ithaca, N.Y. 1992.

Wiesner, Merry. *Working Women in Renaissance Germany.* New Brunswick, N.J., 1986.

"Beyond Women and the Family: Towards a Gender Analysis of the Reformation." *Sixteenth Century Journal* 18/3 (1987), 311–21.

Wiltenburg, Joy D. *Disorderly Women and Female Power in the Street Literature of Early Modern England and Germany.* Charlottesville, Va., 1992.

Wright, William J. *Capitalism, the State, and the Lutheran Reformation.* Columbus, Ohio, 1983.

Wunder, Heidi, and Christina Vanja, eds. *Wandel der Geschlechterbeziehungen zu Beginn der Neuzeit.* Frankfurt a.M., 1991.

Zapalac, Kristin Eldyss Sorensen. *"In His Image and Likeness": Political Iconography and Religious Change in Regensburg, 1500–1600.* Ithaca, N.Y., 1990.

Zeeden, Ernst W. *Deutsche Kultur in der frühen Neuzeit.* Frankfurt, 1968.

D. The Rhineland Palatinate

Alter, Willi. "Von der Konradinischen Rachtung bis zum letzten Reichstag in Speyer, 1420/22–1570." In *Geschichte der Stadt Speyer*, ed. Wolfgang Eger, I:369–571. Stuttgart, 1982.

Ammerich, Hans. "Formen und Wege der katholischen Reform in den Diözesen Speyer und Straßburg: Klerusreform und Seelsorgereform." in *Oberrheinischen Studien*, vol. 6, ed. Volker Press et al. ed. Karlsruhe, 1983.

Baumgartner, Eugen. *Geschichte und Recht des Archidiakonates der oberrheinischen Bistümer mit Einschluss von Mainz und Würzburg.* Kirchenrechtliche Abhandlungen, 39. Stuttgart, 1907.

Bruck, Anton P. "Die Vorreformation in der Kurpfalz." *Archiv für mittelrheinische Kirchengeschichte* 17 (1965), 27–37.

Buchner, Maximilian. "Die innere weltliche Regierung des Speyerer Bischofs Mathias Rammung (1464–78)." *Mitteilungen des Historischen Vereins der Pfalz* 29–30 (1907), 180–255.

Clasen, C.-P. *The Palatinate in European History, 1559–1600.* Oxford, 1963.

Cohn, Henry, J. *The Government of the Rhine Palatinate in the Fifteenth Century.* Oxford, 1965.

Duggan, Lawrence G. *Bishop and Chapter: The Governance of the Bishopric of Speyer to 1552.* New Brunswick, N.J., 1978.

Bibliography

Forster, Mark. *The Counter-Reformation in the Villages: Religion and Reform in the Bishopric of Speyer, 1560–1720*. Ithaca, N.Y., 1992.

Glasschröder, Franz X. "Das Archidiakonat in der Diözese Speier im Mittelalter." *Archivalische Zeitschrift* 10 (1902), 114ff.

Götz, J. B. *Die erste Einführung des Kalvinismus in der Oberpfalz 1559–76; Auf Grund urkundlicher Forschungen*. Reformationsgeschichtliche Studien und Texte, 60. Münster, 1933.

Haffner, Franz. *Die kirchlichen Reformbemühungen des Speyerer Bischofs Matthias von Rammung in vortridentinischer Zeit (1464–78)*. Speyer, 1961.

Hane, Karl T. *Literarische Kulturleistungen des mittelalterlichen Speyer*. Speyer, 1933.

Landsmann, O. *Wissembourg. Un siècle de son histoire, 1480–1590*. Rixheim, 1903.

Lehmann, Johann-Georg. *Urkundliche Geschichte der ehemaliges freien Reichstadt und jetztigen Bundesfestung Landau in der Pfalz*. Landau, 1851.

Dreizehn Burgen des Unter-Elsasses und Bad Niederbronn, nach historischen Urkunden. Strasbourg, 1878.

Lossen, Richard. *Staat und Kirche in der Pfalz im Ausgang des Mittelalters*. Vorreformationsgeschichtliche Forschungen, 3. Münster, 1907.

Nopp, Hieronymous. *Geschichte der Stadt und ehemaligen Reichsfestung Philippsburg*. Speyer, 1881.

Ohler, Norbert. "Alltag in einer Zeit des Friedens, 1570–1620." In *GStSp* I:577–655.

Petri, Franz, and Georg Droege, eds. *Rheinische Geschichte*. Vol. II: *Neuzeit*. Düsseldorf, 1976.

Press, Volker. *Calvinismus und Territorialstaat: Regierung und Zentralbehörden der Kurpfalz, 1559–1619*. Stuttgart, 1970.

"Das Hochstift Speyer in Reich des späten Mittelalters und der früher Neuzeit – Porträt eines geistlichen Staates." In *Oberrheinische Studien*, ed. Volker Press, 251–73. Arbeitsgemeinschaft für geschichtliche Landeskunde am Oberrhein e.V. in Karlsruhe, 7. Karlsruhe, 1985.

Raubenheimer, Richard. "Martin Bucer und seine humanistischen Speyerer Freunde." *Blätter für pfälzische Kirchengeschichte und religiöse Volkskunde* 32/1–2 (1965), 1–52.

Remling, Franz X. *Geschichte der Bischöfe zu Speyer*. 2 vols. Mainz, 1852–54.

Stamer, Ludwig. *Kirchengeschichte der Pfalz*. 4 vols. Speyer, 1949–64.

Vogler, Bernard. *Vie religieuse en pays rhénan dans la seconde motié du XVIᶜ siècle*. 3 vols. Lille, 1974.

Le clergé protestant rhénan au siècle de la réforme (1555–1619). Paris, 1976.

Voltmer, Ernst. *Reichstadt und Herrschaft: Zur Geschichte der Stadt Speyer im hohen und späten Mittelalter*. Trierer Historische Forschungen, 1. Trier, 1981.

"Speyer, Grenzstadt in der europäischen Spannungszone des 17. Jahrhunderts am Oberrhein." In *GStSp*, II:5–113.

Wetterer, Anton. "Geistliche Verlassenschaften in Bruchsal im 16. Jahrhundert." *Freiburger Diözesan–Archiv* 37 (1909), 204–18.

Index

Index

inspectors, ecclesiastical, 161
intermarriage, confessional, 205–6
Isny, 174
ius commune, 149–50; *see also* law, Roman
ius reformandi, 139–40; *see also* marriage jurisdiction

Jedin, Hubert, 95
Jerome, St., 51
Jesuits, 21, 95, 140, 245
Jews, 37, 225, 253
Jöhlingen, 163, 262
Joseph, St., 53
jurisdiction over marriage, *see* marriage jurisdiction
jurors, *see* courts, composition of
Justinian Code, *see* law, Roman

Karlstadt, Andreas Bodenstein von, 62
Keiserberg, Geiler von, 62
Kettenbach, Heinrich von, 33
Kling, Melchior, 149
Köhler, Walther, 86, 131, 163–4, 166

Landau, 176, 189
Landesvater, 39–43; *see also* patriarchy; State, early modern
Langbein, John, 125
Laslett, Peter, 8
Last Judgement, 42, 46
Lasterstein ("stone of shame"), 229, 234 (Figure 7e); *see also* criminal prosecution
Lateran IV (Council), 54, 57–8, 92, 96, 108, 177, 179, 181
Lateran V (Council), 240–1
Lauttenburg, 240
law: customary, 102, 105, 107, 113–14, 117, 119, 126, 129, 144, 165, 171, 173, 193, 224–6, 276–7; Germanic, 105–6, 171, 176, 256; imperial, 125, 148–51, 188, 206, 225, 227–8, 238, 241, 245, 256, 261; Roman, 33, 51–2, 57, 101–

2, 105, 119–20, 122–6, 143, 149–51, 194, 249; statutory (municipal and territorial), 41, 44, 47, 85–6, 88, 92, 98–100, 110, 120–4, 129, 137, 139–41, 144–8, 151–2, 173–6, 181–214, 218–19, 222–4, 228, 238, 240–2, 244–5, 251, 256, 260, 265, 267–70; sumptuary, 123, 145–6, 210–12; *see also* Canon law of marriage; *Sachsenspiegel; Schwabenspiegel*
lawyers and jurists, 12, 39, 43–4, 46–7, 53–7, 86, 92, 100, 103, 124–6, 140, 143–4, 146, 148–52, 200, 273–4; *see also* Canon law of marriage; law; Melanchthon; State, early modern
Laymann, Paul, S.J., 140
Laynez, Diego, S.J., 95
Lenman, Bruce, 225
Leviticus, *see* Bible
licity of marriage, *see* clandestine marriage of minors; marital vows; marital approval
Lindau, 138 (Table 1), 160, 196
Lindner, Klaus, 179
Lombard, Peter, 53–7; *see also* Canon law of marriage; marriage
Lorraine, Cardinal of, 95
Loyola, St. Ignatius of, 82
Ludwig I (prince-bishop), 123
Ludwig VI (Elector), 164
Lußheim, 227
Luther, Martin: against celibate ideal, 35, 61–4; on marriage and social order, 26, 40, 46, 71; on marriage customs, 207; on marriage jurisdiction, 84–5, 101, 150; on marriage law, 28–33, 48, 85–6, 89–90, 146, 148–9, 180, 187–8; on nature of marriage, 48–9, 60 (n. 45), 65–7, 69, 71–2, 101; on own marriage to Katherina von Bora, 82

DATE DUE

NO 22 '0

Demco, Inc. 38-293